D1320208

*International Political Economy Series*

Series Editor:

**Timothy M.** Shaw, Visiting Professor, University of Massachusetts Boston, USA and Emeritus Professor, University of London, UK

*Titles include*:

Leslie Elliott Armijo (*editor*)
FINANCIAL GLOBALIZATION AND DEMOCRACY IN EMERGING MARKETS

Robert Boardman
THE POLITICAL ECONOMY OF NATURE
Environmental Debates and the Social Sciences

Jörn Brömmelhörster and Wolf-Christian Paes (*editors*)
THE MILITARY AS AN ECONOMIC ACTOR
Soldiers in Business

Stuart S. Brown (*editor*)
TRANSNATIONAL TRANSFERS AND GLOBAL DEVELOPMENT

Chang Kyung-Sup, Ben Fine and Linda Weiss (*editors*)
DEVELOPMENTAL POLITICS IN TRANSITION
The Neoliberal Era and Beyond

Gerard Clarke and Michael Jennings (*editor*)
DEVELOPMENT, CIVIL SOCIETY AND FAITH-BASED ORGANIZATIONS
Bridging the Sacred and the Secular

Gordon Crawford
FOREIGN AID AND POLITICAL REFORM
A Comparative Analysis of Democracy Assistance and Political Conditionality

Meric S. Gertler and David A. Wolfe
INNOVATION AND SOCIAL LEARNING
Institutional Adaptation in an Era of Technological Change

Anne Marie Goetz and Rob Jenkins
REINVENTING ACCOUNTABILITY
Making Democracy Work for the Poor

Andrea Goldstein
MULTINATIONAL COMPANIES FROM EMERGING ECONOMIES
Composition, Conceptualization and Direction in the Global Economy

Iain Hardie
FINANCIALIZATION AND GOVERNMENT BORROWING CAPACITY IN EMERGING MARKETS

Jomo K.S. and Shyamala Nagaraj (*editors*)
GLOBALIZATION VERSUS DEVELOPMENT

José Carlos Marques, and Peter Utting (*editors*)
BUSINESS, POLITICS AND PUBLIC POLICY
Implications for Inclusive Development

S. Javed Maswood
THE SOUTH IN INTERNATIONAL ECONOMIC REGIMES
Whose Globalization?

John Minns
THE POLITICS OF DEVELOPMENTALISM
The Midas States of Mexico, South Korea and Taiwan

Matthew C. Murray and Carole Pateman (*editors*)
BASIC INCOME AROUND THE WORLD
Horizons of Reform

Philip Nel
THE POLITICS OF ECONOMIC INEQUALITY IN DEVELOPING COUNTRIES

Marcus Power, Giles Mohan and May Tan-Mullins
CHINA'S RESOURCE DIPLOMACY IN AFRICA
Powering Development?

Pia Riggirozzi
ADVANCING GOVERNANCE IN THE SOUTH
What Are the Roles for International Financial Institutions in Developing States?

Eunice N. Sahle
WORLD ORDERS, DEVELOPMENT AND TRANSFORMATION

Suzana Sawyer and Edmund Terence Gomez (*editors*)
THE POLITICS OF RESOURCE EXTRACTION
Indigenous Peoples, Multinational Corporations and the State

Matthew A. Schnurr and Larry A. Swatuk (*editors*)
ENVIRONMENTAL CHANGE, NATURAL RESOURCES AND SOCIAL
CONFLICT

Adam Sneyd
GOVERNING COTTON
Globalization and Poverty in Africa

Peter Utting, Shahra Razavi and Rebecca Varghese Buchholz (*editors*)
THE GLOBAL CRISIS AND TRANSFORMATIVE SOCIAL CHANGE

William Vlcek
OFFSHORE FINANCE AND SMALL STATES
Sovereignty, Size and Money

---

**International Political Economy Series**
**Series Standing Order ISBN 978-0-333-71708-0 hardcover**
**Series Standing Order ISBN 978-0-333-71110-1 paperback**
(*outside North America only*)

You can receive future titles in this series as they are published by placing a standing order.
Please contact your bookseller or, in case of difficulty, write to us at the address below with
your name and address, the title of the series and one of the ISBNs quoted above.

Customer Services Department, Macmillan Distribution Ltd, Houndmills, Basingstoke,
Hampshire RG21 6XS, England

# China's Resource Diplomacy in Africa

## Powering Development?

Marcus Power
*Professor of Human Geography, University of Durham, UK*

Giles Mohan
*Professor of International Development, The Open University, UK*

and

May Tan-Mullins
*Associate Professor in International Relations,*
*University of Nottingham Ningbo, China*

First published 2012 by
PALGRAVE MACMILLAN

Palgrave Macmillan in the UK is an imprint of Macmillan Publishers Limited, registered in England, company number 785998, of Houndmills, Basingstoke, Hampshire RG21 6XS.

Palgrave Macmillan in the US is a division of St Martin's Press LLC, 175 Fifth Avenue, New York, NY 10010.

Palgrave Macmillan is the global academic imprint of the above companies and has companies and representatives throughout the world.

Palgrave® and Macmillan® are registered trademarks in the United States, the United Kingdom, Europe and other countries

ISBN: 978–0–230–22912–9

This book is printed on paper suitable for recycling and made from fully managed and sustained forest sources. Logging, pulping and manufacturing processes are expected to conform to the environmental regulations of the country of origin.

A catalogue record for this book is available from the British Library.

A catalog record for this book is available from the Library of Congress.

10  9  8  7  6  5  4  3  2  1
21  20  19  18  17  16  15  14  13  12

Printed and bound in the United States of America
by Edwards Brothers Malloy, Inc.

*For Conor Power, Isaac Mohan, Hannah Mohan
and Kyla Meredith Stewart*

# Contents

List of Tables                                                          x

List of Figures                                                        xi

Acknowledgements                                                     xiv

List of Abbreviations                                                 xv

1  **Introduction: Mediating China–Africa**                           1
   Introduction: the geopolitics of representation                    1
   Postcolonial geopolitical economy                                 10
      The political economy of development, globalization
      and international relations                                    10
      Enclaves and surgical colonialism?                             14
      States matter                                                  17
      Neo-liberalization, African agency and the environment         18
   Methodological concerns                                           21
   Book structure                                                    23

2  **Contextualizing China–Africa Relations**                        26
   Introduction: a critical genealogy of China–Africa relations      26
   China in Africa, Africa in China: initial encounters              29
   The 'Overseas Chinese': migration to Africa and
      the Chinese diaspora                                           32
   From 'Afro-Asian Solidarity' to 'South–South' cooperation         36
   China's aid projects in Africa                                    43
   The Tazara Railway (1967–75)                                      48
   China and Africa's 'lost decade'                                  50
   China in Angola                                                   54
   Conclusions: constructing a 'history in common'                   58

3  **Chinese Policies and Their Implications in Africa**             62
   Introduction                                                      62
   The post-millennium mechanisms of China–Africa diplomacy          64
   Differential impacts of Chinese policy in Angola and Ghana         77
   Opportunities and challenges                                      82
      FOCAC: lack of a formal permanent institution                  83
      Lack of coordination                                           83

Sustainability, quality and type of projects                         87
Conclusion                                                           87

4   **Towards a Chinese 'Socialist Market Economy'**                  88
    Introduction: China's economic 'miracle'                          88
    Embracing the market: state socialism and
       the crisis of accumulation                                     92
    China's SOEs and the 'go out' strategy                           100
    The transnational spaces of China's economic development         110
    Neo-liberalism and China: a 'loose hug' or
       an 'intimate embrace'?                                        116
    Conclusions: China as Africa's 'economic role model'            123

5   **Evolving Aid Diplomacy in Africa**                             127
    Introduction: aid, Africa and development                        127
    China's aid 'offensive' and the 'established' donors             128
       Histories and relationships                                   128
       Logics, modalities and conditionalities                       132
       Chinese aid in comparative perspective                        139
    Chinese aid in practice: forms, continuities
       and transformations                                           141
       Contemporary development relations
          in Angola and Ghana                                        141
    Donor responses                                                  151
       At the aid regime level                                       152
       At the country level                                          155
    Conclusion                                                       158

6   **Domestic Governance, Regime Stability and**
    **African Civil Society**                                        160
    Introduction: governance dilemmas                                160
    Making sense of the African state                                161
    China's channels of engagement with Africa                       164
    The politics of hybridity and extroversion                       167
    Beyond elites: migration, social relations
       and micro-politics                                            171
       Multiple flows and communities                                172
       Identity politics, political engagement and shadowy ties      176
       Integration/separation                                        176
    Popular responses and civil society reactions                    178
       Civil society responses                                       181
    Conclusion                                                       188

7  **The Environmental Implications of China's Rise in Africa**  **191**
Introduction  191
Political ecology: understanding power relations
in the environment sector  194
Changing domestic discourses and the
internationalization of China's environmental governance  195
Chinese involvement in Africa's resource sectors  200
The differential impacts of Chinese enterprises on
the environment  205
Illegal activities  207
Roles of multi-stakeholders in global
environmental governance  209
Conclusion: globalizing China's environmental
responsibilities  216

8  **The Geopolitics of China–Africa Engagement**  **221**
Introduction: China's oil diplomacy and 'soft power'  221
The new 'scramble for Africa'  227
Disaggregating Chinese foreign policy:
the diversity of 'actors'  233
Recent shifts in Chinese foreign policy  242
China as a 'responsible' great power:
peacekeeping and security cooperation  250
Conclusion: a 'critical geopolitics' of China–Africa relations  255

9  **Changing Contexts and the Future of**
**China–Africa Relations**  **260**
Introduction  260
Current and emerging patterns of engagement  261
China, Africa and theories of development  265
Future engagements: globalizing Africa–China relations  268

*Notes*  273

*Bibliography*  279

*Index*  323

# Tables

3.1 Areas of cooperation listed in the China–Africa
    White Paper                                          66
3.2 Summary aims of FOCAC action plans                   69
3.3 Projects invested in by the CADFund                  74
3.4 Follow-up committee of FOCAC                         84
5.1 Summary of Chinese aid in Ghana                      148

# Figures

1.1 Cover Image of Adama Gaye's *China and Africa:
The Dragon and the Ostrich*. Harmattan  3

1.2 Cover image of *Red for Danger*, a propaganda pamphlet
from the Rhodesian Ministry of Information
during the ZANU campaign  4

1.3 'Awakened peoples, you will certainly attain the ultimate
victory!' September, 1963. Stefan R. Landsberger collection,
International Institute of Social History (Amsterdam)  6

1.4 Cover image of *The New Sinosphere*, published by IPPR
in 2006. Institute for Public Policy Research  8

1.5 Sign for the Sunon Asogli power plant near Accra, a typical
enclaved investment. Photograph by authors  16

2.1 One of the many Chinese clinics to have emerged in
Lusaka (Zambia) in recent years. Photograph by D J Clark  35

2.2 'The feelings of friendship between the peoples
of China and Africa are deep'. May 1972. Stefan
R. Landsberger collection, International Institute
of Social History (Amsterdam)  36

2.3 'Chairman Mao is the great liberator of the world's
revolutionary people'. April 1968. Stefan R. Landsberger
collection, International Institute of Social History
(Amsterdam)  38

2.4 'Study the Soviet Union's advanced economy to build up
our nation'. June 1953. Stefan R. Landsberger collection,
International Institute of Social History (Amsterdam)  40

2.5 A sign at the front of the National Stadium in Maputo,
Mozambique says 'the friendship between Mozambique
will last for ever like the heaven and the earth'. The
National Stadium for Mozambique, completed in 2011,
was built by Chinese contractors and paid for as a gift by the
Chinese government at a cost of US$ 70 million.
Photograph by D J Clark  46

2.6 The 'Great Wall Casino' in Lusaka, Zambia.
Photograph by D J Clark  59

xi

3.1  The entrance to the Lekki Free Trade Zone in Nigeria.
     Photograph by Ben Lampert                                       76
4.1  'Special Economic Zones – China's great open door'.
     February 1987. Stefan R. Landsberger collection,
     International Institute of Social History (Amsterdam)           94
4.2  'Advance into the 21st century – celebrate the 50th
     anniversary of the founding of the People's Republic
     of China'. 1999. Jiang Zemin succeeds Deng Xiaoping as
     Party leader. Behind him the Shanghai skyline – including the
     Pearl Oriental TV Tower – and a Chinese rocket are shown,
     symbolizing China's economic and technological
     development. Stefan R. Landsberger collection,
     International Institute of Social History (Amsterdam)          102
4.3  Organogram: FDI in the Chinese context (CCCS, 2011: 3)        111
4.4  Pedro Canga, Angolan Minister of Agriculture, Rural
     Development and Fishing (third from left) visits a corn field
     on a farm in Luanda (Angola) being developed by CITIC.
     Wang Bingfei, Newscom                                         116
4.5  The Place, Beijing, China. Photograph by dorz11,
     Flickr, Creative Commons                                      118
4.6  A housing area is destroyed as new apartments rise up
     in the distance in the Yang Pu district of Shanghai.
     Photograph by D J Clark                                       122
5.1  China's foreign aid expenditure increases, 1998–2007         135
5.2  Chinese goods imported with construction projects.
     Photograph by authors                                         144
5.3  The Chinese-built National Theatre in Accra.
     Photograph by authors                                         146
5.4  The Chinese-built Ministry of Defence, Accra.
     Photograph by authors                                         147
5.5  Work Camp for Ghanaian workers, The Bui Dam, Ghana.
     Photograph by authors                                         149
5.6  Ghanaian worker at Bui Dam, Ghana.
     Photograph by authors                                         150
6.1  Chinese and Ghanaian workers, The Bui Dam, Ghana.
     Photograph by authors                                         170
6.2  Chinese medicine distributors, Accra, Ghana.
     Photograph by authors                                         173
7.1  Share of Chinese forest products imports. Source:
     Canby et al., 2008                                            204

8.1   'We will definitely free Taiwan!'. 1971. Stefan R. Landsberger
       collection, International Institute of Social History
       (Amsterdam)                                                      224
8.2   'Vigorously support the anti-imperialist struggle of the
       peoples of Asia, Africa and Latin America'. 1964. Stefan R.
       Landsberger collection, International Institute of
       Social History (Amsterdam)                                       225
8.3   'Awakened peoples, you will certainly attain the ultimate
       victory!' September, 1963. Stefan R. Landsberger collection,
       International Institute of Social History (Amsterdam)             236
8.4   Chinese peacekeepers that are part of the African
       Union/United Nations Hybrid Operation in Darfur
       (UNAMID) form a guard of honour and protect a borehole
       operated by a Chinese engineering company in Nyala
       (South Darfur) for UNAMID contingents. Photograph by
       Albert Gonzalez Farran/UNAMID                                    246
8.5   A large sign, extolling the benefits of China–Africa
       dealings, outside the Xiamen Trade Fair Exhibition Hall
       in China. Source: Speak-it Productions Ltd                       258

# Acknowledgements

The authors would like to acknowledge the support of the UK's Economic and Social Research Council (ESRC) in funding the research project (RES-062-23-0487) from which this book derives. Thanks also to Sylvia Croese for her invaluable research assistance during our fieldwork in Angola. We would also like to thank Editions L'Harmattan for Figure 1.1, the Institute for Public Policy Research (IPPR) for Figure 1.4, Ben Lampert for Figure 3.1, the Centre for Contemporary Chinese Studies (CCCS) at the University of Stellenbosch for Figure 4.3, Wang Bingfei and Newscom for Figure 4.4, dorz11 for Figure 4.5, Albert Gonzalez Farran/UNAMID for Figure 8.4, Speak-It productions Ltd for Figure 8.5, D J Clark for Figures 2.1, 2.5, 2.6 and 4.6 and the International Institute of Social History (Amsterdam) for Figures 1.3, 2.2, 2.3, 2.4, 4.1, 4.2, 8.1, 8.2 and 8.3.

# Abbreviations

| | |
|---|---|
| AAPSO | Afro-Asian People's Solidarity Organization |
| ADB | African Development Bank |
| AFRICOM | US Africa Command |
| AIDS | acquired immunodeficiency syndrome |
| ASEAN | Association of Southeast Asian Nations |
| AU | African Union |
| BBC | British Broadcasting Corporation |
| BHP | Bui Hydropower project |
| BNP | Bui National Park |
| BRIC | Brazil Russia India China |
| CABC | China–Africa Business Council |
| CADFund | China–Africa Development Fund |
| CASS | Chinese Academy of Social Sciences |
| CBRC | China Banking Regulatory Commission |
| CCB | China Construction Bank |
| CCP | Chinese Communist Party |
| CCP-ID | Chinese Communist Party International Department |
| CCPIT | China Council for the Promotion of International Trade |
| CCS | Centre for Chinese Studies |
| CCTV | China Central Television |
| CDB | China Development Bank |
| CEIEC | China National Electronics Import and Export Corporation |
| CEO | chief operating officer |
| CEPAL | United Nations Commission for Latin America |
| CHINCA | China International Contractors Association |
| CIC | China Investment Corporation |
| CICIR | China Institute of Contemporary International Relations |
| CIF | China International Fund |
| CITES | Convention on International Trade in Endangered Species |
| CITIC | China International Trust and Investment Corporation |
| CMAC | Central Military Affairs Commission |

| CMEC | China National Machinery and Equipment Import & Export Corporation |
|---|---|
| CNN | cable news network |
| CNOOC | China National Offshore Oil Corporation |
| CNPC | China National Petroleum Corporation |
| $CO_2$ | carbon dioxide |
| COD | chemical oxygen demand |
| COSCO | China Ocean Shipping Group |
| CRBC | China Road and Bridge Corporation |
| CRI | China Radio International |
| CRS | Congressional Research Service (United States) |
| CSCEC | China State Construction Engineering Corporation |
| CSIH | China Sonangol International Holding |
| CSOs | civil society organizations |
| CSR | corporate social responsibility |
| DAC | Development Assistance Committee |
| DFEC | Department of Foreign Economic Cooperation |
| DFID | Department for International Development |
| DRC | Democratic Republic of the Congo |
| DWF | distant water fishing |
| EC | Energy Commission |
| ECC | economic and commercial counsellor |
| EEZs | exclusive economic zones |
| EIA | environmental impact assessment |
| EITI | Extractive Industries Transparency Initiative |
| EJF | Environmental Justice Foundation |
| EPB | Environmental Protection Bureaus |
| EPC | engineering, procurement and construction |
| ERM | environmental resource management |
| EU | European Union |
| ExIm Bank | China Export-Import Bank |
| FALG | Foreign Affairs Leading Group |
| FAO | Food and Agriculture Organization |
| FCO | Foreign and Commonwealth Office |
| FDI | foreign direct investment |
| FFE | Foreign Funded Enterprises |
| FIE | Foreign Invested Enterprises |
| FNLA | Frente Nacional de Libertação de Angola [National Front for the Liberation of Angola] |
| FOCAC | Forum on China–Africa Cooperation |
| FSC | Forest Stewardship Council |

| GDP | gross domestic product |
| Ghana TUC | Ghana Trade Union Congress |
| GIPC | Ghana Investment Promotion Centre |
| GNP | gross national product |
| GONGO | Government Organized Non-Governmental Organization |
| GRN | Gabinete de Reconstrução Nacional [Office for National Reconstruction] |
| HEP | hydroelectric power |
| ICT | information, communication and technology |
| IBSA | India–Brazil–South Africa Dialogue Forum |
| IEA | International Energy Agency |
| ILD | International Liaison Department |
| IMF | International Monetary Fund |
| INGO | International Non-Governmental Organization |
| IPRCC | International Poverty Reduction Centre in China |
| IR | international relations |
| IRN | International Rivers Network |
| ITEL | Instituto Nacional das Telecomunicaçoês [Institute of National Telecommunications] |
| KMT | Kuomintang [Chinese Nationalist Party] |
| LDC | least developed country |
| LIC | low-income country |
| MDGs | millennium development goals |
| MEP | Ministry of Environmental Protection |
| MFA | Ministry of Foreign Affairs |
| MINURSO | United Nations Mission for the Referendum in Western Sahara |
| MOFCOM | Ministry of Commerce |
| MOFTEC | Ministry of Foreign Trade and Economic Cooperation |
| MONUSCO | United Nations Stabilization Mission in the Democratic Republic of Congo |
| MPLA | Movimento Popular de Libertação de Angola [Popular Movement for the Liberation of Angola] |
| NAASP | New Asia Africa Strategic Partnership |
| NAM | non-aligned movement |
| NBF | NEPAD Business Foundation |
| NDC | National Democratic Congress |
| NEPAD | New Partnership for African Development |
| NGO | non-governmental organization |
| NICs | newly industrialized countries |

| ODA | Official Development Assistance |
| OECD | Organization for Economic Cooperation and Development |
| PBoC | People's Bank of China |
| PLA | People's Liberation Army |
| PRC | People's Republic of China |
| RMB | Renminbi |
| ROC | Republic of China |
| SADC | Southern African Development Community |
| SAFE | State Administration of Foreign Exchange |
| SAR | Special Administrative Region |
| SASAC | State Assets Supervision and Administration Commission |
| SCO | Shanghai Co-operation Organization |
| SEPA | State Environmental Protection Administration |
| SETC | State Economic and Trade Commission |
| SEZ | special economic zone |
| SFA: | State Forest Administration |
| SGCC | State Grid Corporation of China |
| SIIS | Shanghai Institute of International Studies |
| SME | small and medium enterprises |
| SOE | state-owned enterprise |
| SSI | Sonangol-Sinopec International |
| SUCG | Shanghai Urban Construction Group |
| TAZARA | Tanzania-Zambia Railway Authority |
| TICAD | Tokyo International Conference on African Development |
| TNCs | transnational corporations |
| UN | United Nations |
| UNAMID | African Union/United Nations Hybrid Operation in Darfur |
| UNCTAD | United Nations Conference on Trade and Development |
| UNDP | United Nations Development Programme |
| UNITA | União Nacional para a Independência Total de Angola [National Union for the Total Independence of Angola] |
| UNMIL | United Nations Mission in Liberia |
| UNMIS | United Nations Mission in Sudan |
| UNOCI | United Nations Mission in Cote d'Ivoire |
| UNPKO | United Nations peacekeeping operation |
| US | United States |
| USSR | Union of Soviet Socialist Republics |

| WFOEs | Wholly Foreign-Owned Enterprises |
| WTO | World Trade Organization |
| WWF | World Wildlife Fund |
| ZANU | Zimbabwe African National Union |
| ZTE | Zhongxing Telecommunication Equipment Company Limited |

# 1
# Introduction: Mediating China–Africa

## Introduction: the geopolitics of representation

Over the past five years one has not had to go far to find western journalists deriding China's revitalized role in Africa. Typical is Christopher Hitchens, writing in the United Kingdom's *Daily Mail*:

> It is my view...that China's cynical new version of imperialism in Africa is a wicked enterprise. China offers both rulers and the ruled in Africa the simple, squalid advantages of shameless exploitation. (Hitchens 2008)

Similar sentiments were expressed in many other leading international newspapers (see, e.g. *The Economist* 13 March 2008) where China's moves were treated as cynical and self-serving. This zeitgeist is part of a broader concern, expressed in popular culture, about China's 'rise'. For example, the mid-1980s movie *Red Dawn* featured Russian soldiers invading America and a group of teenagers doughtily defending their nation. In the 2011 remake the invaders were to have been Chinese and as if to emphasize the declining economic power of the United States vis-à-vis China it is set in Detroit, the once proud heart of US automobile manufacture. In mid-June 2010 the *Global Times*, a leading Chinese daily, reported on leaked scripts from the film which started a furore under the headline 'U.S. reshoots Cold War movie to demonize China'. Although the film is now due for a 2012 release, post-production editing has changed the invading army from China to North Korea in an effort not to offend such a lucrative market for America's cultural output (Fritz and Horn 2011). Hence, it is not inconsequential at a time when there are serious doubts about the efficacy of capitalist development in Western

1

Europe and North America and challenges to global hegemony that we are seeing an emerging discourse which treats relative newcomers with suspicion, but also as a force not to offend.

Critical geopolitics (Ó Tuathail 1996) has shown us that interpretations of the world are shaped by popular culture and that these discourses also in turn shape geopolitical actions. We take popular culture broadly to include various media, but also (semi)official propaganda and even the more research-oriented work of some think tanks (Shambaugh 2002). But critical geopolitics also shows that academic knowledge, supposedly rational and independent, can also support certain agendas even if this support is unintended. Despite the examples cited so far we do not want to imply that a critical geopolitical analysis is only relevant to 'Western' discourses (Mawdsley 2008). If we accept that power/knowledge are intimately entwined then such analysis is also relevant for content produced from China, African countries *as well as* Western Europe and North America. Given the shifting power relations, different interests and cultural contexts it is important to interrogate all discourses critically to get a rounded and relative sense of how actors might be thinking.

We want to examine briefly some of the recurring tropes in these popular geopolitical discourses as a way of setting out some of the wider problems with the analysis of 'China–Africa' relations that are the focus of this book. But in keeping with our desire to relativize such representations we also highlight some of the more subtle differences within such tropes. The most obvious theme, so evident in the *Red Dawn* remake, is a demonizing of China. Articles are replete with language of rapacity and threat with such terms as 'dragon on safari' (Kohli 2009; Michel et al. 2009) or a Chinese 'take-away' (World Rainforest Movement 2005). Images are of dragons towering over Africa with mouths open ready to consume resources and markets. The two images that follow are interesting. On the face of it the imagery is similar. A towering and angry Chinese dragon eyes up Africa. In Figure 1.1, and reflected in the book's title, Africa is seen as an ostrich, wilfully ignoring the dragon at its door, while a panicked African turns his back. In Figure 1.2 Africa is in the bottom corner – tiny and cowering, unable to resist the onslaught of China's aggression.

But what about the differences? A key difference is in who or what is apparently driving China's Africa strategies. Figure 1.2 was produced by the Rhodesian Ministry of Information during the Zimbabwe African National Union's (ZANU) campaign of opposition to white rule. ZANU was presented as Communist with China's role – represented by the

*Figure 1.1*   Cover Image of Adama Gaye's *China and Africa: The Dragon and the Ostrich*. Harmattan

*Figure 1.2* Cover image of *Red for Danger*, a propaganda pamphlet from the Rhodesian Ministry of Information during the ZANU campaign

uniformed official sitting belligerently with arms crossed – seen as an ideological one of supporting nationalist struggles in Africa. By contrast contemporary Chinese interests – as seen by the Senegalese journalist Adama Gaye in Figure 1.1 – are represented by a well-fed, smiling and open-armed businessman sweating under the weight of his suitcase full of cheap Chinese goods. So, the transition over the past 30 years or so is seen as one of moving from 'ideology' to 'business' or 'Maoism to Markets'. Such representations can, at worst, take a particular case and use it to represent the entire relationship between 'Africa' and 'China' (e.g. Junger 2007). They can, by demonizing China, implicitly present western interests in Africa as more enlightened. However, given that both these images emanate from Africa, albeit at different times and from very different ideological positions, suggests that the issue is more about a circulation of discourses. It is not only western interests that present China as a threat.

Closely related to this is that 'Africa' is treated in hackneyed ways by most commentators. We have already seen in those images coming from Africa that the continent is presented as hapless and helpless, which not only serves to present China in a poor light but might also serve to abdicate responsibility from African leaders. China is simply too powerful to resist. In Chinese representations, Africa is the land of healthy, smiling and non-aligned fellow 'socialists' in cold war propaganda which, as we shall see, is something contemporary African and Chinese leaders draw upon in justifying their renewed interests (Figure 1.3). Sections of the US establishment present Chinese interests as zero-sum and implicitly present the west as genuinely concerned about Africa/ns. By contrast China is concerned about 'containment' and ploughing a separate developmental furrow. In both cases, however, Africa appears as a strategic foil for these greater geopolitical master plans and lacks political identities of its own.

More recently at the 2006 Forum on China–Africa Cooperation (FOCAC) meeting in Beijing we saw images of African wildlife, while on a Chinese website dedicated to Africa (Africaren.com) the images are of Ancient Egyptians and smiling peasants, as well as the obligatory wildlife. Again, these are ways of viewing Africa that have long lineages and it is not just the Chinese that present Africans as happy-go-lucky and rooted in 'tradition' and the continent itself as blessed with abundant natural resources. What is fortunately missing from such representations that often appear in popular depictions of Africa are the disease, famine and war that are assumed to stalk the continent (see Mercer et al. 2003). China's view of Africa is one of strategic opportunity rather

*Figure 1.3*  'Awakened peoples, you will certainly attain the ultimate victory!'. September 1963. Stefan R. Landsberger collection, International Institute of Social History (Amsterdam)

than negativity with the official discourse of the Chinese Communist Party (CCP) based on a realist recognition of business opportunities and 'win-win' relationships with Africa. That said, Shen's (2009) analysis of Chinese websites discussing Africa is that it is a thin line between seeing Africans as rooted in tradition and one where they are seen as lazy and lascivious, and not ready for or worthy of development. So, the representation of Africa as 'traditional' may conceal a self-presentation of China as both a responsible and modernizing power in which it creates 'others' who are in need of assistance (Nyiri 2006), a role often bound up in a growing national(ist) confidence (Callahan 2008).

More academic and policy-oriented representations also suggest that Africa is swamped by China with the Chinese flag appearing as a recurring backdrop and merged with Africa. While less alarmist than towering dragons the other important effect of such a geopolitical imagination is that the specificity of Africa, and China for that matter, is erased. Africa becomes a uniform space for encroachment and exploitation whereas China is symbolized by the official marker of statehood, suggesting – not unreasonably – that the Chinese state is central to this process.

A critical upshot of all of these various representations and their interpretation is that African voices are muted. The 'China Inc.' (Fishman 2005) and 'Beijing Consensus' (Ramo 2004) models see China as acting in a unilateral way according to some singular logic. By contrast the diversity of Africa and Africans is negated (Figure 1.4).

While we are not apologists for China and do not deny the potential for China to exacerbate African development and governance problems these representations tend to generalize from one or two exceptional (bad) cases, present 'China' as a single-minded monolith, treat aid as only ever about enabling resource extraction, and reduce African actors to passive and naïve ciphers in need of 'our' help. Moreover many of these negative views were based on little or no research although this is changing (see Brautigam 2009; Alden et al. 2008).

Now we want to use these representations as a springboard to explore a number of important issues that we feel are vital in analysing the complex and changing relationships between China and Africa. They are addressed here briefly and are developed in detail throughout the book. The first issue we need to factor in is the rise of China in the context of major geopolitical and geoeconomic shifts (Henderson 2008). This is about a changing balance of power in the world system and particularly the waning of US hegemony both pre- and post- the financial crisis, as well as the defensive and 'hawkish' reactions to this (Ikenberry 2008; Kurlantzick 2008). But it is also about China's re-entry into spheres of influence in Africa which have been the purview of the former European colonial powers for two centuries or more (Six 2009). Moreover it is about seeing China as an actor in its own right, one which, as we have seen, is often reduced to stereotypes by many interested parties. Intellectually this means that as scholars of African development we have necessarily had to engage with the literature on Chinese political economy to get a more rounded picture of the interactions between 'China' and 'Africa', but we remain relative newcomers to Sinology.

Second, we need a disaggregated analysis of China–Africa relations in which disaggregation means various things. It can mean the deconstruction of popular images as they are cemented in policy as we have done already. But it can also mean differentiation of nation-states as singular actors and a geographical sensitivity to differences across space in terms of political economic processes. We develop this below. Crucially we also need to disaggregate temporally since Chinese interventions may be similar to other countries' interventions at other times (and so amendable to a comparative analysis) but also that the

*Figure 1.4* Cover image of *The New Sinosphere*, published by IPPR in 2006. Institute for Public Policy Research (IPPR)

conditions on the ground are changing all the time so that any analysis of this fast moving field can only ever be a snapshot. But we hope that by embedding our analysis in historical and geographical context, and by situating it in a broader political economy of development, this book is more than a glimpse of the here and now.

Third, as should be clear by now, we need to re-insert African agency into the picture. Postcolonial theory (Mercer et al. 2003) has argued for recognizing the complex intermingling of the subjectivities of colonizer and colonized so that we do not reduce the colonial relationship to one of singular, external domination. There are a number of ways by which post-colonialism illuminates development and *vice versa*. First, it seeks to shift the primary locus of knowledge production away from the North. This is about the decolonization of knowledge, based on an understanding of colonization as complex, contradictory and geographically varied. In development theory and practice an Orientalist reading links development to hegemony and trusteeship in which colonialism was legitimated through the mission to civilize others. While China has a different relationship with Africa (Snow 1988; Six 2009) which frees the country from some of the guilt exhibited by European powers, we still need to be attentive to the ways in which China exercises hegemony in other ways. Second, although postcolonial theory has been criticized for its lack of a normative political agenda – some of it has engaged with the actions of subalterns. The work of Bhabha (1994) and Spivak (1988) examined the colonizer/colonized relationship and how the colonized exploited the ambivalence of their apparently subordinate position, rendering colonization both differenti-ated and unstable. While Spivak is wary about the possibility of recov-ering these subaltern voices this opens a space for analysing the agency of the colonized and helps us move away from treating Africa as a victim of global forces be they European, Chinese or otherwise.

Hence this book seeks to analyse the dynamics of China–Africa rela-tions in a different way. We ask a series of questions:

- How do China–Africa relations fit into wider and longer term proc-esses of global restructuring?
- In what ways and with what effects have China's internal reforms shaped its engagement with the developing world, and African states in particular?
- How have China's past engagements with Africa shaped its contem-porary relationships?
- What role has 'aid' played in enabling these relationships and to what extent does China 'challenge' other donors?

- How have recent China–Africa interests been shaped through the relationships between Chinese and African states and other 'non-political' actors?
- To what extent and in what ways has Chinese engagement with African states altered domestic politics?
- Have Chinese projects had unusually harsh impacts on the environment in Africa and globally?
- How far is China's African engagement part of a broader geopolitical transition?
- As a result of China's rise do we need to rethink the ways we analyse international development?

The answers to these questions largely structure the rest of the book and we close this chapter with a roadmap for that. Each chapter also progresses a particular area of theory relevant to the discussions therein, but here we set out some of the broad theoretical debates into which our work is speaking.

## Postcolonial geopolitical economy

In order to contextualize China–Africa relations within broader geopolitical and developmental debates we are keen to take the more material concerns of political economy and put them into productive engagement with the culturally centred approaches of postcolonialism (see Power 2003; Mercer et al. 2003).

### The political economy of development, globalization and international relations

First, we base our theoretical approach within a broadly leftist political economy tradition. We follow Gillian Hart's (2001: 650) distinction between 'D' and 'd' development whereby

> 'big D' Development (is) defined as a post-second world war project of intervention in the 'third world' that emerged in the context of decolonisation and the cold war, and 'little d' development or the development of capitalism as a geographically uneven, profoundly contradictory set of historical processes.

Hart's Polanyian view is that the unleashing of markets generates counter-tendencies; the so-called double movement. Hence, 'Far from the counter-movement representing some sort of external intervention in an inexorably unfolding teleology, these opposing tendencies are contained *within* capitalism' (Hart 2001: 650). This forces us to consider how global capitalism must be actively 'created and constantly reworked' (ibid.) – a non-deterministic quest for hegemony. This involves exchanges as opposed to the naked enforcement of hegemony by an 'external' actor, which rests on the belief that development is a 'resolutely dialectical process...(which is)...a sort of mixing, syncretism and cross-fertilization rather than a crude mimicry or replication' (Watts 2003: 23). What we want to do in this book is see how China's hybrid sense of development and modernity works in relation to multiple African rationalities and institutions.

Within this counter-movement the relationship between power and knowledge is a form of governmentality which refers to 'the emergence of particular regimes of truth concerning the conduct of conduct' (Rose 1999: 21). In practice, this means 'analysing the rationalities of rules, the forms of knowledge and expertise they construct, and the specific and contingent assemblages of practices, materials, agents and techniques through which these rationalities operate to produce governable subjects' (Hart 2004: 92). Recent work extends the concept of governmentality to examine international non-governmental organizations (NGOs) and multilateral agencies, and the intersection of different spaces of governmentality (see Ferguson and Gupta 2002; Watts 2003). Hence, knowledge about development and its practical application is very much about control and discipline and feeds into what we later discuss as the process of neo-liberalization. Here Murray Li's (2007) work has been useful since it helps break from those political economy accounts that too easily read off outcomes from interests. The assemblage, for Murray Li, is heterogeneous in which 'programs of intervention are pulled together from an existing repertoire, a matter of habit, accretion, and bricolage' (Murray Li 2007: 6). In the cases that follow of Chinese involvement in Ghana and Angola we see a much more complex and shifting institutional arrangement which both works within the state but exceeds it in important ways.

In terms of explaining broad spatio-temporal dynamism within global capitalism Hoogvelt (1997) elaborates upon the 'inter-connectedness' of globalization which she characterizes in terms of 'widening' and 'deepening'. The widening processes involved the extension of capitalist relations across the globe through trade and productive investment in the nineteenth century. This process was thorough, but still spatially and historically uneven (Smith 2008). With globalization the widening is 'superseded by a phase of *deepening*' (Hoogvelt 1997: 115, original emphasis) whereby capitalist relations are more deeply embedded into social relations. Hoogvelt argues that the previous phase of economically driven global expansion opened up a 'shared' global consciousness and social spaces which now enable novel forms of economic activity. She writes 'If, previously, global integration in the sense of a growing unification and interpenetration of the human condition was driven by the economic logic of capital accumulation, today it is the unification of the human condition that drives the logic of further capital accumulation' (Hoogvelt 1997: 121). So the interconnections established during earlier phases provide the possibilities for new forms of profit-making which necessitates an analysis of the histories of Chinese contact with Africa and the relationships between aid, trade and investment.

These theories help us situate China–Africa relations within the broader dynamics of the global economy and development processes. They foreground capitalism in the explanation and tie together social and economic processes. But how can we understand the (geo) political? Here we consider theories of international relations. Like the post-development critiques of development theory we see mainstream International Relations (IR) as a largely 'American Social Science' (Hoffmann 1977), which tends to neglect the periphery of the world system (particularly Africa) in focusing on European or North American geopolitical discourses (Sidaway 2007; Dalby 2007). In this Orientalist-inspired sense knowledge *about* the international functions to legitimize the structuring *of* international relations in which Africa is marginalized and managed.

Dunn (2001) argues that western IR ignores Africa, because of its neorealist insistence on placing the state at the centre of explanations. Dunn goes on to argue that for Africa the state is largely absent and so IR is incapable of comprehending the 'real' political dynamics of the continent. This is in contrast, he argues, to the clearly delimited and coherent states of Europe which makes IR relevant to them. While Brown (2006) is sympathetic to the broad project of a meaningful analysis of Africa in the world, he criticizes Dunn and others for conflating IR with neorealism. Brown's argument is that neorealism suffers from serious limitations that are evident even *before* one transplants it to Africa. In particular the normalization of the European state as the benchmark for analysis creates certain teleological arguments in which Africa, and some other regions, can only be found wanting. The effect of arguing that Africa shows up the limitations and is so different that it requires an, as yet, unspecified 'new' theory only serves to marginalize Africa from core debates of IR.

So, critiques of certain IR theories mirror those made of development in recent years in their identification of an implicit statism and their construction of hegemonic knowledges. We would however argue that there are other ways of approaching the development/international relations nexus and that China–Africa relations offer the opportunity for de-centring the West from accounts of global politics and looking more closely at the 'intertwining' of knowledges and processes. In developing the critique of the likes of Dunn, Bilgin (2008) argues that these laudable attempts to insert the periphery into IR are based on a reversal of 'Western' theorizing. Bilgin argues we should also ask awkward questions about the 'Westernness' of ostensibly 'Western' approaches to world politics and the 'non-Westernness' of others. What we think of as 'non-Western' approaches to world politics or 'development', in other words, may be suffused with 'Western' concepts and theories (e.g. the importance of modernization discourses to China's scientific or technocratic vision of 'development'). Bilgin argues that this requires becoming curious about the effects of the historical relationship between the 'West' and the 'non-West' in the emergence of ways of thinking and doing that are in Bhabha's (1994) words 'almost the same but not quite'. Rather than becoming fixated with China's exceptionalism it is possible that a process of 'mimicry' may emerge, in other words, as a way of 'doing' world politics or development in a seemingly 'similar' yet unexpectedly 'different' way.

Here then we have been trying to comprehend contemporary approaches to IR coming from China. We know there are close but not unidirectional links between IR theory and foreign policy (Shambaugh 2002; Wang 1994). In reviewing the state of Chinese IR Zhang (2002) identified three contrasting schools. One argues that 'Chinese scholars needed to 'catch up' by 'importing Western IR theories' (ibid. 102). By contrast there is another seeking to re-work Marxism-Leninism to develop an IR 'with Chinese characteristics', what Leonard (2008) refers to as the 'neocomms' (neo-communists). While potentially interesting this is still mired in what Zhang (2002) sees as an 'increasingly anachronistic' Maoist orthodoxy based on Lenin's reading of imperialism tempered with world-systems theory, which he believes fails to produce any new insights. The third approach also seeks to capture the specificity of China's development trajectory and argues that most IR theory has been developed in particular geopolitical contexts which serve to extend the hegemony of the dominant powers. While seeking to capture what is unique about China (see, e.g. Callahan's (2008) discussion of *tianxia*) this third body of theory should 'participate in theoretical debate in the global IR community while addressing theoretical issues in terms of China's national experience' (ibid. 104). Although not explicit and still in what Zhang terms a 'primary stage' this mutual engagement may lead to a more 'international' IR theory.

China's integration into the liberal world order has produced hybrid results that require us to think carefully about 'non-Western' similarity/ difference. However, in valorizing 'non-western' perspectives we are not advocating an uncritical relativism, where, for example, the proclamations of the Chinese government are treated as any more legitimate than claims by rival governments vying for African resources. We would argue for the critical importance of historical context here in order to analyse continuities and identify traces of the past that influence (or are manipulated by) contemporary actors. What we want to avoid here is the suggestion that what China is doing has no historical precedents in terms of Chinese foreign policy or that it is a significant departure from the past practices of other external interests on the continent.

### Enclaves and surgical colonialism?

We saw in discussing IR that some assume the state in Africa is absent or so atypical as to require some (as yet undeveloped) new theory. Clearly as our opening remarks show Africa is rising on the economic and political agenda after two decades (arguably much longer) on the back burner. So, far from being marginalized by globalization Africa is, as James Ferguson argues, selectively incorporated into it.

> ...recent capital investment in Africa has been territorialized, and some of the new forms of order and disorder that have accompanied that selectively territorialized investment...this economic investment has been concentrated in secured enclaves, often with little or no economic benefit to the wider society...see how different the political–economic logic of the privately secured enclave is from the universalizing grid of the modernist state. (2005: 378)

He contrasts the enclave model with a postcolonial 'social' model where mining houses often constructed company towns around a sense of paternalism and thereby had deeper roots in African societies allied to a broader developmental state agenda. Associated with this new mode of insertion into Africa is a bifurcated governance model in which the increasingly *unviable* formal state structures are 'hollowed out' fiscally and in terms of authority and personnel, while the *viable* enclaves are governed efficiently as private entities in a similar vein to pre-colonial mercantilist exploitation. While many Chinese investments in Africa are highly enclaved, as we shall see in subsequent chapters, Ferguson's thesis is flawed insofar as the Chinese use concessional financing to African states to ease their insertion into these lucrative markets (Figure 1.5). China, as one of a number of so-called rising powers, is increasingly pursuing resources, markets and political solidarity, which is accompanied by increases in 'aid' making them 'emerging' donors. The argument is that 'traditional' donors – primarily those represented by the Development Assistance Committee (DAC) – are being challenged by a group of countries that are rapidly industrializing and seeking a greater voice in international affairs. We examine these issues in more detail in Chapter 5.

Harvey's (2003) revitalization of primitive accumulation echoes this. Rather than what he terms 'accumulation by dispossession' being a temporary feature of capitalism, it is an incomplete and recurring phenomenon, given new legitimacy under neo-liberalism in which displacement of people and a violent proletarianization are the norm for many in the developing world. Albert Bergesen (2008) argues a similar line with respect to Chinese engagement in Africa, referring to it as a form of 'surgical colonialism' which 'involves minimum of local disruption'. This return to the mercantilist enclave then opens up familiar neo-Marxist critiques around lack of local multipliers, repatriation of surplus and ultimately a limited sustainability. But where China differs is that it has state backing in the form of aid to effectively subsidize these operations and 'buy off' local elites (again nothing really new), although the discourse of respecting sovereignty does mark the Chinese out as different from western powers.

The other, and more interesting, difference which complicates Harvey's account is China imports cheap labour. Bergesen argues 'traditional' neocolonialism relies on absolute exploitation of African land and labour (e.g. apartheid) whereas the Chinese practice 'national self-exploitation' by importing their labour. Murray Li has also argued that while Ferguson's enclaves enable super-exploitation with minimal contact, 'There is another dynamic, however, that is potentially more lethal: one in which places (or their resources) are useful, but the people are not, so that dispossession is detached from any prospect of labour absorption' (2010: 69). So China may presage a new form of imperialism which connects poverty in China with a surgical colonialism in impoverished Africa. The 'coolie labour' of the late nineteenth century saw the metropolitan powers import labour from colonized Asia to Africa (Mung 2008). The Chinese may be doing similar things to their own

*Figure 1.5*   Sign for the Sunon Asogli power plant near Accra, a typical enclaved investment. Photograph by authors.

workers who ultimately may have been dispossessed in rural China before going to Africa to further dispossess Africans. This scenario is not so much an Africa without Europeans, as Alden (2008) states rhetorically, as it is an Africa without Africans.

## States matter

In countering the tendency to simply treat Chinese involvement in Africa as some *deus ex machina* which robs African actors of any agency we focus on the state and its relations to capital. While not totally dismissing Ferguson's analysis of enclaved capital the relationships between state and capital are more complex, especially given that Chinese capital is, at minimum, split between the large, state-influenced transnational corporations (TNCs) and a myriad smaller, independent entrepreneurs. Whereas in the past Chinese firms and the state were coincidental, now there is some relative autonomy of Chinese firms from state agendas, although the ties between the CCP and the large Chinese multinationals remain quite strong.

Neo-Marxist dependency theories were important in illuminating the relationships between foreign capital and dependent development in the periphery. But sympathetic critics have pointed out (Leys 1996) that dependency theory failed to transcend the limitations of that which it sought to refute, namely modernization theory. For Escobar (1995) the United Nations Commission for Latin America (CEPAL) structuralists still equated development with capital accumulation and technical progress so that 'they lent themselves to a modernization process that international experts and national elites were eager to undertake' (Escobar 1995: 81). Leys is more careful to point out the innovations that the Marxist critique brought which was that, at one level, it was against Eurocentrism and the illusion of statist development. However, Leys (1996) agrees with Escobar that dependency theory 'while radical in intention, really remains within its (bourgeois development theory) problematic' (Leys 1996: 47) and could therefore be easily co-opted into the orthodoxy. Leys focuses on various problems of dependency including its economism, its equation of development with the condition of the metropoles, its confused notion of exploitation and its inability to really analyse the dynamics of class struggle.

As a result of these criticisms it is important to realize that capital is fragmented so that state activity and politics cannot be homogenized by reducing it to the needs of a 'unitary' capital. International capital is never completely 'external' since it combines with fragments of local capital. This fragmentation results in the disarticulation of the domestic capital-owning classes so that the state fails to crystallize these class relations and become their ideological leader as it did in Europe. This counters Alavi's (1972) functionalist claims that state bureaucrats consciously thwart the indigenous bourgeoisie, because their power

derives from their position as mediators in a purely dependent relation to international capital. The reality is that some 'economy' does
exist within the country which the state presides over so that the state
does not simply perform functionalist 'municipal' functions on behalf
of international capital.

Hence the outcomes of China's involvement in Africa will primarily be
shaped by state–capital dynamics, particularly how Chinese capital and
parts of the Chinese state intertwine with fractions of capital and political blocs within Africa. We then have to examine different fractions
of capital – some of which may be enclaved – and what role states play
in enabling these to succeed or how capital itself exploits (unintended)
differences in state policies. This is more complex than Ferguson's bifurcated model of un/viable Africa and it is a profoundly political process
as different classes seek to transform the state in pursuit of their interests. This is also important as Chinese policy responds to local political
conditions while the Chinese doctrine of respecting sovereignty and
non-interference is implicitly based on an assumption that a state exists
in the first place.

## Neo-liberalization, African agency and the environment

The analysis of accumulation by dispossession which we feel is useful
sees its revitalization as given renewed legitimacy under neo-liberalism.
But how far can we characterize China as neoliberal? The idea of China
being 'neo-liberal' is often queried given the traditional understanding
of 'neoliberalism' as entailing strict market features unimpeded by
state planning which is seen to be irreconcilable with the reality of the
Chinese experience. Giovanni Arrighi (2007), for example, argues that
China has refused to follow neo-liberal prescriptions, implementing
reforms gradually rather than by 'shock therapy' and emphasizing a
national interest in stability (see also Schmitz 2007). It could even be
argued that Chinese economic policies are neo-mercantilist in nature
rather than being completely 'neo-liberal'. They are of course fundamentally capitalist and as such, the post-Mao Chinese leadership is
doing precisely what the West wants it to do yet is, on occasion, casti-
gated when processes unleashed by this liberalization play themselves
out in areas formerly held to be within the West's spheres of influence
(e.g. Africa). David Harvey (2005) rightly emphasizes that China is a
'strange case' as the outcome has been a particular kind of neo-liberalism combined with 'authoritarian centralized control'. Our characterization of China's economic vision as 'neo-liberal' is necessarily
tentative and provisional and we develop it in Chapter 4.

By emphasizing the state we wanted to counter the 'Asian Driver' phenomena that African states are relatively powerless and, like the images with which we opened the chapter, behaving in an ostrich-like way. However, the use of governmentality from Watts (2003), Hart (2004) and Murray Li (2007) suggests that 'the political' is much broader than the state and includes multiple actors held together in shifting and heterogeneous assemblages. In trying to understand both the political-economic and this more embedded, hybrid and emergent series of development outcomes there have been some insightful debates in economic geography about the nature of neo-liberalism and the variety of forms it can take.

The general context for this is identifying and explaining capitalist variation. At its heart is a debate around whether capitalism is constituted of transhistorical and universal components or whether meaningful differences are evident in the nature of multiple capitalisms. The 'varieties of capitalism' debate (Peck and Theodore 2007) is essentially a Weberian approach seeking to understand the differences that institutions make to the organization and trajectory of different capitalisms, understood to be nationally centred. Rather than explore this debate in detail we follow Peck and Theodore's attempt to signal a 'variegated capitalism' approach which is not nationally centred but rather looks at capitalism as inherently productive of combined and uneven development. Crucially, due to the co-evolution of capitalism with multiple institutional assemblages we see different forms of combined and uneven development under capitalism rather than multiple forms of capitalism.

In a more focused analysis of neo-liberalism Tickell and Peck (2003) make the case for a process-based analysis of 'neo-liberalization', arguing that the transformative and adaptive capacity of this far-reaching political–economic project has been repeatedly underestimated. Among other things, this calls for a close reading of the historical and geographical (re)constitution of the process of neo-liberalization and of the variable ways in which different 'local neo-liberalisms' are embedded within wider networks and structures of neo-liberalism. It has a geography, with its centres of discursive production (in places like Washington DC, New York City and London), its ideological heartlands (like the United States and the United Kingdom), its constantly shifting frontiers of extension and mediation (such as South Africa, Eastern Europe, Japan and Latin America) and its sites of active contestation and resistance (Seattle, Genoa and Cuba). Neo-liberalism operates at multiple scales and more attention needs to be paid to the *different variants* of neo-liberalism, to the *hybrid nature* of contemporary policies and programmes and to the *multiple and contradictory aspects* of neo-liberal spaces, techniques and subjects. We hope to analyse China as a contingent variant that is neither universal nor particular. There is a need to carefully specify the *discourses, processes and mechanisms of neo-liberalization*, to understand its different institutional variants, and to examine how these are interconnected through new, translocal channels of policy formation. Neo-liberalism has both a creative ('roll out') and a destructive ('roll back') moment and any adequate treatment of the process of neo-liberalization must explain how these moments are combined under different historical and geographical circumstances.

Such processes of contestation and negotiation in multiple sites requires us to treat people of the South as possessing agency in multiple ways, which requires moving beyond formal political spaces and looking to other realms of the political. This is also more than the development studies obsession with 'civil society'. While important in some contexts, civil society whether 'local' or 'international' is only one other arena for politics. As Hecht and Simone (1994: 16) argue: 'Formal governance tends to have a restrictive notion of the public sphere that neglects the desires and efforts of the impoverished to create culture, sociality and solidarity' (see also Chakrabarty 1992; Staeheli and Mitchell 2004). This gives us a more open view of what constitutes political community and what counts as political activity, though only empirical investigation can show whether and how this produces substantive democratic outcomes (Heller 2001; Watson 2004). In our subsequent chapters we examine the lived relations in and around Chinese projects, the perceptions of Chinese entrepreneurs towards 'Africans' and how this shapes their levels of engagement with local society and development, as well as how Africans are adopting and adapting 'Chinese' cultural practices.

The political economy perspective discussed so far clearly relates to resource use, but largely as a factor of production in terms of exports to fuel China's growth. A more complete approach might draw on the insights of 'political ecology' which is a loose body of work drawing on neo-Marxism, post-structuralism and ecology (Peet and Watts 2004). Early political ecology sought to explain environmental degradation using a neo-Marxist perspective around the mode and relations of production, although it was criticized for underplaying 'the political', especially how multiple layers of power and governance impact upon local production and distribution of environmental impacts.

Bryant and Bailey (1997) have developed three fundamental assumptions in practising political ecology. First, costs and benefits associated with environmental change are distributed unequally. Changes in the environment do not affect society in a homogenous way: political, social, and economic differences account for uneven distribution of costs and benefits. Second, this unequal distribution inevitably reinforces or reduces existing social and economic inequalities. In this assumption, political ecology runs into inherent political economies as 'any change in environmental conditions must affect the political and economic status quo' (Bryant and Bailey 1997: 28). Third, the unequal distribution of costs and benefits and the reinforcing or reducing of pre-existing inequalities holds political implications in terms of the altered power relationships that now result.

In addition, political ecology attempts to provide critiques as well as alternatives in the interplay of the environment and political, economic and social factors. For a study of China and Africa relations natural resources and the environment are key for a number of reasons. First, as noted, we have tended to focus on economic flows (e.g. trade) and failed to assess the wider costs/benefits that an environmental analysis would bring. For example, what are the implications for ecosystem sustainability in areas where new oil exploitation is taking place under conditions of lax regulation? Second, China and other rising powers are moving into agriculture which has huge implications for access to land and thereby impacts upon the livelihoods of the poor, which we are only just beginning to comprehend. Third, China is a major producer of greenhouse gases which indirectly impact on low-income economies through climate change so that export production in China for western markets has impacts on the poor in the developing world. In turn this creates complex global governance problems where the relatively powerless developing country governments have little say. Fourth, China not only trades in natural resources but also builds infrastructure, often through 'tied aid' arrangements favouring the use of Chinese firms and inputs. Together these major projects and the importation of supplies over great distances will have hitherto unknown environmental costs.

## Methodological concerns

So far we have argued that both 'China' and 'Africa' are treated in overly simplistic terms and that we need a more fine-grained geographical and historical analysis to determine whether China ultimately is a good or bad thing for African development. We also argued that states matter, but political and economic processes operate within and across such territories and we are seeing new geographies of accumulation and development around the state but also through enclaves and assemblages. In response to these various analytical impetuses we chose a case study approach and here we set out the broad reasons for our choice of these contrasting case studies. Our case study approach involved taking two countries – Ghana and Angola – for the different relationships they offered with China, largely around the different resource endowments they possessed and the types of state. And within them we focused on specific Chinese projects as examples of development assemblages in Murray Li's sense.

First, were we to have undertaken a large-scale data analysis exercise comparing African countries in terms of Chinese aid, trade and investment we would have been confronted with a general paucity of data. Some excellent studies in this vein exist (e.g. Broadman 2007), but they rely on official statistics which we found to massively underestimate the level of activity of smaller, private Chinese firms in particular. Moreover Chinese official data is either not collected for various reasons, is collected but reported differently, or is collected and concealed (Lancaster 2007). Hence, we felt the need for more qualitative approaches involving discourse analysis of various official sources, participant observation in and around Chinese projects and businesses in Africa, and semi-structured and informal interviews with officials and entrepreneurs. A related issue is that of representativeness. One could argue that two case studies still does not address the complexity of the 'China–Africa' relationship. We agree to an extent although logistically multiple in-depth case studies are difficult to undertake consistently and at reasonable cost. To address this we have supplemented our primary data with material from other cases for comparison.

Second, we confronted problems of transparency and causality. For both similar and different reasons the Chinese and African states are opaque in their decision-making processes. Basil Davidson (1992) has talked about the 'black box' of the African state and in China there is CCP domination of agendas, information and the mindset of respondents (Heimer and Thogersen, 2006). This makes attribution difficult so we need multiple interpretations and data sources. It was for this reason, and our recurring experience of being denied access to officials, that we focused on projects as assemblages and examined the multiple relationships they are implicated in and the effects of them on local and national development. Another default strategy we adopted was to go to small-scale entrepreneurs as a possible route into the more official aid projects. It transpired, and we discuss this in Chapter 6, that the state projects hardly interact with any institution besides the in-country Chinese embassy and the Ministry of Commerce (MOFCOM) Counsellor's office. Linkages between small, independent businesses and state-owned enterprises (SOEs) were more or less non-existent. Third, there were issues of inter-cultural interpretation. Culturally 'China' and 'Africa' are relatively new to one another so interpretation by respondents of the others' actions may be hard. This was overlain by 'our' own recent exposure to Chinese literature and debates as part of a broader disjuncture of Sinologists and Africanists having worked in isolation (Mohan 2008). So our research team was assembled for the different experiences we brought to bear. There was a Lusophone Africa expert who spoke Portuguese, a qualitative environmental researcher of Chinese origin who spoke Mandarin and a West Africanist. Hopefully this sensitized us to those exchanges that Watts (2003) and Bilgin (2008) argue characterize development and international relations at both macro and micro levels.

In the next two chapters we deepen the historical comparisons between Ghana and Angola, but our broad reasons for selecting them were as follows. Ghana is the long-standing ideological friend of China and beacon of anti-colonial theorization in West Africa. It is heavily aid-dependent and has been a darling of the Bretton Woods Institutions and has made a successful transition to multiparty democracy. Only recently has oil been discovered, so crucially it runs a trade deficit with China. Angola's independence struggle was much more recent than Ghana's and China was involved alongside major superpowers. Angola's economy has been growing and it is less aid-dependent, but massive wealth polarization exists. It runs a trade surplus with China, and is a target for all oil-producing countries, which makes it an interesting strategic player in Africa.

## Book structure

This Introduction, Chapter 1, has set out some of the conceptual problems in analysing China and Africa relations. We used discourses circulating within popular culture to argue that the analysis has been oversimplified in a series of ways. From there we set out some theoretical agendas around how we understand development, the linkages between development and geopolitics, whether and how neo-liberalism is a useful lens for addressing these emerging connections between China and Africa, and the need for approaches which insert African agency into the mix. Finally we reflected on some of our methodological choices.

Chapter 2 examines the longer history of China–Africa relations. A major error of the more negative and populist accounts is that China is treated as an opportunistic 'new kid on the block'. The reality is that China and Africa have long ties dating back to at least the fifteenth century and certainly intensified during the colonial period through labour importation from China to Africa. These waves of interest, through the cold war to the present day, condition the types of engagement we see and the discourses surrounding them where history is often invoked as justification for China's 'peaceful' interests.

Chapter 3 sets out the recent policy approaches of China towards Africa and the broad-brush impacts of China's growing connectedness to various African states. It reviews the evolving 'FOCAC' process, referring to the Forum on China–Africa Cooperation that is at the heart of the recent policy shift. It shows that in the last decade the policy has become more embedded and that concerns over governance and the environment have risen up the agenda. It also examines some of the problems with this policy approach and the need for African states to manage these relations more effectively.

Chapter 4 turns back into history, though not as far as Chapter 1. Much of China's Africa interests are driven by supply-side issues in China, especially the need for raw materials and markets for the over-accumulation of surplus capital and goods. As such it is important to understand China's recent development experience as a way of understanding how and why it engages with Africa. And in keeping with our theme of disaggregation we look at the multiple actors and motives at work on the Chinese side.

One of the key aspects of China's African strategy is the bundling of aid and concessional financing with other economic ties. It is perhaps this aspect, and the political implications of what some see as the cynical use of 'soft power', that have exercised most critical commentary in the west. Chapter 5 examines these debates around aid effectiveness and the role of China and other 'emerging' donors. Clearly things are shifting but how far China actually alters the terms on which aid is delivered and the choices recipient states have can only be determined empirically so we also look at cases of how these forms of financing actually work.

Chapter 6 picks up this story by looking at the politics of these economic ties. At one level these ties strengthen an illiberal model of involvement in Africa in which elites on both sides carve out deals that bypass channels of accountability and with it any chance to debate the relative merits of these investments. Through looking at smaller scale businesses we also look at more 'everyday' forms of politics in which entrepreneurs are tied into local political processes through patronage and graft. Finally, we examine the responses from African civil society which has been largely class- and interest- based in which the petit bourgeoisie and the labour aristocracy have been most vocal in opposing the Chinese. Moreover it has been international rather than nationally centred civil society organizations that have been most active in contesting China's involvement in Africa.

Chapter 7 looks at another contentious issue surrounding Chinese working practices and popular responses; namely the environment. The limited and lazy analysis that exists tends to argue that China simply exports its poor environmental record to Africa. While Chinese firms do not have a strong environmental record the picture is more complicated with weak African regulatory environments and complicity on the part of powerful African decision-makers contributing to the deleterious ecological effects. Again, civil society responses have been quite mute but moves are afoot to instigate corporate social responsibility measures in overseas Chinese firms.

Chapter 8 picks up various debates by looking at China as a geopolitical actor. With the shift towards a much more internationalized footing the Chinese propound a discourse of a 'harmonious rise' in which the country takes on the mantle of a 'responsible' power. China's development relations with other countries of the 'south' are an important part of this and hence its Africa Strategy is a central plank of its wider geopolitical role. But so too is China's membership of various multilateral forums where it plays a crucial role but one based around being both a member of the world's elite economies and a champion of the developing world. Chapter 9 concludes by addressing some of the major themes we opened with around whether and how we need to rethink international development in an age of China.

# 2
# Contextualizing China–Africa Relations

## Introduction: a critical genealogy of China–Africa relations

> The essence of Zheng's voyages does not lie in how strong the Chinese navy once was but in that China adhere[d] to peaceful diplomacy when it was a big power ... Zheng He's seven voyages to the West [explain] why a *peaceful emergence is the inevitable outcome* of the development of Chinese history. (Xu Zuyuan, Chinese Vice Minister for Communication, cited in Xinhua (2004), emphasis added)

In much of the recent media coverage concerning China's contemporary relationship with Africa there is often little if any recognition that the historical connections between China and Africa run deep and that contemporary China–Africa engagement builds on a longer history of cooperation and interaction. It is as if China's interest in Africa is somehow 'new' and sudden, purely opportunistic or that it has come from nowhere. Yet China has long had a presence in Africa (Yu 1965; Ismael 1971; Larkin 1971; Eadie and Grizzell 1979; Jinyuan 1984) and Africans are also an important part of China's history (Brunson 1985, 1995; Snow 1988; Winters 1984). This chapter traces the *longue durée* of China's historical encounters with Africa, not by offering a simplistic chronology or by focusing purely on the history of formal diplomacy after the birth of the People's Republic of China (PRC) in 1949 but rather by looking at the long-term history of connections and encounters between China and Africa and by rejecting the linearity and seamlessness implied and imposed by the totalizing discourses of official history. These kind of official narrations of China in Africa have particular kinds of ideological uses in the contemporary historical moment and often seek to trace this history to some founding moment or point or origin. Particular regimes of 'truth' are often constructed around such formal and official histories which tend to downplay fragmentation or ignore moments of tension, conflict and contradiction in the name of positing some seamless historical continuity.

In recent years the Chinese Communist Party (CCP) has been attempting to anchor its legitimacy in history and to 'simultaneously patch the chinks in the Party's rusting spiritual-ideological armour with values adopted from traditional schools of thought' (Kallio 2011: 125). China as we understand it today – a unified state with an area equal to Europe and inhabited by the Chinese – is no more ancient than the European nation-states. Nation-building is therefore still an ongoing process in China. With the country's stability at stake, the Communist Party has to anchor its right to rule to something more permanent than economic growth and to strengthen its position as the moral and spiritual leader of the nation and so the Party has been tapping into history and tradition to revamp the basis for its leadership. The Party is also now in dire need of some ideological backing for its capitalist policies, which have led to economic growth but also widening inequalities between rich and poor. Looking for something to patch up and support its failing ideology the Party has apparently turned to traditional, Chinese schools of thought such that 'Socialism with Chinese characteristics' seems to be gradually turning into 'Chinese tradition with socialist characteristics' (Kallio 2011). The revival of Confucianism, a central component in the artificial concoction called 'Traditional Learning', provides legitimization for the Party through such values as harmony and loyalty to the state. With socialism rusting away, the Chinese characteristics have therefore become even more central (Kallio 2011). In the official rhetoric, China's growing strength is dubbed a 'peaceful rise' and China's ambitions are depicted as a 'harmonious world' and so the values of Traditional Learning are increasingly being reflected in China's foreign policy behaviour as well.

One example of how the Party has been tapping into history concerns the way in which the Muslim admiral Zheng He has been enlisted as part of its search for a usable maritime past that it can draw upon to ease worries about its intentions and to amass 'soft power' (Holmes 2007). Capitalizing on the six-hundredth anniversary of the first cruise of Zheng's 'treasure fleet' – named after the silks, porcelains and other valuables it carried to trade with foreign peoples – China's contemporary leadership has woven an intricate narrative that portrays the swift ascent of Chinese economic, military and naval power as merely the latest phase in a benign regional dominance that had its origins in the Ming era. Chinese leaders thus 'summon up Zheng He to help turn the attention of the populace seaward, rousing rank-and-file citizens for seafaring pursuits' (Holmes 2007: 2). Today's communist regime bears scant resemblance to the Ming Dynasty however and drawing a straight line from Emperor Zhu Di's foreign policy to that of the communist regime, or for that matter from the Ming armada to the People's Liberation Army Navy, is dubious at best (Holmes 2007). Clearly the Party-State has a greater need to anchor its role in history than any other preceding 'dynasty' which could all be seen as part of the same continuum of imperial China (Kallio 2011). Weigelin-Schwiedrzik (2006) argues however that in recent years the Party has lost its hegemonic control over the history of the PRC leading to the dissolution of a coherent master narrative about the history of the People's Republic and opening up a space from which to construct potential alternatives from a variety of viewpoints. Particularly in its phase of active revolution between 1949 and 1976 the Party had a stranglehold on understandings of the revolution and its own history which has remained inextricably bound up with regime legitimacy and contemporary politics until well into the 1990s. In recent years there has been a process of depoliticization both inside and outside China which has led to a proliferation of work on the PRC's history (Strauss 2006).

This chapter begins with a discussion of the initial encounters between 'China' and 'Africa' and the earliest historical evidence of China in Africa and Africa in China. It then moves on to explore some of the wider social histories of early Chinese migration to Africa and the emerging presence of a Chinese diaspora and organized Chinese communities in Africa, exploring some of the representations of Chinese workers in Africa produced at the end of the nineteenth century in the context of European colonialism and the use of Chinese indentured labour. The chapter then discusses the birth of the PRC and its coincidence with the end of European colonialism and the movement of decolonization in Africa. The Young PRC came into being at a particularly ideologically charged time as far as the wider international and security environment was concerned and it was led by a group of revolutionaries committed to international socialism at a time when the Cold War was in fact quite 'hot' (Strauss 2006). Kirby (2006) reminds us how deeply important it was to the Chinese leadership at this time to be part of something beyond China's borders – in this case the progressive international socialist world. From the very beginning the CCP was explicitly internationalist in premise and in promise (Kirby 2006) and relations with both Cold War superpowers played an important role in shaping China's early strategies in Africa. The chapter then situates this important history within the context of the Cold War and the wider climate of third-worldism, looking at the major geopolitical forces of change and the wider context of changing global dynamics.

Particular attention is given to questions of ideology and to the evolving attempts to build partnerships for development established around particular principles for cooperation and aid-giving. Throughout the chapter there is a specific focus on the history of Chinese aid practices in Africa and a number of specific aid and development projects (especially the iconic Tazara railway) are examined here. The chapter then moves on to critically explore the emergence of discourses of 'Afro-Asian solidarity' and 'South-South cooperation' before then examining some of the key shifts in China's Africa policy following the growing focus on China's own domestic modernization in the 1970s and during Africa's 'lost decade' in the 1980s. The penultimate section examines the particular example of Angola and the specific history of China's involvement there, a country which has had a very turbulent history of anti-colonialism and complex trajectories of postcolonial state formation. The chapter concludes with a discussion of the idea that China's historical experiences are analogous to those of its African partners and explores the ideological motivations for constructing historical commonalities between China and Africa. Overall the chapter insists on the importance of understanding contemporary China–Africa relations in historical context and explains how past experiences of partnership and cooperation are shaping current trends. In particular the chapter seeks to explore the ideological uses to which the history of China–Africa relations is put in the contemporary era and seeks to ask why China's own articulation of the principles by which it lives in general and towards Africa in particular have been so remarkably consistent for the past 50 years.

## China in Africa, Africa in China: initial encounters

There are indications that the indirect exchange of products between China and Africa could go back two thousand years as Chinese officials were sent to and visited Africa and an African magician[1] came to China, thus starting the earliest human contact between the two continents (Jinyuan 1984). According to Basil Davidson (1959: 158) 'Chinese goods were certainly reaching the Red Sea and the Mediterranean, by the sea routes, as early as the beginning of the Christian era'. By the tenth and eleventh centuries Arab reports and Chinese trade figures indicate that large quantities of African products were reaching China. East African ivory was prominent in this trade along with other products that were attractive for medicinal purposes. During China's Sung Dynasty (960–1279) China's agriculture, commerce and handicraft industry, which included iron-smelting, porcelain-making and ship-building, advanced significantly and thus trade between China and foreign countries as far as Persia and Arabia and even Africa became more frequent and increased in scale (Jinyuan 1984). With the development of trade, China's knowledge about Africa also increased. Zhao Rugua, a Provincial commissioner for maritime trade wrote a book entitled *Ju Fan Zhi* (Records of Foreign Countries) in which he describes a number of African States such as Berbera, Shenli (both in Somalia), Zanj (Zanzibar), Fris and Alexandria (in Egypt), Mulanbi (in Maghrib) and Kunlun Zanj (which historians identify as Madagascar). China's knowledge about Africa further developed in the Yuan Dynasty (1279–1368) when a cartographer named Zhu Siben drew a map in 1315 with Africa shaped like a triangle pointing southward.

Some of the most significant early encounters however occurred during the time of the Ming Dynasty (1368–1644). Between 1405 and 1433, the Ming government sponsored a series of seven naval expeditions designed to establish a Chinese presence, to impose imperial control over trade, to extend the tribute system and to impress foreign peoples in the Indian Ocean basin. The Muslim admiral Zheng He was placed in control of a huge fleet of around 28,000 men and 63 vessels, each at least six times larger than the three small ships sailed by Columbus (Brautigam 2009). In the course of at least two or three of his seven voyages, he and his fleet reached the East African coast and visited Mogadishu, Brava, Juba and Malindi (the former three in present-day Somalia, the latter in Kenya). It is said that a village in north Somalia still bears the name of 'Zheng He Village' in memory of the visit of the 'Chinese Columbus' (Jinyuan 1984; Snow 1988). By the end of Emperor Zhu Di's reign, *baochuan* (treasure ships) had conveyed kings or ambassadors from over thirty foreign states to China on official visits, giving rise to 'a far-flung system of allies who acknowledged Ming supremacy in return for diplomatic recognition, military protection, and trading rights' (Viviano 2005: 37, 41). At the lavish 600th anniversary in commemoration of his voyage in 2005 senior Chinese government officials were quick to celebrate the significance of his travels and to underline that he was an envoy of friendship and peace.

There is also abundant evidence to show that African people within documented historical periods created, nurtured or influenced some of ancient Asia's most important and enduring classical civilizations just as there is evidence of black Africans in ancient China. Brunson (1995) details, for example, some of the significant contributions that Africans have historically made to the Chinese 'race', history and early civilization, particularly during the time of the three major empires of ancient China – the Xia Dynasty (c.2100–1600 BC), Shang/Yin Dynasty (c.1600–1100 BC) and the Zhou Dynasty (1100–256 BC). There are records of African slaves in Canton in the twelfth century, for example, while the founders of Xia and Shang came from the Fertile African Crescent by way of Iran (Winters 1984). In the fourteenth century, Moroccan traveller and scholar Ibn Battuta made a long journey to Africa and Asia, reaching China in April 1345 after a stay in India before serving as an envoy of Sultan Muhammad Tughlaq (of the Indian Tughlaq dynasty) to China. There is also evidence of the arrival of Swahili sailors on Chinese shores in the thirteenth and fourteenth centuries. Van Sertima (1976) notes that the Swahili were actually transporting elephants to the courts in China as early as the thirteenth century but the most famed and well-documented Swahili visits to China centre around the trade links Chinese and African people established during the 1400s. Brunson (1985) includes images of a miniature clay figure of a Swahili sailor that was unearthed in China, made in the likeness of a merchant from the East African island of Zanzibar and dating back to China's Tang Dynasty (618–907 AD).

The period of the Tang Dynasty (618–907) was rich in stories which include references to African servants who spoke and behaved like Chinese people and were treated with respect by their owners (Snow 1988: 17). These few uprooted slaves 'strong, a little frightening, utterly mysterious, excited in Chinese minds a mixture of admiration and awe. Possibly the Chinese hoped to harness their magic' (Snow 1988: 18). There also exists a record of an eyewitness account of Swahili merchants in the Far East from the Portuguese trader Tome Pires who lived in Malaysia from 1512 to 1515 AD. In his memoir Pires reported seeing in Malaysia peoples from the east African cities of Kilwa, Mombasa and Malindi. The Portuguese also began bringing Africans to China. Macao, for example, in the early seventeenth century had a distinctly African flavour. In 1635 it was said to contain some 7000 inhabitants: 5100 of which were slaves and most of them were African men and women (Snow 1988). Whenever Zheng He visited Africa he usually returned to China with African ambassadors and the ambassadors[2] habitually brought exotic animals to present to the imperial court. After Zheng He's visit to the east African city of Malindi in 1414 the ruler of Malindi sent a personal envoy with a giraffe as a present to China on that fleet. Such episodes are today routinely recalled to indicate that China never sought to annexe African territory or to plunder its resources. The Chinese thus claim that they did not seek to colonize Africa or as one Chinese diplomat has put it China took 'not an inch of land, not a slave, but a giraffe for the emperor to admire' (cited in Brautigam 2009: 23). Unlike the Europeans that arrived 70 years after Zheng He the Chinese were not aggressive and unlike the Portuguese they stormed no cities and conquered no land, refraining from plunder:

> Instead they coaxed the coastal rulers into trading by presenting them with gifts of coloured silk. They did not burn, as the Portuguese would, with the urge to impose their religious convictions to lay siege to African souls. All they sought from Africans was a gesture of symbolic acquiescence in the Chinese view of the world. (Snow 1988: 29)

The Chinese came simply to garner prestige and profit for the emperor in Peking which they could achieve perfectly well through their traditional system of exchanging imperial favours for foreign 'tribute' (Snow 1988). As an empire, China had evolved a tribute system: a long tradition of exchanges with smaller nations in its sphere of influence. It is also worth remembering that the Chinese already had many of the natural resources and other forms of wealth (e.g. gold) that Europeans wanted from Africa. Further, the doctors and pharmacists on each of the Chinese ships often took back only African herbs and local medicinal compounds and many of these visits were in fact of a reciprocal nature (Brautigam 2009).

## The 'Overseas Chinese': migration to Africa and the Chinese diaspora

In addition to tracing the earliest recorded encounters between China and Africa and showing that China–Africa engagement does not begin with the birth of the PRC in 1949 it is also important to trace the earliest forms of Chinese migration to Africa and the historical emergence of a Chinese diaspora. The history of Chinese migrants' presence in Africa dates back to the late seventeenth century, to their arrival as slaves, convicts, or indentured labourers working in the continent's goldmines and they have long formed a distinct community on the continent. As Mohan and Tan-Mullins (2009) have argued, however, the term 'Overseas Chinese' has been used too loosely in many contexts, is inherently contested both within China and beyond and tends to subsume identity, class and behavioural differences under an overarching diasporic identity. Moreover 'the Chinese' are very different both culturally and linguistically. Often speaking different languages, let alone identifying as a coherent group, Chinese people in Africa have flexible identities and generate greater or lesser senses of community among themselves depending on a range of factors (Wilhelm 2006; Hsu 2007; Ho 2008). Thus in seeking to trace the growing presence of Chinese migrants in Africa there is a need to understand what Mung (2008: 105–6) terms the 'triangular' perspective in which 'the Chinese diaspora does not only relate to China, but also interacts with the society where it has settled'. There is also a need to recognize that flows of Chinese migrants to Africa have fluctuated across different historical periods, reflecting different economic and political conditions in China and the changing scope of China's international engagements (Mohan and Tan-Mullins 2009).

As far back as the eighteenth century, the Chinese state had policies opposing migrants leaving China (Shen 2006). Systematic Chinese migration to Africa only really began in the mid-nineteenth century (Chang 1968), especially in the aftermath of the abolition of slavery (McKeown 1999). Demand was primarily for plantation, mining and railway construction, although push factors in China included land pressure and conflict. It was after the Opium Wars of the 1840s and 1850s that China was forced by the colonial powers to reduce restrictions on Chinese emigration, which saw the beginning of large-scale movements of Chinese people overseas in the form of the 'coolie trade' (Chang 1968; Park 2006). The 'coolie trade' developed in the nineteenth century in connection with two global events: the gradual abolition of slavery and European colonization. The end of slavery deprived companies of their slave labour while colonization – and more generally the development of the colonial economy – increased the need for hands to work in the plantations, the mines and in the construction of roads and railways. Local recruitment did not cover these needs, and slave labour was no longer a possibility. The colonial companies and governments set in place a system to recruit labour in China and India on contracts lasting several years – from 4 to 8 years, depending on the case. The 'coolie trade' concerned newly colonized Southeast Asia, but also the archipelagos in the Indian Ocean, the South Pacific (Polynesia, Hawaii), the West Indies and Latin America. When their miserable contracts expired, many 'coolies' stayed on because they did not have the means to return home. The 'coolie trade' was the biggest labour migration after the slave trade, and announced the large-scale proletarian migrations of the twentieth century (Mung 2000). European prospectors found the first alluvial gold deposits at Eersteling (Limpopo Province) in South Africa between 1840 and 1870, with the first major gold rush in South Africa in 1873. Thus from the 1870s South Africa became one of the main foci for immigration. These Chinese labourers or 'coolies' were originally recruited by the white colonialists to work in mines in South Africa during the early twentieth century. In the end, it is calculated, about 70,000 to 100,000 Chinese labourers were imported and worked in mines in South Africa from 1904 to 1907 (Robinson 1977). Chinese labourers were also recruited by the French and British to work on plantations in Mauritius, Madagascar and Reunion during the nineteenth century and many were employed by the Germans for building the central railway in Tanganyika at the beginning of the twentieth century (Jinyuan 1984). Most of these labour contracts were highly regulated and workers were sent back after their contracts expired. However, as Mohan and Tan-Mullins (2009) have shown, this 'coolie trade' is often over-represented as the paradigm of Chinese migration. There were also small, but enterprising groups of independent traders that serviced Chinese labour migrants and undertook small-scale export (Pan 2005). From the late nineteenth century in South Africa independent artisans and family trading firms constituted the oldest communities known today as 'local' Chinese in distinction from more recent ones (Wilhelm 2006). The original South African Chinese community was mainly male and from two ethnic groups – Cantonese and the Hakka. Many members of the current South African Chinese community originally immigrated from Taiwan – which maintained diplomatic relations with South Africa during apartheid – in the 1980s and early 1990s. Today there are sizeable and long-standing migrant communities in South Africa and Mauritius as well as Reunion and Madagascar, which can be traced back to the colonial period, as well as to an expansion of Hong Kong and Taiwanese migrants[3] in the 1980s (Li 2005). While Mung (2008) is right to see parallels between late nineteenth-century Chinese contract labour migration to Africa organized by the colonial empires and contemporary forms of labour recruitment from China, there are clearly important differences in terms of the decentralized coordination of recent migration, the nature of the Chinese and African states then and now and the ideologies of development that underpin such movements (Nyiri 2006).

In 1949, when the PRC was formed, there was a reversal of policy, and emigration was officially ended, restricting movement to illegal emigration or people joining existing family overseas. Between the 1960s and the beginning of the 1980s (with the exception of the Cultural Revolution) at least 150,000 Chinese technical assistants were dispatched to Africa (ECOWAS-SWAC/OECD 2006). A significant number of these workers stayed on (Hsu 2007) to engage in commercial activities. At the same time, the perception of Overseas Chinese shifted from being seen as 'traitors' to being viewed as the new vanguards of Third World nationalism (Thuno 2001) and migrants were now freer to engage in tangible activities linking them to home in the form of remittances and charity (Young and Shih 2003). In terms of medical practitioners, Hsu (2007) shows how in Tanzania/Zanzibar, some Chinese doctors who had worked for aid teams in the 1970s stayed on to set up private practices using both Chinese and 'western' medical technologies (Figure 2.1). Hsu (2007) traces the government-sent teams of Chinese experts that were posted for one to two years in Zanzibar but that typically did not settle (Figure 2.2). Noting how different Chinese provinces were assigned responsibility for different African countries, Hsu (2007) documents how during the period of Julius Nyerere's

*Figure 2.1*   One of the many Chinese clinics to have emerged in Lusaka (Zambia) in recent years. Photograph by D J Clark

中、非人民情谊深

*Figure 2.2* 'The feelings of friendship between the peoples of China and Africa are deep'. May 1972. Stefan R. Landsberger collection, International Institute of Social History (Amsterdam)

presidency, Shandong province sent over 200 medical teams to hospitals all over Tanzania (while it sends only two to four nowadays) and neighbouring Jiangsu province was allocated responsibility for the semi-independent Zanzibar. Contrary to the popular story that early migrants in the 1950s and 1960s were aid workers who stayed on, Ho (2008) shows in Ghana that a number of migrants came at the country's independence lured primarily by the promise of a stable and soon to flourish economy. In some cases, the factory owners set up the factories and then brought in managers from Hong Kong while they moved on to start other ventures.

## From 'Afro-Asian Solidarity' to 'South–South' cooperation

For nearly four years after the defeat of Japan in the Second World War a civil war continued to rage in China between the Communist Party of China and the Kuomintang (KMT). By October 1949 Mao Zedong and the communist People's Liberation Army had pushed Chiang Kai-shek's

Peoples Party and the government of the Republic of China (ROC) into retreat on the Island of Taiwan. The two sides (PRC and ROC) faced each other in an undeclared truce across the Gulf of Taiwan. The United States refused to recognize the new government in Beijing and imposed a total economic embargo on China that lasted nearly 20 years (Strauss 2006). Ever since the Korean War of the early 1950s, when Chinese and American troops fought on opposite sides, the United States had posed a threat to the security of the new Communist China. Thus China entered Africa locked in combat with the United States. Further, despite its nationalist rhetoric the PRC was 'born pro-Soviet' and without the Soviet Union there could have been no CCP and no PRC (Kirby 2006). The great Sino-Soviet exchange that ensued in the 1950s was thus part of a larger web of cooperative relationships with all the 'brother countries' of the Soviet bloc. By 1949 a shadow of a 'Soviet model' of state-led industrialization and foreign trade was already evident while Mao Zedong initially had a strong desire to transplant Soviet experience to China, taking the country along a clearly Stalinist path. In political, economic and military terms China became a client of the Soviet Union, guided by Soviet advisors and sustained by Soviet aid (Snow 1988).

Snow (1988) argues that the problems of Africa were far from the minds of the Chinese communists in the earliest years of their rule. After decades of civil war and Japanese occupation, Chinese leaders' first development concerns were to meet the needs of the exhausted population. As the 1950s wore on however the Chinese increasingly came to believe that Africa seemed to be 're-enacting' their own recent past and Chinese leaders soon began to draw attention to a whole series of parallels that they had noticed and to argue that it was thus China's duty to 'explain' these similarities to Africans. China was convinced that events in Africa in the 1950s and 1960s were no more than a 'replay' of their own history. In the 1950s, for example, when Cameroonians were fighting French colonialism Mao is said to have presented one of their leaders with a copy of his work *Problems of Strategy in the Guerilla War against Japan*, inscribed with the greeting: 'In this book you can read everything which is now going to happen in the Cameroons' (Snow 1988: 82). Similarly, during the height of the Cultural Revolution[4] at the end of the 1960s the Chinese media portrayed African national liberation movements as using Mao Zedong Thought as their primary ideological tool for liberation and revolution (Figure 2.3). This was a vital part of the strategic doctrine of 'People's War' which held that the advanced industrial nations constituted the 'cities' of the world, and

*Figure 2.3* 'Chairman Mao is the great liberator of the world's revolutionary people'. April 1968. Stefan R. Landsberger collection, International Institute of Social History (Amsterdam)

the poor nations of Asia, Africa and Latin America were the 'country-side'. By fomenting revolution in the various 'rural' areas of the world, eventually the liberation movements would surround and overrun the urban areas, just as they had in China during its civil war (Jackson 1995).

In a bid to convey the long-term nature and continuity of China's interest in Africa the particular shape of contemporary China–Africa relations is often traced back to the 1950s and specifically to the connections forged during the anti-colonial struggles for independence in Africa and the revolutionary period of Chinese foreign policy beginning in the 1950s. At the moment of the PRC's foundation there were however only four independent countries in Africa: Egypt,[5] Ethiopia, Liberia and the (Apartheid) South African state. China had arms left over from their wars with the Japanese and Chiang Kai-shek while China learned to produce more arms in the 1950s as an ally and technical apprentice of the Soviet Union (Snow 1988) (Figure 2.4). China also specialized in training Africans in the arts of guerrilla warfare, initially at the military academy in the city of Nanjing. Training was also conducted in Africa at a series of remote training camps in countries like Tanzania and Ghana (Snow 1988). The enthusiasm with which many Africans looked upon Beijing in the early years of independence was however offset by widespread fear as most African leaders of the 1950s and 1960s knew very little about China (Snow 1995).

By the mid-1950s however China was increasingly becoming uncomfortable with being confined to the Soviet camp. China saw a chance to establish a separate identity in the world of newly independent Asian and African states (Snow 1988). Two key historical moments stand out here – the Asian–African Conference that met in Bandung, Indonesia in April 1955 and the establishment of the Afro-Asian People's Solidarity Organization (AAPSO) which held its first conference in 1957 (the same year that Ghana became the first black African country to win its independence). Afro-Asian solidarity in particular, forged in the crucible of independence struggles, would go on to provide an important political foundation for the evolving China–Africa relationship. Given China's colonial history and struggle against poverty, the Chinese claimed that their unique understanding of Africa's economic dilemma lies at the root of Sino-African solidarity and could serve as a strong foundation for cordial relations (Tjonneland et al. 2006: 75). Bandung thus became 'a symbol of Afro-Asia as a viable political concept' (Larkin 1971: 28) and China invoked the Bandung spirit (which saw Africans and Asians sharing common political and social tasks) to gain support for

學習蘇聯先進經驗建設我們的祖國

*Figure 2.4*   'Study the Soviet Union's advanced economy to build up our nation'. June 1953. Stefan R. Landsberger collection, International Institute of Social History (Amsterdam)

initiatives that China favoured. China, as an Asian country, was invited to Bandung but the Soviet Union was not. At the conference, contacts were made for the first time between the PRC and African diplomats, leading to the establishment of a Chinese embassy in Egypt as the first on the African continent (Shelton 2005).

It does not appear that Africa was important to China at Bandung however and although it marked the beginning of significant Chinese initiatives in Africa there is little evidence that China foresaw this with clarity (Larkin 1971). Further, only 6 of the 29 states represented were African (Egypt, Ethiopia, Gold Coast (Ghana), Liberia, Libya and Sudan[6]) (Chavan 1979). The AAPSO was the chief institution embodying this Bandung spirit and it established a permanent secretariat in Cairo although the organization was largely unable to translate words into action.[7] Further, Chinese wishes were often stubbornly and effectively resisted within these organizations and by no means did China fully control them (Neuhauser 1968; Larkin 1971). Chinese influence in AAPSO peaked in 1960–61 (Neuhauser 1968: 35–7) but by this time the bitter ideological dispute between the USSR and China had heightened competition for dominance over various organizations of Afro-Asian solidarity and the non-aligned countries (Ismael 1971). By 1963, China and the Soviet Union had finally split 'after three years of increasingly bitter and vituperative polemics' (Jackson 1995: 395). The effect of the split on China's relations with African liberation groups was soon felt as China and the Soviet Union first attempted to influence groups to take sides in their ideological dispute and later demanded that they align with one or the other. This process became increasingly divisive of African groups and as Chinese rhetoric became highly radical, Chinese attention focused on increasingly small splinter groups (Jackson 1995). President Nkrumah[8] of Ghana even offered his services as a mediator between China and the USSR while the Angolan MPLA (Movimento Popular de Libertação de Angola/Popular Movement for the Liberation of Angola) brought Chinese and Russians together at a conference in Tanzania (Snow 1988: 118–19).

In addition to the emergence of the concept of Afro-Asian solidarity we can also trace the emergence of key guiding principles of China–Africa cooperation to the Bandung gathering. The 'five principles' of *pancheela* (alternately *panchsheel* or *panchshila*), agreed upon by India's Jawaharlal Nehru and China's Zhou Enlai at the conference were meant to serve as a model for intra-Asian relations and were partly a response to rising border tensions between China and India (Strauss 2009). These were as follows: 'respect for territorial integrity; nonaggression; non-interference in each other's internal affairs; equality and mutual benefit in relations; and peaceful coexistence' (Jones 2005: 851). By the early 1960s, China had established relations with a number of left-leaning or radical states,[9] including Egypt, Algeria, Somalia, Tanganyika, Ghana and Congo-Brazzaville. By this time then a small nucleus of countries had taken the risky step of establishing formal diplomatic relations with Peking, opening a window for China to 'bring their gospel of independence to African soil' (Snow 1988: 74) and to begin selling its principled packages of aid and cooperation to African postcolonial states. The message was brought directly by Chinese premier Zhou Enlai, who (together with an entourage of 50) began a visit of African countries in the last weeks of 1963 as a wave of alarm rose across the West (Large 2008a). The tour to Africa followed on from two previous tours to Asian countries (in 1956–57 and in 1960) and began as a visit to six states which already had ties with China (Egypt, Algeria, Morocco, Ghana, Guinea and Mali) while calls on four other states (Sudan, Somalia, Tunisia and Ethiopia) were arranged while the tour was in progress. Visits to Kenya, Uganda and Tanganyika were arranged and then cancelled when army mutinies broke out in all three of them (Snow 1988).

One of Zhou's main messages was that the governments that were receiving him were not setting any shocking precedent by doing so and that China had a perfect right to be in their midst. Basing his case on history, Zhou drew attention to Zheng He and the long record of early Chinese contact with the East African coast. China was thus simply 'renewing acquaintances with old friends' (Zhou Enlai quoted in Snow 1988: 75). During the tour Zhou also argued that European colonialism had disrupted the peaceful trade links that existed between Africa and China since the fifteenth century. Zhou also confirmed Beijing's support for African struggles against imperialism (which he called 'the poor helping the poor') and famously declared Africa 'ripe for revolution'. When in Ghana and Mali Zhou announced eight guiding principles for Chinese aid to foreign countries that were a development of *Pancheela* including talk of equality, mutual benefit, non-interference and respect for sovereignty. Building on these principles and as an extension of the wider concept of Afro-Asian solidarity Zhou's tour foreshadowed the concept of 'South-South' cooperation in advocating mutual economic assistance between 'poor friends' and in attacking the bullying of small and weak countries by the 'big and strong' (Snow 1995). Zhou's announcement about support for anti-imperial movements during his 1963–64 tour followed Mao Zedong's August 1963 speech on colonialism and racism, which pointed to the PRC's desire to lead the developing world and confirmed the breakdown of the Sino-Soviet relationship (Shelton 2005). Unlike the Soviet Union, the Chinese emphasized the struggle between the developed and the underdeveloped worlds, between the North and the South. In this context, China placed itself squarely in world politics as the champion of the Third World (Guimarães 1998: 154). By spreading the gospels of nationalism and independence and in its good works, China set out to knit the African countries together into a Third World alliance with China at its head as a counterbalance to the Cold War superpowers and wealthy advanced economies of the North. China thus increasingly emphasized South-South cooperation (even if it did not always explicitly use this language) as a key element in its efforts to oppose unilateral global dominance and as an important way of building a relationship that would support a diplomatic offensive against 'hegemonism'.

Both Chinese and African people have found common ground in the belief that the West's historical experiences in achieving 'development' are distant from the African experience and offer few transferable lessons. Beijing has also argued that both China and Africa are 'cradles of civilization', that both 'belong to the developing world' and face common enemies and that as a result they have common strategic interests and a shared perspective on major international issues. Consequently Beijing has argued that China and Africa should support each other in close cooperation on key global issues while China has often sought to mobilize and maintain African support on those issues. China staged its own conference on South-South cooperation in Shanghai in April 1983 and Beijing's rhetoric of unity and practical backing have constituted an area of broad consensus on which African leaders have been happy to agree. Although China steadfastly refused to join key institutions of South-South cooperation like the Non-Aligned Movement (NAM) or G77, since joining the World Trade Organization (WTO) in 2001 China has become active in trying to address some of the trade symmetries between North and South. It has also attempted to address these questions through the 'G77 plus China' and the G20. In recent years debt relief or the abolition of tariffs are often held up by China as forms of 'south-south cooperation' as China has cancelled nearly US$1.3 billion in debt to 31 African countries and abolished tariffs on 190 different goods from 29 African countries. There is also the International Poverty Reduction Centre in China (IPRCC)[10] which is designed to provide a platform for knowledge sharing, information exchange and international collaboration in the areas of poverty reduction and development along with the Africa–China Forum on Poverty Reduction and Development which met in Cairo in 2010. Some authors (Owen and Melville 2005; Alden 2005; Carroll 2006; Marks 2006) are however sceptical about China's interest in Africa as a form of 'south-south cooperation', which is more progressive and less selfish, suggesting it might be the more familiar and hegemonic 'north-south relationship'. Similarly Snow (1995: 321) questions the way in which China has used 'camouflage tactics' to disguise its private interests and campaigns or has articulated a 'rhetorical unity which has sometimes disguised the pursuit of profoundly different goals'. For all the Chinese rhetoric of seeking to assist African development as a form of South-South cooperation, it is very much the case that development in China itself is immensely uneven, and that the domestic basis for Chinese prosperity is in fact politically volatile (Chan 2008).

## China's aid projects in Africa

The principles for aid and cooperation reflected China's own experience as an aid recipient itself over the preceding 60 years where the Chinese had not appreciated their 'client' status (Snow 1988) and were partly calculated to 'show up the North' (Snow 1995: 287) by contrasting with the assistance then provided by 'first world' countries. Aid[11] would not be 'a kind of unilateral alms but [rather] something mutual' (MFA 2000). Loans would be non-conditional, interest-free, or low-interest and easily rescheduled. Projects would use high-quality materials, have quick results and boost self-reliance. Chinese experts would transfer their expertise 'fully' and live at the standard of local counterparts. The Chinese also brought a refreshing pragmatism in their approach. Brautigam (2009) notes that it was probably fortunate for Africa that China's first aid programmes there were mainly established *after* the disaster of the Great Leap Forward[12] (1958–61) as a pragmatic approach started to prevail in China's aid programme. Snow (1988) notes, for example, how in 1964 Zhou Enlai advised Ghana's President Kwame Nkrumah to scale down his industrialization plans because they were 'too ambitious' while when in Algeria Zhou suggested that China was not a model to emulate but instead a kind of 'reference point'.[13] In the wake of Zhou's tour China committed a total of nearly US$120 million to Congo-Brazzaville, Ghana, Kenya, Mali and Tanzania (Brautigam 2009). For its first official aid project in sub-Saharan Africa China built a cigarette and match factory just outside Conakry in Guinea (Brautigam 2009). Guinea was 1 of only 14 sub-Saharan African countries to forge diplomatic ties with the PRC immediately after independence. Others followed the US lead and recognized the ROC or delayed making a decision due to other more pressing domestic concerns.

China's first official aid recipients reflected ideological interests. Along with Sekou Touré, socialist leaders took power in Ghana (Kwame Nkrumah) and Mali (Modibo Keita) with both countries promptly receiving aid from China. Aid was also used to encourage each new government to recognize Beijing as 'China' instead of Taipei. According to Snow (1988) Chinese assistance to Africa during the phase of China's active revolution between 1949 and 1976 was considered to be a 'heroic endeavour', with the continent as the 'object of a philanthropic crusade' (Snow 1988: 146) and China seeking to discharge its 'missionary duty of setting Africa free' (ibid: 153). From 1956 to 1973, out of the total US$3.38 billion aid granted by China, just over half the amount (US$1.73 billion) was granted to African countries (Brautigam 2009). China's method of giving aid, it can be argued, has displayed certain distinctive historical features. It was usually given as a grant, or as an interest-free loan, which was different to the Soviet model where interest was charged at 2.5 per cent (Snow 1988). Strictly bilateral in nature and only given where the relationship was mutually beneficial to donor and recipient alike, Chinese aid workers were also unique in their approach, not being permitted to 'loll in hotel suites and run up expenses as other expatriates did [having to] content themselves with the same standard of living as the ordinary Africans they worked with' (Snow 1988: 146).

Chinese aid went to various sectors of African 'development' such as light industry, transport, agriculture, water control and irrigation, public health, power and communications, sports and cultural complexes and heavy industry. In 50 years of cooperation some 900 infrastructure and public benefit projects have been built by China in Africa most of which were small or medium sized (Brautigam 2009). Africa tended to receive proportionately more projects concerned with agriculture, irrigation, medicine and sports facilities (Eadie and Grizzell 1979). China funded state-owned factories in Africa, where skilled technicians from Shanghai's pre-war industries trained Africans to churn out substitutes for exports (Brautigam 2009). Cotton textile mills dominated. Medical teams of doctors and medics were also sent out. Chinese construction teams built bridges, roads, power plants and ports and always a popular 'prestige' project or two: a very visible 'friendship' conference hall, a modern government ministry building or a stadium named in honour of a friendly president (Brautigam 2009). China seemed happy to work on projects that were effectively inessential monuments to the glory of the African regimes they worked with such as conference halls, sports stadia (Figure 2.5) and party headquarters and on projects that 'seemed calculated less to promote the development of a country's economy than to win for Peking the favour of the [recipient] regime' (Snow 1988: 156). Up until the early 1970s many African leaders believed that Chinese assistance was given to them for wholly altruistic reasons with no strings attached whatsoever (Yu 1977).

At the start of the 1970s Chinese teams were building close to 100 different turnkey aid projects around the world (three in Latin America, six in the Middle East and twenty-nine in Africa by 1973) and had committed aid to seven countries in Asia (Brautigam 2009: 41). The level of aid and the number of large, costly projects initiated during the Cultural Revolution had however far outpaced China's capacity (Brautigam 2009). Zhou Enlai and Mao Zedong had embraced 19 enormous '100 million RMB' projects (each worth about US$50 million in the 1970s) during their terms in power. Between 1967 and 1976 China's aid had reached an average of 5 per cent of government expenditure while the State Council sponsored five national conferences on foreign aid between 1972 and 1977 (Brautigam 2009). One of the reasons for

*Figure 2.5* A sign at the front of the National Stadium in Maputo, Mozambique says 'the friendship between Mozambique will last for ever like the heaven and the earth'. The National Stadium for Mozambique, completed in 2011, was built by Chinese contractors and paid for as a gift by the Chinese government at a cost of US$ 70 million. Photograph by D J Clark

this was the fundamental change in the diplomatic relations of the PRC between October 1970 and October 1972 as China established or re-established diplomatic relations with 15 African states in this period (Jackson 1995). Many of these states in turn voted for China's admission to the United Nations in autumn 1971 (the seat previously occupied by Taiwan). Chairman Mao Zedong described the situation bluntly: '[w]e were brought back into the United Nations by our black African friends' (cited in Weng Ming 1995: 9). China then started aid programmes in 13 different African countries.

By 1978 some seventy-four countries were receiving aid from China, the largest group of which were in Africa and by then China had aid programmes in more African countries than the United States. Aid was dispensed in the very early years by the Ministry of Foreign Economic Relations (Snow 1988: 147) but later on what other countries would call development assistance became part of the Ministry of Commerce (King 2006). Each Chinese province also had a foreign aid bureau that the Ministry could draw upon if it needed to locate expertise for its Africa missions. In the sphere of medical aid a kind of twinning system was organized where a province of China would be 'twinned' with an African country (Snow 1988). By the early 1980s nearly 150,000 Chinese aid technicians had been sent to Africa in a call to Chinese national glory and sacrifice. Many aid workers made an effort to speak local languages and were often keen to 'muck in' to avoid hierarchies and to show what could be achieved with dedicated effort (Snow 1988). Many Chinese projects however did not anticipate how difficult it would be to ensure long-term sustainability through training and to 'transfer' the technology they had brought with them and many did not cooperate very closely with African countries about the detail of the planning processes involved (Brautigam 1998).

The Chinese often made a point of supporting schemes which the West had rejected on narrowly economic grounds or which were important to African states for political or psychological reasons and they also made a point of 'doing something' for districts which the Europeans had been content to leave as backwaters (Snow 1988). Aid was also an important geopolitical tool for the Chinese in the contest with Taiwan (also an aid giver) and the USSR (where the Chinese aimed to shame the Kremlin by stepping up their charity and economic aid and by providing fewer arms). Aid thus became an important way of exposing the limitations of China's opponents, both Western and Soviet. Thus in the 1960s Beijing had a 'tendency to launch spectacular rescue operations' (Snow 1995: 288). There was often a reluctance however to coordinate efforts with other foreign powers and a deep-seated tendency to 'go it alone' sometimes resulting in active hostility to other aid personnel. However, domestic, economic and social difficulties as well as China's Cultural Revolution undermined the PRC's efforts to implement ambitious foreign policy objectives in Africa due to the domestic upheaval in China that resulted and the confusion that spread among China's official representatives overseas.

According to Neuhauser (1968) Peking's failure in Africa during the late 1960s may also be attributed to the ignorance of PRC leaders and their failure to grasp the significance of regional antagonisms and cultural and historical differences between the various countries while trying to apply a general model of revolution to all African 'liberation movements'.[14] During this time China tried to provide support to liberation movements in Angola, Mozambique and South Africa, for example, but 'backed the wrong horse in all three cases' (Cheng and Shi 2009: 89). Similarly Snow (1995) argues that the Chinese were not especially interested in domestic developments in African countries let alone in actively propagating Communism there. China's relations with its 'third world partners' and 'poor friends' were 'either thin or troubled through much of the Maoist period' (Harding 1995: 394) as it refused to join key organizations like the G77 or the NAM. China's uncompromising call to revolution, her subversive activities and her support for African Communist and revolutionary parties, often in opposition to the established government, thus led to a period of decline in Chinese influence on the continent.

## The Tazara Railway (1967–75)

All previous aid efforts were dwarfed however by the massive Tanzania–Zambia Railway Authority (Tazara; 1967–75) which cost over US$600 million (more than the Aswan dam had cost the Soviet Union) (Brautigam 1998). The enormous and costly railway project had been envisioned by Cecil Rhodes in the late nineteenth century and was briefly considered by the British colonialists a decade later. Rejected as unfeasible by a World Bank mission, China, Tanzania and Zambia signed off on the project in 1967 to widespread scepticism (Brautigam 2009). Running from Dar-es-Salaam to Kapiri Mposhi, the Tazara railway (which includes ten kilometers of bridges and 300 tunnels) took only five years to build and was finished two years ahead of schedule in 1975. Before construction work began, 12 Chinese surveyors travelled for nine months on foot from Dar es Salaam to Mbeya in the Southern Highlands to hack a path for the railway through the bush (Monson 2009). Later some 50,000 Tanzanians and 25,000 Chinese toiled on the actual construction.

The Tazara railway has since assumed almost iconic status as a symbol of the first heroic stage of China's involvement in Africa and an ideologically inspired symbol of anti-imperialist solidarity, in contrast with today's more pragmatic and market-driven Chinese engagement with the continent. That was certainly how it was seen at the time it was built in the early 1970s (Brautigam 2009). China came forward to build the railway and fund it with a US$450m loan after western donors – including the World Bank and the UN – rejected initial approaches to back the project. The news was greeted with alarm in the West. The *Wall Street Journal* warned that 'the prospect of hundreds and perhaps thousands of Red Guards descending upon an already troubled Africa is a chilling one for the West'. One US Congressman luridly described it as a 'great steel arm of China thrusting its way into the African interior' (US Congress 1973: 286). Monson (2009) discusses the origins of the African leaders' aspiration to build the railway and the Sino-African goal of achieving economic independence from the former colonial regimes and from Rhodesia, South Africa and the Portuguese colonies. The themes of nationalism, self-reliance, Pan-Africanism and development espoused by Sino-African leaders made Western critics decidedly anxious about the prospects of China's role and ambitions in Africa. Monson (2009) suggests however that the construction, use, and operations of the Tazara line mirrored that of colonial administrations, despite Tazara being an anti-colonial project. More specifically, African leaders asserted that the train would bring development based on the exportation of raw materials, an idea previously promoted by colonial administrations.

According to Brautigam (1998) the success of Tazara was limited however as it failed to understand local political and institutional factors; there were limited evaluations in the early period and a persistent over-centralization in decision-making. There was also a lack of transparency and more project linkages were held with Chinese agencies than with local institutions. During the building of the Railway, the training and continuing tenure of skilled African workers and technicians were challenges to the sustainability of the project (Snow 1998; King 2006). The fall of the white supremacist regimes in Zimbabwe and South Africa reopened the Zambian copper belt's earlier established rail and road links to the south, which Tazara was intended to circumvent, and so lost it much of its profitable traffic. Economic changes in Tanzania also increased the economic pressures on the railway, at the same time as its Chinese sponsors were withdrawing from their earlier African involvement. The dissolution of the Ujamaa villages planned and located along the route as part of Nyerere's own brand of socialist vision only seemed to confirm the view of the railway as an inevitably decaying and predictably run-down relic of an earlier age (Marks 2009). Interestingly the Tazara Railway, once the showpiece of the early heroic phase of Sino-Tanzanian relations, now looks likely to be rescued from the state of disrepair into which it had gradually fallen to become a key link in one of the most ambitious projects of China's new African strategy. After years of under-investment and mounting competition from road transport had brought the rail link to the verge of financial and structural collapse, it is now being rehabilitated by Chinese firms as a key link between two of China's Special Economic Zones [SEZs]. One in Chambishi, in Zambia's copper belt, centres on a US$250 million anchor investment in a copper smelter, and is promoted as creating up to 60,000 jobs through duty and tax incentives for Chinese firms (Marks 2009). The other SEZ is in Dar es Salaam where China has already invested in the modernization and extension of the port. This reconstructed Tazara railway will link up in Zambia with the Benguela line crossing Angola to the Atlantic coast (which is also being reconstructed by Chinese firms). The two lines together will create a first-ever functioning east-west corridor across the continent.

## China and Africa's 'lost decade'

Immediately after the deaths of Zhou Enlai and Mao Zedong, a period of constant evaluation, reevaluation, investigation, experimentation, debate and criticism commenced (Brautigam 2009). It seemed that everything was under scrutiny. Radical Maoist idealism had indeed been replaced by economic pragmatism, but a sharp division existed between those proposing the pursuit of a Maoist-inspired modernization strategy that relied on collectivist principles and policies and an alternative strategy based on individual initiative, economic rationality, market forces, and an open door to the West. Within years then of the completion of the flagship Tazara project major shifts were underway within China's domestic and foreign policy which saw a gradual dilution of the ideological focus in policy-making in favour of a greater emphasis on economic cooperation. In the post-Mao era Chinese leaders have sought to assign highest priority to economic modernization and to maximizing their access to foreign markets, technology and capital (Harding 1995). As the Cultural Revolution wound down in the 1970s China's foreign policy began to lose its strong ideological inflection although it did continue to make active efforts to export its domestic experiences to its foreign clients (Harding 1995). Few international partnerships were sought until the late 1970s partly because Chinese leaders regarded established third world governments as 'reactionary' or 'neo-colonialist' and distrusted allies of the United States and Union of Soviet Socialist republics (USSR). Between 1976 and 1982 total Chinese aid pledges to Africa fell from US$100.9 million to just US$13.8 million (Snow 1995: 306). At the start of the 1980s China itself qualified as one of the world's 20 least-developed countries (LDCs) and its annual per capita income of US$208 per head placed it between Mozambique and Burma.

During Africa's 'lost decade' of the 1980s Chinese economic attention was firmly directed towards Japan and the United States while Sino-African trade was increasingly marginalized (Taylor 1998). In 1982, Chinese foreign policy took a subtle but very significant shift away from the position of extreme hostility towards the Soviet Union that had characterized it in the late 1970s. A resurgence in American power, and the diplomatic and economic stagnation of the Soviet Union, prompted China to move towards a middle position between the two super-powers (Jackson 1995). At precisely the time when China's policies in Africa came closest to resembling a regional view, however, its interest in the continent declined from an already fairly low point (Jackson 1995). Chinese interest in Africa became sporadic, as their attention increasingly focused on domestic economic development and pros-perity. Chinese premier Zhao Ziyang's[15] four-week visit to 11 African countries, starting in December 1982, was part of a shift of attention towards the Third World during an ebb in Sino-American and Sino-Western relations. During this period, China extended its diplomatic relations to all but two Black African states on the continent (Malawi and Swaziland). Zhao was 'greeted like a visiting rock star' (Brautigam 2009: 53) and when in Dar es Salaam he announced four sets of princi-ples that would guide the new China as it worked out its economic rela-tions with other developing countries. Many of these echoed the eight principles of aid announced by Zhou Enlai in 1963–64 but crucially they did not mention the word 'aid',[16] emphasizing a broader *cooperation* instead. Zhao explained that cooperation would build capacity and foster growth in China and in Africa and that each side could comple-ment the other (Brautigam 2009). Zhao's visit thus sent a strong signal that China wanted to remain engaged in Africa (Yu 1988). Throughout the 1980s and well into the 1990s China focused the bulk of its aid on rehabilitating the dozens of former aid projects that had collapsed or were barely limping along and began developing ways to make their initial benefits more sustainable. For every new project launched during this period, three were being consolidated (repaired, renovated, restored) (Brautigam 2009). The return of Chinese aid workers and their growing involvement in the management of these Chinese-built aid projects raised some awkward questions for China concerning its hallowed 'non-interference' principle but during his 1982 tour Zhao declared that this was helping Africa to build self-reliance and was not therefore 'interference'.

In a major policy speech delivered in June 1985, Deng Xiaoping laid the foundation for China's post-Maoist foreign policy, by suggesting that the PRC would become a 'modern, powerful socialist economy' and stressing that a revival of China's own economic development and modernization was *the* primary objective. In the same year China roundly turned on Africa and criticized the developing world's 'errors in policy-making' but China's direct influence was beginning to wane by this time due to its inability to compete with Western aid programmes and the fact that China was no longer fearful of Taiwan's presence.[17] Africa policy shifted from support for Maoist-inspired revolution to the search for new commercial engagements that would strengthen the PRC's economy. Combining the promotion of Chinese exports with the giving of aid, from 1983 onwards China's aid contribution to Africa stood at an average of US$200 million a year (Snow 1995: 311). Deng continued the policy of non-interference, encouraging African countries to find political and economic models of development to suit their own particular circumstances (Qinmei 1998; Fei 1995) and explaining the mistakes that China itself had made in pursuit of development during official Chinese visits to African countries. China had 'readjusted' its economy and once again there was an assumption that African partners could learn lessons from Chinese history (so they too would have to 'adjust').

By the end of the 1970s then the 'four modernizations' had become the stated goal of Chinese economic policy-making in the post-Mao era. First articulated by Zhou Enlai in the mid-1970s, the 'four modernizations' ordered the priorities of Chinese economic development in the following order of importance: agriculture, industry, national defence, and science and technology. It required enormous resources at home, leaving little extra for overseas aid. The pursuit of the 'four modernizations' represented a shift in emphasis from 'putting politics in command' to 'putting economics in command'; from stressing political goals to stressing economic goals; from transforming the social relations of production to transforming the forces of production; from employing idealism and utopianism to employing pragmatism ('seek truth from facts') in designing socio-economic policy. In other words, the 'four modernizations' programme represented the rejection of Cultural Revolution ideology and what were perceived to be the excesses of the radical left. Virtually all political factions in post-Mao China accepted the broad goals of the four modernizations yet how these modernizations would be accomplished remained extremely controversial. In March 1978 China announced an ambitious ten-year plan that focused on 120 key modernization projects, including thirty electric power stations, seven trunk railroads, eight coal mines, ten new steel plants, five harbours and ten new oil and gas fields (Brautigam 2009: 45). Japan was the earliest to enter the Chinese market using low-interest loans to finance the export of its modern plant, industrial technology and materials with China agreeing to pay by exporting its equivalent in crude oil and coal to Japan (an experience that Chinese officials would draw on again in developing cooperation and trade agreements with Africa more than two decades later). More broadly Japan and the other 'Asian tigers' provided a model of the developmental state that China looked to (using control over finance and other government tools as both carrots and sticks to propel its industrialization and exports forward).

Beijing continued however to engage the African states in the promotion of the 'Four Principles' of Chinese cooperation with Africa advocated by Chinese premier Zhao Ziyang in 1982 (Wang and Lim 2007). By the mid-1980s Chinese companies were bidding on aid projects offered by Germany and the World Bank[18] and the first wave of Chinese joint ventures in Africa had begun (providing valuable experience for China's new companies). Chinese construction companies also began to stick around after building an aid project, registering as a local company and then bidding on construction projects (Brautigam 2009). After joining the UN system China's contributions frequently became the seed capital for tripartite cooperation projects with various UN agencies. The state-controlled Red Cross was also used to channel some humanitarian aid in disaster situations. The peaceful democratic transition underway in Taiwan at the end of the 1980s however was to have significant implications for China's aid to Africa. China's new aid commitments in 1990 rose by some 68 per cent reflecting the diplomatic battles with Taiwan (Brautigam 2009). The rivalry sparked a bidding war as offers of aid escalated on both sides. Some African countries switched their allegiance to Taiwan, Liberia being the first in 1989 and Saõ Tomé and Principé the last in 1997. It also sparked a new round of diplomacy beginning with Foreign Minister Qian Qichen's visit in 1989 to Botswana, Angola, Mozambique, Zimbabwe and Lesotho. In January 1991 he initiated a tradition of starting each New Year by travelling to a group of selected African countries for high level meetings, a tradition repeated every January by his successors.

After June 1989, China underwent a major re-evaluation of its foreign policies as it ended its 'honeymoon' relationship with the West. The self-interest of African elites under threat from democratization projects and the longer history of Third World solidarity and resentment at Western 'neo-imperialist' interference in the affairs of a fellow developing country meant that African leaders were muted in their criticism (if not openly supportive) of China following Tiananmen square and were fearful that Beijing could easily end Chinese development aid at any time. Given their numerical weight in international organizations, African states played an important role in the Chinese stratagem (Tull 2006: 460–1). Africa thus played a critical role for China in its struggle to be free of the overt influence of any one power (mindful of its past domination by outsiders) and in regaining its eminence in the international system (Taylor 1998).

## China in Angola

The armed struggles for independence in Portuguese Africa during the 1960s and 1970s posed a number of questions for Chinese foreign-policy makers: 'whether to become involved in the Lusophone African struggles, to what extent to be involved and in what form (supplying arms, money, publicity, training)' (Jackson 1995: 388). The Chinese involvement in the Angolan civil war is quite atypical of the overall Chinese involvement with the liberation organizations of former Portuguese Africa, most of which was low-level, involving little more than small amounts of money or arms and it was only during the Angolan civil war that China attempted to assert itself 'strongly (and unsuccessfully) in the complex and shifting currents of African politics' (Jackson 1995: 389). Differences between liberation movements over the issues of race, assimilation and miscegenation, ethnicity, and the roles of the Organizations of African Unity (OAU) and South Africa were critical in the Lusophone African colonies yet as Jackson (1995: 392) notes:

> The Chinese seldom if ever mentioned these purely African issues and as no analogous controversies had existed in their own revolution, it is questionable whether they in some fundamental sense appreciated the gravity of these questions.

The revolutions in Lusophone Africa were far from being a simple repetition of the Chinese revolution but it does not seem that China fully appreciated this or the uniqueness of the Angolan context in particular. Chinese policy during the initial period of involvement in Lusophone Africa was to give low-level (largely rhetorical) support, informed by a Chinese world view that envisaged a global struggle against American imperialism. Armed rebellions led by nationalist groups started in Angola in 1961 (Marcum 1981) and China had initial contacts with elements of all three of the major guerrilla groups which eventually formed in Angola during this early period (Jackson 1995; Esteves 2008). One of China's first encounters with Angolan nationalist movements came in December 1958 when a Chinese diplomatic observer, Yang Shuo, attended the first All-African People's Conference in Accra. It is clear that the Angolan party initially favoured by China was the MPLA and that China may have supplied arms to the MPLA through AAPSO (Jackson

1995). Chinese funds were, moreover, critical for the early survival of the MPLA (Snow 1988; Jackson 1995) although this preference did not however preclude Chinese attempts to build support for a 'united front' between the Angolan groups. The Chinese press closely followed the activities and statements of the MPLA until the summer of 1963, when the Chinese temporarily switched their attention to the Frente Nacional de Libertação de Angola/National Front for the Liberation of Angola (FNLA; the MPLA had previously held strong ties with the Soviet Union). The MPLA once again had some contact with the Chinese in early 1966, but the MPLA was 'an elitist, pro-Soviet and urban organization at a time when the Chinese increasingly wanted to show Africa to be populist, peasant-oriented, anti-Soviet and rural' (Jackson 1995: 396). Thus, the Chinese turned to the União Nacional para a Independência Total de Angola/National Union for the Total Independence of Angola (UNITA) for a 'compatible object of propaganda and support (Jackson 1995: 397) opening contacts with the leaders of UNITA in 1964 as they began to explore relations with other organizations in the Lusophone colonies.

When Jonas Savimbi and his supporters left the FNLA in 1964, he turned to China for support (Jackson 1995) and in August and September 1964 Savimbi took a short course at the Nanjing Military Academy, the main guerrilla training institute in China, before returning to China in January 1965 to gain support for the formal establishment of UNITA (Bridgland 1986; Jackson 1995). Given that Savimbi had previously condemned other Angolan leaders for being too 'pro-Chinese' trust was a key issue and the Chinese leadership were wary of him but they did agree to train some of his followers in guerrilla warfare and Savimbi himself underwent a more extensive course at Nanjing in guerrilla strategy in 1965 (Jackson 1995). In the early 1970s Chinese reports on UNITA began to decline, supplanted by those focusing on the MPLA instead and if Jonas Savimbi had expected that his lavish praise of the Chinese would produce major volumes of Chinese aid for his organization 'he was sadly disappointed' (Jackson 1995: 398). According to M. J. Marshment, Savimbi indicated in an interview that total Chinese aid amounted to approximately £5000 during this period.[19]

Led by Agostinho Neto, Lucio Lara and others an MPLA delegation visited Beijing and met Zhou Enlai in July 1971 (Jackson 1995) and China thereafter channelled its assistance to the MPLA through the OAU liberation fund but in late 1973 China also entered into a patron–client relationship with the FNLA, partly as a reaction to Soviet support for the MPLA (Jackson 1995). From around 1974 onwards, Chinese foreign policy became ever more rigidly concerned with checking the Soviet bloc's 'wild ambitions' around the world and in Africa. The Chinese and Soviet bloc states tried to 'translate their past support of national liberation in the Portuguese colonies into influence in post-independence governments' (Jackson 1995: 404). In Angola three parties were all competing for formal recognition and power not just within Angola but also within the OAU and around the world and armed clashes between the three groups commenced as early as February and March 1975. Internationalization of the conflict escalated rapidly, first in the form of arms shipments by the Soviets, Cubans, Americans and others, and later by direct intervention. During the Angolan civil war foreign policy strategists in China sought primarily to prevent a Soviet victory in Angola while preserving good relations with the majority of Black African states (Jackson 1995) thus publicly supporting all three parties in Angola and calling for a peaceful transition to independence but covertly attempting to arm anti-MPLA groups before and during the civil war. Chinese policy favoured the FNLA and UNITA simply to preclude a Soviet victory,[20] 'not because of any ideological merits of these organizations themselves' (Jackson 1995: 405). Delegations from all three Angolan parties were invited to Beijing after the ceasefire in 1974 in an effort to cultivate relations with all potential leaders of Angola and to underline China's ostensible policy of supporting all liberation groups.

The Angolan civil war was embarrassing for China's leaders and shifted Chinese foreign policy in Africa:

> support for the remaining liberation struggles in Zimbabwe, Namibia and South Africa declined or was cursory. Instead of supporting armed struggle as the only means to achieve liberation, Chinese leaders began quietly urging negotiated or mediated settlements, afraid that civil wars would turn again to the Soviet Union's advantage. (Jackson 1995: 413)

The initial Chinese reaction to the new government in Luanda was to ignore it, arguing that it was a country 'under occupation'. The Chinese media referred only to the 'Soviet revisionism and its mercenary occupation army' in Angola during 1976 and 1977 (Jackson 1995: 413). Numerous articles appeared at this time describing the economic deterioration of Angola, caused by 'Soviet social-imperialism' but by the end of the 1970s China was beginning to characterize the foreign policy of the Angolan government as somewhat more independent than it had done in previous statements. Just as Sino-Soviet talks began to reopen in the late 1970s Sino-Angolan relations seem to have come very close to normalization, when the Angolans announced that they had accepted a Chinese invitation to open talks regarding the establishment of diplomatic relations (Jackson 1995). Tensions remained however. Agostinho Neto, Angolan President from 1975 to 1979, condemned the Chinese invasion of Vietnam in February 1979 for example (Winrow 1990: 115). Sino-Angolan relations in the period 1982–89 started to ease however and in July 1982 the Chinese made a new offer indicating their willingness to normalize relations. On 22 October 1982, it was announced that the two countries would recognize each other in 1983. This was partly a consequence of a brief resurgence of Chinese attention to Africa and a drive by the Chinese to establish diplomatic relations with all Black African states on the continent. Subsequently, in June 1984 Angolan Foreign Trade Minister Ismael Gaspar Martins visited China and a trade agreement was signed (Jackson 1995). A Chinese trade delegation visited Luanda in December 1985 and China also donated some food aid to Angola in the same year. A Joint Economic and Trade Commission was created in 1988, but its first meeting was held as late as December 1999, with a second meeting in May 2001 (Esteves 2008). This normalization of relations between China and Angola was not merely a Chinese effort to broaden its diplomatic representation; it was also meant 'to put the Angolan civil war behind them, a quiet end to a nagging historical embarrassment' (Jackson 1995: 419). As one Chinese official[21] described the situation:

> We made mistakes in Angola, perhaps because we simplified the issue, reacted blindly, without proper analysis, to the position taken by the Russians. As the Angolan civil war went on, the affair became for us more and more of a fiasco. When we recognized this we tried more than once to normalize relations with the Luanda government but our approaches were premature. (Chinese official quoted in Jackson 1995: 411)

The final step in the process of normalization of Sino-Angolan relations was the visit of President Jose Eduardo dos Santos to Beijing in October 1988 (Campos and Vines 2008) in response to an invitation extended five years earlier. Deng Xiaoping's recommendation to the Angolan government in the late 1980s, besieged by the continuing UNITA insurgency, is indicative of how far China had removed itself from the struggles of Southern Africa: 'Dialogue is better than confrontation, and relaxation is better than tension'. Ironically, Dos Santos and his defence minister had come to China hoping to purchase counter-insurgency weapons (Jackson 1995).

## Conclusions: constructing a 'history in common'

Contrary to the historical amnesia that characterizes many accounts of contemporary China–Africa relations in the western media this chapter has sought to demonstrate that China has not 'suddenly' entered Africa in the last two decades and that there is a long and complex history of China–Africa cooperation and interaction. This history does not just commence with the birth of the PRC in 1949 but instead can be traced back thousands of years to the earliest trade and diplomatic exchanges between China and East Africa and to the connections forged in Africa by some of China's imperial dynasties. Indeed it could even be argued that both 'China' and 'Africa' have played a key role in each other's historical development: some of the founders of China's dynastic empires came from Africa while China itself has played a significant role in the liberation and state-formation of many of its contemporary African partners. Much is made today, for example, of the contemporary 'waves' of Chinese migration to Africa in the aftermath of China's economic reforms and its deregulation of labour recruitment but the historical roots of Chinese migration to Africa are complex and run deep, while the Chinese diasporic presence in Africa (as with the wider history of China–Africa relations) does not always begin and end with state intervention[22] (Figure 2.6).

In many ways official Chinese narrations of the history of engagement with Africa depict a seamless continuity running from the voyages of Zheng He to the present day along with the impression that China's historical presence in Africa has been constant and uniform. This is part of a wider move by the Communist Party to strengthen its position as the moral and spiritual leader of the nation by tapping into history and tradition to revamp the basis for its leadership and generate further ideological backing for its capitalist policies (Kallio 2011). Chinese officials and commentators conjure up the treasure fleet to make a geopolitical point: 'reminding foreign governments and their own countrymen that China boasts a proud tradition as a seafaring power, notwithstanding its reputation as a wholly land-oriented power' (Holmes 2007: 6). Zheng He also allows China's political leaders to indulge in a kind of 'one-upmanship' at the expense of the West. On a recent trip to Europe, for example, Premier Wen Jiabao reminded audiences that the Chinese explorer had 'sailed abroad earlier than Christopher Columbus'.[23] Chinese spokesmen habitually contrast the size and technical sophistication of Zheng's vessels with the relatively backward fleets put to sea in fifteenth-century Europe (Holmes 2007). In support of Beijing's claims that it is pursuing a 'peaceful rise' to great-power status, Chinese

*Figure 2.6* The 'Great Wall Casino' in Lusaka, Zambia. Photograph by D J Clark

spokesmen also play up the predominantly non-violent nature of Zheng He's voyages and use Zheng's expeditions of commerce and discovery to draw a favourable contrast with Western imperialism. In a speech delivered in South Africa in 2007, President Hu asserted that Zheng He's armada 'brought to the African people a message of peace and goodwill not swords, guns, plunder or slavery' (Jintao 2007). Chinese officials also intimate that, had the Ming Dynasty not outlawed maritime pursuits after Zheng He's final voyage, Asian history might have taken a different – and more humane – course under China's beneficent dominance. In short, Beijing has used Zheng He to fashion a diplomacy that bestows legitimacy on China's overseas aspirations (Holmes 2007).

More generally Chinese officials regularly invoke the long-term nature of China's connections with the African continent to demonstrate that China has been an 'all-weather' friend and therefore by implication that its contemporary interactions with Africa are also legitimate and build sensitively but directly on historical precedents. Thus this history has come to serve as a kind of discursive field through which China's contemporary forays into Africa are constructed as a legitimate form of 'cooperation' rooted in the past (Power and Mohan 2010). The project of constructing a 'common history' (of revolution and 'peoples war', of colonial exploitation or of mutuality in experiences of development) serves a particular function in the present historical moment then in demonstrating that historically there have always been commonalities between China and Africa and therefore that China and Africa must also share common strategic objectives in the contemporary era. Stressing that China has also historically been a victim of colonialism helps to counter fears that what China is doing in Africa today is a contemporary form of imperialism. Underlining that China has been through many similar historical phases already (especially in its experiences of modernization) helps to construct China as an authoritative and experienced partner in development that Africa can and should learn from.

The construction of a seamless continuity in Chinese official narrations of China–Africa engagement is perhaps best illustrated by China's own articulation of the principles by which it lives in general and towards Africa in particular, which have been remarkably consistent for the past 50 years (Strauss 2009). Principles of non-interference, mutual benefit and absolute state sovereignty that were worked out with India around the Bandung conference in the interests of lessening border tensions in the mid-1950s and then expanded more generally, have since been 'set in aspic' (Strauss and Saavedra 2009: 558), leaving very little rhetorical room for the Chinese government to encompass other discursive rhetorics to legitimate and explain its actions domestically and abroad. Yet clearly there have been significant changes in China's foreign policy over the last half-century. Muekalia (2004: 7) sums up the transformation in Sino-African relations since 1949 in the following terms:

> China had gradually changed its tactics from confrontation to co-operation, from revolution to economic development, and from isolation to international engagement.

Particularly since the late 1970s, there has been a sea change in China's Africa policy as China announced its plans for the 'four modernizations' and cast aside the ideology of the Cultural Revolution, focusing increasingly on China's domestic modernization and replacing Cold War ideology with the 'pragmatism' of economic growth. Strauss (2009) sees a partial, but still only very tentative, adjustment to the old rhetoric of common suffering at the hands of imperialism, analogous underdevelopment and China's unique moral claims to be Africa's 'all-weather friend'. Although some newer notions of an international division of labour and complementarity have begun to enter some of the official rhetoric, most official and semi-official pronouncements continue to be framed by appeals to China's unselfishness in its dealings with Africa, its spirit of co-equal partnership, and its exceptional morality in, for example, the 'heroic' Tazara railway project. Given how shopworn this rhetoric is in the light of China's current wealth, and how divorced it is from most contemporary realities either in China or Africa, this begs the question of why. Strauss (2009) suggests that the sheer longevity of the rhetoric has more to do with the relative importance of elite audiences in China (and until recently, in Africa) and a set of images about China that those audiences find comforting, legitimating and credible: that China has a long history (in Africa and elsewhere) of separateness, difference and implicit superiority to the colonial and exploitative West.

Yet there is not a seamless continuity to China's engagement with Africa – China's interest in the continent has peaked and troughed at different historical moments and has been subject to a wide range of national, regional and global geopolitical dynamics. China has also not had a constant and uniform presence across the African continent and as can be seen from the example of Angola, China's interest in particular African states has been historically uneven and dynamic and not always characterized by 'friendship' and 'cooperation'. Further, China has historically made some big mistakes in its relations with some of its African partners: Jackson (1995) concludes, for example, that it took China nearly 30 years to understand the indigenous roots of war in Angola. One of the reasons China made some of these mistakes was that it tried to interpret the revolutions under way in the dying days of colonialism in Africa through the lens of its own historical experience. Particularly during the 1950s and 1960s China increasingly came to believe that what was happening in Africa was a re-enactment and replay of their own recent past as Chinese leaders regularly drew attention to a series of historical parallels that they had noticed. Partly what motivated China's interactions with Africa at this time then was a sense that it was thus China's duty to 'explain' these similarities to the people of Africa. China's historical experience of importing modern plant, industrial technology and materials from Japan in the 1980s for its own modernization and of paying for this with its own coal and oil reserves has also come to shape China's contemporary practices of financing 'aid' and investment projects in Africa today, along with the other historical 'lessons' that China has learned from the developmental states of East Asia.

# 3
# Chinese Policies and Their Implications in Africa

## Introduction

Despite some accounts which treat China's African interests as opportunistic and short-term, Chapter 2 showed that China's engagements with Africa in fact go back many years. Having said that, the past decade or so has seen the pace of China's 'charm offensive' (Kurlantzick 2008) intensify with a series of high profile political events and policies. This chapter sets out the broad dimensions of China's renewed engagement with Africa.

In 2009 a meeting of the Forum on China–Africa Cooperation (FOCAC) was held in Sharm El-Sheikh in Egypt. Formed in 2000, this was the fourth meeting of FOCAC and at the meeting Chinese Premier Wen Jiabao announced that the objectives set by the 2006 FOCAC meeting were nearing completion, which included the cancellation of 168 debts owed by 33 African countries, US\$5 billion of concessional loans, and the US\$1 billion China–Africa Development Fund (CADFund). Premier Wen announced a new set of eight measures at FOCAC IV, with less emphasis on loans or grants and a greater focus on capacity building and technological transfer to African states. China also announced its intention to support the African Union (AU), allowing it to play a bigger role in regional and international affairs (*China Daily*, 9 November 2009a). Despite the economic downturn China seems to be honouring its commitments.

The success of Chinese diplomacy with African states has been impressive and is hard to ignore. In terms of trade, for example, Chinese trade with Africa stood at US\$817 million in 1977 just before the reforms (Servant 2005), but from 2000 to 2009, bilateral trade rose from US\$10.6 billion to US\$91.07 billion (CAITEC 2010). In the first half of

2011, China–Africa imports and exports totalled US$79.01 billion, an increase of 29.1 per cent year-on-year (Chinese Customs 2011). China's direct investment in African countries reached US$1.44 billion in 2009 (Han 2011), in which non-financial direct investment soared by 55.4 per cent from the previous year (*China Daily* 14 October 2010). In the same period revenues from China's contracted and engineering projects in Africa rose from US$1.1 billion to US$28.1 billion (CAITEC 2010). In 2008, nearly 1600 Chinese enterprises had started business in African countries with a direct investment stock of US$7.8 billion (Wen 2009). Some 180 of these companies were spearheaded by the 'going out' policy and have been designated by the Chinese state to benefit from preferential finance, tax concessions and political backing in order to 'go global' and become true multinationals (Alden and Davies 2006).

In Africa, these extensive Chinese activities have translated differently in terms of aggregate gains and losses for the continent (Kaplinsky 2008). Concerning aggregate gains, Africa has benefited from commodity exports such as oil, mineral, cotton and logs; building of infrastructure, for example, transport and construction of public buildings which are seen as a means of assuring social gains such as education and healthcare in the future; imports of machinery equipment and auto-parts and finally welfare gains from consumer imports from China. However, these Chinese imports also brought about losses due to the low quality products and competition. For example, to cut costs, the Chinese tend to import older equipment often resulting in lower quality production. At the same time, cost concerns also mean lower skills training translating into poor workmanship. Besides this, low cost Chinese products meant competition with local industries amounting to the closure of local enterprises and job losses (Amankwah 2005). This in turn contributed to losses in export to third country markets and further capacity losses in terms of labour and management deskilling (Kaplinsky and Messner 2008). More importantly, in terms of governance, although the Chinese system of aid disbursement theoretically limits corruption of procurement, because funds are transferred to the Chinese contractors, it ultimately increases governance corruption due to the lack of transparency in these procedures (Morris 2010, pers. comm.). We return to these issues in the next two chapters.

In terms of development cooperation – which, as Chapter 4 discusses, is tightly linked to trade and investment – according to Wen (2009), by September 2009, China had delivered to African countries US$2.647 billion of concessional loans to support 54 projects in 28 countries and US$2 billion in preferential export buyer's credit to support 11 projects in 10 countries. The White Paper on China–Africa economic and trade cooperation published in December 2010 also indicated that by the end of 2009 China had constructed over 500 infrastructure projects, such as 107 schools and 54 hospitals, and offered 29,465 scholarships to African students. China further dispatched 17,000 medical practitioners to the continent, and cancelled 312 liabilities of 35 African countries totalling 18.96 billion yuan (MOFCOM 2010; CAITEC 2010). In the agricultural sector, China had helped build 142 agricultural projects and 14 agricultural technology demonstration centres in Africa. By June 2010, China had provided training for over 30,000 people from African countries covering over 20 fields such as economics, agriculture, medical care, and science and technology (MOFCOM 2010). To promote integration of the African countries, China is now helping to build the AU Convention Centre in Addis Ababa (CAITEC 2010).

Accompanying these economic and political ties are concerns from some western observers pertaining to the broader developmental discourses, such as transparency, fair competition and good governance. These debates are revisited throughout the rest of the book but in this chapter we have two aims. First, it aims to provide the more general context of China–Africa engagement in terms of increasing trade and investment relations. Outlining and tracking through the many policy directives of the Chinese government, we will demonstrate the broad-brush impacts of these directives. Second, we will then examine more critically the contending discourses surrounding this partnership and how Chinese, African and western observers regard the supposed cooperation. The next section will detail the main aims of the policies and the objectives of the FOCAC and then discuss the economic tools being used here including the CADFund, Special Economic Zones and ExIm Bank loans, in which the evolving discourses surrounding this economic partnership will be evaluated.

## The post-millennium mechanisms of China–Africa diplomacy

There are two main components to the political directives regarding the direction of China–Africa relations. According to W. P. He (2007: 36), 'China's African Policy' comprises China's White Paper on Africa in 2006, which is the blueprint for future relations, and FOCAC which is the vehicle to explore and implement effective methods to realize the goals of the White Paper (Taylor 2011).

Turning to the first of these, the White Paper adhered to the five principles of peaceful coexistence, discussed in the previous chapter, with the Ministry of Foreign Affairs (MFA) stressing that the China–Africa strategic partnership is based on 'equal treatment, respect for sovereignty and common development' (Ministry of Foreign Affairs PRC 2006). According to the White Paper peace and development remain the main themes of international diplomacy, and enhancing solidarity and cooperation with African countries has always been an important component of China's foreign policy. The guiding principles of China–Africa relations are built on the following concepts: sincerity, friendship and equality, mutual benefit, reciprocity, mutual support and common and sustainable development. However, the one-China principle was indicated in the White Paper as the only conditionality for the establishment and development of China's relations with African countries. Listing 29 areas of cooperation including political, economic, education, science, culture, health, peace and security (see Table 3.1 for more details), the White Paper put forward the objectives of China's policy towards Africa and the measures to achieve them.

With the White Paper outlining various areas of cooperation between China and Africa, the FOCAC became the engine to implement these stated aims. According to Xinhua (2006), the FOCAC is considered a 'platform established by China and friendly African nations for collective consultation and dialogue and a cooperation mechanism between the developing countries, which falls into the category of south–south cooperation'. As a collective multilateral consultative mechanism between China and Africa, this forum is intended to allow Africa to 'speak with one voice' and to increase efficiency in diplomatic interaction, especially among 54 African states (W. P. He 2007). Accompanying the triennial meetings at the top ministerial level, there are also the biennial senior officials meetings and yearly ambassadorial meetings.

The first FOCAC was held on 10–12 October 2000 and 44 African nations were present. The Beijing Declaration was signed as the founding working document for the forum and its main principles are based on the Five Principles of Peaceful Coexistence, such as non-interference and mutually beneficial cooperation. A programme for China–Africa Cooperation in Economic and Social Development was then released. The first action plan (Programme for China–Africa Cooperation in Economic and Social Development 2001–2003) was also signed during this forum. The two main areas of cooperation (which continued into

*Table 3.1* Areas of cooperation listed in the China–Africa White Paper

| Categories | Areas of Cooperation |
| --- | --- |
| Political | – high level visits<br>– exchanges between legislative bodies<br>– exchanges between political parties<br>– consultation mechanisms<br>– cooperation in international affairs<br>– exchange between local governments |
| Economic | – trade<br>– investment<br>– financial cooperation<br>– agricultural cooperation<br>– infrastructure<br>– resource cooperation<br>– tourism cooperation<br>– debt reduction and relief<br>– economic assistance<br>– multilateral cooperation |
| Education, science, culture, health and social aspects | – cooperation in human resources development and education<br>– science and technology cooperation<br>– cultural exchanges<br>– medical and health cooperation<br>– media cooperation<br>– administrative cooperation<br>– consular cooperation<br>– people-to-people exchanges<br>– environmental cooperation<br>– disaster reduction, relief and humanitarian assistance |
| Peace and security | – military cooperation<br>– conflict settlement and peacekeeping operations<br>– judicial and police cooperation<br>– non-traditional security threats |

the second, third and fourth action plans) focused on intergovernmental relations and trade and investment.

The second FOCAC meeting took place on 15–16 December 2003 in Addis Ababa. The then new premier, Wen Jiabao, presided over the meeting indicating the importance the Chinese Communist party (CCP) attached to the meeting and the initiative more broadly. The theme of this forum was 'Pragmatic and Action-Oriented Cooperation' and the emphasis was on peace and security issues, on increasing consultation between China and Africa and strengthening cooperation in areas such as infrastructure, agriculture and trade. The first China–Africa Business Conference was also held in parallel with the 2nd Ministerial Conference. Over 500 Chinese and African entrepreneurs attended the conference with 21 cooperation agreements signed with a total value of US$ 1 billion (FOCAC 2006b). The aftermath of the FOCAC II saw a phenomenal expansion in Afro-Chinese trade and investment (Centre for Conflict Resolution 2009).

The third FOCAC meeting held in Beijing on 4–5 November 2006 catapulted China's increasing involvement in Africa into the media spotlight and this meeting brought over 1700 delegates from China and Africa together under the banner of 'friendship, peace, cooperation and development' (Hon et al. 2010: 5). Commitments to 'south-south' and 'win-win' cooperation were also reiterated during this summit. Proposals were put forward by Vice Premier Wu Yi in the same summit, calling for the forum to be the lead organization in advancing China–Africa relations. She suggested that China and Africa should fully utilize each other's strengths to expand and upgrade the cooperation and more importantly, recommended that the two entities should strengthen coordination to facilitate both bilateral and multilateral interaction (Hon et al. 2010: 5) The FOCAC III action plan is divided into four main sections, namely: political, economic, and international affairs and social development. New areas of concern included information, air and maritime transport, social development and encompassed development assistance and debt relief, human resource development and environmental protection. The China–Africa Chamber of Commerce was also established as part of the FOCAC III initiatives. Scholars such as Corkin (2009), Hon et al. (2010) have argued that the FOCAC III plan was by far the most successful in terms of deliverables, especially in trade and investment. However, we must acknowledge that unlike previous plans, this included more quantifiable targets which are easier to measure in terms of outcomes.

As noted at the start of this chapter, the fourth FOCAC was held in Sharm el Sheikh on 8–9 November 2009, with 49 African states participating in the discussions. Two documents, the FOCAC Sharm el Sheikh Declaration and the FOCAC Sharm el Sheikh Action Plan (2010–12) were adopted at the conference. A new US$1 billion fund for small and medium enterprises in Africa announced at this meeting is intended to help African entrepreneurs wishing to set up businesses in the Special Economic Zones (SEZs), first elaborated in FOCAC III. This marks a shift away from the focus on state-owned enterprises (SOEs) and links to the questions of economic migrants, raised in the last chapter and picked up in detail in Chapter 5.

The similarities and differences of the four FOCAC action plans are summarized in Table 3.2. From the table, we can observe that the major shift has been a move away from material support to issues around building local capacity. New areas of cooperation, such as environmental governance and climate change have also come into play due to changing global and domestic demand. In some ways this could be interpreted as a move towards the 'norms' of international development cooperation and a recognition after half a decade or more 'in the field' that African capacity is key to the success of Chinese investments and that this is sorely lacking.

Since the first FOCAC action plan, a whole series of economic tools have been utilized by China in seeking cooperation with the African continent. The CADFund and SEZs were launched in FOCAC III and there has been considerable progress in dispensing CADFund loans and in construction of the SEZs. The CADFund, one of President Hu Jintao's eight measures aimed at forging a new type of strategic partnership, revolves around financing the market entry of Chinese firms into the African economy (Chen and Orr 2009) and promoting economic cooperation between China and Africa. It was officially launched in June 2007 with an initial capital of US$1 billion (SAIIA 2009) and an additional funding of US$5 billion to be gradually added by China Development Bank.

The CADFund is the first equity investment fund in China focusing on investment in Africa (Tradeinvest Africa 2009). Other than providing funds for companies, CADFund provides various consultancy services and information sharing for investment in Africa, partner sourcing, finance structuring, initial public offering (IPO), operation and management and environment and social issues (CADF 2010). Its target industries and sectors are agriculture, manufacturing, infrastructure and energy industries, natural resources, and industrial parks set up by Chinese firms. However, access for African enterprises to this fund can only be achieved through joint ventures with their Chinese counterparts, which will then apply on their behalf. The opening of the first CADFund representative office in Africa on 16 March 2010 also made the fund more accessible to the Africans (Gu and Schiere 2010: 19). By the end of 2009, the CADFund had earmarked US$700 million for over 35 projects, covering agriculture, electric power, construction material, mining, machinery and industrial parks (CAITEC 2010: 4).

*Table 3.2* Summary aims of FOCAC action plans

| Category | FOCAC I 2000 | FOCAC II 2003 | FOCAC III 2006 | FOCAC IV 2009 |
|---|---|---|---|---|
| **Agriculture** | – | Work plan on China–Africa agricultural cooperation for 2004–06. Support and encourage strong and viable Chinese enterprises through financial and policy incentive schemes, to develop agricultural cooperation projects in Africa. | 10 demonstration centres (later increased to 14 due to African demand) and 100 agriculture experts. | Increase total number of demonstration schools in Africa to 20 and send 50 agricultural technology teams. Contribute US$30 million to UN Food and Agriculture Organization (UNFAO) to set up trust fund for Africa. |
| **Investment** | Set up special fund to encourage Chinese enterprise to invest in Africa Establish China Africa joint business council | Designate China Council for the Promotion of International Trade (CCPIT) to help African countries and regional groupings. Creation of China–Africa joint ventures aimed at encouraging the transfer of technology and the creation of employment. | $5 billion China–Africa Development Fund, three to five Special economic zones. | Increase the size of the China–Africa Development Fund to US$3 billion to support the expansion of investment from Chinese businesses to Africa. |

Continued

*Table 3.2*   Continued

| Category | FOCAC I 2000 | FOCAC II 2003 | FOCAC III 2006 | FOCAC IV 2009 |
|---|---|---|---|---|
| **Trade** | Establish China–Africa Products Exhibition centre in China to promote two-way trade and facilitate African products to Chinese market. | Open China market by granting tariff, free access to some commodities in least developed countries (LDC) in Africa. | Zero tariff from 190 to 440 items to China. | Zero tariff for 90 per cent of African items to China. |
| **Development Assistance and debt relief** | Reduce or exempt debts worth RMB 10.5 billion for a total of 156 loans. | Continue to increase assistance to African countries. Cancel 31 LDC and HIPC in Africa ahead of its committed schedule, reduce or cancel 156 matured debts totalling RMB 10.5 billion yuan. | Increase preferential loans to US$3 billion and export buyers credit to US$2 billion. Cancel interest-free loans to LDC and HIPC in Africa. | US$10 billion concessional loans debts. US$1 billion special fund for African SMEs. Cancel debts for HIPC and LDC by end of 2009. |
| **Human resource development** | Establish African Human resources development fund to train professionals for economic development. | Train up to 10,000 personnel in various fields in three years. | Train 15,000 Africans. | Train 2000 African agricultural technicians, 3000 doctors and nurses, 1500 principals and teachers. |

Continued

*Table 3.2*  Continued

| Category | FOCAC I 2000 | FOCAC II 2003 | FOCAC III 2006 | FOCAC IV 2009 |
|---|---|---|---|---|
| **Education** | – | Sponsor "Meet in Beijing" international art festival focusing on African arts and the "Voyage of Chinese Culture to Africa". Exchange teachers and new scholarships and set-up channels of communication for exchange of ideas between their institutions of higher learning and Technical and Vocational Education and Training (TVET). | Build 100 rural schools and increase scholarships from 2000 to 4000 a year. | 100 joint demonstration projects on scientific and technological research. 100 postdoctoral fellows to China Build 50 friendship schools. Increase number of scholarships to 5,500 by 2012. Launch China-Africa joint research programme. |
| **Medical care and public care** | Convocation of China-Africa forum on traditional medicine and plan of action for cooperation for traditional medicine between china and Africa. | Continue cooperation on traditional medicine and continue to send teams to Africa. | Build 30 hospitals and 30 malaria prevention centres, donate RMB 300 million anti-malaria drugs. | Donate RMB 500 million of anti-malaria drug US$1.5 million contribution to support NEPAD's projects to train nurses and maternity assistants. |

Continued

*Table 3.2* Continued

| Category | FOCAC I 2000 | FOCAC II 2003 | FOCAC III 2006 | FOCAC IV 2009 |
|---|---|---|---|---|
| **Environmental protection** | – | – | Step up cooperation in capacity building, prevention and control of water pollution and desertification, maintenance of bio-diversity and the development of environmental protection industry and demonstration projects. | Launch 100 clean energy projects involving biogas, solar power and small hydro power dams. |
| **Security** | Strengthen capacity of African states for peacekeeping missions through provision of finance, material and training. | Extend China's active participation in the peacekeeping operations and de-mining process in Africa. Strengthen the capacity of African States to undertake peacekeeping operations. | Strengthen its cooperation with the AU and sub-regional organizations and institutions in Africa; support the AU's leading role in resolving African issues. Continue to take an active part in UN peace-keeping operations in Africa. | Continue to support the UN security council and peace keeping missions in Africa. Intensify cooperation with African countries in peacekeeping theory research, peacekeeping training and exchanges. |

Continued

Table 3.2 Continued

| Category | FOCAC I 2000 | FOCAC II 2003 | FOCAC III 2006 | FOCAC IV 2009 |
|---|---|---|---|---|
| Others | – | Increase tourism cooperation with Ethiopia, Kenya, Tanzania, Zambia, Mauritius, Seychelles, Zimbabwe and Tunisia with approved destination status. | Expand the 'Chinese Young Volunteers Serving Africa' program and dispatch 300 young volunteers to African countries to work in medical, health, sports, agriculture, education and other fields. | Hold a FOCAC Science and Technology Forum and proposed to launch the China-Africa Science and Technology Partnership Plan to help African countries develop their own science and technology capacity. |

Source: UNCTAD, WEN Jiabao speech 2009; FOCAC website (2000, 2003, 2006, 2009); Brautigam and Tang 2009; Guerin 2008.

Some of the projects invested by the fund are summarized in Table 3.3. The investment amounts in some projects are however unavailable. (Yu 2011; Brooks 2011).

The SEZs have been receiving a lot of attention due to their potential for spillover economic growth, transfer of technology and skills, and vertical and lateral industrial integration. It is expected that these proposed SEZs will focus on value-added industries and provide liberalized investment environments for investors (*China Economic Review* August 2010). According to Davies (2010: 26), the emergence of a Chinese-funded cluster zone could contribute to African domestic and export markets but most importantly the zones are seen as facilitators for creating employment opportunities and generating greater foreign exchange reserves through more diversified sources of income. Over the past four years, Chinese companies have been taking responsibility for designing, building and managing the planned zones: two in Nigeria and others in Egypt, Ethiopia, Mauritius, Zambia and possibly a sixth in Algeria (*China Economic Review* August 2010). Companies operating in these zones have cumulatively invested US$920 million (CAITEC 2010: 4).

In the Zambian copperbelt, an US$800 million zone was set up in Chambishi, known as the Zambia–China Economic and Trade

*Table 3.3*   Projects invested in by the CADFund

| Country | Amount | Chinese partners | Details |
|---------|--------|------------------|---------|
| Ethiopia | US$90 million | China Machinery and Equipment | Glass factory (40,000 tons per year) |
| Ghana | | Import and Export Corp, China National Agricultural Development Group | Gas-fired power plant, building material project |
| Zimbabwe | | | Chromite project and building material project |
| Johannesburg Ethiopia Zambia | | | CADFund office |
| Malawi and Mozambique | | China Colour-Cotton (group) Co Ltd, Qingdao Ruichang Cotton Co Ltd, Qingdao Huifu Textile Co Ltd | Cotton planting and processing (Company + farmer) targeted for 100,000 farmers |
| Ethiopia | US$26 million | | Leather processing project through development of capacity of local stockbreeding industry |
| Ghana | US$450 million | Shenzhen Energy Investment Co Ltd | Ghana Power Station (560,000kw) |
| Egypt, Nigeria and Mauritius | US$ 100 million | | Egyptian Suez Park, Nigerian Lachish Trade Zone and Mauritius Tianli Park |
| South Africa | US$220 million | Jidong Development Group | Cement Plant |
| Zambia | US$1 million | | Hydroelectric Project |

*Source*: SAIIA 2009; Tradeinvest Africa 2009; *China Economic Review* August 2010.

Cooperation Zone. The only zone that is operational at present (*China Economic Review* August 2010) this SEZ was established partly to offset criticism about the effects of Chinese imports on local manufacturers and some fifty companies have pledged investments worth up to, by some estimates, US$900m so far (Mwanawina 2008 quoted in Carmody and Taylor 2010: 11). The anchor investment is a copper smelter project with a project value of US$250–$300 million built by China Nonferrous Metal Mining (Group). Total investment in the zone is expected to reach between US$800 million and US$1 billion (Davies 2010). By early 2009 it was reported that more than ten Chinese firms had established operations in the zone, creating over 3500 local jobs (Davies 2010).

The second SEZ was announced in mid-2007 and to be established in Mauritius. Named the Mauritius Jinfei Economic and Trade Cooperation Zone, it is a joint venture between the Mauritius government and provincial SOEs like the Shanxi Tianli Enterprise group, Shanxi Coking Coal Group and Taiyuan Iron and Steel Group (Brautigam and Tang 2011). The zone is expected to earn about US$200 million in export earnings per annum once fully operational contributing to the island's economic diversification process. This country was chosen due to its strategic geographical location to become a hub of Sino-Africa trade and services (Brautigam and Tang 2011), The third SEZ is located near the Suez Canal in Egypt. Tianjin Economic-Technological Development Area (TEDA) Suez International Cooperation Company is the major shareholder of the Egypt-TEDA zone initiative – a Sino-Egyptian joint venture overseeing the development of the zone. Investing companies include China Textile Machinery Corporation, Brilliance China Automotive Holdings and an oil equipment industrial cluster (*China Economic Review* Aug 2010). The first phase of the zone was completed in 2011 while construction of the entire zone will take up to 2018 to be completed (China Daily 19 April 2009).

Two zones are being established in Nigeria – the Lekki Free Trade Zone and the Ogun Zone (see Figure 3.1). The Lekki Free Trade Zone is receiving investment from the China Civil Engineering Construction Corporation, Jiangning Development Corporation, Nanjing Beyond and China Railway while the main investors of the Ogun Zone are the Guangdong Xinguang and South China Developing Group (Brautigam and Tang 2011). Totaling investment of US$869 million, these two zones mainly focus on industries such as transportation equipment, textiles, housewares and electronics. In eastern Ethiopia, US$101 million was invested in 2006–07 by Qiyuan Group, Jianglian International Trade and Yangyang Asset Management but this zone is still in its planning stage. This zone aims to draw in industries such as electric machinery, steel, metallurgy and construction materials. The zones in Mauritius, Egypt and Nigeria are partially supported by the CADFund (Teng 2009), which is assisting both with zone construction and, infrastructure roll-outs and supporting Chinese companies looking to expand into these zones. The Egypt zone is expected to create 10,000 jobs mainly for local

*Figure 3.1* The entrance to the Lekki Free Trade Zone in Nigeria (photograph by Ben Lampert)

workers (Davies 2010: 28). Although these zones are mainly invested in and built by the SOEs, their main occupants are small and medium enterprises (SMEs), amounting to 85 per cent of the businesses (Tang and Zhang 2011).

While these developments are still in an early stage, there could be potential benefits to the industrial development of these economies through these Chinese invested SEZs. One of the major benefits of these SEZs is that they not only attract Chinese investments but also come with economic spillover effects such as upgrades in technology, increases in employment, foreign exchange and rent, and the promotion of socio-economic development. An example is the China–Mali joint venture 'SUKALA S.A.' which produces 35,000 tons of cane sugar and has created nearly 10,000 job opportunities for the local population of Mali (CAITEC 2010: 5). Also, these SEZs could form clusters of industry which, according to Porter (1998), is an important factor to promote productivity, innovation and creation of new businesses. The emergence of these zones could also contribute to backward (country's hinterland) and forward (to export markets) linkages in the economy (Davies 2010: 26).

One of the most contested economic tools in China–Africa relations is perhaps the Export–Import Bank (ExIm) loans. Key recipients of ExIm Bank loans in Africa include Angola, Equatorial Guinea, Congo Brazzaville, Ethiopia, Guinea, Nigeria, Sudan and Zimbabwe – countries with questionable regimes, some of which may not qualify for funding from the traditional developmental finance institutions (Davies 2010: 12). Established in 1994, the ExIm Bank is a government bank that provides foreign and domestic aid administration and looks after trade and investment guarantees. As a state bank, its market strategies are mainly determined by the Chinese government, and many of its commercial activities are in line with the political directives, such as providing concessional loans and financing China's going global strategy (see Chapter 4).

In principle, these concessional loans are used for procuring equipment, materials, technology and services, with no less than 50 per cent of the contract's procurement coming from China. But in practice our research shows that most projects are implemented at closer to 70 per cent. The loan is denominated in Chinese Renminbi (RMB) and has a maximum maturity of 20 years. A grace period of three to seven years may be granted to the borrower, during which the borrower will only repay interest payments and not the principal. The interest rate is subsidized and underwritten by Chinese Government finances. By June 2008, China ExIm Bank had financed more than 300 projects in Africa worth at least US$6.5 billion, of which 80 per cent were committed to infrastructure development (IDE-JETRO 2010). Despite the large uptake of ExIm loans by African governments, the financing model employed is coming under a great deal of scrutiny and suspicion by external stakeholders, especially pertaining to debt sustainability issues in the long run (Davies 2010: 12).

## Differential impacts of Chinese policy in Angola and Ghana

From the above, although we have been discussing China and Africa as two entities through the multilateral framework of FOCAC, the actual implementation and monitoring of the FOCAC commitments remains largely bilateral (Guerin 2008: 5–6). As such, it is important to examine the differential impacts of China's policy directives on individual African states. This difference is also partly attributed to the varying geographies, energy endowments, make-up of the economy (agricultural or manufacturing sectors) and political regimes of the countries, which are then translated into differential gains and losses from involvement with the Chinese state. In this section, we will specifically look at Angola and Ghana and how the mechanisms are translated on the ground and its developmental impacts.

Angola is now China's largest African trade partner with US$24.8 billion in bilateral trade in 2011 (MacauHub 3 February 2012). China has been active in Angola's post-war reconstruction and has been involved in a range of major infrastructural projects in the country in recent years. For example, the China Road and Bridge Corporation (CRBC) is rebuilding the national road that links the Angolan city of Uíge to the municipality of Maquela do Zombo. Reconstruction work on the road, as well as the Negage-Bungo section, began in 2008 at an estimated cost of US$79.6 million and is due to be concluded in 2010 (ANGOP 2009a). As for rail networks, the Ango-Ferro 2000 project involves the rehabilitation of 3100 kilometres (km) of railway, 8000 km of extensions, 36 bridges, and rehabilitation and the construction of 100 stations and 150 new substations. The project, contracted to China Railway 20 (China Ferrovia 20), may be the single largest infrastructure project that has been awarded to a Chinese company in Angola (Hon et al. 2010: 29). Other infrastructural projects under the umbrella initiative of the FOCAC include the Kilamba Kiaxi Housing Project and African Cup of Nations stadiums.

The Kilamba Kiaxi Housing Project was launched in August 2008. The China International Trust and Investment Corporation (CITIC) and the Angolan government launched a US$3.5 billion housing project spanning 880 hectares of land and consisting of 10,000 workers (approximately 4000 are locals) (Hon et al. 2010: 28). It will accommodate around 200,000 people upon completion by October 2011. The four African Cup of Nations stadiums were completed in January 2010 by the Shanghai Urban Construction Group (SUCG) and Sinohydro in Benguela, Cabinda, Luanda and Lubango.

There are four major contentious issues with these infrastructure projects which are not exclusive to Angola. First, many established communities living in informal settlements in the area have been forcibly evicted. This affected an estimated 3000 homes housing some 15,000 people in 2009 alone, many of whom are children and adolescents below the age of 15 (Power 2011: 19). Second is that the Chinese model provides minimal employment opportunities for the locals and did very little to alleviate the country's skills shortage (Kiala 2010: 3). Although the Angolan government recognized the need to improve employment opportunities and upgrade skills in these projects, China's model for infrastructure development with significant imported

Chinese labour provides minimal employment opportunities for locals and little technological and skills transfer (Kiala 2010: 54). In our field-work, local labourers were rarely used except as security guards and in minimal numbers. These firms justified their actions so as to complete their projects rapidly (Davies 2010). Third, the surveillance and inspection process of these infrastructure projects (*fiscalização*) in Angola was limited with a lack of effective auditing (Kiala 2010: 4). Fourth, the question over the sustainability of the sovereign-backed debt was also raised, especially for African countries who are heavily indebted. For example, the Democratic Republic of the Congo's (DRC) US$9 billion deal with ExIm Bank for infrastructure in exchange for mining concessions raises questions about the ability of the DRC to repay these huge debts and deal with the growing debt burden (Davies 2010). However, infrastructure is vital to help improve the competitiveness of African economies as a major constraint to sustainable economic development is the poor state of the infrastructural system. The cost of transportation is five times higher in Africa compared to the rest of the world. It has been estimated that Africa requires at least US$40 billion per annum to fund and maintain its core infrastructure capacity (Davies 2010).

In the telecommunication sector, China's Zhong Xing Tele-communication Equipment Company Limited (ZTE) first entered Angola in 2004 on a deal with Mundo Startel – Angola's fixed line telecommunications utility and assumed the management of Movicel, Angola's second mobile operator and a state-owned enterprise in October 2008. China's Information and Communications Technology (ICT) firm Huawei Technologies is also setting up the national back-bone for Angola's operators in wireless technology and a fourth generation network, with funding from China's ExIm Bank. Huawei has invested US$7 million to transform the former *Instituto Nacional das Telecomunicaçôes* (ITEL) (Institute of National Telecommunications) into the *Universidade de Telecomunicações*, as well as building a new Telecom Technical Training Centre.

In addition to telecommunications, a significant investment has been made in the manufacturing of motor vehicles. In 2007 China's Dongfeng and Japan's Nissan invested US$30 million to establish a car manufacturing plant in Viana's industrial zone – north of Luanda. From their joint venture with Angola's CGS Automovel, operations at the Zhengzhou Nissan (ZZNissan) plant began in 2008. Angola desperately needs a manufacturing sector and this joint venture will be valuable in promoting value-added production and developing local manufac-turing industries.

To date Angola has not yet taken advantage of the provision to allow zero-tariff treatment on export items to China as it currently exports only six products to China – that is crude oil, diamonds, granite, copper waste, furniture parts and aluminum scrap (CCS 2010: 42). Moreover, investments or assistance to promote long-term sustainable development and capacity building have thus far been minimal, though there have been reports of Chinese involvement in funding a $40 million cotton growing project (ANGOP 2006). Moreover, there is limited evidence that Chinese credit lines are boosting Angola's productive capacity and the limited employment opportunities created for Angolan workers have been the cause of some tension locally (Interview with Mr. Xu Ning, Industrial and Commercial Association Angola–China). Where Angolans have been able to find work on Chinese construction sites it has often been as security guards rather than on equal terms as waged labourers.

In terms of medical aid, Luanda's Central Hospital, which contains an anti-malaria centre, was financed by the Chinese government prior to the FOCAC 2006 Ministerial Meeting. After 15 months of construction, the hospital was inaugurated in February 2006. It accommodates 100 patients and cost an estimated US$ 8 million to build (CCS 2010). However, Terra Daily (6 July 2010) reported of the hospital that 'four years after its inauguration (it) is basically collapsing and in July patients and staff were evacuated due to safety concerns'. In 2008, the Chinese government has also donated anti-malaria medication to Angola's Ministry of Health and an additional RMB 2 million (approximately US$440 million) on 9 April 2009 (CCS 2010). More vitally, the key to sustaining the medical facilities after the physical infrastructure is in place is a dedicated team of medical professionals, which is lacking in Angola. Hence, human resource development and filling the shortage of skilled and knowledgeable personnel is of the utmost importance.

By contrast the scope of China's involvement in Ghana has been quite distinct and comparatively less intense. In recent times, following the first FOCAC summit in 2000, China undertook to finance a series of projects aimed at helping Ghana to close the infrastructural gap, amounting to US$1 billion over the last eight years. In 2007, Ghana received a total of US$1.15 billion (OECD 2007a) from all donors (not including China) and Chinese aid is still only a small percentage of the total development assistance Ghana receives.

In 2008 China exported US$1.4 billion to Ghana and imported only US$91.8 million of goods from Ghana, creating a trade surplus of US$1.33 billion (MOFCOM 2008). This trade deficit with China, in particular the export of mainly traditional primary goods, did not help Ghana in terms of the industrialization process. China's subsidy of agricultural exports to Ghana also hurts Ghana's agricultural exports to China (ACET 2009: 1). Moreover, Chinese tariffs discourage many kinds of African imports to China, especially on higher value added goods. For example, China levies a tariff of 6.5 per cent on raw hides but 14.6 per cent on manufactured leather (ACET 2009: 6). The 'Going out' policy has also had an impact in Ghana. According to the Ghana Investment Promotion Centre (GIPC), a total of 314 Chinese projects were registered between 1994 and 2007. The manufacturing sector accounts for about 30 per cent of the projects, while 19 per cent were in the general trade sector. From 1 January 2007 to 30 September 2008, there were a total of 104 new Chinese investments in Ghana, amounting to US$28.5 million (GIPC 2008). By August 2010, Chinese businesses in the country had invested in over 400 projects (Ghana Business News Website 16 August 2010).

Ghana began to receive grants and interest-free loans directly from China in 2004/5, including a US$24 million package of debt relief on interest-free loans. Similar to Angola, Ghana's recent experience with the deleterious effects of difficult to service debt raises questions about the sustainability of Chinese debt (ACET 2009: 2). In the 2006 FOCAC, Ghana and China signed six agreements, including a US$66 million loan for the expansion of Ghana's telecommunication infrastructure and a US$30 million concessionary loan for the first phase of the National Fibre-optic and e-government project. This project, estimated to be $70 million in total, was executed by the Chinese telecom giant Huawei and is aimed at linking all the 10 regional capitals and 36 townships on fibre routes (Idun-Arkhurst 2008). This will serve as a catalyst for the implementation of the national ICT development policy (*Daily Graphic* 15 August 2007).

China has provided US$10.4 million assistance to Ghana's agricultural sector, funding irrigation, agro-processing, agricultural technology and infrastructure (ACET 2009: 20). The agricultural sector has also benefited from training offered by the Chinese government to fisheries officers and young graduates in agricultural technology. The rehabilitation of the Ashaiman Aquaculture Demonstration Centre in Accra was financed by China, as a means of diffusing fish farming expertise in the country. Ghana also received assistance from China for the rehabilitation of the hatchery in the Ashanti region, making fingerlings more affordable to the local fish farmers. Finally, China also provided a US$99 million interest-free loan for the construction of landing sites for fishing communities in Ghana (Idun-Arkhurst 2008) and supported the Afefi irrigation project and grain depot (ACET 2009: 20), which contributed to the food security of the nation. However, this interest in the country's fishing industry has improved access rights for Chinese fishing companies leading to the exploration of offshore processing opportunities in Ghana (Idun-Arkhurst 2008).

Perhaps the most significant feature of Chinese engagement with Ghana is the Bui hydroelectric dam which is predominantly funded by China ExIm bank at a cost of US$622 million. The Bui hydropower project (located in the Tain District of Brong-Ahafo region) employed over 580 workers. Constructed by the Sinohydro Corporation Ltd, it is expected to generate about 3000 jobs at its peak (Yaw Baah and Jauch 2009: 81). However, this project is plagued with numerous Corporate Social Responsibility (CSR) issues, such as those concerning labour conditions, the resettlement of villagers and environmental impacts. Sutcliffe (2009) has assessed the compliance with the environmental impact assessment (EIA) recommendations and found that many of them – such as consultation with the local people, health and livelihood security and adequate compensation – were blatantly flouted. These issues will be discussed in greater detail in Chapter 7.

Most stakeholders agree that Ghana's economic engagements with China have been beneficial, bringing affordable manufactured imports and some investments, job creation, technology transfer and salutary competition for local industries (ACET 2009: 1). Moreover, infrastructural investment by the Chinese such as the Accra-Kumasi highway (provided through an interest-free loan) will reduce the domestic transport costs and will benefit the local people in terms of cost and pricing effectiveness. Low-priced Chinese imports enable Ghanaians to improve their standard of living and has enabled competitive pricing for local consumer products. Although Chinese investors are expected to allocate 15 per cent of jobs created in Ghana to Ghanaians, competition from these Chinese firms has also damaged Ghanaian manufacturing and jobs (ACET 2009).

## Opportunities and challenges

The above sections have provided the background of the various FOCAC plans' objectives and the numerous tools for implementing these aims. We have also highlighted some of the achievements from the broad spectrum of cooperation programmes through quantifiable targets. The next section will examine the challenges and issues surrounding the FOCAC platform and implementation mechanisms in Africa.

## FOCAC: lack of a formal permanent institution

Formally, FOCAC is under the aegis of the MFA (although it integrates the minister and vice minister of commerce as co-chairpersons) and has no multilateral permanent body. A secretariat based in the premises of the African Department of the Chinese Ministry of Foreign Affairs serves as a follow-up mechanism in between FOCAC meetings (FOCAC, 20 March 2009). However, the 27-member follow-up committee is very ad hoc and impermanent and cooperation policies and strategies are largely based on the FOCAC process, which is renewed every three years with new action plans and targets being adopted. Hence it is difficult to have a long-term plan in terms of planning for schools and human resource needs (Nordtveit 2010: 7).

Moreover, there is a dilemma between the multilateral mechanism of FOCAC and the bilateral reality of China's negotiations with African countries. According to Guerin (2008: 5–6), the collective dynamic at a continent scale struggles to emerge as China prefers to keep up privileged bilateral relations with politically and economically important countries. It hides behind FOCAC's multilateral screen to give the impression of diplomatic support to Africa as a whole. FOCAC meetings are largely a formality, while the 'real development' takes place in the ongoing bilateral dialogue and the preparatory meetings that are coordinated in each African country by the President's office and the MFA. In China, this process is managed by the Foreign Ministry and the Ministry of Commerce (MOFCOM). Hence it is difficult to align bilateral interactions with the broader aims of the FOCAC platform.

## Lack of coordination

As multiple actors arrive in growing numbers in Africa, alongside with its poor business practices and low quality produce, it is becoming increasingly important and urgent that the Chinese government develop a better mechanism to govern their activities in the continent. This problematic multitude of actors was obvious as early as the first FOCAC, with the establishment of the follow-up committee of 27 members. To varying degrees however each of these ministries and agencies play a part in carrying out the objectives of the FOCAC action plans, either in China or Africa. The members are listed in Table 3.4.

*Table 3.4*   Follow-up committee of FOCAC

| Ministry of Foreign Affairs | Ministry of Commerce | Ministry of Finance | International Department of CCP Central Committee |
|---|---|---|---|
| National Development and Reform | Ministry of Education | Ministry of Science and Technology | Ministry of Land and Resources |
| Ministry of Communications | Ministry of Information Industry | Ministry of Agriculture | Ministry of Culture |
| Ministry of Health | People's Bank of China | General Administration of Customs | General Administration of Quality Supervision, Inspection and Quarantine |
| State Administration of Taxation | National Tourism Administration | Information Office of the State Council | Chinese Communist Youth League |
| China Council for the Promotion of International Trade | Bank of China | Export-Import Bank of China | Beijing Municipal Government |
| Ministry of Environmental Protection | General Administration of Civil Aviation | State Administration of Radio, Film and Television | |

The highest organ of executive power in China is the State Council while the MFA advises Chinese leaders and helps implement African policy. The MOFCOM is the administrative department authorized by the State Council to oversee foreign aid. However, there are more actors involved in foreign aid and these include the Ministry of Finance, the MFA, various Chinese embassies based in Africa and especially the Economic and Commercial Counsellors' offices, the ExIm Bank and other ministries such as Ministry of Education and Health who are in charge of the provision of scholarships and other medical programmes (CCS 2008: 30). The CCP's International Department interacts with African counterparts to lay the foundation for commercial and diplomatic cooperation, exchange visits and to ensure that policies are implemented in accordance with CCP strategic objectives (Brown and Chun 2009: 10). Realizing the need to coordinate the departments, the Ministries of Commerce, Finance and Foreign Affairs set up a foreign aid liaison agency in 2008, which was upgraded to an inter-agency coordination mechanism in February 2011, called the Department of Foreign Aid (MOFCOM 2011a).

We also can observe from Table 3.4 that most of the committee members are state agencies/ministries including finance institutions such as Bank of China and ExIm Bank. Missing from this list however are peripheral state actors such as provincial governments, SOEs and non-state agencies such as the China–Africa Business Council (CABC). Although China is a unitary state, provincial governments and leaders have not been insignificant players in Africa. Many SOEs, including the provincial branches of national foreign-trade companies, are handed over to provincial governments (Chen and Jian 2009: 3). The central government is able to rely on the provinces' international activities to advance its own foreign policy goals, while the provinces can use the central government's endorsement to realize local objectives internationally (see Chapter 4).

Through the sister city and multinational companies networks, these provinces are able to command a variety of channels to gain access to foreign countries' foreign policy making process (Chen and Jian 2009: 7). In addition, China's 31 provinces, autonomous regions, municipalities and two special administrative regions (Hong Kong and Macau) each have their own relationships with African countries and cities (Brown and Chun 2009: 10). Local governments such as the Shanghai municipal government also issued their own directives on an investment strategy in Africa in 1998. To encourage local companies to invest in Africa, a special fund of RMB 100 million was set up to support local companies by providing them with low-interest loans. In 2003, encouraged by the government's 'going out' strategy, provinces such as Fujian and Zhejiang also developed comprehensive subsidy systems to encourage local enterprises to invest in Africa (Chen and Jian 2009: 11–12). The provinces also help develop grassroots contacts between China and Africa to strengthen the societal base of sustainable Sino-African relations. Examples of successful provincial-based companies in Africa include Shanghai Construction Corporation and Ningbo C.S.I Power & Machinery group (in Zhejiang province), which has built 20 power plants in Nigeria (Gu 2009).

Other actors include the CABC, a joint project of the United Nations Development Programme (UNDP), the Chinese Ministry of Commerce and the Guangcai programme. The Guangcai programme was established in 2005 to deepen the economic relations between China and Africa and to inculcate the idea of corporate social responsibility in Chinese companies. According to Bai Xiaofeng, the secretary of CABC, 'We have started to emphasize CSR to our member companies investing in or trading with African countries' (pers. comm., 11 September 2008). In April 2008, a 63-member delegation under the leadership of Mr Hu Deping, President of CABC, undertook a four-day business tour to seek investment opportunities in Africa (Baah and Jauch 2009: 87).

With this multitude of actors and in the wake of several incidents of Chinese labour unrest in Africa, it is imperative for the Chinese government to mitigate the negative impacts of its Chinese practices, brought about by various Chinese actors in Africa. The Chinese government, realizing the importance of managing negative impacts and perceptions arising from the lack of good business practices, urged the ministries of Commerce and Foreign affairs to jointly hold a national conference with the aim of creating a management system composed of the functional ministries of the central government, overseas embassies, local governments and the various enterprises to ensure that all the investment or construction projects in Africa are under comprehensive supervision (Chen and Jian 2009: 19).

Indeed, although efforts are made at the national and provincial level to manage this complex coordination, there is still an obvious gap in communicating especially with the smaller players such as SMEs. An effective mechanism bridging the gap between China's Africa policy and its implementation in terms of private sector is lacking (Jing Gu 2009). According to Jing Gu (2009), many local firms and enterprises do not have much knowledge or understanding of the policies relating to going out and investing in Africa. One CEO observed: 'We don't know whether they have policies or, if they do, what kind of policies our local government has towards this. We do not know the policies or exactly how they operated in reality' (cited in Gu 2009: 18). This issue of coordination is particularly problematic in the SEZs, especially issues of communication, governance, political factors, poor infrastructure and the lack of transparency, as exemplified in studies by Brautigam and Tang (2011), Davies (2010) and Centre for Chinese Studies (2011). For example, in Mauritius, delay in construction of the SEZ was attributed to the lack of environmental, labour and safety concerns (Brautigam and Tang 2011), while in Zambia issues such as special taxes and concessions granted to Chinese investors have been raised because it is felt they might undermine good governance if not monitored cautiously and effectively (Davies 2010).

## Sustainability, quality and type of projects

One of the main concerns of the FOCAC and its mechanisms is the sustainability and quality of the projects. As exemplified in Angola, a poorly built hospital building poses concerns over the sustainability of such Chinese aid projects in Africa. Moreover there is an increasing awareness of the need for environmental protection among Chinese companies operating in Africa as exemplified in the Bui Dam case, which was partly a result of domestic conditions in China. Typically, in a state-owned or state-invested enterprise, political directives, rather than market directives, tend to be more influential in the business strategy. The lack of corporate governance codes and a developed system of commercial law within China fail to regulate Chinese SOE practice in the international economy (Alden and Davies 2006: 5–6). Also, to ensure sustainability of a project, there is a need for skills transfer and training a professional team of staff, especially to fill in for the Chinese after they have gone. This is particularly critical in the medical and education sector. Last but not least, there is a need to shift the type of projects from 'bricks and mortar' to building the manufacturing sector of the African countries. In most African states, what is more vital is to industrialize and encourage the manufacturing sector, which will have a more sustainable lifespan and bigger economic spillover effect in terms of employment, capacity, skills and technology build-up. The SEZs could play a bigger role in enhancing the manufacturing capacities of these nation-states.

## Conclusion

Generally, the FOCAC commitments and various implementation mechanisms have been praised by African leaders and international observers as a successful initiative, with measurable outcomes in terms of trade, aid, infrastructure and capacity building. However, there are also long-term governance issues, ranging from effectiveness of aid, sustainability of projects, obvious gaps between formulation and implementation and transparency. This chapter detailed the various FOCAC plans, its aims and highlighted its outcomes in the Africa continent. It has also outlined the differential impact of Angola and Ghana, giving this multilateral initiative a more grounded evaluation.

# 4

# Towards a Chinese 'Socialist Market Economy'

## Introduction: China's economic 'miracle'

> Reform is China's second revolution. (Deng Xiaoping, 28 March 1985)

On 6 September 2010 President Hu Jintao led celebrations marking the thirtieth anniversary of the Special Economic Zone (SEZ) in Shenzhen, where China's economic transformation first began. In August 1980 Shenzhen became the first area in China to be designated an SEZ that could accept foreign investment under Deng's reforms. The site of a former fishing village on the border with Hong Kong, the Shenzhen SEZ has since evolved into a thriving metropolis over the past three decades and is now home to the headquarters of many high-tech companies along with the Shenzhen stock exchange. Tens of billions of US dollars in investment have since flooded into Shenzhen, where thousands of factories produce goods for export around the world. Shenzhen has since become one of China's most productive cities, rising from a gross domestic product (GDP) per capita of 606 Yuan in 1979 to rank first by 2008 with 89,814 Yuan per capita (Yiming et al 2011). According to Hu, the Shenzhen SEZ had 'created a miracle in the world's history of industrialization, urbanization and modernization, and has contributed significantly to China's opening up and reform'. Only weeks before Hu's visit the State Council decreed the southern city in the province of Guangdong as 'a national economic centre' and 'a city of global clout' in cultural, economic and technological exchanges. Praising the reforms ushered in by Deng, Hu observed that the achievements made by the Shenzhen SEZ had proved that the Party's basic theories, guidelines and experiences formed since the Third Plenary Session of the Eleventh

88

Central Committee of the Chinese Communist Party (CCP) in 1978 were 'completely correct' and that the decision made by the CCP to establish such zones was 'absolutely right'. For President Hu 'Socialism with Chinese characteristics' is the only way to realize the continued revitalization of the Chinese nation (*China Daily* 7 September 2010) and (along with further reform and opening up) the only path to China's development.

It is now almost *de rigeur* to acknowledge that the rapid transformation of China's economy and the enterprise zones that this has been centred upon has been something of a 'miracle'. China's ability to lift millions of its citizens out of poverty as a result of this 'miraculous' transformation has been widely heralded. According to Shaohua Chen and Martin Ravallion of the World Bank, between 1981 and 2005 over 600 million Chinese people moved out of poverty (Chen and Ravallion 2008). Since the late 1970s, China has experienced extraordinary economic growth (exceeding 9% per year over more than 20 years) brought on by the privatization and de-nationalization of economic enterprises, the opening of export markets and the new partnerships of state cadres with transnational investors, and with local township, provincial and national domestic entrepreneurs (Nonini 2008). What we are witnessing is 'perhaps the most explosive and long-sustained period of economic advance that the world has ever seen' (Nolan 2004: 1). Inspired by the impressive economic performances of its East Asian neighbours, such as Japan, Singapore, South Korea and Taiwan, China's reform and 'opening up' (*Gaige Kaifang*) involved a series of wide-ranging reforms that would radically refocus China's economic development strategy with the domestic social, political and economic systems undergoing massive change around the focus of the 'Four Modernizations' (see Chapter 2). This 'opening up', which began with the process of rural reform (that was itself to act as the guiding path for all reform), has since seen exports grow from US$18.1 billion in 1978 to over US$1.19 trillion in 2009 (Nolan 2004; Workman, 2009). China's manufactured exports rose from US$9 billion in 1978 to US$1.3 trillion in 2008 (WTO 2009) while their share in China's total exports rose from 50 per cent in 1978 to 93 per cent in 2008. By 2009 China's manufacturing output represented some 15 per cent of the world's total (*Xinhua* 2009). Together with high levels of public investment, foreign direct investment (FDI)[1] in China (implying the entry and expansion of transnational companies) has been crucial to this growth and in the wider restructuring of the Chinese economy. From 1985 to 2010, FDI inflows rose from US$2 billion to US$105.7 billion (MOFCOM 2010).

There has also been *a significant outflow of investments from China into the global economy* over the past five years, a period which corresponded with a massive upsurge in foreign reserve accumulation and a significant expansion of China's domestic economy, which grew 13 per cent year-on-year in 2007, 9.6 per cent in 2008 and 8.7 per cent in 2009 (*China Daily* 25 December 2009, 21 January 2010) despite the global economic downturn. In 2010, China's outward FDI reached US$57.9 billion, nearly 20 times that of 2003 levels, and accounted for over 5 per cent of the global total (Huang 2011). It is estimated that by the end of 2008 there were around 12,000 businesses with Chinese capital in 174 countries (MOFCOM 2009).

Once China set out on this 'socialist' course, powerful 'path-dependent' effects were created and it has become harder and harder to shift the country off this development trajectory. Since 1989, commodification in China has become ruthless and pervasive throughout society (Wu 2008) as the state has pursued an export-oriented development strategy based on 'market socialism'. The consequences of this commodification are being played out across China and can be seen clearly in the changing landscapes of some of China's largest cities. Housing demolitions and the forced relocation of some of the poorest and most marginal urban citizens to make way for new private urban developments have become a regular feature of China's neo-liberalized urban development policy. Unemployment, which officially stands at 4.1 per cent but, in reality, might be around 10 per cent or more is a growing concern, particularly given China's population growth. In the countryside, mechanization and the replacement of collective socialist motivations with private and profit motivations resulted in the loss of an average of six million workers a year in the 1990s (Breslin 2004). A significant proportion of the rural workforce are without work for most of the year leading to a significant growth in migration – both state sanctioned/supported and illegal, particularly from China's poorest provinces. When we examine China's global economic standing today then, by many yardsticks, it remains a poor developing economy, with more than 10 per cent of the population stricken in absolute poverty (UNDP China 2008). Estimates from various sources, including the World Bank and the Chinese government, suggest that income inequality has increased at least 50 per cent since the late 1970s, making China one of the most unequal societies in Asia. According to one study less than 1 per cent of Chinese households control more than 60 per cent of the country's wealth (Pei 2006). These widening inequalities are a real concern for the CCP who have made plans for income redistribution, 'balancing development' and social reform key features of China's twelfth five-year development plan covering the period 2011–15.

This chapter critically explores China's recent economic transformation and the nature of the reforms and 'open door' policies first instigated at the end of the 1970s by Deng Xiaoping. Reviewing China's own economic transformation is an important and necessary part of understanding China's escalating global economic outreach and the contemporary push into new regions and markets such as Africa. In particular the chapter seeks to trace the origins of China's recent attempts to build a socialist market economy and interrogates the proclaimed uniqueness of 'Socialism with Chinese characteristics'. The chapter also focuses on China's 'go out' (*Zǒuchūqū Zhànlüè* ) strategy and looks at the specific Chinese banks, institutions and companies (state-owned and otherwise) that Beijing sees as the 'champions' of this strategy. This includes a critical analysis of the changing roles of China's state-owned enterprises (SOEs) and of recent attempts to restructure them along with a discussion of the 'Chineseness' of Chinese businesses and the role of transnational Chinese business networks. The global expansion of Chinese enterprises does not just involve the SOEs however – China's more dynamic and more profitable small- and medium-sized enterprises (SMEs) have also been expanding beyond China's borders. As Jing Gu has shown, these enterprises are characterized by high flexibility, a strong entrepreneurial spirit and work ethic, and are highly concentrated by provincial origin, with Zhejiang having the largest representation (Gu 2009). China has more than 40 million SMEs, which account for 99 per cent of all registered Chinese companies, making up 60 per cent of Chinese exports (MOFCOM 2007) although most (78%) of these are focused on the Asia-Pacific region (*China Daily* 21 September 2010). Our primary focus here however is on the SOEs since they are currently playing an important role in China's aid, partnership and cooperation projects in Africa and because the fluctuating strategies adopted by the state for their management reveals a great deal about China's changing economic vision. The entwinement of Chinese economic development with the fate of many other economies and corporations is also discussed here as is the global interconnectedness and transnational dynamics that shape China's economic development strategies both domestically and overseas. The chapter also looks at domestic debates about (and critiques of) China's economic philosophy and engages with debates about the emergence of 'neoliberalism with Chinese characteristics'. In particular the chapter seeks to explore some of the processes, practices, institutional mechanisms, interconnections and flows that are involved in China's global economic outreach. In so doing the chapter will attempt to disavow the illusion of 'China Inc' by unpacking the myth of a unitary, singular and coherent Chinese economic actor, by drawing out some of the contradictions within China's policies (and the multiplicity of actors involved) and by highlighting the fragility of China's regulatory hold over state-owned enterprises (SOEs) and private companies operating overseas.

## Embracing the market: state socialism and the crisis of accumulation

Following the death of Mao Zedong on 9 September 1976 China faced a number of complex challenges. The power struggle between the Gang of Four (that wanted to continue the policy of revolutionary mass mobilization) and the reformers led by Deng Xiaoping (that wanted to overhaul the Chinese economy based on market socialism and to de-emphasize the role of Maoist ideology in determining economic and political policy) had led to considerable political flux and turmoil. China was on the verge of ruin and still coming to terms with the collective trauma that resulted from the failures of the Great Leap Forward and the Cultural Revolution, combined with the additional threat of impending aggression from Communist Vietnam. Even the State Bureau for Statistics admitted that national economic progress had 'got stuck' and was 'in a state of collapse' (cited in Weil 1996: 293). Between 1960 and 1970, China's GDP showed an average annual increase of only 1.8 per cent, which was considerably lower than the growth figures posted by Japan (14.5%) and South Korea (7.7%) (Holslag 2006).

China's post-1978 economic liberalization has already been well-documented elsewhere (see Wang 2003; Lardy 2005; Zweig and Chen 2007; Lampton 2008; Zhang and Ong 2008). The main objective of the reforms was not so much to foster a fully fledged market economy, but rather to replace the tight centralist dirigisme with a more relaxed regime of 'planning through guidance' (Gao 1996). The five-year development plans were drafted in more flexible terms: fixed production targets were abolished and immobile prices became subject to international market prices. In 1980, provincial authorities received substantial autonomy to adapt national guidelines to their own local contexts (Goodman and Segal 1994). In 1979 peasant communities were reformed and farmers were allowed to retain surpluses. Consequently, China's agricultural output rose 49 per cent in five years and peasants' household incomes increased significantly (Holslag 2006). The transportation, communication and energy grids were upgraded and extended, and the mining sector revitalized to improve the supply of raw materials.

In this context the 'Open Door Policy' was launched to entice foreign entrepreneurs to invest their cash and skills in China's huge market. This 'invite-in' strategy comprised several far-reaching measures and legal modifications. In 1979, the investment law was relaxed and the so-called foreign exchange retention system was changed to permit local governments and companies to retain a part of the foreign currency earned on exports, with a view to enlarging the industrial output and stimulating the import of technology. Whereas foreign investors were initially compelled to set up joint ventures with their Chinese counterparts, a new directive in 1986 also allowed the establishment of 100 per cent foreign-owned branches. From 1984, the first Special Economic Zones, Open Coastal Cities, Inland Cities with expanded authority, and Open Coastal Economic Areas were created. Thus international economic contacts were originally limited to just four SEZs with the (limited) freedom to conduct international economic relations. These SEZs were conceived as 'windows on the world' for China – allowing international economic contacts to grow (Breslin 2004) (Figure 4.1). China's SEZs were very similar both in intention and policy to the Export Processing Zones (EPZs) that had previously been established in other regional states. Following the example of the Kandla export-processing zone in India, Taiwan opened its first EPZ at Gaoxiong (Kaohsiung) in 1966 to attract inward investment to produce exports. A similar strategy was pursued in South Korea, which opened its own EPZ at Masan, and by Malaysia which established EPZs in and around Penang in the early 1970s. In 1984, China opened 14 coastal cities[2] to overseas investment and in the following year announced an expansion of the open coastal areas, extending the open economic zones into an open coastal belt.[3]

The government also attempted to create a more beneficial environment for foreign investors including lower fees for labour and rent, tax rebates for exporters, and making it possible for foreign companies to convert limited profits earned in RMB into foreign exchange for repatriation. It quickly became clear however that most investors were not interested in the local consumption market in which purchasing capacity was very modest, but rather in China's abundant cheap labour (Chan et al. 1999). The People's Republic swiftly developed into the world's assembly factory: at the end of the 1980s more than half of its GDP consisted of export earnings (Holslag 2006). To stimulate exports, Chinese companies were allowed to engage directly in international trade while Beijing decided to keep the Yuan currency at low rates to

*Figure 4.1* 'Special Economic Zones – China's great open door'. February, 1987. Stefan R. Landsberger collection, International Institute of Social History (Amsterdam)

retain a competitive edge over other competing exporting nations. The Yuan was first devalued against the dollar from 1989 to 1994, and then resolutely maintained at a fixed rate before the crawling peg system was implemented in 2005 (Xing 2006). A system of import and export licensing was also established to permit the government to go along more smoothly with the exigencies of interior and international markets. While foreign invested enterprises (FIEs) only accounted for 2 per cent of exports and 6 per cent of imports before 1986, the figure increased to 48 per cent and 52 per cent respectively by 2000 (Braunstein and Epstein 2002: 23). Since then, export-based investment has not only dominated investment into China, but has also been a major motor of Chinese export growth. From 1993, exports increased by 60 per cent in two years (53% in real terms), and doubled in the space of five years (Breslin 2004). Trade deficits turned into surpluses. As a result of the heavy focus on foreign investment 'the way in which capitalism is emerging in China – or more correctly, in those parts of China that are inserted into the global economy – owes much to the preferences of external economic actors' (Breslin 2004: 14–15). The decision to join the World Trade Organization (WTO) in 2001 for example, and join on the conditions negotiated in 2001, was partly[4] down to the need to secure access to major markets in the global North.

Many reforms were not originally the product of central government directives but would be introduced by local leaders and if successful and promising would then be adopted by larger and larger areas and ultimately introduced nationally. Local municipalities and provinces were allowed to invest in industries that they considered most profitable, which encouraged investment in light manufacturing. The short gestation period, low capital requirements, and high foreign-exchange export earnings meant that revenues generated by light manufacturing could be reinvested in more technologically advanced production and further capital expenditures and investments. It is thus important to acknowledge the role of the local state in China's economic transformation (Oi 1995) and that state power exists at different levels of the 'local' from the still relatively centralized provincial level right down to towns and villages. Township and village level governments were not only crucial in establishing new enterprises but were also the basic level of revenue collection across the country, often deploying innovative and proactive means of generating income (Bernstein and Lu 2003) and absorbing many of the surplus workers who were without employment following the abandonment of collective socialist objectives and the restructuring of SOEs. These market-oriented public enterprises under the purview of local governments and based in townships and villages proved to be one of the main engines of economic growth, and a major source of China's export boom in the 1990s. In recent years power has been selectively delegated to provincial governments (Lin 1999) meaning that central directives are increasingly shaped and limited by local autonomy. As a result of China's decentralization process 'local leaders have become significant economic actors and not simply local agents of the state' (Goodman 2009: 442).

Abandoning Mao's mass campaign style of economic construction Deng's reforms actually included the introduction of planned, centralized management of the macro-economy by technically proficient bureaucrats. Deng sustained Mao's legacy however to the extent that he stressed the primacy of agricultural output and encouraged a significant decentralization of decision making in the rural economy and among individual peasant households. At the local level, material incentives, rather than political appeals, were to be used to motivate the labour force, including the decollectivization of agriculture and allowing peasants to earn extra income by selling the produce of their private plots at free market prices. According to Deng, China's socialist modernization should proceed in three steps (as outlined in the 13th national congress of the CCP): (1) to double the 1980 GNP to solve the problem of clothing and feeding the Chinese people; (2) to quadruple the 1980 GNP by the end of the century to achieve a good standard of living for the people and (3) realizing the goal of modernization by 2050 so that China had a GNP comparable with an intermediate-level developed country.

It is important to recognize here that at the inception of China's economic liberalization, Deng and other Party reformers turned to markets not to restore Chinese capitalism of the pre-1949 period or to create a new capitalist class. As Breslin (2006: 115) puts it, 'China's post-Mao leadership did not begin with an ideological commitment to neoliberalism – far from it'. Chinese leaders initially identified markets as part of a necessary capitalist stage of freeing the forces of production in order to 're-socialize' them within a prosperous future socialist economy (Meisner 1999). The idea that they might be left uncontrolled by China's political authority – the Communist Party – was anathema. Consequently China's state and its governing logics since 1978 have represented 'a recombinant or hybrid assortment of oligarchic institutions, practices and disciplines of power' (Nonini 2008: 156) that have juxtaposed older elements of Maoist governance (e.g. central planning and an ideology of socialist paternalism toward 'peasants' and 'workers') with elements of market liberalization in a kind of 'slow-tempo improvisation' (Nonini 2008: 156) aimed simultaneously at developing China's forces of production, preserving the position and legitimacy of the CCP, and, particularly since the 1980s, consolidating the base of economic accumulation of China's 'cadre-capitalist' class (So 2005). The 'market socialism' ushered in by Deng has thus been combined with pre-existing Maoist developmentalist, nationalist and socialist discourses and practices in an uneasy synthesis held together by the authoritarian rule of the CCP (Lin 2006). As Breslin (2004: 1) notes, the recent development of the Chinese economic system may thus be dysfunctional in that the system that has emerged:

> owes more to the agglomeration of numerous initiatives to interpret and implement economic change to serve particular interests than it does to the plans and strategies of national level decision making elites ... China has moved from a state planned and state owned economy towards state regulation of a hybrid economic system with the existence of a private economic sphere that remains very close to the state system that spawned it.

Thus the programmes of economic intervention developed since 1978 in China can be considered products of accretion and bricolage and are interesting examples of the kinds of assemblages that Murray Li (2007) writes about. Much of the non-state sector in contemporary China has its origins in the party-state sector that spawned it. Further it is all but impossible to distinguish between the public and the private while much of what is considered 'non-state' remains heavily connected to offi-cialdom through various mechanisms (Breslin 2004). The relationship between state and economy is, to say the least, blurred and strong elements of state control remain in place. The Chinese state remains deeply entrenched in the economy, accounting for 38 per cent of the country's GDP and employing 85 million people in 2003 (about one-third of the urban workforce and down from 99.8% in 1978). It is either a monopolist or a dominant player in the most important sectors, including financial services, banking, telecommunications, energy, steel, automobiles, natural resources and transportation. The government maintains tight control over most investment projects through the power to issue long-term bank credit and grant land-use rights while the party appoints 81 per cent of the chief executives of state-owned enterprises and 56 per cent of all senior corporate executives (Pei 2006).

In the early years of reform, when enterprises of more than eight employees were illegal, larger private enterprises 'camouflaged' themselves as collective enterprises (Tsai 2007). This practice, known as 'wearing a red hat' was eventually accommodated at an official level, paving the way for private entrepreneurs to become legitimate 'red capitalists' and eventually party members, thus internally altering the membership composition of the CCP. As a result there has long been a tendency for emerging private enterprises to form an alliance with local governments, often resulting in what are effectively private companies being officially classified as collectively owned 'in order to obtain the security and privileges that those governments extend to collective firms' (ADB 2003: 63). Dickson (2003) focuses on the emergence of new entrepreneurial elites from the ranks of the political elites, concentrating on the children of party state officials, and those entrepreneurs who have left formal political office to become economic elites – the process of *xiahai*. Particularly at the local level, power holders are switching the prestige, influence and wealth that came from forming part of the political structure for the wealth that comes from being a factory manager, or a member of the board. SOEs, for example, were typically transferred into the hands of previous factory managers, or relatives of local party-state officials who have used their political positions to increase their economic potential and bargaining power. Rather than own or run the enterprises themselves, officials more often retained control by proxy, establishing new enterprises run by their relatives, or transferring ownership of publicly owned assets to private enterprises owned by 'cadre kin'. These enterprises were then allocated state contracts and were provided protection through local state power. This form of privatization[5] did not entail government officials directly taking control of public enterprises and assets, but a form of 'insider privatization' (Walder 2002: 13) whereby officials directed the privatization process towards close contacts or relatives, and ensured that the success of these enterprises remained contingent on the new owners' relationship with the local government. Ding (2000a) has referred to the resulting relationship between political and economic elites as 'nomenklatura capitalism' and considers this process of privatization as comprising illegal asset stripping (Ding 2000b).

Economic reform in China has thus transformed relationships between existing state actors and the changing basis of their power, leading to a reformulation of class alliances within China (Breslin 2004). The party leadership increasingly resembles an authoritarian executive leadership acting on behalf of (and in many ways generating) the bourgeoisie 'whilst providing palliatives for social groups that could jeopardize stability if they lost too much' (Breslin 2004: 24).

It is an economic system where the state creates the space for the private sector to dominate and regulates the market to ensure that the new bourgeoisie can appropriate surplus value thanks to the bourgeoisie's close relationship with the party state – capitalism with Chinese characteristics (Breslin 2004). The new classes which have emerged with different private rights over the means of production include *geti*, 'small business people', *minying*, 'private entrepreneurs', *guoying* and *dajiti*, two related kinds of 'managers in the public sector', and *guanshang/guanying*, 'former officials-turned private owners of sold State Owned Enterprises' (Lin 2006: 255). They have been formed by what So (2005: 486) refers to as 'the embourgeoisiement [*sic*] of cadres'. Government cadres and Party officials have been in the vanguard of those profiting from privatization and liberalization, while private entrepreneurs have also emerged. In this environment, local cadres formed prosperous partnerships with business people, including foreign corporate investors. Cadres provided entrepreneurs with vital information and access to credit and to markets; they shielded their capitalist partners from exactions by other cadres and from official or irregular taxes; and they accorded their partners the political protection they have needed to evade labour, health, pension and other welfare regulations. In return, capitalists provided 'their' cadres with money (via fees) and gifts, integrated them into valuable social networks, mobilized overseas connections and provided them with shares in the enterprises they formed (So 2005: 487).

It is also important to recognize that a key part of what drove Deng's economic reforms was the crisis under state socialism (Wu 2008) whereby effective accumulation supported by state-led extensive industrialization had reached its limit. There was no alternative accumulation space within the state system and so economic reform brought in a 'market discipline', creating an internal space for accumulation while opening a door to the space of external expansion (Wu 2008). In short, the market was initially introduced as a survival strategy for the state: faced with increasing competition between nations, globalization and the 'inevitability' of market reorientation, the state needed to find new space for accumulation, and thus legitimized itself through shifting its priority from 'class struggle' to 'promoting economic growth'. Ironically, the Cultural Revolution, with its detrimental effect on the productive forces and disillusion regarding utopia, paved the way towards the great transformation: ideological fetishes had been swept away, long before the official cosmetic surgery on the ideology into 'market socialism' or the 'socialist market economy' (Wu 2008). This opened a period of pragmatism: 'it is glorious to become rich'; 'no matter whether it is a white or black cat, as long as it can catch a mouse, it is a good cat'; 'there is no need to ask whether its name is socialism or capitalism'. During this time China could also not help but notice the impressive economic growth underway in the 'tiger' economies of Hong Kong, Taiwan, Singapore and South Korea.

The increasing importance of the non-state sector and the concomitant decline in the significance of state planning made the concept of a planned socialist economy increasingly out of step with reality. At the Fourteenth National Congress of the CCP held in 1992, the idea of 'developing a socialist market economy with Chinese characteristics' proposed by Deng was first designated as the leading strategy of the Party. This gave the green light to privatization and the commercialization of SOEs but it also proclaimed the end of the command economy, implying that both investment and consumption were to be left increasingly to the 'market'. As a result 'market economy' would become the law of value replacing state planning as the main means of allocating and distributing resources. To reassert his economic agenda, in the spring of 1992, Deng made his famous southern tour of China, visiting Guangzhou, Shenzhen, Zhuhai and Shanghai, using his travels as a method of reasserting his economic policy after his retirement from office. The tour marked his attack on the 'Conservative' and the inauguration of full-scale integration to global capitalism. It also began a period when China's overseas investment began to increase dramatically. While China's initial opening-up strategy mainly focused on the attraction of foreign investors, it now increasingly wanted its own companies to explore foreign markets.

## China's SOEs and the 'go out' strategy

China's economic diplomacy is now increasingly focused on the execution of the 'going-out' strategy rather than the 'invite-in' policy. Although the amount of overseas investment in the early period of the reform era was relatively small (accounting for less than 5% of total investment by the early 1990s) it helped Chinese firms to accumulate the necessary experience and to cultivate partnerships and contacts for more overseas investment in the following years. In 2001, the Chinese Vice-Premier Wu Bangguo officially announced his two-way investment strategy: it was an explicit dictate of the Party that the 'invite-in' approach had to be complemented by a 'going-out' strategy to realize 'trade-ownership'. In the same year Premier Zhu Rongji, in his policy address to the People's Congress, officially used the term 'going global' in outlining a strategy for Chinese firms. Thus a number of Chinese officials and government think tanks increasingly came to see the relationship between *Yinjinlai*, literally meaning 'inviting in' (inflow FDI) and *Zouchuqu*, or 'going global' (outflow FDI), as supplementary to the course of modernization. In 2001 the government released its tenth five-year plan (2001–05) which officially included the 'going out' strategy and aimed to raise the rate of outflow FDI. The National Development and Reform Commission, together with the Ministry of Commerce (MOFCOM) and the Ministry of Foreign Affairs (MFA) then began to mobilize firms to 'go out' and purchase resources around the world, promulgating a 'Guidance Catalogue on Countries and Industries for Overseas Investment' in 2004 which listed resources and industries which the state saw as the appropriate targets for foreign investment. MOFCOM subsequently issued new guidelines in April 2009 drawing on information supplied by the business departments of Chinese embassies and consulates around the world and pointing out potential problems that firms might encounter and how they might be solved in a more systematic attempt to promote the policy of 'going out' (Zweig 2009). The 'go out' strategy was then comprehensively implemented in the eleventh five-year plan drafted in 2006 (CCPIT 2010).

As Deng's reforms began, the challenge of keeping the SOEs afloat was costing billions in subsidies and loans contributing to the near bankruptcy of the Chinese financial system. In 1996, prior to the Company Law which put into operation real SOE reform (see below) around half of all SOEs officially made a loss. Further, unpaid loans to various levels of government by SOEs accounted for around 10 per cent of Chinese GDP (Breslin 2004). At the outset of reform, China desired change in order to increase productivity and improve living standards, but at no time did the leadership think of introducing a fully-fledged market system (Perkins 1994) and for the first 15 years the official ideology was one of 'combining plan and market together'. In 1993, the Communist Party's Economics and Finance Leading Group, headed by Party Secretary General Jiang Zemin, worked together with economists to prepare a grand strategy of transition to a market system (Qian and Wu 2000) (Figure 4.2). Several research teams were formed to study various aspects of transition, ranging from taxation, the fiscal system, the financial system and enterprises, to foreign trade. The final output was the 'Decision on Issues Concerning the Establishment of a Socialist Market Economic Structure' adopted by the Third Plenum of the Fourteenth Party Congress in November 1993.[6] This sought to replace China's centrally planned system with a

*Figure 4.2* 'Advance into the 21st century – Celebrate the 50th anniversary of the founding of the People's Republic of China'. 1999. Jiang Zemin succeeds Deng Xiaoping as Party leader. Behind him the Shanghai skyline – including the Pearl Oriental TV Tower – and a Chinese rocket are shown, symbolizing China's economic and technological development. Stefan R. Landsberger collection, International Institute of Social History (Amsterdam)

modern market system, eventually to incorporate international institutions recognized as 'best practice'. It called for the building of market-supporting institutions, such as formal fiscal federalism, a centralized monetary system, and a social safety net. It also decided to transform SOEs into 'modern enterprises' with 'clarified property rights, clearly defined responsibility and authority, separation of enterprises from the government, and scientific internal management' (Qian and Wu 2000). Also, for the first time, it left the door open regarding the privatization of SOEs, permitting the management of some small SOEs to be contracted out or leased while others could be shifted to the partnership system in the form of stock sharing, or sold to collectives and individuals. SOEs that had evolved from former ministries such as PetroChina (Ministry of Petroleum), Sinopec (Ministry of Petroleum and Ministry of Chemical Industry) or China Telecom (Ministry of Post and Telecommunications) were to become listed companies in Chinese and overseas stock markets (Zhang 2004: 1).

As Arrighi (2007) rightly explains, centralized politico-economic control is an enduring legacy from the Mao-era planned-economy model and one important legacy of this is the central government's control of productive enterprises within China. The central government continues to support SOEs with a view to enhancing their economic competitiveness (Nolan 2002; Chen 2005; Pei 2006), ostensibly so that they could become 'national champions' analogous to those in other East Asian economies. China did not privatize any of its SOEs prior to 1992 but by then the ratio of total profits and taxes to capital in SOEs had declined from 24.2 per cent in 1978 to below 10 per cent in 1993 (Qian and Wu 2000). Losses from SOEs had increased dramatically and non-performing loans had begun to accumulate in state banks, accounting for around 20 per cent of total outstanding loans. Moreover, the rise of the non-state sector increased the competitive pressure, which made holding on to the SOEs costlier than before. Although SOEs remain the main revenue source for the government they also represent a big financial burden for it. For instance, SOEs' share of bank lending stood at nearly 60 per cent by the end of 1998 (Hope et al. 2003). In the planned economy, SOEs were an integral part of the state budgeting system, with all their financing needs being covered by the state, and profits and losses directly included in the state budget. In the late 1970s, more than half the budget revenues were drawn from SOEs (World Bank 2005). Until recently the Chinese government did not collect dividends from state-owned companies (Mattlin 2009) and in 1994 Chinese SOEs were exempted from having to pay dividends to the state. However, stock market-listed SOEs still had to pay dividends to their non-listed wholly state-owned parent companies that often, in effect, are holding companies. They in turn have, as a rule, retained all profits rather than passing them on to the government (Allen et al. 2005). At the time then, SOEs were in dire straits, with lots of loss-making firms and few profitable ones. Consequently, collecting dividends for state coffers was not seen as a priority. Keeping the SOEs afloat was regarded as a more pressing concern. In 1998 the now dissolved State Economic and Trade Committee released a policy document entitled *Index of Over-Invested Products for Moving Abroad* (Loong Yu 2009). By then this objective of trying to export China's excessive capacity to solve growing domestic problems had become particularly urgent due to rising numbers of bad loans. While there are still many loss-making SOEs, some parts of the state-owned economy are now highly profitable.

Thus the 'going global' strategy is closely related to reform of China's SOEs. The guiding principle of the SOE reform strategy became the expression *zhua da, fang xiao*, or 'grasp the big and let the small go', a reference to a policy enshrined in the ninth five -year plan (1996–2000) concentrating the government's resources on the larger SOEs, while relaxing state control over smaller SOEs. Parallel to what Japan and Korea realized in the recent past, Beijing has pursued an active policy to create an elite corps of 'national champions'[7] that would lead the 'going out' process: large, vertically integrated business groups that encompass entire industries from upstream to down. In 2002 the government began selecting some 50 globally competitive 'national champions' from the most promising or strategic SOEs in China. These large corporations enjoy a range of benefits from the government, including information-sharing networks, domestic tax breaks, cheap land, diplomatic support and low-interest funding from state-owned banks. For example, Chinese construction firms operating in Africa receive export credit for feasi-bility studies, government guarantees for bank loans, export credits for financing the operational cost of projects, and lines of credit for capital goods and machinery. The policy is designed to develop these corpora-tions' technological skills, exploit China's comparative advantages, gain access to key inputs, open new markets abroad, create global Chinese brands and help China to avoid becoming overly dependent on export-led development (Accenture 2005). To meet the logistical demands of the 'going out' strategy, the government has also founded several ship-ping companies whom in turn have since expanded to 'global cham-pions'. As of October 2011 the China Ocean Shipping Group (COSCO) and the China Shipping Group are now respectively the fourth and eighth largest shipping companies in the world (Alphaliner 2010).

In many ways the 'going out' strategy has been a success for China – in 1995 there were only 3 Chinese companies in the Fortune 500 list but by 2011 there were 61. Government controls over enterprises' investment and management decisions have loosened, and government supervi-sion in general has progressively entered a state of disarray following the break up of links between ministries in charge of specific industries and enterprises, and the corporatization and partial public listing of big SOEs. More than 7000 Chinese enterprises had invested in 160 countries and regions around the world, with a total outward foreign investment stock and flow estimated at $50 billion and $5 billion, respectively, by 2005. By 2006, China's 'going out' policy reached 200 countries and regions (IPR 2005), resulting in an estimated 750 Chinese companies operating in 50 countries on the African Continent (WorldMarkets Analysis 2006). Outgoing Chinese FDI grew significantly from US$2.7 billion in 2002 to US$57.9 billion in 2010 (Lim 2010; Huang 2011).

It is worth remembering however that the newly crowned 'national champions' leading the going-out strategy are the same large-scale, inefficient, highly subsidized SOEs that have resisted previous reform efforts in China (Gill and Reilly 2007). Indeed, the World Bank recently reported that one-third of Chinese enterprises had lost money on their foreign investments and that 65 per cent of their joint ventures had failed (Accenture 2005).

Privatization of small-sized SOEs began to emerge on a large scale in 1995 (Cao et al. 1999). It initially began with experiments by local governments in a few provinces, such as Shandong, Guangdong and Sichuan as early as 1992. Yet the government has also enforced clearer demarcations on which industries it considers strategic, and has backed this up with a number of prohibitions on their sale or privatization that will probably also be extended to cover SOE subsidiaries. Since the 1980s the policy of *zhengqi fenkai* formally separates government functions from business operations yet the line between SOEs and private-sector companies has blurred considerably in recent years (Woetzel 2008). Many observers define a Chinese state-owned company as one of the 150 or so corporations that report directly to the central government yet thousands more fall into a grey area, including subsidiaries of these 150 corporations, companies owned by provincial and municipal governments, and companies that have been partially privatized yet retain the state as a majority or influential shareholder. The oil company China National Offshore Oil Corporation (CNOOC) and the Chinese utility State Grid Corporation of China (SGCC), for example, are clearly SOEs under the first classification, while the computer maker Lenovo and the appliance giant Haier are less clear-cut cases, in which the state is the dominant shareholder.

If China had to open up its market to foreign capital, then only after immense downsizing could the big Chinese SOEs be able to compete domestically and then, later, internationally, with foreign capital. About ten million workers from SOEs and urban collectives were laid off in each year between 1996 and 1998 (Mattlin 2009). Between 1998 and 2004, a further 21.6 million workers were laid off from SOEs as they struggled to become leaner organizations, although some 19.4 million subsequently found new employment opportunities (Lu and Feng 2008). Transforming SOEs into joint stock companies provided them with the necessary legal and economic conditions to float first in the domestic market and then in Hong Kong and New York. The first wave of flotations in Hong Kong provided the companies with huge amounts of capital for further expansion both domestically and globally. The creation of SOE giants, and hence the oligopoly of key industries, not only enabled them to enjoy economies of scale, but also allowed them to acquire monopoly rent, which enhanced their ability to invest overseas. The growing oligopoly in key industries meant that medium-size firms rapidly lost their market share and had to look to overseas markets as compensation. For example, in the oil industry, because of the three giants' dominant position (CNPC, Sinopec and CNOOC), medium-size firms like the Sinochem have been forced to invest overseas.

A key aspect of the 'going out' strategy (especially in China's engagement with Africa) is the undertaking of overseas contracts, from infrastructures like roads and dams to telecommunication. Chinese companies such as Zhong Xing Telecommunication Equipment Company Limited (ZTE), Sinohydro and the China Road and Bridge Corporation (CRBC) are thus indirect beneficiaries of Chinese foreign aid programmes to African and other developing countries. As a result, in recent years the value of overseas contracts has increased significantly. By the end of May 2010 the total value of China's overseas contracts had reached US$605.7 billion (*China Daily* 20 July 2010) and this now accounts for a considerable proportion of all Chinese overseas investment (excluding portfolio investment). Accompanying this trend is a growth in the exportation of workers. More than 340,000 Chinese people worked abroad in 2009 according to MOFCOM statistics but this figure would rise considerably if un-documented Chinese workers are included. China currently has around 500 authorized labour agencies for hiring overseas workers but there are also a growing number of illegal labour agencies and sub-contractors (*China Daily*, 28 August 2010). An emergency circular prohibiting illegal labour agencies from exporting Chinese labour abroad was jointly issued by MOFCOM and the MFA in August 2010.

Despite three decades of economic reforms in the PRC, the restructuring of large SOE groups has proceeded at a slow pace. The establishment of the State Assets Supervision and Administration Commission (SASAC) under the State Council in 2003 marked a new phase in efforts to deal with the outstanding challenges and unresolved problems of China's SOEs. The SASAC's remit is to 'advance the establishment of a modern enterprise system in state owned enterprises' and to manage the 'strategic adjustment of the structure and layout of the state economy'. The SASAC can also assign so-called supervisory panels to large enterprises on behalf of the state, it appoints and removes the top level executives of enterprises and 'either grants, rewards or inflicts punishments based on their performances (...) in accordance with the requirements of the socialist market economy system and modern enterprise system' (SASAC 2011). The SASAC is either the sole owner of any given Chinese SOE or maintains a controlling share of stock in any public SOE. The founding of the SASAC launched a process of redefining the relationship between the central government and the so called central enterprises[8] (*zhongyang qiye*), the key SOEs selected by the government to form the basis from which China's future top global companies will be created. In addition to these key SOEs there are hundreds of others that are equity-funded by different government agencies (Chen et al. 2009; Woetzel 2008; Imai 2009). Local SASACs (those at the provincial and city levels) handle SOEs within their respective jurisdictions, with independent powers over SOEs delegated to the local level. Province-level SOEs make up approximately 88 per cent of all Chinese firms investing abroad, making provincial governments a key player in China's corporate engagement strategy overseas (Gill and Reilly 2007). A majority of the equity in the car manufacturer Chery, for example, belongs to the municipal government of Wuhu. Major export-oriented cities, such as Shanghai and Shenzhen, often encourage local SOEs and private companies to expand their operations in Africa. Although the central enterprises under the management of the central-level SASAC comprise only 150 major companies out of a total of nearly 120,000 SOEs, their size and importance to the national economy surpasses that of all the other SOEs combined.

As Beijing rolled out its 'going out' strategy it has also mobilized China's banking sector to implement the policy (Chan-Fishel and Lawson 2007). China's central bank exhorted other Chinese banks to 'play a key role in facilitating international capital flows, mergers and acquisitions in the country's efforts to seek resources' (*Business Daily Update* 2006). Similarly, Beijing's African Policy Paper specifically promised that Chinese banks would play a key role by providing preferential loans and buyer credits to support Chinese companies' investment in Africa (see Chapter 3). China is now the world's largest exporter of financial capital and notionally the world's biggest creditor country (Lim 2010). The availability of highly centralized capital holdings in China (through the People's Bank of China, PBoC and the China State Administration of Foreign Exchange, SAFE[9]) offers the state tremendous flexibility to influence credit-creation and foreign lending policies within the domestic banking sector as well as create barriers-to-entry for foreign financial institutions. Financial institutions such as the PBoC, China Development Bank (CDB) and Sinosure also offer foreign exchange, financing and insurance services to Chinese companies expanding abroad. In December 2004, for example, the CDB issued a low-cost US$10 billion loan to Huawei, a major Chinese communications technology company, to promote its international operations. Soon afterwards, Huawei won contracts worth US$400 million to provide cellular phone services in Kenya, Nigeria and Zimbabwe (*Shenzhen Daily* 5 January 2005). Huawei was formed by a former People's Liberation Army (PLA) officer and active CCP member and its ease of access to finance from China's policy banks has enabled it to undercut other global competitors (Gonzalez-Vicente 2011).

Both China's official policy banks, as well as its state-controlled commercial banks (such as the PBoC), are active on the continent; two financiers which play a particularly important role include the CDB and the China Export-Import Bank (ExIm). China Exim Bank and CDB are two of three banks established by the Chinese government to further national economic policies (the third being the Agricultural Development Bank of China). Whereas ExIm focuses on infrastructure development in Africa, CDB is more focused on investment, yet both institutions actively bankroll individual firms' 'going out' expansion activities, coordinating with the MOFCOM to authorize Chinese firms to bid for China's aid projects (in the case of ExIm) and playing a key role in China's Africa policy by making foreign capital available to Chinese corporations for investment abroad, often with political intervention or encouragement from top leaders. Given that Chinese diplomatic visits to Africa frequently encompass large business delegations and result in prominent economic agreements, diplomats from the MFA responsible for Africa often work closely with the banking and business communities and with MOFCOM. The CDB is however less focused on international affairs than China's Exim Bank. Although its US$560 billion asset base is larger, only around 5 per cent of its loans are extended to parties overseas. Only recently has CDB played a significant role in Africa, largely due to its establishment of the China-Africa Development Fund (CADFund) (see Chapter 3).

The ExIm bank is a government export credit agency set up in 1994 which finances the overseas operations of Chinese businesses, promoting Chinese exports by offering loans to foreign buyers who want to purchase Chinese-made goods. ExIm Bank's main focus is on international loans and export credit and as much as 80 per cent of its funding activity in Africa is dedicated towards infrastructure projects. It also finances Chinese companies' 'going out' pursuits, offering interest rates that can be 3 per cent lower than commercial rates (Gill and Reilly 2007). ExIm differs from most countries' export credit agencies because it serves as Beijing's sole agent bank for extending concessional (low interest or subsidized) loans to governments abroad. Since ExIm Bank's founding, its impact overseas has grown substantially. Its asset base of US$292 million in 1994 expanded dramatically to US$116 billion by the end of 2009, with African assets accounting for as much as one-third of the total. Although Angola, Ethiopia, Nigeria and Sudan have been the traditional recipients, the range of projects announced in 2010 suggests a more diverse group including Zimbabwe, Mozambique, Kenya and Ghana. In September 2010 Ghana signed agreements for loans totalling US$13 billion with two of China's policy banks. This involved a US$9.87 billion loan from ExIm for road, rail and dam projects and US$3 billion from the CDB for funding oil and gas infrastructure (*AllBusiness* 23 September 2010). Also allied to the broader 'going out' policy is the establishment of the China Investment Corporation (CIC) in September 2007. The CIC essentially functions as a global sovereign wealth fund to strategically utilize US$200 billion of China's foreign reserves[10] and clearly indicates that China intends to diversify its capital accumulation strategies. CIC can not only make purchases directly, but also indirectly supports the overseas strategies of other Chinese firms after the Central Huijin Investment Corporation (which holds majority stakes in several big state-owned banks) became a CIC subsidiary. The CIC's assets had grown to some US$410 billion by the end of 2010 (CIC 2011).

In recent years, various government agencies such as the National Development and Reform Commission (NRDC), the Ministry of Finance, the MOFCOM and the SAFE have also developed policies encouraging Chinese companies to expand overseas. In 2003 the Ministry of Foreign Trade and Economic Cooperation (MOFTEC) was merged with the State Economic and Trade Commission (SETC) to create a new Ministry of Commerce as the relationship between the international and the domestic was officially accepted. In combination, the reforms established a governmental structure designed to regulate the economy rather than control it (Breslin 2004). Within MOFCOM responsibilities are divided across four departments, each with its own set of interests. The Department of West Asia and African Affairs provides policy advice on Africa to top policymakers and encourages investment as well as trade with Africa by distributing information on the local economic, political, legal and social environments in Africa to Chinese firms. The Department of Foreign Economic Cooperation (DFEC) of MOFCOM is responsible for regulating all Chinese companies involved overseas. All Chinese corporations with overseas investments greater than US$10,000 are required to register with MOFCOM before investing abroad. The

DFEC has the authority to fine or revoke the permission to operate overseas for corporations that fail to adhere to MOFCOM regulations and Chinese laws. The DFEC also regulates Chinese overseas labour corporations, in effect making MOFCOM responsible for the treatment of China's overseas workers by Chinese corporations (Gill and Reilly 2007). MOFCOM's Department of Aid to Foreign Countries plays the central role in administering China's aid projects, approving all corporations permitted to tender bids on aid projects, managing the bidding process, and overseeing the project itself. MOFCOM also has operational authority over the office of the Economic and Commercial Counsellor (ECC) and staffs these offices. MOFCOM treats the ECC office as the local MOFCOM representatives in Africa, even though the ECC offices are located inside local Chinese embassies or consulates and are subject to the Embassy's administrative authority. In addition, MOFCOM offices at the provincial and city levels have regulatory authority over all companies registered at that level. China thus relies heavily on coordination among a complex array of corporations and government bureaucracies to achieve its policy objectives in Africa (see Figure 4.3). MOFCOM, for example, does not have direct authority over any of the SOEs operating in Africa and has conflicting internal interests, given its dual responsibilities to support Chinese corporations going overseas and to regulate these companies. The combination of multiple oversight bureaucracies, competing companies and their conflicting interests suggests that Chinese firms are likely to act in ways that are not always in complete synchrony with the diplomatic objectives of the aid programme (Gill and Reilly 2007).

## The transnational spaces of China's economic development

The rise of the Chinese economy, in the view of Dirlik (1997: 304), coincides with 'an intensified [Chinese] interest in what has been called "Global Capitalism" or "flexible production"'. From 1985 to 2010, FDI inflows rose from US$2 billion to US$105.7 billion (MOFCOM 2010). In the period 1985 to 2005, China took in more than US$600 billion in FDI, 12 times the total stock of FDI Japan received between 1945 and 2000 (Pan 2009). Since 1993, China has consistently been the largest recipient of FDI among developing countries (Minqi Li 2005). In parallel to the massive inflows of FDI is a growing trend for transnational corporations (TNCs) to outsource and subcontract production and even services to China. Unable to compete with the cost of labour in China,

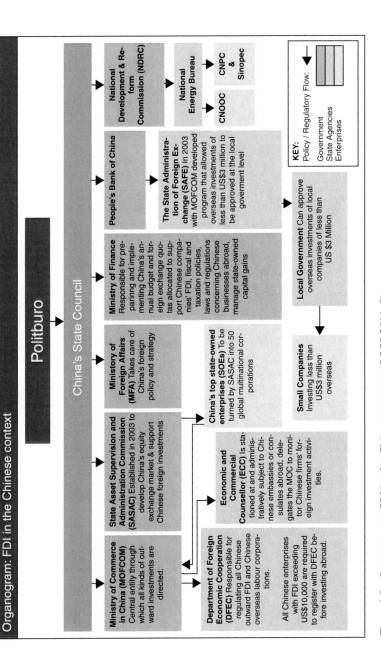

*Figure 4.3* Organogram: FDI in the Chinese context (CCCS 2011: 3)

manufacturers of apparel, footwear, electric appliances and plastics products have been rushing in droves to shut US factories and relocate them elsewhere, including China. Fernández-Gilberto and Hogenboom (2007) note that in the industrialized countries China is now considered as the decisive factor in the process of the deterritorialization of global production, which in the United States caused a loss of 15 million jobs in the industrial sector between 1995 and 2002 (Si Zoubir 2004). To date, corporations from 190 countries and regions, which include 450 of the Fortune global top 500 multinational corporations, have invested in China and some 60,000 foreign-owned factories were opened between 2003 and 2005 alone (Pan 2009). Chinese manufacturers initially serve as component suppliers to foreign buyers and Original Equipment Manufacturers (OEMs) and it has been estimated that between 60 per cent and 80 per cent of the value of all Chinese exports are processed (imported) components (Ravenhill 2006: 670). As a result a transnational production chain takes shape, linking together the world's most advanced economies such as the United States and Japan, semi-periphery economies such as Taiwan and developing states like China.

As Pan (2009) has argued, the penetration and dominance of non-Chinese elements in the Chinese economy, taking the form of foreign control over major processes and components of production in China, such as exports, technology, marketing, and profit, calls into question the conventional understanding of 'Chinese businesses'. There is thus an implicit and rarely questioned assumption that takes for granted the Chineseness of Chinese businesses (Pan 2009) which are believed to both operate within, and are inexorably linked to, a coherent, unproblematic actor called 'China'. Some 70 per cent of China's overseas investment consists of joint ventures or foreign–China collaboration projects. In relation to exports, what are commonly labelled as 'Chinese' businesses can in many cases be more suitably described as Chinese subsidiaries of global multinationals and Chinese joint ventures with businesses from industrialized countries. Those Chinese subsidiaries, or foreign-funded enterprises (FFEs), accounted for about two-thirds of the total growth in Chinese exports between 1994 and mid-2003. The dominant position of 'non-Chinese' businesses in China's production and exports is echoed and underpinned by a similar pattern in relation to technology, services, branding and marketing (Pan 2009). Since the early 1990s, FDI inflows have further accelerated in light of Beijing's decision to allow a new form of FDI called wholly foreign-owned enterprises (WFOEs). By the early 2000s WFOEs accounted for 65 per cent of new FDI in China (Pan 2009).

Many of the so-called non-Chinese businesses in China, upon a closer examination, are overseas Chinese businesses in 'Greater China' or the Chinese Diaspora: Hong Kong, Macau, Taiwan and overseas Chinese in Southeast Asia and elsewhere (Pan 2009). Variably known as the 'bamboo network' (Weidenbaum and Hughes 1996) and an 'invisible empire' (Seagrave 1996) the Chinese network not only seems to share common Chineseness, but it also indicates the far-flung reach of Chinese businesses in the global economy. China's integration into the global production networks has been at the expense of the national coherence of Chinese businesses. As part of a push to join tracks with international standards (*yu guoji jiegui*), many Chinese companies have not only developed a dependence on transnational capital and technology but some have also shied away from horizontal collaboration with their domestic counterparts, especially if such collaboration crosses regional or bureaucratic boundaries (Pan 2009). As a result a variety of terms have been used to capture the uniqueness of the Chinese economy (e.g. 'cellular', 'federalism'); even if those Chinese businesses share the same national space and are all run by Chinese 'they may still be a long way from, if ever, forming a unitary, coherent Chinese economic actor' (Pan 2009: 22). That said, China's political and business leaders clearly do want to construct a coherent national economy. The locations of the four original special economic zones, for example, have been chosen by the Chinese government 'with a view to maximizing their attraction to investment from ethnic Chinese living outside China' (Dicken 2003: 189). Further, as the main driving force behind Chinese companies' 'going out' strategy, Beijing has sought to assemble a team of national economic 'champions' in global economic competition. Thus, as Kerr (2007: 78) has noted, 'China is "nationalising" globalization, pursuing a policy of selective and strategic integration that bends globalization to China's long-term nation-building goals'.

Freedom of access to strategic markets is critical to enhancing the success of outbound FDI and so much of China's recent diplomatic engagement with the states in which the markets are located has been focused on securing this access (see Chapter 8). Further, many of China's initial overseas 'aid' projects are geared to providing a point of entry for Chinese companies into overseas markets from which they can then expand and develop further market share (e.g. in the construction business). It is worth noting however that the emergence of some Chinese business giants is not because of state support, but rather in spite of state neglect and bias against them. For example, current privately owned vanguards, including Huawei Technologies and TCL (a telecoms and an electronics manufacturer respectively), were not designated as 'national champions' in the first instance. Also, the much-taunted Haier success story had its humble beginnings as a loss-making enterprise, which had to borrow money from local villagers as it was unable to secure credit from state banks (Lunding 2006: 7). Further, the latest 'going out' strategy of many Chinese companies, often perceived as orchestrated by the state, reveals that they were not so much supported by an ambitious, monolithic state as they were 'pushed' out by intense competition in domestic markets from FFEs and by the need to deal with over-production and over-investment domestically. The foreign aid and loans provided by the Chinese state does however allow Chinese SOEs to transcend geopolitical boundaries and penetrate new markets, perfectly in line with capitalist logics (Lim 2010). Such processes of territorialization, as Brenner (1999: 53) explains:

> remain endemic to capitalism, but today they are jumping at once above, below and around the national scale upon which they converged throughout much of the last century. Consequently, state territoriality operates less as an isomorphic, self enclosed block of absolute space than as a polymorphic institutional mosaic composed of multiple, partially overlapping levels that are neither congruent, contiguous, nor coextensive with one another.

What we need to attend to then is the consequent entwinement of Chinese economic development with the fate of many other economies and corporations (Lim 2010). Rather than simply being the commercial and economic 'arm' of China, many Chinese businesses are a prime example of transnational or global interconnectedness at work and their strength, identity and characteristics need to be understood in relation to broader, transnational dynamics in the global economy today (Pan 2009). China's economic development is thus co-produced by capital accumulation strategies both on the 'inside' (the domestic restructuring of SOEs and macroeconomic strategies) as well as the 'outside' (the global search for new markets and corresponding foreign demand for financial capital) (Lim 2010). The social origins and production of various production materials, labour, capital, information, technology, design, management, marketing and consumption are no longer rigidly tied to fixed, singular localities or nationalities, thus making it increasingly difficult and problematic, if not impossible, to identify businesses and their practices in exclusively national terms.

Although there are some forms of Chinese business networks across 'Greater China' their existence cannot be viewed in isolation from the larger global economic networks (Pan 2009). Hong Kong, for example, has been a major source of 'foreign' direct investment in China yet this does not mean that the origins of the investment are necessarily based in Hong Kong or even come from China itself. To broaden the Yuan's global role, China is evidently capitalizing on Hong Kong as a 'space of exception'. Designated a Special Administrative Region (SAR) of China, the Hong Kong economy operates on a free-market model, with a separate currency, jurisdiction and administrative government. Hong Kong is also a favourite destination for Chinese 'round-trip'[11] investments. Hong Kong is hence effectively considered a quasi-autonomous offshore financial centre, protected by laws analogous to major global financial centres, and yet well within Beijing's governance influence. Above all, Hong Kong offers 'an ideal conduit – or more precisely, a significant geographical advantage – for China to leverage on neo-liberal practices without implementing them throughout the whole country' (Lim 2010: 685–6).

Further, some Chinese businesses based in Hong Kong have been a key feature of China's push into African markets. Angola has received oil-backed loans amounting to as much as US$10 billion from the private equity firm based in Hong Kong, the China International Fund (CIF). As Levkowitz et al. (2009) have shown many of the Chinese companies currently operating in Angola have the same Hong Kong address (88 Queensway, Hong Kong) while a handful of individuals control over 30 companies at this address. The CIF also has created numerous other companies registered in Hong Kong (most of which are located at the 88 Queensway address) to spread its investments abroad. By posing as a private firm, the Group creates numerous companies within a complicated organizational structure to invest globally, thereby enabling the Group to acquire assets 'unnoticed'. In presenting itself as a private entity based in Hong Kong, it is unclear whether its companies would receive the same scrutiny from regulatory institutions and the foreign media that a Chinese state-owned company would receive. Key personnel involved in this firm have ties to Chinese SOEs and state agencies including the China International Trust and Investment Cooperation (CITIC) (Figure 4.4), the China National Petrochemical Corporation (Sinopec) and possibly China's intelligence apparatus. Hong Kong is also the home of a joint venture set up in 2004 between the Angola national oil company Sonangol and Hong Kong-based private business interests, known as China Sonangol International Holding (CSIH).[12] Similarly, the parent

*Figure 4.4*   Pedro Canga, Angolan Minister of Agriculture, Rural Development and Fishing (third from left) visits a corn field on a farm in Luanda (Angola) being developed by CITIC. Wang Bingfei, Newscom

company of the China International Fund (CIF), Dayuan International Development, which is also based in Hong Kong, controls a range of oil trading and infrastructure construction operations in Angola, worth as much as US$30 billion. The cosy relationship Dayuan (previously known as Beiya) has developed with the Angolan government and military circles in particular helped them to obtain twelve big projects including an airport, railways, roads and housing projects. The structure of such companies is complex and the nature of their connections to African economies are opaque while the lack of transparency creates further difficulty in distinguishing between Chinese state and non-state actors.

## Neo-liberalism and China: a 'loose hug' or an 'intimate embrace'?

An interesting point of debate in some of the literature concerning China's recent economic transformations concerns the extent to which neo-liberalism can be said to prevail in China. 'Neoliberalism' is a term that is difficult to theorize with since it has been referred to variously as an ideology, an hegemony, a doctrine, a rhetoric, a discourse, a discursive formation, a logic of governance and a govern-mentality (Nonini 2008). In recent years there have been claims made about the 'neoliberal restructuring' of China (Hairong, 2003: 511), about 'a dominant rhetoric of neoliberal developmentalism' (Anagnost 2004: 197), about a prevailing 'neoliberal biopolitics' in China (Greenhalgh and Winkler 2005: 9) and about neo-liberalism in China as 'a national project about global reordering ... a national imaginary about a post-Cold War world' (Rofel 2007). Many commentators have also noted the growing evidence of neo-liberalism in China's cities and the role it is now playing in reshaping China's urban landscapes. He and Wu (2009) argue, for example, that neo-liberal shifts have fundamentally restructured the regulatory–institutional architecture and urban spatial structure in China. They also argue that a new mode of urbanization, namely neo-liberal urbanization, is emerging (He and Wu 2009). Similarly Thornton (2010) notes how, in consolidating its claim to Rising Power status, the post-Mao generation of the CCP and state leaders have committed to the distinctly entrepreneurial rebuilding of the nation's cities to attract private investment and stimulate consumption-based development. The emergence and success of large-scale shopping malls in Beijing like *The Place* (Figure 4.5) demonstrate how the regime's increasingly enthusiastic embrace of market reform has substantially reshaped the political geography of the capital, including that of its symbolic centre, Tiananmen Square (Thornton 2010). More broadly the change in social welfare provision in China has been phenomenal and the state has indeed retreated from welfare provision. Public housing has dwindled while the rate of home ownership increased to 80 per cent of urban residents, according to the 2000 Population Census (although a large proportion is ex-public housing). China is now a 'nation of homeowners'.

In his book *A Brief History of Neoliberalism* David Harvey (2005) includes China as a country embarking on the course of neo-liberalism and comes to justify why China is neo-liberal by saying that 'in so far as neoliberalism requires a large, easily exploited, and relatively powerless labour force, then China certainly qualifies as a neoliberal economy, albeit "with Chinese characteristics"' (Harvey 2005: 144). Harvey does however emphasize that China is a 'strange case' as the outcome has been a particular kind of neo-liberalism interdigitated with authoritarian centralized control (2005: 34–41). For Harvey then the presence of the 'authoritarian centralized control' in combination with 'neo-liberal' policies seems to mean that China has deviated from the neo-liberalism model. Ong (2007: 4) picks up on the tension between Chinese reality and neo-liberal ideology in Harvey's work, arguing that he 'has trouble fitting China into his "neoliberal template"'. Instead Ong (2007: 4) proposes to understand neo-liberalism as a technology of

*Figure 4.5* The Place, Beijing, China. Photograph by dorz11, Flickr, Creative Commons

governing 'free subjects'. Implicitly, authoritarian control may well be part of such governance technology.

Wu (2008: 1093) argues that the term neo-liberalization 'does capture some basic features of market re-orientation in China' but instead tries to show that 'authoritarian control' is not a legacy of previous institutional forms, but rather a reaction to marketization. For Wu the presence of control does not make the Chinese case 'strange' and it may show that under some specific conditions neo-liberalization may have to consolidate rather than reduce control. Therefore the process of marketization has not always led to the waning of state power while continued state intervention has been justified by the need to enhance competitiveness as a 'latecomer' to industrialization. The new export-oriented development strategy relies very much on the state's ability to maintain social order. Highly reliant on foreign investment and trade, competitiveness is built upon cheap labour and land while the rural–urban divide and the state ownership of land are becoming key methods for forging structural competitiveness (Wu 2008). However, the exploitation of cheap production factors relies on sustaining such a social order, which requires the strong intervention of the state. The consequence is not the diminishing and minimum state as advocated by orthodox neo-liberalism, but rather a transformation from the 'redistributive state' to the 'entrepreneurial state(s)'. In other words such a growth model strengthens 'state capacities'. Zhang and Ong (2008: 4) characterize this as 'sociliasm from afar' by which certain strains of neo-liberal ideology proliferate in symbiosis with socialist authoritarian rule. Similarly Pei (2006) refers to the 'neo-Leninism' that blends one-party rule and state control of key sectors of the economy in China with partial market reforms and an end to self-imposed isolation from the world economy. Through becoming a market actor, the state(s) can tap into a great pool of resources. Containing and conducting the market society towards a 'harmonious society' is therefore not only ideologically but also practically imperative. Thus the state's presence in the economic sphere and its regulation may strengthen the market logic rather than reducing it (Wu 2008).

While China's search for alternative investments worldwide has undoubtedly contributed to the sustainability of global capitalism and has stabilized an otherwise volatile capitalist system it is important to recognize that neo-liberalism in China is not a single and coherent formation. Much of the recent literature on neo-liberalism and neo-liberalization recognizes the diversity, embeddedness, scalar unfolding and path dependency of neo-liberalism. Thus actually existing neo-liberalism in China is multiple and contradictory rather than singular and consistent. Interestingly the unashamedly pro-neo-liberal Heritage Foundation ranked China as 135th out of 179 countries in a league table[13] of economic freedom in 2011, several years *after* the liberalization policies that had been put in place following admission to the WTO (Heritage Foundation

2011). Lim (2010) thus cautions against essentializing the Chinese political economy and construing its growth through a zero-sum lens and argues that it is more productive to place China's economic policies in a broader context, or more specifically within what Peck and Theodore (2007) call the variegated global system of capitalism, to gain a deeper grasp of the specific processes shaping China's growing geo-economic influence. For Peck and Theodore (2007: 761), understanding capitalism as a variegated whole, with different constituents (of which China is one) and outcomes, allows analysts to avoid the pitfalls of the varieties-of-capitalism approach because 'reading [economic] differentiation primarily through the lens of (national) institutional coordination runs the risk of exaggerating and reifying some forms of geographical difference, while obfuscating threads of commonality and interdependence'.

As Gibson-Graham (1996: 15–16) argue, 'a capitalist site (a firm, industry or economy) or a capitalist practice (exploitation of wage labour, distribution of surplus value) cannot appear as the concrete embodiment of an abstract capitalist essence. It has no invariant "inside" but is constituted by its continually changing and contradictory "outsides"'. As a result it is important to recognize that 'Chinese policymakers are proactively and simultaneously negotiating capitalist logics and macroeconomic constraints even as they mould their own version of domestic politico-economic governance' (Lim 2010: 678). Thus it is necessary to explore the various ways in which the Chinese state has reacted reflexively to its self-imposed macroeconomic constraints and to changes in other economies by seizing emergent opportunities to create new markets in new geographical regions. For Lim (2010) this is effected through a dualistic politico-economic strategy which involves firstly the regulation of the domestic financial system and the restructuring of SOEs and secondly the selective adoption of neo-liberal principles as a sovereign geopolitical entity and through capitalist vehicles (e.g. SOEs and sovereign wealth funds) on the global stage. Put differently, China's economic expansion 'is co-produced by the Chinese state's strong interventionist strategies domestically as well as the structural changes in the global capitalist system' (Lim 2010: 678). Thus for Lim (2010: 682) China is arguably adopting a 'neo-mercantilist politico-economic approach that is leavened by selected neo-liberal principles already in practice globally'. These 'neo-mercantilist' policies at home (export-orientation, import-substitution, capital controls and control of currency exchange value) have enabled China to become a colossal capital-exporting entity while notions of 'freedom of capital flows' and unfettered markets (fundamental neo-liberal tenets) are now employed to 'contour and broaden the geographical reach of Chinese SOEs' investments abroad as well as gradually reduce dollar-usage in international trade' (Lim 2010: 682).

In a similar vein Nonini (2008) argues that although it may make sense to speak of the prevalence of 'neo-liberal' ideology among certain privileged urban residents of China, and specific leaders and factions of reformers within the CCP, recent claims about neo-liberal processes of restructuring, neo-liberal capitalism and the dominance of neo-liberalism in China cannot be justified, and in fact are 'overstatements unsupported by evidence' (Nonini 2008: 146). In support of this contention Nonini points to the tensions arising between different sections of Chinese society along with evidence of increasing social polarization and argues that the existence of widespread social protests against state cadres, and the market socialist reforms with which they are identified in China, strongly suggests the absence of neo-liberal hegemony. Observers agree that social inequality within China has increased greatly since the early 1990s (Guan 2001: 246–9) with many pointing to the de-nationalization of large numbers of SOEs which has meant that millions of urban workers were released and cast into conditions of widespread pauperization and the misery of finding casual work in the informal sector. Indeed there is growing evidence that rural farmers, urban workers and the floating population have all undergone dispossession in recent years. The rapid redevelopment of some of China's cities, for example, has involved many social tensions and conflicts while marginalization and dispossession have been common outcomes for many of China's poorer citizens, especially as a consequence of some of the demolitions and forced relocations involved in neo-liberalized urban development policy (Wu 2004; Meyer 2008; He and Wu 2009) (Figure 4.6). Further, Nonini (2008) reminds us that these social protests are not entirely external to the Party, but also characterize it internally as well – in a dialectic of conflict between factions about the course of China's future society and who should benefit from, and pay for, its emergence. There is also evidence that China, through the Party's direction, has departed radically from IMF/World Bank and WTO neo-liberal dictates over capital controls (Liew 2005: 332). Instead, state policies and cadres' practices have channelled foreign corporate investments through the Party to selected industries, regions and 'special economic zones' in a classic instance of what Aihwa Ong (1999) refers to as 'graduated sovereignty'. Nor does China's government show much commitment to free trade in commodities, placing restrictions on foreign investors who might compete with Chinese domestic firms through controlling where foreign firms can invest while it also tolerates extensive software and luxury-goods piracy.

*Figure 4.6*   A housing area is destroyed as new apartments rise up in the distance in the Yang Pu district of Shanghai. Photograph by D J Clark

Therefore, it may be the case that the central government's engagement with neo-liberalism is only a 'loose hug rather than an intimate embrace' (Liew 2005: 331). As Smart observes: 'the adoption of market-based reforms continues to generate serious debate within China... there has been consistent concern with the social and cultural implications of the market-based reforms and the opening to the capitalist world economy' (Smart 1997: 179–80). This is not to say that there are no ideological 'neoliberals' in China – especially among CCP factions, entrepreneurs (e.g. guanshang/guanying) and among intellectuals – there clearly are (see e.g. Wang 2003). Yet alongside such groups there is also China's 'New Left' – a heterogeneous group of disgruntled writers and academics who advocate a 'Chinese alternative' to the neo-liberal market economy, one that will guarantee the welfare of all those left behind by the recent reforms. Edited by Wang Hui, a professor of literature, the journal *Du Shu* is a venue that allows for criticism of the calibre of governance and the impact of policies that favour an export-oriented economy at the expense of the well-being of several sectors of the population, especially subaltern groups in the countryside. Many such critical intellectuals are fundamentally opposed to the decision to allow private entrepreneurs to join the Communist Party, a decision that has raised concern and bitter protests from many party members (Dickson 2002, 2003). Despite the protests, the party constitution was amended at the 16th Party Congress in November 2002 to include Jiang Zemin's theory of the 'Three Represents' (Marxism–Leninism–Mao Zedong Thought) as the Party's guiding principle.[14] Yet many on the New Left are concerned by the proposition that the communism that aims to build a socialist market economy and which represents all of China's traditions – the three represents – is linked by a golden thread to China's great Confucian past. Wang Hui and others on the New Left have thus spoken of the way in which local officials have used their arbitrary power to become successful entrepreneurs *at the expense of the rural populations they were meant to serve* or have joined up with real estate speculators to seize collectively owned land from peasants.

Moreover a discourse resistant to market-led and state-induced globalization is emerging in the expanding space carved out by China's nongovernmental organizations (NGOs) (Mittelman 2006: 9). Thus when the Party speaks about environmental and social 'harmonies' in China's development or articulates the 'harmonious society' ideology, this should be regarded as devices that are being used to alleviate the inherent tensions and controversies of neo-liberalism (He and Wu 2009). Evolving from a non-market system, the neo-liberalizing process in China inevitably involves lots of contradictions and inconsistencies within which a strong state presence is expected. As He and Wu (2009: 301) have argued 'since the state possesses very powerful tools to effectively regulate market operations by controlling the most important resources, this particular setting actually creates a more effective management system to cope with the contradictions and imbalances produced by neo-liberalism itself'. Thus rather than as a deliberate design, neo-liberalization in China is perhaps better understood as a response to multiple difficulties/crises and the desire for rapid development. As a result the neo-liberalization process in China is full of controversies and inconsistencies, which involve conflicts between neo-liberal practices and social resistance, as well as tensions between central and local states (He and Wu 2009).

## Conclusions: China as Africa's 'economic role model'

China's recent experience of rapid economic transformation today plays an important role in shaping the nature of contemporary China–Africa engagement. The focus on developing export-oriented industries and facilitating the flow of FDI is particularly important in this regard as is China's experience of concentrating this in SEZs, which are now providing a template for Chinese SEZs in several African countries (Zambia, Ethiopia, Mauritius, Nigeria and Egypt). China regularly claims to be sharing this recent experience with its African partners in the name of South-South cooperation and China is regularly held up as a 'model' of economic development and (as a consequence) poverty alleviation that African countries can learn from. In recent years many African leaders have heralded the relevance of a Chinese 'model' of development even though Deng Xiaoping once told an African head of state in 1985 that there was no Chinese model to emulate and noted that all nations must adopt growth policies suitable to their own particular circumstances (Alden 2007: 131). Others see this 'model' as an alternative 'to the American model' (Zhang 2006) or as 'defying the conditionalities of the Bretton Woods institutions' (Manji and Marks 2007: 136) even though Chinese lending does come with its own conditions. Joseph Stiglitz (2002) even touts China as a 'model' for how developing nations should rise and escape the prescriptions of Anglo-American neo-liberalism! Further many commentators have been quick to note the 'lessons' that Africa can learn from this 'model' (Dollar 2008) and even to suggest that China can be Africa's 'economic role model' (Juma 2007). Yet Deng was right, there is no single, coherent 'Chinese model' (Friedman 2009). Many observers seem to conflate the various possible and often overlapping meanings of this term in problematic and contradictory ways. It is thus often used simultaneously to refer to a Chinese model of development in China (which serves as an example for others to follow), a Chinese development model enacted in Africa to steer the continent's development (in an analogous sense to the Washington Consensus) and as a global model of interaction around development cooperation.

Neither is there a unitary, singular and coherent Chinese economic actor. Implying that there is such coherence considerably downplays the global interconnectedness and transnational dynamics that shape China's economic development strategies both domestically and overseas. There is a danger here of overlooking the co-production of china's economic development (in which Africa is playing an increasingly important role) and missing the many ways in which China's economy is intertwined with the fate of many other economies and corporations. Thus the singularity and coherence of a Chinese 'model' has often been considerably overstated, despite the internal variation within China (between say rural and urban areas and even between SEZs) and the growing difficulties the Chinese state is facing in managing the complex range of corporate agents now active overseas. We might also question the supposed 'Chinese' nature of this 'model' given the extent to which China has looked to and drawn from East Asian examples of state practice in pursuing 'development' (Power and Mohan 2010), following the tracks of Japanese and Korean mercantilism, the so-called developmental state model. Further we might also question some of the taken for granted assumptions about the 'Chineseness' of Chinese businesses. Constructing this myth of a singular coherent economic actor and focusing only on those enterprises that are state owned also downplays the considerable importance of China's SMEs which represent a significant proportion of Chinese firms investing in Africa (Gu 2009). The complexity involved in managing such a large and diverse group of enterprises makes it very difficult for the Chinese state to regulate their activities in Africa, particularly when we consider that few of these Chinese private sector firms share a sense of being part of an overall project, strategy or expectation and that most have followed commercial rather than policy objectives in deciding to establish themselves in Africa (Gu 2009). As Gonzalez-Vicente (2011: 2) argues 'the political economy of China's development is not determined by centralized geographing alone'.

China's primary oversight agencies do not enjoy direct lines of authority over Chinese corporations overseas (Gill and Reilly 2007) while the recent fragmentation of authoritarian power (Breslin 2004) also further complicates the management of 'national' economic space. As a capitalist site the Chinese economy should not be read as a self-enclosed, 'concrete embodiment of an abstract capitalist essence' (Lim 2010: 678) with an invariant 'inside'. Rather it is China's engagement with its continually changing and contradictory 'outsides' that is important here. What is particularly challenging about this however is that there has been a considerable blurring of the lines that separate inside and outside, domestic and foreign, state and non-state and public and private in contemporary China. As Dickson (2007) has shown, notwithstanding its communist rhetoric, the CCP's strategy has been to incorporate and co-opt entrepreneurs into its party-state system. The overaccumulation of financial capital in China and its accelerated outflows should thus be regarded as part of a wider global capitalist logic to secure profitable 'spatio-temporal fixes' (Lim 2010). The 'going out' strategy reveals that Chinese companies were not so much supported by an ambitious, monolithic state as they were 'pushed' out by intense competition in domestic markets from FFEs, by the need to deal with the crisis of accumulation under state socialism and by the desire to export China's excessive capacity.

The comprehensive transformation of China's economy that resulted from this has rested on a silent pact 'between on the one hand an elite that was in an existential crisis and struggled to survive, and on the other the millions of Chinese citizens who were desperate to escape poverty and arbitrariness' (Holslag 2006: 2). Thus the move towards a socialist market economy has fundamentally been a survival strategy for the Chinese Communist party. Rather than 'converge' towards a singular, coherent neo-liberal model (cf. Harvey 2005), however, the Chinese government seems to have developed what Tickell and Peck (2003: 181) call the 'capacity to morph into a variety of institutional forms, to insinuate itself into, and graft itself onto, a range of institutional settlements, and to absorb parallel and even contending narratives of restructuring and intervention in response both to internal contradictions and external pressures'. As a result the Chinese government has applied an assortment of neo-mercantilist and neo-liberal principles as a state and has actively participated in shaping geo-economic configurations at the global scale through capitalist entities like the WTO. The existence of China's New Left and the rising tensions and protests that are the outcome of China's growing inequalities and social polarization further suggest that it may be premature to proclaim the emergence of a neo-liberal hegemony in China.

The discourses surrounding the objective of a 'harmonious society' suggest that the inequality and polarization resulting from China's recent economic growth are a growing concern for the Chinese state. Rural farmers, urban workers and the floating population have all undergone dispossession yet it is important to remember that these same groups of the Chinese population today comprise a substantial proportion of the labour force utilized by Chinese companies overseas and that many of the labour agencies and sub-contractors that employ them are in fact illegal. In October 2010 when the CCP was meeting in Beijing to draw up the twelfth five-year development plan concerns were articulated that instead of seeking a high rate of economic growth, China should in future look to close the gap between rich and poor and between coastal and inland areas. Indeed a striking feature of China's re-engagement with the global economy is a continued uneven geographical distribution, with the vast majority of investment and trade still concentrated on the coastal regions. Further, having located China as a low-cost assembly site in an international division of labour, it is now proving difficult for the Chinese government to progress to a new stage.

# 5
# Evolving Aid Diplomacy in Africa

## Introduction: aid, Africa and development

So far we have discussed how Africa has gained in importance and the ways in which the Chinese are among a number of rapidly industrial- izing nations that see the continent in strategic economic and political terms (Carmody 2011). With this seems to have come a renewed interest in the role of aid in enabling development marked by a raft of publica- tions dealing with Africa and/or the failure of aid (e.g. Calderisi 2007; Easterly 2007; Riddell 2007; Bolton 2008; Collier 2008; Easterly 2008; Warah 2008; Amin et al. 2009; Moyo 2009; de Haan 2009; Sorensen 2010). Those dealing with aid in general (Easterly 2008; Riddell 2007) focus on Western donors and those of the Organisation for Economic Cooperation and Development (OECD)'s Development Assistance Committee (DAC). The Chinese are not members of DAC and, as we will see, Chinese aid levels are still relatively low, but given the entwining of aid with other financial flows and market dynamics it is having a significant impact on the development fortunes of Africa.

In an important recent intervention entitled *Dead Aid* the Zambian economist Dambisa Moyo argued, among other things, that the emer- gence of China is a 'golden opportunity' for Africa (Moyo 2009: 120) offering the continent a 'win-win' alternative to the scenario of an 'aid-dependent economy' by focusing on trade and investment and by providing the infrastructure that will enable Africa to 'move up the development curve' (Moyo 2009: 122). Moyo's optimistic argument very much echoes the pronouncements of the Chinese Government in its analysis of its relations with Africa (Ministry of Foreign Affairs of the PRC 2006). The pessimists, by contrast, focus on the aid–governance nexus where the Chinese are accused by some of unscrupulous behaviour that undermines African good governance (Naim 2007), and concomitantly has been used to justify the more enlightened goals and modalities of the west.

This chapter builds on the previous two chapters which dealt with China's reforms and evolving international policies by focusing in on Chinese 'aid', its goals and modalities, and the way in which it is negotiated on the ground. But we also look at the relationships between Chinese and DAC aid and the responses of the 'established' group of donors to China's growing role in international aid. The first section will discuss the emerging debates and issues on Chinese aid in Africa. In particular, we will examine the logics, modalities and conditionalities of the Chinese model. The second section will examine Chinese aid in Africa in general and the two case study countries in particular, focusing on its forms and continuities with the past. This sets up our analysis of recent aid and investment in Angola and Ghana before a conclusion which examines the similarities and differences between the two cases and suggests policy responses to such emerging features of Sino-African development relations.

## China's aid 'offensive' and the 'established' donors

Ever since researchers and policy watchers became aware of China's revived interests in Africa, there have been a number of contributions dealing with the levels, destinations and implications of Chinese aid (e.g. Lancaster 2007; Huang 2007; Davies et al. 2008; Kragelund 2008; Staehle 2007; Woods 2008; Brautigam 2009). They raise critical issues around the novelty and significance of Chinese aid, the levels and modes of delivery and the nature of conditionality. We deal with each of these presently, but it needs stating that these studies tend either to be pitched at the aid regime level in terms of geopolitics and donor relationships or they simply map the key flows without analysing the impacts on recipient countries. We use the debates around histories, modalities and conditionalities as a way of generating further research questions that we will interrogate through the case studies of Angola and Ghana.

### Histories and relationships

One of the recurrent themes about China as aid-giver is that it is part of a wider group of 'emerging' donors (Manning 2006; Woods 2008; King 2010). The argument is that 'traditional' donors – primarily those represented by DAC – are being challenged by a group of countries that are rapidly industrializing and seeking a greater voice in international affairs. Some are OECD members who are not in DAC, others are new European Union (EU) members or Middle-Eastern states, and the final group is a more disparate one that includes the 'heavyweights' of China and India. The implications of this are manifold in that these countries not only add new sources of finance for developing countries, but have wider effects by introducing, as Woods (2008) argues, 'competitive pressures' among established donors and bringing about a 'silent revolution' in aid. Woods also argues that while China gets criticized, the promises of the G8 at Gleneagles in 2005 have not been honoured so it is hypocritical to criticize either China which has brought new finance or those impoverished countries which accept China's aid and investment. While we broadly agree with Woods, we also need to monitor whether established donors really do feel pressurized and, if so, is this at the aid regime level or the recipient country level. And, crucially, do these competitive pressures open up policy space for recipient countries to escape the strictures of aid conditionality, or is it as Tull (2006) argues, more of the same for African economies?

A further implication of the 'emerging donor' discourse is, as Kragelund (2008) observes, that China and many others deemed 'emerging' have been active donors for most of the Cold War period and beyond (King 2010). For example, Snow (1988) and Brautigam (1998) showed how China has been active in technical cooperation around infrastructure, health and agriculture since the 1950s and, as we shall see below, these modes of engagement are found today in the recent upsurge in Chinese aid. What is more extraordinary is that through the 1980s and 1990s DAC members dominated aid-giving to an unprecedented degree (*c*.95%) (Manning 2006) when it had been closer to 65 per cent during the 1970s. So this 'emergence' of new donors needs to be seen in this longer context which is tied to an ideological and geopolitical shift from what McMichael (2000) terms 'developmentalism' in the post-war period to a neo-liberal 'globalism' in the 1980s and 1990s that saw hegemonic powers project their development vision outwards via Structural Adjustment (Mohan et al. 2000) lending and the complicity of domestic elites (Harvey 2005; Tickell and Peck 2003).

Like any classification the blanket term 'emerging donor' covers a diversity of actors with quite different approaches to development cooperation (King 2010). Moreover while 'emerging donors' are set against 'established' or 'traditional' donors, the former group is also diverse (Wissenbach 2010). So, for example, while we have seen the Washington Consensus, a putative Beijing Consensus and an EU

Development Consensus, the idea of consensus masks major differences *within* and *between* particular donor countries. Additionally, many of the criticisms of China and other emerging donors that we discuss shortly are not dissimilar to the criticisms levelled at the established donors in times gone by. For example, China is criticized for its large-scale project focus which was something that was raised in the 1960s and 1970s regarding European and American aid.

The current trepidation about 'emerging' donors is, therefore, part of a wider concern about the rise of China and India as major global competitors that may signal a new orthodoxy in the political-economy of development (Schmitz 2007), though we feel it is too early to say how far China really changes the terms on which development is conceived and enacted (Mohan and Power 2009). This warning about the histories of aid raises important questions about how multilateral institutions, such as the OECD, function to police and protect the privilege of western powers. As Kapoor (2008) observes the DAC is in effect an elite 'club' which acts as 'moral book-keeper' of international development and in doing so seeks to cement a particular vision of development that is relatively immune from critique or reform. Eyben (2006) examines how there were missed opportunities to re-orient the aid paradigm away from seeing aid as simply managing finance towards people-centred approaches during the Copenhagen and Beijing Summits of 1995. Eyben argues that the debates served to distance the causes of poverty away from western consumption towards developing countries' policy failure and to exclude different perspectives on aid and development. While Eyben makes a case for social-centred alternatives one could easily argue that another alternative that the established donors are seeking to distance is the so-called Beijing Consensus (Ramo 2004) that potentially stands as a critique of the neo-liberal Washington Consensus. So, the debates around aid are at one level about the self-satisfied self-representation of the western donors, but at a deeper level concern the very balance of global power and the discourses enabling it.

In some policy circles China's 'aid' offensive has been greeted with scepticism and concern, captured in the concept of 'rogue aid' (Naim 2007). More imperatively, one of the biggest criticisms of Chinese aid is the lack of political conditionalities, which some argue will undermine good governance and lead to deepened debt and governance crises in Africa (Chidaushe 2007; Schoeman 2007). Naim (2007: 95) represents China and other 'rogue' states as a 'threat to healthy, sustainable development' arguing that they 'are effectively pricing responsible and well meaning organizations out of the market in the very places they are needed most' while 'underwriting a world that is more corrupt, chaotic and authoritarian'. Similarly, the US Treasury Department has called China a 'rogue creditor' practising 'opportunistic lending' (Phillips 2006). According to Tull (2006: 476), 'Beijing uses the pillars of its foreign policy, notably unconditional respect for state sovereignty and its corollary, non-interference, in the pursuit of its interests, be they energy security, multipolarity or the "One China" principle'. Many (Manji and Marks 2007; Trofimov 2007) have taken this focus on aid and conditionality further to argue that China is essentially a neo-colonial power, where African resources are 'plundered' by Beijing and sent back in the form of Chinese goods which cements the long-standing uneven division of labour between Africa and the rest of the world. Whether these condemnations are justified or not demands empirical testing, but they have added costs to China's efforts at establishing 'soft power' in its foreign diplomacy (Zhao 2007). In terms of putting Chinese aid in the wider context of other 'older' donors Dreher et al. (2010: 18) point out that new donors 'do not generally exhibit a stronger bias against better governed countries', the corollary being that older donors, despite their criticisms of China, have also been willing to support corrupt and authoritarian states when it suits their strategic interests.

Although we have criticized the DAC for seeking to protect certain privileges the organization has not gone unchanged. One of the key debates about the different approach of China as a donor is that it sharpens a set of existing criticisms from within the donor community. These revolve around the effectiveness of aid. Sometime before China began to be criticized for its concessional financing the DAC donors were aware of the need for change. The Structural Adjustment Programmes of the 1980s and 1990s were seen as dogmatic and inflexible (Mohan et al. 2000), aid conditionality created dependent 'governance states' (Harrison 2004), western aid had limited or even negative impacts on growth (Easterly 2007), and the mixture of bilateral and multilateral channels created a confusing operating field for recipient states (de Renzio 2006).

So, the 2005 Paris Declaration on Aid Effectiveness was the culmination of these growing concerns with its emphasis on coordination and efficiency of aid. China is an aid receiver, although this status is diminishing as inflows of aid fall away. It is beyond the scope of this chapter to evaluate the Paris Declaration process though some of the criticisms of the dominant aid paradigm are germane to our discussion. In brief the critique is that aid delivery is fragmented, comes through a confusing array of modalities, places too much pressure on recipient states and increases transaction costs (see de Renzio 2006; Collier 2006; Birdsall 2008). The move towards Direct Budget Support, Poverty Reduction Strategies and Sector-Wide Approaches (SWAPs) were part of the response to these critiques and moved away from project-based approaches which are seen as easily manipulated by patrimonial pressures. Yet the Chinese, as we will see, primarily deliver aid through discrete projects and despite the goals of the Paris Declaration Moss et al. (2008) report a proliferation of project funding among all donors (see also Riddell 2007: 180). The rationale given by the Chinese for a project focus is to avoid any avenues for possible corruption and a preference for quick and tangible results. Collier (2006) raises the question of whether aid is like oil, in terms of creating rents for African states and while he argues that project aid can lead to embezzlement and patrimonialism equally it can be a useful public good. Similarly, Woods (2008) points out that all countries' own standards which inform aid are at odds with these normative goals set out in multilateral forums (e.g. the 0.7% of GDP aid target) so we must be careful to single out emerging donors who do not adhere to these initiatives as recalcitrant. Where the new donor countries were acknowledged in the Paris Declaration it was rather patronizing in being a 'valuable complement to North-South cooperation' (para 19e, cited in King 2010: 10) which clearly reveals an implicit power relation that 'Northern' donors should set agendas and others should contribute where appropriate.

The 2008 meeting in Accra to monitor the implementation of the Paris Declaration produced the Accra Agenda for Action, which reported reasonable progress, yet nowhere near fast enough or far enough (Davies 2009). Interestingly in the intervening three years the importance of Southern donors had been acknowledged with one of the Round Tables at the Accra meeting being on 'Non-DAC' donors in recognition of the growing role they are playing or might play. Crucially, Chinese aid is seen by recipients as much more streamlined and speedy in reaching its target. The argument in favour is that this makes it much more effective and efficient; yet, the downside is that this effectiveness is at the expense of considerations around the governance, human rights and environmental implications. It is to these debates that we know turn.

### Logics, modalities and conditionalities

In terms of the practices of aid delivery that the Paris Declaration seeks to normalize, much of China's rationale for its aid and development cooperation has been to place it in a distinctive relation (often in opposition) to western aid logics and practices. This dates back to the height of the Cold War when the Chinese sought to distance themselves from both the United States and Soviet Union, and to lead a Third Worldist movement (Eadie and Grizzell 1979; Ismael 1971; Larkin 1971; Snow 1988; Mohan and Power 2008). Zhou Enlai elaborated the Eight Principles for Chinese aid that grew out of his five principles of Peaceful Co-existence. These centre on aid being mutually beneficial, that all countries are equal and that their sovereignty is respected. Moreover they are expounded today as characterizing China's development relations with the 'South' since the idea of 'donor' and 'aid' are anathema to China's vision of itself.

As we saw in Chapter 3, the populist concept of 'scientific development' currently guides the socio-economic ideology of the Chinese Communist Party (CCP), seen as the latest version of 'socialism with Chinese characteristics'. What does 'pursuing development in a scientific way' mean and how does it shape foreign assistance? Further, what does it mean for African states on the receiving end of China's development cooperation? According to more official accounts coming from China on China's approach to development cooperation there is a significant difference between China and the West in their approach to Africa with China's strategy being 'one of humanitarian and development aid plus influence without interference, in contrast to the West's coercive approach of sanctions plus military intervention' (Qian and Wu 2007). According to Huang Chinese aid centres on 'the real needs of the recipient countries, free from the shackles of unpractical ideas' (Huang 2007: 84) or in the words of the 2011 White Paper 'China's actual conditions and the needs of recipient countries' (Xinhua 2011a). Like Japan's aid these 'real needs' are focused on infrastructure and agriculture, and assisted without being 'tied-up with a package of political or economic reforms' (Huang 2007: 82). Indeed, the comparisons with Japanese aid are instructive since both countries have recently undergone a phase of rapid, export-oriented industrialization, been aid recipients and drastically reduced poverty (GRIPS 2008), which influences their focus on infrastructure and growth. In turn this affects the modalities, discussed below, of aid and concessional financing being connected and tied to China's commercial needs. In concrete terms China's engagement with Africa has gathered pace in the past 5–10 years, culminating in the Forum on China-Africa Cooperation (FOCAC) meetings in late 2006 and 2009 which we discussed in Chapter 3.

One of the problems of assessing Chinese aid is that it is not measured in the same way as 'normal' aid and a lack of domestic transparency compounds the uncertainties, although the publication of an aid White Paper in April 2011 went some way to clarify these issues

(Xinhua 2011a). For most calculations of aid, or Overseas Development Assistance (ODA), analysts use the DAC definition, which is that it is official finance, seeks to promote economic development and welfare, and is concessional in character containing a grant element of at least 25 per cent (Riddell 2007). For reasons we will discuss below, China does not use this definition which makes comparing like with like difficult (Glosny 2006; Jacoby 2007; Kragelund 2008). China does not separate Official Development Assistance from economic cooperation or investment as long as the intent is to expand the local capacity. Respondents in Beijing used the famous analogy: 'it is better to teach them how to fish' as opposed to giving poor countries handouts as the West has been doing. Moreover China pursues a principle of 'diversity in forms of interaction' or 'multi-form and mutually-beneficial cooperation' (Xinhua 2011a). According to the Chinese, China offered scholarships to nearly 16,000 Africans from 52 countries and more than 600 Chinese teachers and 1500 Chinese doctors have worked in these countries in 2005.

That said the volume of Chinese aid is often regarded as a state secret (Lancaster 2007) and data on this is not collected in the same way as it is by western aid donors. According to Lancaster (2007), the Chinese justify this secrecy to avoid criticism and competition from major donor countries, and domestic criticism of providing aid to foreign countries instead of eradicating poverty domestically. Given these caveats Brautigam (2007) put Chinese aid worldwide in 2005 at US$970 million but World Bank estimates put the figure at US$2 billion while Lancaster (2007: 4) estimated a figure of US$1.5–$2.0 billion. The Chinese Government's Ministry of Finance website also indicated total foreign aid expenditure as 10.8 billion yuan (US$1.6 billion) (Figure 5.1).

The 2011 Chinese White Paper on aid gave a breakdown of aid disbursement as of 2009 as 256.29 billion yuan of aid including 106.2 billion yuan in grants, 76.54 billion yuan in interest-free loans and 73.55 billion yuan in concessional loans (Xinhua 2011a). Of the latter category – concessional loans – 61 per cent went on economic infrastructure, 16.1 per cent on industry, 8.9 per cent on energy and resource development, 4.3 per cent on agriculture and 3.2 per cent on public facilities. In terms of geographical distribution 45.7 per cent has gone to Africa, 32.8 per cent to Asia, 12.7 per cent to Latin America and the Caribbean and 4 per cent to Oceania. Hubbard (2008) notes that like many western donors China often publicly pledges large amounts of aid but does not disburse this amount, though given the preceding discussion on transparency it is hard to verify or calculate this alleged shortfall.

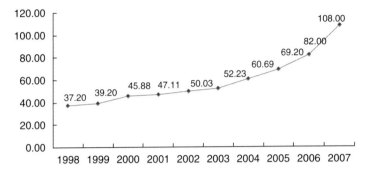

*Figure 5.1* China's foreign aid expenditure increases, 1998–2007 (Unit: RMB 100 million)

*Source*: Ministry of Finance.

However, in terms of assessing the impact of this aid what is more important than levels of aid *per se* are the modes of delivery as it is tied to other financial and trade flows, involving different amounts of leverage and, hence, developmental impact. Many of the features of China's contemporary aid-giving were laid down during the Cold War period. It was usually given as a grant, or as an interest-free loan, which was different to the Soviet model where interest was charged at 2.5 per cent (Snow 1988). Strictly bilateral in nature and only given where the relationship was mutually beneficial to donor and recipient alike, Chinese aid workers were also unique in their approach, not being permitted to 'loll in hotel suites and run up expenses as other expatriates did [having to] content themselves with the same standard of living as the ordinary Africans they worked with' (Snow 1988: 146). Chinese aid went to various sectors of African 'development' and many aid projects have had the word 'friendship' in them. All previous aid efforts were dwarfed however by the massive Tanzania-Zambia (Tazara) railway (1967–75) which cost over US$600 million and was built with the help of 15,000 Chinese workers (Brautigam 1998). Finally, there was often a reluctance to coordinate efforts with other foreign powers and a deep-seated tendency to 'go it alone' sometimes resulting in active hostility to other aid personnel.

In terms of sector the Chinese have been much more focused on growth and productive investment as opposed to the 'software' of governance that might underpin economic development. This is much more about mutual benefit than a discourse of charity or of 'catching up' (King 2010: 11). This is echoed in Sachs' observation (2007) that the real solution to Africa's problems is not really economic. It is not a matter of the right monetary and fiscal policies but of roads, fertilizers, hospital beds, malaria nets and AIDS treatments – readily available technocratic solutions which are missing only for lack of funds. In early 2007 Sachs noted that while the World Bank was mired in the scandal surrounding the then President Paul Wolfowitz, clinging to rigid free-market ideology and having forgotten 'the most basic lessons of development' (Sachs 2007), China was busy offering 'much more practical advice' as it 'skilfully raises its geopolitical profile in the developing world' (2007: 1). As China set about stressing the crucial role of public investments in infrastructure and agriculture as the basis for private sector growth the World Bank is portrayed here as 'preferring to lecture the poor', forcing African countries to privatize rather than invest in infrastructure.

China is a recipient of development aid, though this is diminishing, and so avoids the status of 'donor' and the word 'aid' is often avoided altogether when talking about Africa. As King (2006: 2) has suggested, this is not just about semantics but is part of the almost 50-year history of China seeking to avoid the status of donor, and of presenting itself as a friendly developing country (with much historical experience of external oppression) helping other developing countries, to the best of its ability.

Today, much of the aid is bilateral, which necessitates a country-by-country analysis as we do in the following sections. The aid disbursed by the Chinese is generally delivered through three modes of grant aid, interest free loans and concessional loans (Davies et al. 2008), and can be grouped into six categories, ranging from financial and technical assistance for key investments to peacekeeping (see McCormick et al. 2006). Aid is also project based (often turnkey) rather than sectoral or programme aid as encouraged by the OECD in its Paris Declaration on aid effectiveness (Glosny 2006; Davies et al. 2008).

In concrete terms, however, there is a blurring of aid and investment. The routes for aid and investment are the privileged Chinese corporations selected as part of the Chinese Government's 'Go Out' Policy of 2002 (Reilly and Na 2007). These 'national champions' form the brunt of China's internationalization strategy, but as more companies internationalize it becomes harder for the Chinese state to maintain a coherent strategic and regulatory hold over them (see Chapter 4). China's corporate engagement with Africa has been exaggerated while the 'China Inc.' model is far less efficient and monolithic than is often assumed (Gill and Reilly 2007) with Chinese corporations competing with one another (Downs 2007). Thus as China's Africa strategy comes to rely on a growing number of bureaucratic principles and corporate agents, contradictions will increase.

Decision-making around aid usually involves the recipient country approaching China, either through the embassy or at a higher diplomatic level. Indeed, it seems Chinese Embassies are crucial nodes in these negotiations. At the Chinese side there is a range of ministries responsible for aid and overseas investment (Sautman and Hairong 2006; Glosny 2006; Brautigam 2008). If consensus is reached, a framework agreement is signed and the finance is assembled with the Ministry of Commerce (MOFCOM) playing the lead role in grants and ExIm Bank for loans, although Brautigam (2008) shows how MOFCOM may pay the difference between a commercial loan rate and a concessional rate, thereby cross-subsidizing ExIm Bank. Once details have been negotiated a more detailed agreement is signed at which point MOFCOM assigns a Chinese company as contractor (Glosny 2006: 19–20, see also Davies et al. 2008; AFRODAD 2008: 12–13). MOFCOM also liaises with relevant ministries, notably Ministry of Foreign Affairs and the Ministry of Finance plus some other departments of State Council. In 2008 these ministries formed an inter-agency liaison mechanism around aid which has been upgraded to an inter-agency coordination mechanism in 2011.

One of the contentious elements besides the lack of political conditionality discussed below is that much of China's aid is tied, though arguably it is a form of commercial conditionality (Kragelund 2008). This goes against the OECD's efforts to untie aid, although Riddell (2007) notes that despite these efforts many DAC donors still have significant proportions of tied aid. A similar issue is raised around export credits which are the preferred currency used by ExIm. Again the OECD has instituted a 'gentleman's agreement' about the use of export credits, though this is limited to OECD members. Export credits are not classified as aid and potentially allow for more tying (Manning 2006), but Reisen and Ndoye's (2008) study for the OECD suggests that despite China not being part of the DAC their lending is not 'imprudent' despite the accusations of some China hawks that the country is a 'rogue creditor' (Phillips 2006).

Hubbard (2008: 225) asserts that the Chinese insist that the Chinese contractor appointed by MOFCOM should 'purchase and import from

China as much equipment, technology and services as possible', which is similar to the earlier Japanese model. Moreover claims abound about the importation of Chinese labour, which is part of the tying agreement. Glosny (2006) notes the labour importation issue is often overlooked though research is needed into the actual levels of Chinese labour importation as opposed to speculative hyperbole that we noted in the introduction to this book. More recently too, most notably in the Democratic Republic of the Congo (DRC), the recipient government stipulates the overseas labour content so such matters are negotiable. We discuss these issues later in the chapter and the next.

One of the key criticisms emanating from China's apparent insistence on non-interference and its blurring of concessional finance with other financial flows concerns conditionality. Conditionality has long been a part of ODA and became most prescriptive during the Structural Adjustment Programmes of the 1980s and early 1990s when it was attached to economic reforms and later to good governance. Why China exorcizes some commentators and activists is that it seemingly attaches no such conditions to its loans and therefore undermines, 'undercuts', in Manning's (2006) terms, the good works of western donors around governance, human rights and environmental protection (French 2004; Naim 2007). The ideological caveat of this critique of China by some western commentators is that despite people arguing that there is such a thing as 'pure' (Natsios 2006) or 'altruistic' (Kragelund 2008) aid, all aid is strategic. We are not defending China's non-interference stance *per se*, since the outcomes on the ground determine its efficacy, rather China bashing serves to bolster western interests as opposed to any deep concern with the rights of Africans.

The Chinese defend their non-interference line in various ways, which usually fall back on evoking historical ties between China and Africa as well as a shared sense of injustice by the west. Typical is Liu Guijin, China's special representative on Darfur, who argued:

> We [China] have never, and will never in the future, attach any kind of political conditions to these aid and development projects, because we think that providing assistance is just for the benefit of the people, it is not for political purposes, not for showing off to the outside world. (Liu Guijin cited in Xinhua 2008a, see also Huang 2007)

This reinforces the non-interference policy and the projected image that China is now 'non-ideological' and pragmatic, since its concerns are commercial or altruistic rather than transforming hearts and minds. An interview respondent in Beijing (CASS 2008) argued that the emphasis shifted in the early 1990s from 'south-south solidarity' to one of 'mutual benefits', which by the turn of the millennium morphed into exhortations of 'win-win' scenarios.

However, the backlash against China's role in Sudan, combined with an increasingly hazardous operating environment, has pushed China to weaken its 'non-interference' line and to become more involved in diplomacy (Large 2008b; Carmody 2011). The question remains open as to whether this weakening on non-interference is impacting on the ground in Africa in terms of China's engagement with domestic governance and capacity issues. Additionally Glosny (2006) argues that the Chinese are aware they need to understand local institutional cultures to maximize the benefits from their interventions, but how this translates into practice is another matter.

That said, and something we examine more in the next chapter, the 'emerging' donors introduce competitive pressures among existing donors which gives recipient countries some leverage, what has been termed the 'revival of triangulation' (Large 2008c). For the first time since the end of the Cold War African countries have some choices about aid and investment, which might open a policy space for alternatives, but this remains an empirical question. On the face of it China's interests do not radically alter the role Africa plays in the global division of labour but what is interesting to analyse is whether individual African states are able to harness this hegemonic rivalry for their own ends. The following sections will power the debates with concrete examples from Angola and Ghana.

## Chinese aid in comparative perspective

So far we have examined some of the key modes of aid-giving by the Chinese and set this in the wider context of 'emerging' versus 'established' donors. We noted that this is a somewhat false distinction given that the Chinese are not 'new' donors and many of the supposedly negative actions they take are practised, or have been, by the 'established' donor countries that initiate the criticisms. However, many of these criticisms are at the technical level about, say, bilateral project approaches versus in-country harmonization. In terms of wider understandings of development and geopolitical tensions there are some key areas where China differs from established donors but also where aid is used in all too familiar strategic ways and where the criticism of China is much more about the self-presentation of western 'liberal' donors.

Clemens Six (2009) argues that a key difference that China and India bring to the aid agenda is 'they do not share the same history of colonial and postcolonial relations ... and thus do not use historicist development rhetoric to legitimize their interventions' (1108–9). As such, according to Six (2009: 1110) they occupy a 'dual position' being both of the developing world but also key drivers of growth in the global economy. This means they do not need to fall back on ideological constructs around certain teleologies of emancipation bound up in western development discourse but are freer to be honest about their interest-based engagements with African countries. Indeed, Six sees this new honesty as potentially liberating for all concerned, including established donors, who no longer need to conceal their interests behind legitimatory discourses. Six's insistence on the transparency of China's interests is fair although questions of 'partnership' and 'solidarity' (King 2010) that are the watchwords of China's discourse of development cooperation also need to be empirically tested rather than taken at face value as inherently better for African states and peoples. King (2010) also points out, using the example of the former UK Prime Minister Gordon Brown, that western donors also use aid to further their interests. Brown's argument shifted from the early New Labour position (Slater and Bell 2002) that Africa was a 'moral' concern for western donors to one which was both a moral issue *and* a potential source of insecurity that could threaten western countries such that aid could ameliorate insecurity thereby indirectly benefiting western interests. That aid is not purely altruistic is hardly a new insight in critical development studies (Hayter 1971), but what is more surprising is how a discourse of 'apolitical' aid became so prominent in the 1980s and 1990s such that China's new 'honesty' could puncture it.

In terms of more focused comparisons with western donors Wissenbach (2010) argues that many western criticisms of China are picking the wrong fights insofar as they exaggerate the differences between China and others, around good governance for example. In practice, and echoing the previous discussion on interests, there is a lot of overlap between China and western donors around the importance of economic growth for development and the role of business in driving this (e.g. Conservative Party 2010) although Wissenbach rightly points out that China uses different benchmarks. Indeed, an interesting ideological and practical issue is that despite the seemingly bounded scope of 'south-south' cooperation much of the activity that new donors engage in is delivering on the goals established by 'northern' donors (Steiner-Khamsi 2010) either at the macro-level in terms of structural adjustment and liberalization programmes creating the conditions for Chinese trade and FDI or the more focused issue of development targets, most notably the Millennium Development Goals (MDGs). It was noted in one of our interviews with a US-based Chamber of Commerce that China was not a threat and in fact benefitted everyone:

> I basically don't see the Chinese presence in Angola as being, I suppose, any more competitive say than a South African firm or an Indian firm or a Portuguese or whatever. The fact is of course also that a lot of the stuff that they are involved in particularly the infrastructure projects, it 's going to be of benefit to all of us, so you have to look at the larger picture that way.

In this sense China benefits from liberalizations driven during the Washington Consensus period and now western firms benefit from the soft power projects of the Chinese.

## Chinese aid in practice: forms, continuities and transformations

So far in this chapter we have examined discourses and debates around China's growing role as a donor. In most cases the 'rogue aid' argument of the China hawks is massively exaggerated and more balanced arguments basically suggest that China is not so different and hence there are areas of overlap and, as we will see towards the end of this chapter, potential areas of collaboration. However, what we still lack is an analysis of aid 'in action' which is really what the rest of this, and much of the next two, chapter does. In terms of China's engagement with Africa we saw in Chapter 2 that there was a period of intense activity during the Cold War where between 1956 and 1977, approximately US$2.4 billion Chinese official foreign aid was extended to Africa (Yu 1980). This waned in the mid-1970s, but picked up again in the mid-1980s where between 1983 and 1995 China's aid contribution to Africa stood at an average of US$200 million per year (Snow 1995: 311). We have already seen how the past five years have witnessed a massive increase in Chinese aid under FOCAC.

### Contemporary development relations in Angola and Ghana

In the previous section, it was argued that China's recent interests in Africa are built on longer histories of cooperation which have tended to be couched in terms of solidarity and development rather than aid.

Current 'aid' is tied into geopolitical agendas, economic cooperation as well as to specific resource acquisitions. The governance of this aid is increasingly complex and diffuse as the Chinese state becomes privatized and fragments into different ministries and regions, all having some part to play in African interventions. In many senses, given that all aid is politically and economically motivated, the Chinese are not behaving much differently from previous industrial powers intent on accessing African resources. But where they do appear different from western powers is the types of political relationships they operate through, as well as envisage for, Africa. It is to these that we now turn.

Following the end of decades of internecine civil war in Angola in April 2002 rapid post-conflict reconstruction became the government's priority (Campos and Vines 2008) as it began to seek partners in the international community that could help to make this happen. At the end of the war the International Monetary Fund (IMF) and many Western donors wanted Angola to adopt a staff-monitored programme (SMP) demonstrating good performance against certain criteria in a way that would lend credibility to Angola's economic policies and open the way for a donor conference that would raise funds for national reconstruction. The government refused to agree to the conditionalities however and announced in 2003 that they no longer sought to conclude an agreement with the IMF. As in many other previous instances where negotiations between the IMF and Angola collapsed, commodity prices at the time were very high (Hodges 2001). It was in this context that China (in need of access to energy resources to fuel its own development) sought to offer Angola a series of oil-backed credit lines with far fewer conditionalities, paying more than lip-service to the need for local 'ownership' and leadership of these projects. China's ExIm Bank provided the first funding for infrastructure development in 2002 and a 'framework agreement' for new economic and commercial cooperation was formally signed by the Angolan Ministry of Finance and the Chinese Ministry of Commerce in 2003 while in March 2004 the first US$2-billion financing package for public investment projects was approved. This oil-backed loan (which guarantees China a supply of 10,000 barrels per day) is payable over 12 years at a deeply concessional interest rate, Libor plus a spread of 1.5 percent, with a grace period of up to three years and was divided into two phases, with US$1 billion assigned to each. The loan operates like a current account. When ordered by the Ministry of Finance, disbursements are made by ExIm Bank directly into the accounts of the contractors. Repayment starts as soon as a project is completed.

Two separate additional ExIm loans of US$500 million and US$2 billion were made in 2007 with the repayment terms increased to 15 years with a revised interest rate of Libor plus 1.25 per cent (Campos and Vines 2008). A further $1 billion loan from the China Development Bank was granted in March 2009 (rising to US$ 1.5 billion in 2010) with a view to supporting the development of Angolan agriculture. In the first official estimate of Chinese credit to Angola, Chinese Ambassador Zhang Bolun said in early 2011 that an estimated US$14.5 billion in credit had been provided since the end of the war from the three Chinese state banks (ExIm Bank, the Commercial and Industrial Bank of China and the China Development Bank) (Power 2011).

These credit lines have opened up well over 100 projects in the areas of energy, agriculture, water, health, education, telecommunications, fisheries and public works including key elements in the governments postwar National Reconstruction Programme such as the rehabilitation of 371 kilometers of road between Luanda and Uige. This corresponds to the Angolan government's strategy of giving top priority to the reopening of the country's transportation corridors and the construction and reconstruction of infrastructures such as road, rail, power and telecommunications networks, airports, seaports, housing, schools and hospitals. Project proposals identified as priorities by the respective Angolan ministries are put forward to the *Grupo de Trabalho Conjunto,* a joint committee of the Ministry of Finance and the MOFCOM (China). For each project put to tender, the Chinese government proposes three to four Chinese companies and all projects are inspected by third parties not funded by the credit line while sectoral ministries are in charge of managing these public works and making sure that sufficient staff are trained.

Additionally, oil-backed loans amounting to as much as US$10 billion have also been provided by a private equity firm based in Hong Kong called the China International Fund (see Chapter 4). This credit facility has been managed by Angola's Reconstruction Office, the *Gabinete de Reconstrução Nacional* (GRN), which has been exclusively accountable to the Angolan presidency and originally managed most of the major infrastructure projects. In the major government reshuffle of March 2010 (in which the President called for a crackdown on corruption) a replacement was sought for the GRN in what was widely seen as a vote of no confidence in the agency and later in the same year the President announced that a company called Sonangol Imobiliária [Sonangol Real Estate] would be taking over responsibility from the GRN for implementing various projects relating to construction and the rehabilitation of infrastructure (Power 2011).

Tied to the original ExIm loans is the agreement that the public tenders for the construction and civil engineering contracts tabled for Angola's reconstruction will be awarded primarily (70%) to Chinese enterprises approved by the Chinese Government. To date some thirty-five Chinese companies have been pre-approved by the PRC Government to bid for projects that are put to tender in China. Furthermore, in principle, at least 50 per cent of all procurement for China ExIm Bank funded projects (in terms of equipment, materials, technology or services) must come from China but in practice our research shows that most projects are implemented at closer to 70 per cent. As a result almost everything down to the cement and nails for these works are imported from China ensuring a large portion of the loan money returns to China's domestic economy and addresses China's domestic challenge of structural unemployment by restricting competition from local and other foreign firms (Figure 5.2). Further, there is limited evidence that Chinese credit lines are boosting Angola's productive capacity and the limited employment opportunities created for Angolan workers has been the cause of some tension locally. Where Angolans have been able to find work on

*Figure 5.2* Chinese goods imported with construction projects. Photograph by authors

Chinese construction sites it has often been as security guards rather than on equal terms as waged labourers.

Angola is now China's largest African trade partner with US$24.8 billion in bilateral trade in 2010 (MacauHub, 31 January 2011). From having one of the most protracted conflicts in Africa, Angola has within five years become one of the most successful economies in sub-Saharan Africa. The country is now considered by some to be 'Africa's foremost emerging market' (Frontier Advisory 2009) with the fastest growing economy in the world in 2007 and 2008 based on growth rates of 22.30 per cent and 18.60 per cent respectively (World Bank 2007a, 2008, 2009a). As a result of these phenomenal rates of growth Angola is receiving increasing recognition for its oil wealth leading to a growing number of attempts to engage Angola as a strategic partner. Angola was chair of OPEC from 2008 to 2009 and was invited to take part in the G8 summit in Italy in July 2009 while the United States appears to have 'woken up to the importance of Angola' (Vines 2009a: 3) with US Secretary of State Hilary Clinton visiting the country in August 2009. Lord Malloch Brown's visit to Angola in June 2009 was a clear sign of the escalating strategic importance of Angola both regionally and globally and the growing strength of the relationship between Angola and the United Kingdom (FCO 2009). Thus China is not the only show in town and the Angolan state has been very shrewd and pragmatic in managing its relations and establishing partnerships with a range of potential suitors including Brazil, South Africa and Portugal. Far from being monopolized by its ties with China, the Angolan state thus welcomes closer relations with a range of other partners and the agency and ingenuity of Angolan officials in managing these relations and in creating a competition among partners seeking strategic influence in Angola has often been overlooked. We discuss this further in the next chapter. The fiscal impacts of low oil prices in late 2008 and early 2009 once again led to the government reopening negotiations with the IMF over the terms of a 27-month Stand-By Arrangement (a type of loan facility) amounting to as much as $890 million (Global Witness 2009).

This presence and intensity of Chinese involvement is comparatively less evident in Ghana, largely due to the lack of strategic minerals although this will change due to the discovery of offshore oilfields in the Ghanaian coast in late 2008. Given the relative lack of Ghanaian exports to China Ghana has a trade deficit compared to Angola's trade surplus with China. From 2000 to 2008, China's exports to Ghana increased manifold from US$93 million to $1512 million and China now ranks first as an importing country to Ghana with a 15.9 per cent share (Jiang and Jing 2010). Although China has had a long-standing relationship with Ghana since the 1960s, it is only in recent years that the relationship has been taken to a higher level with the value of bilateral trade reaching US$2.05 billion in 2010 (AllAfrica 2011). In 2007, Ghana received a total of US$1.15 billion (OECD 2007a) from all donors (not including China) and Chinese aid is still only a small percentage of the total development assistance received by the Ghanaians, as exemplified by below.

Over the years, Chinese aid has been used to build physical infrastructure like roads (e.g. the Ofankor-Nsawam section of the Accra-Kumasi road) and buildings (the National Theatre)(Figure 5.3). It was in 2004/2005 when relations improved tremendously that Ghana began to receive grants and interest-free loans directly from China such as a US$24 million debt relief on interest-free loans. Table 5.1 details the main Chinese projects in Ghana (see also figures 5.3 and 5.4). In the 2006 FOCAC, Ghana and China signed six agreements, including an agreement on a US$66 million loan for the expansion of

*Figure 5.3* The Chinese-built National Theatre in Accra. Photograph by authors

*Figure 5.4*  The Chinese-built Ministry of Defence, Accra. Photograph by authors

Ghana's telecommunication infrastructure, mainly the US$30 million concessionary loan for the first phase of the National Fibreoptic and E-government project. The project was executed by the Chinese telecom giant Huawei and aimed at linking all the 10 regional capitals and 36 townships on fibre routes (*Daily Graphic* 15 August 2007). In late 2008, when fieldwork was conducted, the network was not working and we were told by a senior executive of a mobile phone company that the Government of Ghana had not planned strategically for this e-infrastructure nor did they possess the necessary technical skill to do so, yet refused advice from the private sector that had. China also provided a US$99 million interest-free loan for the construction of landing sites for fishing communities in Ghana. This interest in the country's fishing industry by China, in itself, has improved access rights for Chinese fishing companies leading to the exploration of offshore processing opportunities in Ghana.

In general the process is one where the Chinese sign a framework document for construction and then engage their own contractor from China and procure the materials from the mainland. Upon completion,

*Table 5.1* Summary of Chinese aid in Ghana

| Project | Date | Modality | Amount |
|---|---|---|---|
| Ofankor-Nsawam stretch of Accra-Kumasi Road* | 2002 | Interest-free loan | US$30 million |
| The National Theatre* | 2003 | Grant | US$2 million |
| Police and Military Barracks* | 2003 | Grant | US$3.9 million |
| Expansion and upgrading telecommunication network, building of a school and malaria centre@ | 2006 | | US$66 million |
| Security communication between agencies* | 2006 | Concessional loan | US$30 million |
| The Bui Dam Project@ | 2007 | Concessional loan and buyers' credit | US$622 million |
| Various developmental projects+ | 2007 | US$4 million interest-free loan and US$1.33 million grant | US$5.33 million |
| Landing Sites for Selected Fishing Communities* | 2008 | Interest-free loan | US$99 million |
| Office Complex for the Ministry of Defence* | 2008 | | US$7.5 million |
| Pedause President Lodge* | 2008 | | US$1.34 million |

Compiled from various sources (Tsikata et al. 2008*; Davies et al. 2008@, internet news sources (modern Ghana news)+)

the Chinese effectively donate the building to the Ghanaian government (Xi, counsellor, Ghana). There is a perception among ministers and think tanks in Ghana that the Chinese are serving genuine infrastructure needs. As one think tank told us the 'Chinese also got it right from the beginning as countries must get infrastructure in place before any development can take place', which they set up in opposition to the liberal governance agendas of DAC donors. Other sectors that have benefited from China's technical support include education (three schools), the public sector and military cooperation. For example, the Chinese government has trained over 700 professionals in various sectors of the economy in addition to other training for public sector functionaries. Moreover, there are 34 scholarships to Ghanaian students annually.

Undoubtedly the most significant Chinese engagement with Ghana is the Bui hydroelectric dam, which is the focal point for a series of major energy-related investments by the Chinese (see figures 5.5 and 5.6). The Bui Dam and others built by Sinohydro are 'EPC' projects, meaning 'engineering, procurement, construction' and is the preferred route for many African governments since the price is agreed up front and fixed. It also suits the Chinese since it creates time-bound projects but Hensengerth (2011) notes that Chinese state-owned enterprises (SOEs) also engage in 'build-operate-transfer' (BOT) schemes where the Chinese operate the facility for a fixed period after construction before giving it over to the government and also undertake supply contracts for other non-Chinese construction firms.

Like many Chinese-funded infrastructure projects the majority of the money comes from ExIm Bank, which increasingly rivals the World Bank even though the two have been exploring ways of working together. The

*Figure 5.5* Work Camp for Ghanaian workers, The Bui Dam, Ghana. Photograph by authors

*Figure 5.6*   Ghanaian worker at Bui Dam, Ghana. Photograph by authors

Bui Dam will cost US$622m – US$288m from buyer credits and US$298 as a commercial loan, whose interest will kick in after September 2012, when the electricity is delivered. It should bring 400 MW of much needed electricity to Ghana's struggling grid and even allow some for export to West African neighbours. The remaining US$40million or so will come from Ghanaian sources, though exactly from where is not clear. The Chinese favoured the dam project as opposed to the Ghanaian Government's preferred option of a railway from the coast to Burkina Faso, because the sale of electricity to Mali, Cote d'Ivoire and Burkina Faso would guarantee repayment in a way that a railway could not. This revenue will be paid into an escrow account and funds used to service the debt. In addition there is a special arrangement with the Ghana Cocoa Board to supply cocoa at current market prices as part payment of the debt, with the Chinese keen to promote chocolate consumption in China.

Sinohydro and other Chinese firms are looking to deepen their footprint in Ghana and Africa more broadly. Although the Chinese seemed to have got a foothold in Africa through these Chinese government-supported projects they are now competing more openly for tenders and as one European aid official told me 'winning in straight fights'. For example, one Chinese firm is building roads in Northern Ghana funded by French aid. The Chinese presence in construction is threatening to local firms who have lobbied under their trade organization to limit the number of Chinese firms operating, but to date the government has not responded. And after the Bui Dam the planners are working on Bui City, which is a new city benefiting from the water made available in this arid part of Ghana and which one Ghanaian official optimistically noted would be 'like Dubai'. Here the infrastructure of modernity holds great power even as the vision is increasingly a privatized one of home ownership. The interesting thing is that a Chinese firm is working on the plans for it and Sinohydro also has plans for four smaller dams in Ghana. But these are essentially turnkey projects and so have limited multipliers locally, which is why it is so imperative that African governments ensure that local content agreements are written into contracts.

## Donor responses

The whole 'emerging' donor debate implicitly and explicitly concerns whether and how 'established' donors can or should respond. As we saw, the debate was somewhat polarized between an extreme reaction that China is a threat to sustainable and democratic development cooperation and to one where China is doing nothing different. In between was recognition that China does do things somewhat differently and in this difference there is opportunity for learning and collaboration on delivery. We will explore these in more detail, first at the more discursive and general level and then in more focused empirical ways.

## At the aid regime level

As we saw, the Paris Declaration was about donor harmonization and the subsequent Accra Agenda noted reasonable but slow progress and a recognition of the role of non-DAC donors. But what is the substance of these moves? We have noted that China does do things somewhat differently but is also similar to the East Asian newly industrialized countries (NICs) in focusing on tied aid and infrastructural development. We also noted that some see China as a complement to other initiatives around growth and MDGs. It is this difference and complementarity that is at the heart of potential cooperation based on the 'comparative advantage' of each donor (GRIPS 2008). The start of this is dialogue with the Chinese which over the past five years or so has become one of the mainstays of the European donors, although Copson (2007) warns that dialogue is not the same as policy. Some calls seek to socialize China into the western aid paradigm by suggesting dialogue between China and the rest through existing forums. Again, it is a proposal which acknowledges that China needs to be brought into the fold of multilateral cooperation, but it cannot be forced to do so as this would risk alienating a lucrative market opportunity. That said Zhao (2007) sees China becoming more involved in multilateral institutions as signalled by developments such as the Olympics, membership of the WTO as well as international condemnation of and China's response to the Darfur situation. All this is presented as a part and parcel of China's ongoing 'responsible' and 'peaceful' ascendance on the world stage which we discuss in Chapter 8.

In keeping with this general thrust, the UK Government's response to China is based on 'constructive cooperation' over the MDGs and Africa (Benn 2004; Thomas 2005). A concern for the Department for International Development (DFID) is China's lack of experience in maximizing the 'effectiveness' of aid with Hilary Benn, the minister responsible for DFID at the time, arguing that effectiveness can only be through coordinated national programmes, the implicit corollary being that bilateral actions which undermine this are unwelcome. In recognition of this, Tony Blair invited Chinese representatives onto his Africa Commission. A DFID official Thomas (2005) urged China to use its 'soft power' and experience to enhance aid impact and that lessons could be learnt from China's different approach to aid. DFID also sees trade as a critical issue where China is well placed as a 'bridge' between developed and developing nations. More recently the Foreign and Commonwealth Office (2009) set out its programme of working with China in which the document:

> sets out ambitious aims and outcomes for co-operation with China across the board. And it shows that China's own sustainability and development are in our national interest as well. Two examples: China's decisions on its energy, transport and building infrastructure over the next five years will establish the path of its carbon emissions over the next thirty. And China's growing engagement with Africa has the potential to help African countries make real strides towards the Millennium Development Goals – China itself being one of the biggest global MDG success stories. (Milliband/FCO 2009: 4)

The new government of 2010 echoed this (Hawksley 2010) and stressed the need for partnership with the Chinese. An example of this in DRC is where DFID is working with the Chinese on a road construction project. The Chinese are providing the bulk of funding through a resource-backed loan and it is Chinese firms that undertake construction. The UK Government are funding a small part of the road construction but also working with the Chinese on HIV-AIDs prevention in which it feels it has greater expertise. Part of this collaboration and dialogue is around learning and here DFID have worked on projects in China through their now defunct aid programme. Begum (2010: 112–13) notes that 'China has showed considerable willingness to learn from innovative pilot projects from donors' and foresees the enlargement of 'space for south-south collaboration and lesson learning ... as developing countries look east towards China for more lessons'.

The EU's Consensus on Development (2005) sees development involving poverty eradication and sustainable development, both of which are enshrined in the MDGs. This document shapes much of the finer policy around Africa, China and aid effectiveness. Much of the discussion is about country ownership and partnership. Gone are ideas of aid recipients and instead, and in keeping with wider post-Structural Adjustment Programme debates, the emphasis is on respecting low-income country (LIC) sovereignty and allowing LICs to develop their own development strategies based on an appreciation of local context. This has interesting parallels with China's notion of 'non-interference' though coming from different ideological and practical experiences and honoured to varying degrees and in different ways. The EU sees its role as one of facilitating dialogue and ensuring coordination and complementarity in aid delivery based on its size, global presence and coherence. Again, this has some affinities with China's bilateralism and non-interference. It is these potential affinities that are at the heart of the EU, Africa and China trilateral dialogue (2008). The watchwords of this initiative are 'dialogue' and 'coordination' to see where overlaps and potential synergies exist in terms of promoting African development. The potential areas are agriculture, infrastructure, environment and security.

Such dialogue is likely to continue although the intention, if not always the practice, of initiatives like the EU trilateral cooperation is that African actors input into the policy process. This, then, is not just a dialogue between existing powers and rising ones but also with the supposed beneficiaries of aid. Some are sceptical of trilateral processes insofar as they can be a smokescreen for the most powerful axis of the 'triangle' using the apparent cooperation to push through its agenda, and even defray some of the costs in the process by encouraging the Chinese to pay for it (King 2010). The IPPR (Wild and Mepham 2006) concluded that solutions must be *by and for Africans*, although outsiders do have a legitimate concern with China's role on the continent. It remains to be seen how far this is borne out and the extent to which Africa once again becomes a canvas against which superpowers play out their strategies. Hopefully, the triangulation that African states have been able to achieve will continue but how far a real policy space is opened up by doing this remains to be seen.

However, most agree that some form of donor coordination is critical (de Haan 2010), that relationships should be more transparent, and that partner countries' needs should be more accurately reflected in policies (Davies 2010). Indeed, these are much the same as the original Paris Declaration goals. Deutscher (2010) of the DAC also sees the need for global stability and security as something which will drive cooperation between DAC and non-DAC donors and certainly China's recent exasperation with North Korea (November 2010) suggests that old ties may no longer be as strong or useful as they once were. We discuss the geopolitical implications in more detail in Chapter 8. The Chinese White Paper on Aid concedes that 'China has a long way to go in providing foreign aid. The Chinese government will make efforts to optimize the country's foreign aid structure, improve the quality of foreign aid, further increase recipient countries' capacity in independent development, and improve the pertinence and effectiveness of foreign aid' (Xinhua 2011a). Deustscher adds that a broader development agenda is required which means engaging with other policy areas and dealing with factors hitherto believed to be beyond the remit of 'development'. Importantly this means altering the architecture of development aid and we have seen recent moves to enlarge the role played by China in the IMF (Strauss-Kahn 2010).

## At the country level

These debates are pitched at the aid regime level even though they have implications for national donor processes. The harmonization agenda is clearly one which is brokered on a country-by-country basis and evidence suggests that the Chinese do not enter into multi-donor arrangements (Brautigam 2009; King 2010). A DFID official stated:

> No I think what's happening they (the Chinese) are willing to send observers, certainly not a full blown participant ... They (the Chinese) want to be very clear about if I join this, what am I expected to do, oh that's sounds a good idea we will join that, so I think they have been reluctant to join in that kind of way ... Our (DFID's) way is just to keep the door open, well to say, look do come along and see sort of thing.

In terms of donor harmonization Ghana has been a leading light, but has played a shrewd game of agreeing to donors' demands while also backsliding to fit in with domestic concerns (Whitfield and Jones 2007). In terms of donor harmonization invitations to become more involved in the Ghana Joint Assistance Strategy were rejected by the Chinese suggesting they are wary of throwing themselves in with the 17 'established' donors, although they often attended meetings as observers. One interpretation is that, as noted earlier, the Chinese do not see themselves as donors. One western aid official spoke rhetorically from a Chinese perspective:

> we are not a donor, we are a poor country so we can't really afford to give grants, on the other hand we want to trade and that would benefit everyone. So they don't seem to see themselves as donors and even though we have invited them to join in the donor harmonisation coordination groups, they don't seem interested.

At the same time, the Chinese officials were often frustrated during meetings with DAC officials, who they argued often start the conversation with 'let us set up some standards first and how much money could you contribute?!' For the Chinese, there is still much apprehension about these standards and reaching them. They are more concerned with the concrete outcome of aid projects, mostly involving infrastructural projects. Most importantly, there are no benefits to the Chinese in abiding by the OECD norms and standards, except to increase approval ratings from DAC counterparts.

Like Angola's recent return to the IMF it appears that the Government of Ghana has turned to the Chinese aid/investment packages – often uncritically in the case of the fibreoptic spine discussed earlier – when other avenues for commercial financing have been closed. As one aid official noted:

> a package of tied lending is only interesting when there is more limited access to the international market and I think that is why many African countries find this package interesting, because they don't have access to the markets.

The coming years are likely to see market access to finance even more limited and so China's leveraged option may well be much more appealing.

Senior aid officials were divided on whether the Chinese development banks, like ExIm, were a threat to the World Bank with some seeing them as complimentary by adding additional finance whereas others suggested they were capable of 'putting the World Bank out of business in Ghana'. In terms of World Bank projects Chinese contractors actually undertake 50 per cent of them and the World Bank has been exploring a memorandum of understanding with ExIm for joint funding of infrastructure although this appears to have stalled for the time being.

Since the turn of the millennium China's engagement with Ghana was through these focused projects, but in 2008 off shore oil was discovered. For a country dependent on oil imports and a massively over-stretched energy infrastructure this was great news. Production is estimated at 490 million barrels placing it in a similar league to Chad and Equatorial Guinea but well below Angola and Nigeria. New Gulf of Guinea reserves tend to deplete quickly with an estimated lifespan of around 25 years so it is a small window of opportunity for Ghana. The oil producers soon began arriving. Initially the discovery was through a UK–US consortium – Tullow and Kosmos – but before long a range of applicants was seeking drilling blocks. Importantly the Chinese SOE China National Offshore Oil Corporation has sought to purchase Kosmos for a reported $3 billion on the basis of its Ghanaian and Ugandan oil discoveries.

Estimates of revenue are difficult to determine due to untransparent contracts and uncertainties over the price of oil but the World Bank (2009b) calculates around $20billion over 20 years, peaking between 2011 and 2016. This was dealt a blow in late 2010 when reserve sizes were downgraded following further testing. The danger is that with a high budget deficit the government will be tempted to emulate what has been dubbed the 'Angola model' where the state collateralizes the oil in return for credit. Major multilaterals are urging the Government of Ghana to sort its underlying structural problems first rather than simply use the windfall rents to shore up budget deficits which will simply re-emerge once the boom ends. Additionally there are worries about a 'Dutch Disease' scenario where this resource export-ation discourages investment and taxation in non-oil sectors (Oxfam 2009). Agriculture is one of the key sectors likely to suffer under this scenario.

Importantly, with the discovery of oil Asian deals have stepped up in scale with a potential US$10 billion housing deal with Korea's STX Group being paid for with future oil revenues. The negotiations for this were untransparent and accusations circulated regarding corrup-tion. Moreover local realtors and building contractors have opposed the deal for the damage it will do to domestic firms since the Koreans would tie the finance to extensive use of Korean contractors. As yet the final signing of the contract has been postponed for 'technical reasons'. In mid-September 2010 the Chinese announced a US$15 billion fund for oil-related infrastructure development which was negotiated at the highest levels, with Ghana's President Atta-Mills eschewing a high level meeting in New York, about the future of aid, to stay on in Beijing for the signing ceremony (*The Independent* 2 October 2010). This signals the changing power balance in African development relations and the established donors in Ghana are already expressing concern about the transparency of these deals (Ghanaweb 27 September 2010).

The situation was similar in Angola where 'Efforts had been made to include them (the Chinese embassy) in on some projects, but they never receive any response' (fieldnotes) although a key difference as noted by the World Bank in Luanda is that:

all the Western donors all together probably represents 1% of the budget of the government budget, very different than in Mozambique for example, that 50% of the budget is financed by aid. Here is not aid now.

The implication of this is that the donor lobby is much weaker. However the established donors do see a need to collaborate with the Chinese with a virtuous link between 'harder' infrastructure projects and 'softer' institutional development. As one aid official in Luanda explained:

> the focus is to rebuild infrastructure and its based on the country that's borrowing the money wants to do, our approach is a bit different because we are looking at the reduction of poverty so we are looking in much more in terms of training and improving institutional capacity of the government, both are needed you need to have infrastructure but you also need to have other areas looked at.

They went on to say that this collaboration needs to be transparent 'as long as the credit lines are transparent and the projects are clear, I will have no problem. I think that the relationship with China can be very positive, they have lots of savings that they can lend to these countries, they have lots of technologies and lots of know how and they could help these countries, for me the principle point is how transparent these relationships are'.

## Conclusion

As a result of the increasing Chinese aid and engagement with African counterparts, a political outcome of the new aid landscape is that China's presence as an 'alternative' to Washington, and demonstrated amply by the Angola and Ghana cases, permits African leaders to 'triangulate' between donors. This 'fiscal triangulation', which is not simply a rejection of 'western' donors and their conditionalities, gave the Africans an option about who to turn to for investment and aid for the first time since the end of the Cold War. This, as a result, has carved out some room to manoeuvre. It is this leverage that the Chinese offer and the potential that resources could flow elsewhere that is really exorcizing western critics to sharpen their knives over China. But they gain no friends in Africa by repeating the patronizing message that Africans need saving from some venal power, when Africans are sorely aware of what venal powers have done, and continue to do, across the continent. Moreover, in welcoming the non-interference policy, African leaders were more willing to look to the Chinese model of successful economic development for guidance given that it is clearly massively successful and has not been forced upon African countries as a condition of aid.

As discussed above, Chinese modalities of aid in both Angola and Ghana are different in nature and definition from the OECD countries. Mainly tailored to the political and socio-economic conditions of the two countries, what we saw was more concessional loans in bricks and mortar projects in Angola and Ghana. The lack of transparency in credit lines and bidding procedures further complicate the situation. This non-interference policy reinforced the projected image that China is now 'non-ideological' and pragmatic, since its concerns are commercial or altruistic rather than transforming hearts and minds.

While preaching non-interference in domestic politics China's interventions have undoubtedly exacerbated existing political problems in some countries; either by design or by default. The Sudan case is pivotal for showing how China is changing in the management of international relations, and also for the ways that western donors are seeking to cooperate with China in finding solutions to African development. So, in contrast to the hawkish take on China a more conciliatory response to China assumes that China can be 'socialized' into the norms of the international aid business/community. Such critics contend that China's engagement with Africa should still be guided by Western values and should conform to established patterns of Western involvement on the continent (Wilson 2005), but rather than outright criticism they prefer a 'dialogic' approach (see Tjonneland et al. 2006). However, Beijing has no economic incentive to fall in line with Western views on issues such as fiscal transparency and accountability. 'By rejecting regulation efforts on the grounds of non-interference, China can position itself as a free-rider and is prone to win the political favour of, and by extension economic benefits from, sovereignty-conscious governments (e.g. Angola)' (Tull 2006: 474). Some critics thus challenge that international donors engage with governance in ways to fit their own specific mandates.

# 6
# Domestic Governance, Regime Stability and African Civil Society

## Introduction: governance dilemmas

As we have seen earlier, China's re-entry into Africa was greeted with much scepticism. Perhaps nothing exercized critics more than the potential impacts of China on African governance systems. This concern is captured by Paul Collier's warning about authoritarianism: 'the Chinese are making it worse, for they are none too sensitive when it comes to matters of governance' (Collier 2008: 86). In Chapter 5 we discussed the idea of 'rogue aid' and this chapter picks up on that not by looking at what critics *think* will happen to Africa's governance, which was often about seeking to present western aid in the best possible light, but by analysing what *actually happens*. This chapter is also distinct from Chapter 8 where we look at international politics and multilateral governance, though clearly the idea of discrete 'national' and 'international' spheres of governance is artificial and we will be examining the interacting scales of governance.

The 'mainstream' analyses of China's impact on governance include the following observations: they support corrupt regimes with aid and concessional loans (e.g. Zimbabwe), their business-orientation and non-interference *de facto* fails to sanction poor governance and/ or could exacerbate it, that while they formally support various good governance initiatives (e.g. the African Peer Review Mechanism) they do little in practical terms to honour them, they rarely undertake environmental assessments, and they undermine local labour standards. This tendency is seen by some as an extension of China's own lack of concern for human rights and accountability at home – the Chinese simply export the capitalism they know best (Alden 2007). A related line of argument around mineral-based development strategies is the resource curse thesis, which some have used to warn against further Chinese engagement. This tends to be a more subtle argument and is much more about the position of Africa in a global division of labour *per se* rather than being simply about the Chinese, though the Chinese are seen as the latest and most bullish actors in these 'extroverted' economic relationships.

The official Chinese response is complex and changing. One counter-critique, which we are very sympathetic to, is that the concern in the west for 'ethical' foreign policy is hypocritical. Too often a discourse of human rights is championed by the very powers that undermine them. The Chinese critique then restates the principle of non-interference as evidence of a 'respect' for African states and regimes and that good governance by its very nature implies the imposition of some normative standard of governance which denies the sovereignty that should be at the heart of any governance agenda. More recently the Chinese have become more involved in governance (e.g. Sudan) and the Forum on China-Africa Cooperation (FOCAC) 2009 had much more to say about these matters as we discussed in Chapter 3.

We will be examining the veracity of these claims in light of evidence from Ghana, Angola and other examples. Analytically what we have argued throughout the book is that we cannot read off an entire continent from one or two cases and so need a disaggregated approach. Crucially, for this chapter, this relies on a much deeper engagement with the nature of the state in Africa and of state–society relations. Arguably it also rests on understanding Chinese actors in more detail which we have already done in Chapters 1–3, particularly the changing relations between state and non-state actors and the discourses of development. We begin by examining debates around the African state and its relation to international capital. We then analyse the impacts of Chinese aid, trade and investment on African economies and how this is bound up in changes to governance. Part of this is also about the many small firms that are proliferating across Africa and how these are entwined with local social relations and forms of governance. We conclude by looking at popular and political responses to China.

## Making sense of the African state

We are not alone in arguing for a disaggregated analysis that deals with the nature of state–capital relations. Alden (2007) and Tull (2006) have both made similar calls. For example, Alden's political economy is based around regimes such that 'it is best to look at the nature of the individual African regimes in place and the underlying economy of particular countries' (p. 59). Alden sets out a broad typology of states (see also Tull 2006) – pariah states, illiberal regimes and weak democracies and democratic countries with diversified economies. This tendency to focus on regime types over states is a little problematic since 'it is the state – scaled at various levels – which sets and controls the parameters for regime formation in the first place' (MacLeod and Goodwin 1999: 508). Hence we need to focus on states rather than regimes. A state-based approach to political economy is echoed by Ian Taylor (2007b: 22) where he argues: 'Understanding how the state in Africa really functions and its attributes has critical implications for China's initiatives on the continent'. Taylor takes a more Weberian approach to the African state in looking at organizational structures and culture and, as a result, tends to see states' articulation with international capital in terms of how it impinges upon personalized rule.

Much of the 1970s Marxist theory on the peripheral state dealt with the question of the state's autonomy from international capital and its ability to engender autonomous national development (e.g. Alavi 1972; Leys 1996) and so remain relevant for our analysis of China in Africa. Hamza Alavi (1972) began these debates by using Poulantzas's ideas to analyse the state in Pakistan and Bangladesh. He argued that 'The essential problem about the state in post-colonial societies stems from the fact that it is not established by an ascendent native bourgeoisie but instead by a foreign imperialist bourgeoisie' (Alavi in Gouldbourne 1979: 41). In order to rule, this imperialist bourgeoisie 'over-developed' certain parts of the state which at independence was taken over by a domestic political elite to form what Alavi called the 'bureaucratic-military oligarchy'. From here radical Africanists tended to take Alavi's analysis and apply it to quite varied states across the continent. The limitations of this approach were soon realized:

> neo-Marxist theorists have too often sought to generalize – often in extremely abstract ways – about features and functions shared by all states within a mode of production, a phase of capitalist accumulation, or a position in the world capitalist system. (Skocpol 1985: 5)

Similarly, Jessop (1990: 44) argued,

> It is debateable whether it is possible to develop a theory of the capitalist state in general. For, since capitalism exists neither in pure form nor in isolation, states in capitalist societies will necessarily

differ from one another...(so that the aim is)...explaining how the different systems come to be articulated in a contingent, non-necessary manner which sustains capital accumulation.

At the root of the neo-Marxist analysis was a tendency to reduce the 'political' to a function of the dependent 'economic' despite the 'relative autonomy' of the overdeveloped state apparatus. It is important to realize that capital is fragmented so that state activity and politics cannot be homogenized by reducing it to the needs of a 'unitary' capital (Glassman 1999). Similarly, international capital is never completely 'external' since it combines with fragments of local capital. As Ferguson (2006) notes the internationalization of capital makes the relationships between capital and the state more complex, and breaks away from a rigid territorialization of the political and economic which assumes capital has a nationality. This fragmentation results in the disarticulation of the domestic capital owning classes so that the state fails to crystallize these class relations and become their ideological leader as it did in Europe. This counters Alavi's claims that state bureaucrats consciously thwart the indigenous bourgeoisie, because their power derives from their position as mediators in a purely dependent relation to international capital. The reality is that some 'economy' does exist within the country which the state presides over so that the state does not simply perform 'municipal' functions on behalf of international capital.

From a more developmentalist perspective the African state has increasingly been referred to in the negative – as failed or collapsed – which presupposes some norm of statehood against which these states are deemed to be lacking (Mbembe 2001). It also leads to programmatic solutions to 'build' or 'strengthen' the state by external agents, such as donors and international non-governmental organization (NGOs), as though only one trajectory of statehood is desirable or possible. While the Marxian position on the relationship between capital and the state determines certain structural possibilities for state autonomy they are less able to focus on some of the actual dynamics of state/society interactions and the enactment of politics. One attempt to do this was through the work of Bayart (1993) and others (Chabal and Daloz 1999) who argued that 'Africa works' through social networks comprised of particular forms of 'social capital'. The African state is seen as an external imposition and lacking in political purchase but things 'work' in spite of this. Yet this attempt to explain African politics through a societal lens tends to assert rather than demonstrate the existence of these networks and, crucially, downplays the importance of the state as a set of institutions with meaning and effect (Nugent 2010). Hence we also need some concepts capable of analysing African politics in non-normative ways and that show us how, in Nugent's words, 'institutions actually work' (p. 37).

Here the work of Hagmann and Peclard (2010) is instructive in seeking to 'understand how local, national and transnational actors forge and remake the state through processes of negotiation, contestation and bricolage' (p. 544). Their 'analytic of statehood' is about the dynamic and always undetermined, but not random, process of state (de)construction which is a multi-level phenomenon (Nugent 2010). Their heuristic framework comprises diverse actors, many of whom lie outside formal political structures and the resources and repertoires they deploy in shaping their political authority. Crucially resources not only enable political action but political action mediates the production and reproduction of social inequalities. The process of negotiation takes place in particular political spaces called 'arenas' which are simultaneously social, temporal and spatial and often hard to locate and delimit. More focused and formalized processes occur at 'negotiating tables' and there are iterative links between the wider 'arena' and these more formal spaces. This echoes Migdal's (1994: 15) 'anthropology of the state' which investigates 'different levels of the state, including the lowest rungs on the organizational hierarchy where direct engagement with society often occurs' and moves away from a totalizing analysis of the state towards a spatialized understanding of political praxis. Such politics is also historically conditioned, with previous rounds of negotiation or stabilization of a social contract shaping the playing field for subsequent negotiations. Doornbos (2010) rightly cautions against universalization of the idea of 'negotiation' because there are many instances in African politics of 'negation', something Nugent (2010) captures in his idea of the 'coercive social contract'. Despite this, the framework of Hagmann and Peclard (2010) is useful to help us capture the ever-changing balance of power in African polities among a plurality of actors often not deemed as relevant.

## China's channels of engagement with Africa

So far in this chapter we have argued for the need to disaggregate notions of Chinese capital and the African state in order to understand the fine-grained impacts on governance. In chapters 2, 3 and 5 we examined the bundling of Chinese aid, trade and investment. One way of disaggregating these relationships is through a framework developed as part of the wider Asian Drivers programme (e.g. Kaplinsky and Morris 2006; Kaplinsky 2008). We can distinguish different channels of impact transmission, the distinction between complementary and competitive impacts, and between direct and indirect impacts. These channels are contingent and change over time, and vary in significance depending on such things as location, resource endowment, trade links and geo-strategic significance.

In each of these channels of interaction, there will be a mixture of complementary and competitive impacts. For example, with regard to trade, China may both provide cheap inputs and consumer goods to sub-Saharan Africa and be a market for African exports. On the other hand, imports from China can displace local producers. In relation to foreign direct investment (FDI), China can be a direct source of inward FDI into sub-Saharan Africa and perhaps crowd-in FDI into Africa from third countries as parts of extended global value chains. These are complementary impacts. But China may also compete with other economies for global FDI. China and other rising powers in a western dominated global governance system may strengthen the voice of developing countries in international organizations as we discuss in Chapter 8. The emerging conflicts between China, the United States and Europe on energy, resources and markets might also marginalize development policy issues in world politics. Similarly, financial flows environmental spillovers and migration may be either complementary or competitive, which we discuss in this chapter and Chapter 7.

In terms of thinking through the developmental and political impacts the key aspect of these interactions is the 'for whom' component. Countries may be affected differentially – in some cases, for example, the export of fabrics from China to sub-Saharan Africa may feed productively into a vibrant clothing and textile value chain; in other cases, it may displace a country's exports and production for the domestic market. However, these effects are not just felt at the national and economy-wide level, but affect groups within countries differentially. For example, cheap clothing imports from China may displace clothing and textile workers, but cheapen wage goods and hence reduce wage costs for producers in other sectors. These impacts on a complementary–competitive axis may also change over time, and most importantly, they will vary for different classes, regions and groups within economies.

The complementary–competitive axis of impacts is generally quite well recognized and understood. What is less widely acknowledged is the distinction between direct and indirect impacts. In part this is because the indirect impacts are difficult to measure. Indirect impacts occur in third country markets and institutions. For example, China's trade with the United States may open or foreclose the opportunities for sub-Saharan African economies to export into that market. Similarly, China's high savings rate has had the effect of lowering global interest rates, indirectly facilitating investment in sub-Saharan Africa. As in the case of the complementary/competitive access, the effect of the direct and indirect impacts can be gauged either at the country level, or at intra-national levels, for example with regard to different regions, sectors, classes and genders. And in many cases the indirect impacts may in fact be much more significant than the direct ones.

As a heuristic it is also important to stress that these channels are clearly not discrete. For example, we will be looking at how Chinese migrants, as small-scale traders and investors in Africa, interact with the local state. Or in Chapter 7 we look at how Chinese aid-backed infrastructure projects built by major Chinese SOEs sometimes overlook internationally recognized environmental standards. One of the important differentiating factors across many of these channels is the scale and type of Chinese enterprise. While we talk about the bundling of aid, trade and investment – and much of the debate on China–Africa has focused exclusively on this – it largely relates to the ties between key Chinese ministries, development banks and large state-owned enterprises (SOEs). Although there is no typical package we may see the Ministry of Commerce (MOFCOM) and ExIm Bank agreeing on a concessional loan and using a Chinese SOE as the main contractor which procures inputs from China and may bring in significant parts of the labour force (Hubbard 2008). These are often spatially enclaved investments with relatively few multipliers in the local economy or 'deep' linkages to local society. By contrast we see Chinese private transnational corporations (TNCs) entering under 'open' commercial contracts such as in the IT sector, where they lack any of the protection afforded by the tying of loans to investment. And finally there are the myriad small Chinese private firms that date back, in some cases, to the colonial period. These range from one-person 'suitcase multinationals' to quite large conglomerates with stakes in multiple sectors such as construction, catering and manufacturing (Michel et al. 2009). Each type of firm has different levels of engagement with local capital, the state and society and we will explore these differences through our case studies. Moreover, we also need to distinguish between 'Chinese' firms in the sense of whether they originate from Taiwan, Hong Kong,

Macau or the mainland, or as we shall see complex networks straddling more than one of these territories.

## The politics of hybridity and extroversion

In Chapter 3 we examined the continental and national level economic impacts and touched briefly upon the different forms of enterprise and the social relationships bound up in them. But what of the effects on the political process in Africa? This is necessarily complex and the data is often hard to confirm given the clandestine nature of many of these processes. In the introduction we touched upon how we might combine postcolonial theory with political economy. The former has argued for recognizing the complex intermingling of the subjectivities of colonizer and colonized so that we do not reduce the colonial relationship to one of singular, external domination. In the case that follows of Chinese involvement in Angola we see a much more complex and shifting institutional arrangement which both works within the state but also exceeds it in important ways.

In the previous chapter we outlined the loans made to Angola over the past decade or so. In spite of the growing magnitude of China's projects in Angola very little is known about them and many of the details remain shrouded in secrecy. As a result there have been many myths and popular misconceptions about the terms of cooperation. In many ways this is because both governments have largely conducted their bilateral cooperation in the form of a 'narrow elite business dialogue' (Campos and Vines 2008: 15; Carmody 2011). Assessing the impact of China's 'foreign assistance' projects in Angola is further complicated by the 'bundling' or aggregation of this 'assistance' together with direct foreign investments from the approved Chinese companies. Thus oil-backed loans and credits are intertwined with massive investments by state-led enterprises such as the China International Trust and Investment Corporation (CITIC), the China Road and Bridge Corporation (CRBC) and the privately owned China International Fund (CIF). This is not 'aid' in any conventional sense therefore. In many cases it is unclear how money has been spent in the projects that have resulted from bilateral cooperation as the funds are often tracked so far off the books that they do not appear in any budgets while the bidding process for the lucrative contracts themselves has also often been rather opaque.

Indeed opacity is one of the defining characteristics of China–Angola cooperation so far leading to some decidedly tangled webs. There is a great deal of opacity around the CIF and its relations to the Gabinete de Reconstrução Nacional (Office for National Reconstruction) (GRN) for example and the World Bank has estimated that some $8 billion of CIF loans to Angola have not been made public while there have also been repeated allegations about the misappropriation of GRN funds. There are also companies like Sonangol Sinopec International (SSI) a joint venture between Sinopec (China's state-owned oil company) and China Sonangol International Holding (CSIH) itself a joint venture between Sonangol (Angola's state-owned oil company and the centre of power in contemporary Angola) and Hong Kong-based private business interests (Vines et al. 2009). Thus in several cases a rather opaque clique of interests lies at the heart of this 'partnership' dominated by informal and personal relations between Chinese and Angolan investors that have proven difficult to trace and document.

The Angola case points to this particular 'China–Africa' relationship being organized through inter-elite brokerage and an insulation of the state from popular forces. Indeed the CIF-GRN could be seen as a hybrid assemblage that sits within the state apparatus but is only connected to selected and clandestine elements within the state, which bears out some of the 'network' type analysis of Bayart et al. that we discussed earlier in this chapter. It also supports Ferguson's idea of an enclave insofar as these assemblages are not connected to wider society or subject to public scrutiny within Angola. Such relationships only strengthen authoritarian and patrimonial modes of governance in Africa by cementing the position of strategically placed elites within and around the state. However, these high-level and inter-state relationships are only one part of the picture and many Chinese people, financial and commodity flows and social relations are by their very nature far less state-driven or enclavic, something we analyse in the next section on Chinese migrants.

The 'Angola-mode' of resource-for-equity swaps is often hailed as *the* paradigm for Chinese engagement with African states. But like so much analysis of China and Africa it is generally the Chinese that are seen to hold the authority in the relationship. But looking comparatively across states we get a different picture of African agency. Vines et al.'s (2009) study of Asian investment in Angolan and Nigerian oil shows how the Chinese attempted an 'Angola mode' relationship with Nigeria but that due to internal political dynamics of the Nigerian state the success of the arrangement for both sides was less smooth. In keeping with our approach Vines et al. (2009: vii) argue that 'Neither Nigeria nor Angola fits into the stereotype of weak African states being ruthlessly exploited by resource-hungry Asian tigers'. Angola's state structures – like the GRN – and President Dos Santos' leadership combined to see successful oil exploitation by China to the exclusion of other Asian countries. The Chinese combined business and diplomacy through hybrid institutions like the CIF to produce a series of successful joint ventures with Angolan oil companies that extended through the infra-structure deals into housing, road building and the like. By contrast Nigerian oil politics is much deeper and older, with the state-owned Nigerian National Petroleum Corporation treated as a cash cow for political elites. The period around 2007 when Chinese and other Asian interests in Nigeria oil stepped up a gear coincided with the transition of power away from President Obasanjo and so there was a fluid and contested political arena which meant that many of the agreements entered into with the Chinese were not enforced. As a result China's entry into the Nigerian oil economy was disrupted though remains at high levels.

The fragmented, weak and sometimes chaotic nature of many African states also has implications for the regulation of inward investments, though arguably this is not just an issue for Chinese investors or donors. While statutes and regulatory bodies relevant to inward invest-ment – such as immigration, labour, health and safety, and environ-mental protection – usually exist in some form within African states the willingness and ability to monitor and enforce legal codes is frequently poor. Given that the Chinese allegedly have a cavalier attitude to labour rights and environmental protection one could foresee a mutually reinforcing spiral of institutional undercutting in an attempt to gain access to African resources. Data is limited and we discuss this in more detail later in this chapter and the next, but the process of consultation and planning around the Bui Dam in Ghana, which we discussed in the last chapter, showed both obedience in some areas and non-compliance in others (Hensengerth 2011).

The Bui Dam had a long genesis and in the process a feasibility study and environmental impact assessment (EIA) were undertaken not long before the Chinese showed a willingness to fund and build it (Figure 6.1). Securing the right to proceed with construction requires, under Ghanaian law, various permits and consultations to take place. In terms of the environmental permits one respondent in Hensengerth's research commented: 'the government sometimes jumps steps... For Bui, the river had already begun to be diverted when the Bui Power Authority applied for the Diversion Permit' (2011: 15). The EIA process also stipulates a consultation with affected citizens but these hearings took place in Accra or other towns, a long and expensive journey from these largely impoverished rural communities around the dam site, and relied on a

*Figure 6.1*   Chinese and Ghanaian workers, The Bui Dam, Ghana. Photograph by authors

narrow set of representatives from local government and other statutory bodies rather than direct representation from the communities. When it came to the resettlement itself Sinohydro have not been involved at all reflecting their Engineering, Procurement and Construction (EPC) contract, and construction of the 'temporary' villages was undertaken by Ghanaian contractors. This process suggests that where the African state is determined to see a project realized then regulatory short cuts can be taken. While not confined to Chinese investments these large, elite brokered turnkey projects are likely to encourage this flouting of due process in favour of the Chinese; something we discuss shortly with regard to labour.

Comparing across states reveals neither a monolithic Chinese state nor powerless African states. Rather we see a flexible and hybrid engagement between a range of actors and institutions in pursuit of resource access. Carmody and Taylor (2010) term this 'flexigemony' whereby 'Chinese actors adapt their strategies to suit particular histories and geographies of the African states with which they engage' (Carmody and Taylor 2010: 497). These strategies are essentially between elites and utilize not just 'soft power' in the form of aid but also hard power in terms of military spending and arguably hard economic power in terms of the business-oriented bundling of aid which we discussed in the last chapter. Some (Jacques 2009) have likened this strategy to the historical tribute system that characterized the Chinese Empire in times gone by and hypothesize whether future international relations – driven by China – might be neo-tributary in nature.

## Beyond elites: migration, social relations and micro-politics

In Chapter 2 we mentioned that Chinese migrants were an important part of China's engagement with and impact on Africa over a considerable period of time. In chapters 3 and 5 we focused on the inter-state politics of aid diplomacy which have been one of the key foci for analysis of China–Africa relations. Yet the more recent engagements have also involved large-scale migration and Alden (2007: 128) is right to note that 'the behaviour of thousands of newly settled Chinese businessmen and the conduct of the African communities in which they live and work will matter as much as the diplomacy and concessions made at the government level'. This forces us to look at social interactions and their micro-politics. In many cases these micro-politics – questions of identities, networks and relationships – are bound up in more formal political structures and processes as we suggested in our framework for looking at the African state. In this section we want to map out some of these migrant organizations as a way of examining their political effects in Africa.

## Multiple flows and communities

Key to understanding the dynamics of these migrants and their relationships with African societies is an appreciation that they are multiple
and differentiated, with three distinct groups. The first are temporary
labour migrants usually associated with large infrastructure projects.
Official Chinese figures put this number at around 80000 (Mung 2008)
working in an estimated 800 Chinese 'state-influenced' companies
across Africa (CCS 2007). These projects are quite bounded with Chinese
personnel living in compounds and having little contact with African
communities (Corkin 2008b). They are run by Chinese expatriates on
fixed term contracts who return home after a few years. A World Bank
study (Broadman 2007) found that 93 per cent of Chinese-owned firms
were run by Chinese nationals.

The second group is petty entrepreneurs who largely operate in trade,
services and light manufacturing (Haugen and Carling 2005) and lack
any government backing (Ho 2008). From the start Chinese traders
have been involved in cheap consumer goods, what are called in Kenya
'down street' merchandise rather than 'up market' products producing
in Nigeria what Ogunsanwo reports as 'illegal Chinatowns' (2008: 202).
They are welcomed due to the low-cost commodities they bring, but
as we shall see have excited tensions among trade unions and business associations due to displacing local manufacturers and traders.
These traders' flexible use of networks helps explain their ability to
out-compete African firms (Brautigam 2003). Part of this flexibility has
seen strategies of geographical movement, expansion or diversification
(Haugen and Carling 2005). Moreover some of the smaller manufacturing firms recruit low-wage Chinese labour through agencies (Wong
2006) who are in direct competition with unskilled Africans, which
coupled with poor conditions have led to disputes in Zambia (Fraser
and Lungu 2007), South Africa and Mauritius (Wong 2006). Third are
undocumented migrants that purposefully evade state surveillance. An
unknown number of illegal sojourners use African states as 'soft' locations where they can break their journeys on a quest to enter North
America or Europe (Mung 2008). As such they may take up petty trading
to remain solvent as opposed to a longer-term strategy of becoming
embedded in African economies (Figure 6.2).

In all cases the motivation is primarily economic though in some
cases bound up with discourses and expectations of wider modernity
and nationalism (Nyiri 2006). Most of our respondents in Ghana and
Angola saw a period in Africa as more lucrative than staying in China,

*Figure 6.2* Chinese medicine distributors, Accra, Ghana. Photograph by authors

but some also reflected on a broader 'mission' of bringing development to Africa even if, as we shall see, this was often couched in quite patronizing and hierarchical terms. These two factors – motivations and type of migrant – also played into different types of business organization and a disposition towards mobility. Park (2009) notes that at minimum Chinese migrants can be categorized into two groups: sojourners and transnationals. The former are intentionally and avowedly 'temporary' and see Africa as a short-term opportunity to make money but ultimately to return 'successful' to China. By contrast, and this is not simply a factor of longevity, some are much more transnationally oriented. They organize their business across multiple territories, have family in various international localities, shuttle between sites, and have no firm plans to settle back in China. A further distinguishing feature that Nyiri (2009) notes is that Chinese private enterprises work through and require local patrons. These can be to navigate hostile host societies and access contracts, but can also be a more formal requirement of investment codes that require a local partner. Our research showed that these more legal patrons were often frustrating for the Chinese entrepreneurs as they were effectively 'silent' and failed to deliver benefits to the business.

These traders seem to use limited African labour, except for menial tasks such as waiting, cleaning and security. A lack of trust – or more often a racist proxy – is usually cited as the reason for employing Chinese labour over Africans. In our interviews we heard cultural assumptions about 'blacks', which made them unsuitable for higher level roles. Many felt that Chinese productivity was too intense – 'Our tempo is too fast for the local people'. We were told by different businessmen that one problem with Ghanaian productivity was 'too much culture' insofar as Ghanaians, it was argued, were forever disappearing for funerals or clan events and so could not be relied on. Poverty was also seen to undermine the ability of African employees to plan ahead with the result that the Chinese businessmen saw them as money grabbing and untrustworthy – 'They don't care about tomorrow'. This was exacerbated by poor infrastructure such as regular power failures and a lack of public transport so that they could not operate shift systems as they would in China. A study of Chinese internet sites discussing Africa (Shen 2009) echoes this where Africans are discussed in terms of laziness, lasciviousness and immorality.

Arising out of diversification strategies and partly as a legacy of the cold war aid programmes Chinese migrants are also involved in a range of services: mainly restaurants and medicine. Catering has partly grown out of retailing, but also to service the growing Chinese populations in Africa's capital cities and resource frontiers. Our research showed how traders had diversified into manufacturing. Contrary to the popular story that early migrants in the 1950s and 1960s were aid workers who stayed on in Ghana a number came at the country's independence lured by the promise of a stable and soon to flourish economy. In some cases the factory owners set up the factories and then brought in managers from Hong Kong while they moved on to start other ventures. Our interviews also revealed a number of Chinese employees who came over with Taiwanese firms in the 1980s and 1990s and who set up their own businesses once they were au fait with the local economy and/or the original company failed.

Many businesses were looking to reinvest in Ghana as opposed to the usual depiction of the Chinese as simply remitting profits and undermining African growth. Remittance levels varied depending on the stage in the life course and wealth of the family back home. For temporary migrants working on state-backed projects wages were paid directly to their bank accounts in China and they only received petty cash for out of hand expenses. Many of the private businesses were run by middle-class graduates who did not need to support family, although clearly married men travelling alone did send money to wives and children. All respondents saw Africa as an opportunity. For the SOE workers overseas wages were 2–3 times those in China plus there was nothing to spend money on locally. For private businessmen they saw Africa as a real opportunity, especially as the financial crisis was seen to have hit China hard. One respondent noted of Angola: 'This place is like China, very undeveloped in the past but now is the time ... It is always the first pot that is most profitable'. Some did acknowledge that the civil war meant the country was in need of infrastructure and commodities. A Chinese businessman told us in an interview we conducted in Ghana, 'I don't think I will be able to make more money in China than I can do here. The conditions in China are getting quite bad, and will be worse with this world crisis. I will stay overseas and support my family until my son has graduated. Wow, that's like another 15 years (sigh)'. The implications are that migration to the developing world may increase with some countries of Africa and Latin America acting as a vent for domestic underemployment.

For these smaller private entrepreneurs, who lack formal state backing, it is important to analyse what role existing diasporic communities play in enabling integration into African society and how they are organized to facilitate connection back to China. In general, recent Chinese migrants in Ghana remain relatively self-contained and are unconnected to the Chinese embassy or state projects, which questions the 'China Inc.' and 'Beijing Consensus' representations. Ho (2008) shows in the case of Ghana that formal organization is generally less important than informal sociality. We were told that while karaoke rooms in the restaurant were a bit unstylish they were the only form of sociality to be had. The theme of 'boredom' came through time and again, with the sense that 'there is nothing to do here'. This was used to explain the tendency to socialize with other Chinese, and belies a lack of integration with local society. However, in Angola a number did say that 'the Chinese are hated' and they saw thieving and rudeness towards them as signs of their unpopularity, which in turn was used to explain their own lack of engagement with Angolans.

However, there is also evidence of divisions within the 'Chinese' community in Ghana. Ho argues that 'their social bonds are loose and uneasy and that their idea of belonging to a place and group is fluid' (ibid.: 53). He shows how suspicion and distrust mark the business relationships between the Chinese, built upon a sense of transitioning and moving on, yet Chinese-ness may be evoked at certain times. Dobler (2008: 247) also argues that the 'Chinese who are living in Oshikango are no homogenous, close-knit community' and have not cooperated among themselves. Yet he speaks of the 'intensification' of social life among the Chinese as more traders arrive and socialization begins to increase, possibly leading to a more unified sense of diasporic community.

## Identity politics, political engagement and shadowy ties

These migrants are not overtly 'political' but their presence and their practices do have political implications. Here we will examine how Chinese businesses engage with the African state formally and informally, which relates to questions of identity, otherness, citizenship and patronage. Zetter et al. (2006) argue that for migrants what appears as inherent social capital may be a survival strategy in a hostile society, which urges us to study the geographical contexts and 'relationality' of identity formation (Gilroy 1987). For example, for the Chinese in Apartheid South Africa racial categorization meant they were encouraged to hold onto a sense of Chinese-ness (Park 2006) and they do have a diasporan identity (Wilhelm 2006), which urges a deeper understanding of how state policy of both sending and receiving states affects migrants' identity and mobilization.

Since the early 1980s the PRC governments have been keen to attract the wealth of the Chinese diaspora (Young and Shih 2003) through laws and less direct appeals to the cultural affinities of migrants. This is a development strategy found in other developing countries (Levitt and de la Dehesa 2003), but has been especially successful in the case of China where as much as 70 per cent of China's foreign direct investment, a major motor of economic growth over the last two decades, has come from overseas Chinese. This inflow of diasporic investment into Southern China has, in part, spurred that region's economic growth which further attracts migrants from impoverished parts of China.

## Integration/separation

During the colonial period Chinese migrants to Africa were usually met with hostility, if not outright racism, which sometimes generated their sense of togetherness as opposed to any innate Chinese identity (Park 2006; Wilhelm 2006). Indeed the Chinese, as the derogatory phrase 'Jews of the East' suggested, were treated as outsiders and often scapegoated as the reasons behind a society's ills, be it crime or drugs.

However, despite this ambivalent identification, Chinese communities in Africa have generally remained relatively self-contained. One important upshot of this for integration and business more generally is that language and communication has been and remains a problem. Very few recent migrants speak any local languages and have rudimentary English or Portuguese at best. Some innovative solutions to this are emerging such as Chinese translators in Sierra Leone giving themselves English names to ease communication with Africans and Europeans (Hilsum 2006) and in Angola firms recruiting from the former Portuguese colony Macau to ease language barriers.

Alongside the family and clan as important institutions of diaspora are more formal organizations which serve to cement and connect disparate communities (McKeown 1999). These organizations have, at times, played a political role. For example, during the early twentieth-century in South Africa the Chinese community lobbied hard to oppose restrictive citizenship laws and even up to the post-Apartheid period the Chinese Association of South Africa has made deputations to Parliament to secure employment equity (Wilhelm 2006). There has also been a long history of Chinese Chambers of Commerce and business associations, with the one in Mauritius forming in 1908 (Brautigam 2003). Indeed it was the Chinese entrepreneurs in Mauritius that helped persuade the government to establish an export processing zone, and then travelled to Asia, inviting co-ethnics from Taiwan, Hong Kong and Malaysia to join them in joint ventures.

The Taiwanese in South Africa are also well organized and have entered formal politics with a number of MPs (Wilhelm 2006: 356). Given that this is a well-established community it may serve as a template for the gradual involvement of a migrant community in national politics. Politically, there may be parallels with other 'ethnic' merchant classes such as the Indians in East Africa and the Lebanese in West Africa. On the face of it these merchants may be less interested in domestic political issues so long as they can accumulate wealth. This could be attractive to authoritarian African regimes (Lee 2007), because their sojourner status means they are less likely to press for openly democratic changes. However, studies such as those by Reno (1995) of Sierra Leone suggest politics will be organized via a 'shadow state' which ties ethnic entrepreneurs into circuits of state power. For example, it appears that elements in the Chinese community in Sudan are 'attempting to penetrate Sudanese society and be able to influence the course of things' (Large 2008b), though details are not surprisingly sparse (see Askouri 2007: 73).

## Popular responses and civil society reactions

Like so much China–Africa reporting, one case is often used to represent the entire relationship. One such example was the election campaign of Michael Sata in Zambia in the 2006 Presidential elections and 2008 Presidential by-elections. Here the Patriotic Front led by Mr Sata played the anti-China card to win votes in Lusaka and the Copperbelt. The campaign whipped up popular resentment that had been stirred by industrial accidents and plant closures on the back of Chinese imports. It also depicted the Chinese as taking over other sectors of the economy. Guy Scott, a former agriculture minister and the Patriotic Front leader in parliament, said 'If you go to the market, you find Chinese selling cabbages and beansprouts. What is the point in letting them in to do that? There's a lot of Chinese here doing construction. Zambians can do that. The Chinese building firms are undercutting the local firms. Our textile factories can't compete with cheap Chinese imports subsidized by a foreign government. People are saying: "We've had bad people before. The whites were bad, the Indians were worse, but the Chinese are worst of all"' (quoted in McGreal 2007). While the Patriotic Front had some success, the overall campaign was unsuccessful, but it may signal the shape of things to come should these tensions grow.

The government of the time were critical of Sata's 'racism', but they clearly had a vested interest in maintaining good relations with the Chinese state and investors, although in reality there were genuine concerns about losing out to the Chinese, though not as extreme as Sata's propaganda would suggest. In another newspaper piece about Sata's subsequent campaign in the Presidential elections people in the street talked to the journalist about the Chinese as the backdrop to how the Patriotic Front were championing a 'pro-poor Zambians' ticket. In an impoverished part of Lusaka one respondent (in Berger 2008) said of the Chinese 'They are like the British and the Americans, they come, they steal and they go. We can't share these resources'. Others were critical of the importation of relatively unskilled labour by the Chinese: 'You can't have somebody coming to lift a brick to build a house, we need experts, we need proper collaboration and partnership in this country'. Both quotes suggest a sense of how the Chinese are both similar to other 'imperialists' but also different in usurping low-skilled labour, what we referred to in the introduction as 'national self-exploitation'. These concerns are repeated across Africa and begin to tell us something about the ethnic, class and political dynamics of China's engagement with African economies.

According to one scholar 'Among ordinary people, a very strong resentment, bordering on racism, is emerging against the Chinese...It's because the Chinese are seen as backing the [African] governments in oppressing their own people' (Melber in Trofimov 2007). This adds a complexity to the debate by seeing African states as complicit in aiding Chinese 'exploitation'. It also begins to point to a more differentiated understanding of this resentment as conditioned by economic and political factors that affect the level of exploitation and its effects. The levels of opposition to the Chinese are shaped by the degree to which they expropriate resources – however defined – and the extent to which the local state and domestic political elites fail to regulate or sanction such activity. Put crudely where exploitation is perceived to be greatest we are more likely to see opposition. As Gong (2007) notes, given the involvement of Chinese SOEs in extractive industries and with the backing of the Chinese state it is these groups that have become the targets for more violent and criminalized animosity among Africans, such as attacks on oil facilities in Ethiopia and kidnappings of oil workers in southern Nigeria (Powell 2007). However, in some of these cases – notably the Niger Delta – kidnapping is endemic and part of a wider political economy of ethnic, petropolitics (see Watts 2003) so that it is issues of inequality and exploitation *per se* which are key rather than an explicitly ethnicized anti-Chinese motivation.

But the talk of exploitation skews the debate towards cases where tensions are greatest and is not an accurate reflection of how China is perceived by 'ordinary' Africans. Although our knowledge base is still thin there are a few attitude surveys, which suggest a much more positive feeling towards the arrival of Chinese (Ngome 2009; Sautman and Hairong 2009), although as with any survey data we cannot straightforwardly rely on the veracity of these attitudes or easily explain how they relate to actual processes of engagement. While Ngome (2007) extracts some quotes very similar to those surrounding Sata in Zambia, such as the Chinese taking jobs and being comparable to former colonialists, his general survey results show a high approval rate towards the Chinese. Although 70 per cent of respondents were concerned about the growing number of Chinese, 81 per cent welcomed Chinese products, 92 per cent felt the Chinese helped Cameroon's economy in some way, and 79 per cent recommended relations between China and Cameroon should continue though not without some conditions. Sautman and Hairong's (2009) survey across nine countries was among university students and faculty so does not reflect a cross-section of Africans. In general respondents were positive about the role that Chinese small businesses played, felt that the Chinese model of development is a good one and are impressed by the work ethic of Chinese migrants. In tying back to the Zambia case they argue that patterns of attitudes are similar across Africa, but where more negative sentiments have been expressed it is the politicization of the issue by political leaders that explain the differences.

The results of these suggest various forces at work. On the one hand we have the politicization of the relationship for domestic political advantage. In turn these reflect some genuine concerns about the extent to which China's engagement with Africa will benefit ordinary Africans, though these concerns are not in general decisive except in a few localized cases. Further, for most Africans China's presence is relatively unexceptional and relationships – whether face-to-face or mediated by the commodities they trade – are simply part of Africa's ensuing engagement with globalization and modernity. These are much more everyday exchanges than the vitriolic and confrontational politics whipped up by the likes of Sata and jumped upon by some sections of the western media.

These everyday exchanges are at the level of what Gilroy (2004) terms 'convivial culture', the everyday minutiae of living together through which much integration occurs. Amit (2002) argues that it is through such localized practices that 'community' is created as opposed to some ascribed similarities that migrants might share. That said, like any cultural contact, we see interesting hybridization where Chinese cultural practices are adopted and adapted by Africans. Hsu (2007) provides an interesting example of this in the case of noodle production on Zanzibar. Originally produced for the local Chinese community in the 1950s they started to become popular with locals through the restaurants on the island. Over time they have become a staple of Ramadan feasting at the same time as diasporic Chinese have shunned them for not tasting good enough, being 'unhygienic' and inauthentic. However, a couple of Chinese firms produce for this growing African demand, employing a local workforce. Sylvanus (2007) also discusses how 'African' cloths, once produced in Holland, are now copied by Chinese factories at cheaper costs. Set against this conviviality are growing tensions among Africans, some of which are built on stereotypes and prejudice, although they conceal genuine economic concerns (Sylvanus 2007). In some senses this is a convenient way to explain the success of the Chinese, rather than face the fact that their business networks and contacts with Chinese manufacturers have helped them succeed.

## Civil society responses

In this section we will examine responses from civil society contrasting the normative with the actual. We start with a few points about the debates around African civil society in general regarding its potential, abuse and limitations. Then we will look at the normative case for the role of African civil society in debating and shaping China's engagement before looking at actual civil society action.

Civil society emerged as the key arena for various governance initiatives in the 1990s. The recent emphasis on civil society as a motor for development has, paradoxically, seen a convergence between the neoliberals who champion freedom of choice and the 'new' left uniting around a post-Marxist critique (Mohan and Stokke 2000). While debate exists over the meaning of civil society, it is generally held to occupy the political space between the state and the household (McIlwaine 1998). The mainstream liberal discourse on civil society and development argues that civil society is not only distinct from the state, but confronts the state and is comprised of associations whose interests are primarily non-economic. Leading from this civil society is seen as being at the heart of the democratization struggle.

We have argued elsewhere (Mohan 2002) that any analysis of civil society in Africa must situate African countries within the global capitalist economy and the ways in which this structures state–society intersections. Additionally it is not simply a case of states dominating and civil society resisting, but a more subtle interplay of power through which subjects are incorporated into structures of rule (Mamdani 1996). We need to see civil society as constituted across local, national and international territories. If we accept that state and society are not separate spheres we must examine the shifting processes of rule operating in the interstices between them. This means focusing on the ways in which political actors mobilize discourses of civil society, locality and the state and utilize organizations for political gain. It also involves examining the way in which the state manipulates civil society and the relationships at a micro-level between state and civil society organizations.

Obiorah (2007) argues that China provides a powerful development model which urges economic growth before human rights, which has a number of possible effects on African development debates. First, African leaders can use this model to deny political rights to their people and rebuff efforts at building good governance and promoting democracy. Second, China exports its model via growth-oriented aid and overlooks the social impacts of its actions under the banner of non-interference.

Ultimately this can entrench authoritarian leaders so Obiorah feels it is the duty of African civil society to debate and discuss China's role, because rentier regimes will not engender such debate. If African countries are to avoid another (or deeper) resource curse, the benefits must be distributed by a democratic developmental state. This is echoed by some European policy debates which support this encouragement of civil society organizations to lead the critique and debate around African countries' (and by implication China's) development model (Tjønneland et al. 2006; Wild and Mepham 2006). But championing civil society has been on the donor agenda for twenty years without much success and civil society is not a homogenous realm unilaterally acting in the good of poor Africans. The conundrum is that it is not in the interests of either the Chinese or rentier elites to transform the African state.

In practice African civil society responses to China's activities have been relatively mute. That said, a number of Africa trade unions and business associations have led the critique of China's role in national economies. For example, the South African TUC was one of the first to recognize the threat and organized debates around the future of African clothing and textile industries (Amankwah 2005). More recently a pan-African trade union project (Baah and Jauch 2009) has identified some common traits across Chinese firms in Africa and suggested potential areas where African trade unions could be more active. The common traits that Baah and Jauch (2009) identify are an absence of contracts and a casualization of labour (see also Lee 2009). In turn this is linked to the arbitrary determination of wages and benefits, with wages in Chinese firms lower than many locally owned firms and other foreign firms. However, their research shows that where trade unions are relatively strong and have been active then wage rates are better and they cite Nigeria as an example. On top of poor wages there are only the most basic benefits and for these to be provided they have to be enshrined in local law. So, in general, there are basic holiday allowances and the like, but no insurance, pension or health care provision. Moreover there were cases where Chinese firms ignored local legislation and violated many rights, most notably the enforcement of over time and very weak health and safety provisions. Unilaterally trade unions are not welcomed by Chinese firms and on the flip side many African workers doubted the ability of their respective unions to represent and defend them.

These general trends are well demonstrated in the case of Zambia. We have seen that Chinese investment in Africa has largely been in resource extraction and infrastructure projects. In Zambia the Chinese

SOE Non-Ferrous Company-Africa (NFCA) owned the Chambishi Mine in the Copperbelt. As an SOE they project the image of a single entity but within the zone there is also Sino-Metals and Beijing General Research Institute of Mining and Metallurgy (BGRIMM) which ran an explosive factory making dynamite for the neighbouring mine. In 2005 there was an explosion at the BGRIMM plant which killed 52 Zambians yet no Chinese workers were harmed. A strike in 2006 also resulted in the death of two protestors shot by unknown security personnel. In the aftermath of the debacle a damning report by the Civil Society Trade Network of Zambia (Fraser and Lungu 2007) openly accused Chinese firms of malfeasance and urged the Zambian government and mining firms to develop and enforce better standards.

Lee's (2009) comparative study of Chambishi and the Urafiki textile plant in Tanzania is instructive in how we understand Chinese work practices and the power of organized African labour. Like Baah and Jauch (2009) Lee (2009) focuses on the casualization of labour as a feature of neo-liberalism and how this is allied to the 'shallow' social inks of the enclave model (Ferguson 2006). Lee's (2009) study of the Chambishi incident suggests that the official unions were relatively corrupt and colluded with the Zambian government in favour of the Chinese investors. In both case studies the strikes had not been instigated by the union. A quote from one of Lee's interviewees regarding the Zambian strikes shows how useless the official union was seen to be:

> We started the strike right away. The corrupt union [Mine Workers Union of Zambia] was able to convince us to go back to work and I guessed they were just bought off by the management (p. 660)

Despite this cynicism the union-backed negotiations did get better terms and conditions with the Chinese firm. This was in contrast to the case in Tanzania where the union was much more corporatist and less confrontational. In the case of the Urafiki textile factory there were strikes but each one led to greater demoralization and a lack of concessions by the Chinese parent firm. Again, there was a perception that the Tanzanian government favoured the Chinese investors over internal pressures:

> The Prime Minister is backing the Chinese so they dare to ignore us because they know the government is supporting them...No party dares to declare itself anti-Chinese because they are big investors (p. 662)

This comparative study backs up Baah and Jauch's (2009) point about the power of organized labour, especially the importance of different forms of working-class history and struggle. And in the case of Zambian copper the world price is listed publicly on the London Metals Exchange which makes it easier to get a sense of the rate of profit compared to wage levels. By contrast the profit rates for textile products are harder to determine.

We have noted that Chinese labour has been a part of African economies for many years, but with Chinese reforms labour recruitment by private firms has increased and we see labourers coming to countries like Namibia, Mauritius and South Africa where they compete with African workers. The working and pay conditions in these Chinese factories are poor which prompted worker protests (2002, 2005) in Mauritius by contract labourers (Wong 2006). A China International Contractors Association (CHINCA 2005) report disclosed that a total of 20 disputes involving more than 2500 workers have occurred between Chinese workers and management in Mauritius. While displaying limited solidarity with African workers or trade unions the flexibility, efficiency and low cost of this imported labour encourages a race to the bottom, which harms workers in Africa and China. Dispatched Chinese workers are explicitly banned from participating in trade unions and political activities in the host country both in the dispatch contracts as well as in the voluntary codes of CHINCA. Although labour laws and trade union laws in Namibia and Mauritius cover both local and migrant workers, the extraterritorial extension of this Chinese labour control mechanism detaches Chinese workers from trade union protection of the host country as well.

In terms of union responses the rank and file in Lee's case study clearly see the union as relatively powerless and even corrupt. Part of this is the legacy of neo-liberal structural adjustment programmes of the 1980s and 1990s which actively undermined the power of African organized labour (Andrae and Beckman 1999; Baah and Jauch 2009). While the future looks bleak for organized labour in the face of a 'race to the bottom' economic model and a seemingly blind willingness of African leaders to encourage foreign investment at any cost Baah and Jauch (2009) suggest possible activities like boycotting Chinese goods and firms, learning Mandarin in order to more effectively negotiate, lobbying for national legislation on a minimum wage, building regional and continental coordination of trade unionism and building union capacity.

In terms of business associations the response to China has been somewhat less confrontational than strikes although traders have protested in

Ghana in 2007. In Uganda the local business organizations, mainly the Kampala City Traders Association (KACITA), spearheaded a campaign challenging the issues of cheap and unfair competition and shoddy goods. Their argument was based on a series of related points about a perceived manipulation of the price mechanism, the discouragement of other investors, the promotion of unemployment, and undermining revenue through tax evasion (Lee 2007: 34). Dobler (2008) has shown how local graft in Namibia, in terms of paying off customs officials, has enabled Chinese firms though local firms are also subject to such pressures. Our work around Chinese small and medium enterprises (SMEs) in Ghana suggested that paying local officials to expedite various official requirements was common but noted that it was not too severe and, tellingly, not dissimilar from practices in China.

Other responses to the Chinese by local traders have been less formalized but equally steeped in negative stereotypes about the Chinese. Sylvanus's (2007) study of market women in Lome's *Grand-Marche* examines the transit of Chinese-produced 'African' print textiles. These cheaper fabrics are contrasted by the traders as inferior to the long-established European cloths such as the Dutch Wax. This sense of difference and inferiority is projected onto the Chinese traders and evokes nostalgia among the Togolese market women for colonial ties: 'You could depend on them (colonial trade partners), and they would not sell to everyone'. By contrast the Chinese are described as criminals, violent and amoral. There is then a relationship between the object and the peoples trading it, where the fabric embodies prejudices against the Chinese although this animosity has not hindered ongoing expansion of Chinese trade.

While the KACITA members of Lee's (2006) study were critical of the Chinese one positive difference they cite is that when it comes to them buying goods in China the Chinese are more respectful of them and require less stringent travel restrictions. Arguably one response, then, has not so much been voice against the Chinese *in situ* as 'exit' in the form of African traders travelling to China to source merchandise and compete with Chinese traders in Africa. The study by Li et al. (2007) looks at African traders in *Xiaobei* Guangzhou, which the authors characterize as a 'transnational ethnic enclave'. Guangzhou's economic success has seen an explosion of temporary business migrants coming in to purchase goods for export. The African traders have been coming since the turn of the millennium with around 1000 officially registered long-term residents being African in 2005 and upwards of 30,000 temporary migrants, though accurate figures are clearly hard to determine. In one enclave the Africans occupy high-rise apartments where they live and work from, and Li et al. found over 400 residents from 52 African countries though most came from Mali, Togo, Gambia, Guinea, Ghana, Senegal and Congo. These traders buy general merchandise and ship it back to Africa where it is generally wholesaled on. A typical example is a Tunisian trader:

> He started to do business in Guangzhou since 2003, and visited Guangzhou 4–5 times per year. Each time he stayed about 15 days in the city, focusing on several large-scale footwear wholesale markets. As short-term residents, they would choose to live in hotels, and it is quite common that several traders sharing one room. (p. 17)

This 'response' to Chinese trade in Africa is interesting and suggests even more complex linkages between China and various localities in Africa.

Other forms of civil society response have been around major infrastructure projects, notably dams. In Chapter 5 and earlier in this chapter we touched upon the Bui Dam in Ghana, which is part of a much broader entry by Chinese firms into large dam building across the global South (Bosshard 2009; Watts 2010). When the World Bank got out of loans for dams following international pressure and the World Commission for Dams the Chinese had built up local expertise by using joint ventures for technology transfer (Watts 2010). By the early 2000s these Chinese companies, such as Sinohydro, were ready to internationalize and have continued apace albeit through contracts which are weak on environmental and social considerations. Profitability on servicing domestic Chinese markets was limited and with the international reluctance to fund dams set against chronic energy shortages in Africa these Chinese SOE 'champions' had a relatively free reign. They were also enabled by the ExIm concessional loans we have already discussed. But what about the reaction to these projects, which we have seen often use imported labour and inputs and are heavily enclavic?

We saw above that with trade union responses to the Chinese histories of labour struggle in different localities with different types of production process engendered quite different responses, even if the political elites in power were similarly seen to collude with the Chinese. Similar patterns of difference can be seen in responses to dam building. The Merowe dam in Northern Sudan had been debated since the 1970s but it was the Chinese who took on the mantle and construction was underway by 2005 by the China International Water and Electrical Corp (Askouri 2007; Bosshard 2009). The resettlement colonies were poorly planned and the soil around the villages was very low quality forcing many resettlers to abandon farming and migrate to Khartoum. The period 2006–08 witnessed various flooding incidents which destroyed houses, killed large numbers of livestock and ruined various crops (Bosshard 2010). A lobbying group led by Ali Askouri has been contesting the dam and resettlement scheme and in 2010 they brought a legal case against the German Company – Lahmeyer GmBH – that supervised the project construction for recklessness and violation of human rights. As Askouri (2006) notes, the dam is part of ongoing Chinese engagements with Sudan in the oil sector and elites on both sides are colluding to conceal the truth.

In contrast at Ghana's Bui Dam there has been tension around the dam over resettlement. Studies show that although new accommodation seems adequate affected residents were hardly consulted and some people have yet to be rehoused or compensated, resulting in the involvement of local chiefs. The new government of January 2009 sent high level representatives to the area to calm matters which is part of an electoral pay-back since there was a re-run of the presidential vote in the Tain constituency where Bui is located which went the National Democratic Congress (NDC)'s way. In response to the Bui Dam, and longer debates around the impacts of the Akosombo Dam, the Ghana Dams Dialogue started in 2006. Its mission is to lobby for greater transparency and dialogue in dam planning and construction and has to date organized a series of high profile forums. They have also got involved in the Bui resettlement issue through fact finding visits and brokering between local communities and the Bui Power Authority. However, their activities are more accurately described as accommodatory than confrontational, reflecting the differing nature of China's engagement in Ghana compared to Sudan and longer histories of political activism.

What the Merowe Dam case shows also is that much of the debate around China's role in Africa and elsewhere is being driven by civil society actors that are not Africa based, but attached to international human rights or environmental organizations elsewhere. In the case of dams it has been the International Rivers Network that has produced evidence of China's practices and lobbied ExIm and Sinohydro to adopt better environmental and social standards. This is a case of international civil society groups seeking to effect change within sovereign states, be they China or Sudan, and is an example of what Keck and Sikkink (1998) term the 'boomerang effect'; that is, local conflicts cannot be addressed by domestic civil society lobbying its own government so it links with international civil society organizations (CSOs) that can pressure states from without in order to effect change within the affected state territory.

Another high profile example was the 'Genocide Olympics' campaign in the run up to the 2008 Beijing Olympics. The call for a boycott of the 'Genocide Olympics' came from a wide range of groups, including US Senators, Hollywood actors, journalists, Burmese activists and Taiwanese political parties. They all used China's human rights abuses domestically and internationally as the justification. Notably it was the Darfur crisis which exercised most people citing the oil revenues that the Chinese brought combined with ignoring the al-Bashir Government's ethnic cleansing of the oil producing areas and China's willingness to sell arms to the government (see Large 2008b, 2008c). Celebrities such as Mia Farrow and Steven Spielberg were highly vocal, with Farrow initially berating Spielberg for his role as artistic advisor to the Olympic organizers. The use of the Olympics as a highly visible public event was intended to shame China into reform as well as hurting China economically through lost revenue although it is hard to say what impact the campaign had. Similar debates arose around the 2010 Nobel Peace Prize going to the jailed Chinese dissident Liu Xiaobo with the Chinese authorities urging a boycott of the ceremony at which an empty chair was prominent to represent Liu's glaring absence. In the next two chapters we pick up these debates around international environmental standards and the ways in which governance mechanisms are attempting to transform these relationships.

## Conclusion

China's engagement with African states is through context specific and flexible 'assemblages' which create new institutional forms. Crucially these institutions are clandestine and elite-based and so undermine democratic accountability and simply serve to entrench a narrow authoritarianism in many African states. At an everyday level of politics, where Africans and Chinese actually encounter one another as employers, employees, customers, neighbours, or friends we see a different kind of ambivalence. On the whole 'the Chinese' are welcome for the commodities and infrastructure they bring, but at times there is resentment, tempered on both sides by a measure of racial stereotyping. Jacques (2009) sees Chinese 'civilization' as inherently hierarchical and racist, so that these encounters which seemingly reinforce Chinese superiority are not surprising. They do however question how far enduring encounters in situ will transform these mutual perceptions and lead to greater integration. If these tensions persist then public proclamations of 'South-South co-operation' begin to look rather thin.

The complicity of African elites in championing the Chinese at any cost seems to be leading to over-riding of established legal norms around labour rights, social protection and the environment. And it is not in the interests of the Chinese or these elites to challenge such a model of governance. That said the international furore over Darfur seems to have pricked the Chinese government's conscience, but more pragmatically it is a realization that accumulation requires stability that is seeing enhanced efforts to intervene in African governance. Parallels might be made between the pre-colonial Charter companies who were in the Tropics simply for business and the subsequent need to secure territory and security that saw more formal colonization. We are not predicting that the Chinese will formally colonize Africa – largely since colonization in the nineteenth century was about inter-imperial rivalry which is lacking in the same way today – but they will be forced to engage with questions of African politics. The Nigerian oil debacle was evidence of how they misread the nature of the state and Nigerian politics.

If these inter-elite negotiations lock out the wider citizenry what options are left? The trade union activism shows that where unions are powerful and able to enforce local laws then wages and conditions in Chinese firms appear better. But the weakness of unions and collusion with political elites often renders them relatively non-confrontational. It speaks to a wider issue about whether 'Africa' has a China strategy compared with China's Africa strategy we discussed in Chapter 3. While policy responses have been quite weak to date the Angola case shows that the state is far from passive and has been able to carve out a hybrid space of elite collaboration with the Chinese, although this clearly has limited benefits for wider society. The deal with the Chinese struck by the DRC sought to secure contracts for local firms and set a minimum threshold for use of local labour. However, as the cases discussed above show not all firms honour such obligations although the intention is a good one. Recent calls by the Managing Director of the World Bank – Dr Ngozi Okonjo-Iweala – set out a clear agenda for leveraging greater and more strategic benefits from China's engagement in the resource sector (All Africa.com, 16 November 2010). She urged the Chinese to make investments consistent with national development priorities, which at root means creating jobs. She added that Chinese firms should also demonstrate transparency and operate legally as well as add value by locating more elements of the value chain in Africa.

Moreover they should pay the taxes due and avoid bribery and finally should engage with local communities. In short this is partly about breaking free from an enclavic mentality and deepening the footprint that Ferguson (2006) argued has been eroded not just by Chinese firms but by TNCs more generally.

# 7
# The Environmental Implications of China's Rise in Africa

## Introduction

In 20 years, China has achieved economic results that took a century to attain in the west. But we have also concentrated a century's worth of environmental issues into those 20 years. While becoming the world leader in GDP growth and foreign investment, we have also become the world's number one consumer of coal, oil and steel – and the largest producer of $CO_2$ and chemical oxygen demand (COD) emissions ... China is a socialist country and cannot engage in environmental colonialism, nor act as a hegemon, so it must move towards a new type of civilization. Ideas such as the scientific view of development and building a harmonious, resource-saving and environmentally-friendly society, as put forward by the Central Committee in recent years, have laid the foundation for doing so.

Mr Pan Yue, deputy director of the China State Environmental Protection Administration (SEPA), 27 October 2006

As early as October 2006, the Chinese State increasingly came to realize the scale of the domestic and global tasks that China would have to take on in terms of tackling environmental issues. Domestically, as we have seen, thirty years of reforms saw huge improvements in China's economic development and living standards. However, China's natural resources have been the subject of widespread exploitation with significant implications for the pollution of the natural environment as documented by scholars such as Economy (2004, 2005), Hayes (2007), Magee (2006) and Smil (1980, 1998, 2004). China now emits more $CO_2$ than the United States and Canada put together and its emissions are up by

171 per cent since the year 2000 (EIA 2011). China's insatiable appetite for natural resources to fuel its domestic growth and satisfy its domestic energy needs has thus left an unparalleled and increasing footprint on the world's environment (Liu and Diamond 2005; Mol 2011). Shortages of domestic commodities and global oil price spikes in 2004, 2006 and 2007 has led China to increasingly turn to resource-rich regions such as Africa and central Asia in search of these resources and in the interests of energy security. China relies on coal, for example, for almost 70 per cent of its total energy supply, yet it is estimated that in 2020 the shortage of coal in China will reach 1 billion metric tons per year, with significant implications for domestic manufacturing businesses (Dickinson 2010).

Africa is believed to possess a significant proportion of global mineral reserves: 30 per cent of bauxite, 60 per cent of manganese, 75 per cent of phosphates, 85 per cent of platinum, 80 per cent of chrome, 60 per cent of cobalt, 30 per cent of titanium, 75 per cent of diamonds and nearly 40 per cent of gold (France Diplomatie 2008). The continent also has substantial quantities of oil and gas reserves. According to the 2011 BP Statistical Energy Survey, Africa had proven oil reserves of 132.1 billion barrels at the end of 2010 or 9.5 per cent of the world's reserves and in 2010 the region produced an average of 10098 thousand barrels of crude oil per day (12.2% of the world total) (BP 2011). According to the same survey, Africa had proven natural gas reserves at the end of 2010 of 14.7 trillion cubic metres (7.9% of the world total) while natural gas production for 2010 was 209 billion cubic metres (6.5% of the world total). This wealth, however, has had a variety of implications for African development. On the one hand, Africa's fabulous mineral and natural resource endowment, combined with high global demand and rising prices, should bring revenues that benefit its people. Many African countries have historically relied on their mining sectors to attract foreign direct investment, earn export revenues and provide much needed employment (Grant 2009: 5). On the other hand, it is these very resources which have promoted the rise of corruption and conflict, in which 'rentier states' have emerged in some African countries as the mainstream models of governance. As a result, it is perceived to be of urgent need to promote global governance initiatives in the extractive and natural resources sectors along with transparency and good governance within these African states.

It is against this background that China's reinvigorated entry into Africa was initially greeted with scepticism by many analysts in the west (Carroll 2006; Bennett 2007). At the same time, many African commentators noted with trepidation the environmental degradation of

China's own landscapes and resources, and expressed serious concerns about an uncritical acceptance of Chinese development initiatives in Africa (Rupp, in Rotberg 2008: 75). China's lack of environmental diplomacy with international agencies and non-governmental organizations (NGO) in the past has also put China in a negative light in debates about global environmental governance issues.

In the past few years things have begun to change (Brautigam 2009). For one, better data now exists with which to assess China's impacts, although this is still patchy and often poor (Kaplinsky 2008). As greater global engagement drew increased regulatory attention to the environment (Jahiel 2006), China's domestic record of dealing with environmental problems, participation in global environmental governance building and acceptance of international norms has also improved tremendously since 2003, when the term 'peaceful ascendance' entered Chinese policy discourse. Aware of its growing global responsibilities as a 'rising power', China has also increasingly come to incorporate renewable energy projects into its aid, loan and investment portfolios in Africa (Hon et al. 2010: 84–6; Conrad et al. 2011) and has been keen to invest in renewable energy in Africa. This is partly driven by the desire to improve China's image in the South and its reputation in dealing with climate change issues but also by the fact that China has become the world's largest producer of wind turbines, photovoltaic cells, solar water heaters, small hydropower plants and that it has taken a significant role in the geothermal and biomass sectors (Watson et al. 2011).

With this in mind this chapter seeks to examine the environmental implications of China's rise in Africa and explores the extent to which China has become more 'responsible' environmentally in its engagement with the continent and what this might mean for African development. Using the political ecology analytical framework discussed in Chapter 1, this chapter begins by setting out in more detail this important theoretical framework. The chapter will then move on to explore the changing domestic discourses around China's environmental governance. The next section will then discuss Chinese involvement in various natural resource sectors in Africa (using the case studies of Angola and Ghana). In particular, we will focus on three themes: (1) the differential impacts of Chinese enterprises on the environment, (3) illegal activities and (2) the changing roles of multi-stakeholders in global environmental governance. Finally, the chapter will examine China's increasing responsibilities as a global actor in tackling cross-boundary environmental issues and its changing role in global environmental governance structures.

## Political ecology: understanding power relations in the environment sector

Power relations between different actors are at the heart of the political ecology framework. Assessing the abilities of state and non-state actors to impose their preferences on how resources are extracted and used, and from which resource sectors, can often shed light on the relative power of each actor. Assessing these unequal power relations between various actors in turn provides a way to explain the uneven distribution of environmental resources. Power is conceptualized as the differential ability to control access to valued environmental resources, the main objective of which is control and/or access the economic benefits ensuing from resource exploitation (Bryant 1997: 11; see also Peluso 1992; Dauvergne 1994; MacAndrews 1994; Bryant 1996).

Previously in much of the political ecology literature the state tended to be the primary foci of analysis. Due to its 'unique remit to act in the "national interest"' (Bryant and Bailey 1997: 48) or for the 'common good', the state has been regarded as the 'steward' of the environment and an important actor in the often contradictory role of promoting 'development' and capital accumulation in line with its own political and strategic interests (Bryant and Bailey 1997: 188). Adopting this perspective, Le Billion (2001: 567) has illustrated how tight economic and political control of a dominant resource sector by a ruling elite leaves little scope for accumulating wealth and status outside of state patronage.

However, failure to regulate effectively, combined with increasing globalization and economic and ecological interdependence, requires rigorous national policies and effective international collective action (Esty and Ivanova 2004: 17). This was exemplified by a shift in the environmental management literature from state-centric approaches towards a focus on collaborative management, involving a diversity of players. This came about partly because traditional government institutions can no longer respond effectively to these new and complex problems and changes (Griffin 2008: 461). This 'shift in the policy making process' has at times been referred to as a 'hollowing-out of the state', involving a 'partial transfer of responsibility and authority for policy decisions from the central agencies of government to networks of public and private bodies at national, regional and local levels' (Rhodes cited in Symes 2006). Jessop (2002: 199) refers to this shift of power from the government to other societal actors in the environmental arena as the 'destatization of the political system', while Himley (2008: 435) notes that this change from studying 'government' to 'governance' has been prompted by the growing importance of non-state actors and institutions.

At the same time, the different interests maintained by the variety of actors involved also translates into differing interpretations and actions within each group or agency, and at various levels. Scholars are also interested to explore how 'society exercises different levels of power, authority and action to determine "who gets what?" and "who decides"?' (Reed and Bruyneel 2010: 646). Furthermore, the traditional top-down centralized system of management, and between government planning and implementation at the national, provincial and local levels, illustrates the tensions between and within agencies. This often contributes to failed environmental governance as effective governance often requires 'multiple links across levels and domains, and seeks overlapping centres of authority' (Berkes 2009: 1694), along with the 'collective efforts of state (that is, public) and non-state (private) stakeholders at the global, regional, national, sub-national, and local levels' (Selby 2003). This is especially important in today's globalized investment context, as failed domestic environmental governance often results in negative environmental impacts overseas, when the same actors transpose their poor business practices onto another sovereign space. Political ecology hence provides the necessary basic framework for thinking about the conflicts and struggles engendered by the varied forms of control over access to natural resources. By examining new forms of transboundary Chinese political practices and their impacts in Africa we aim to examine how the power relations between the Chinese state, African agencies and international organizations are played out in the natural resource arena. In the case of China and Africa, an examination of the key Chinese domestic developments in environmental governance will help us to comprehend the rationales and aims of Chinese actors in the overseas African context (Mol 2011).

## Changing domestic discourses and the internationalization of China's environmental governance

State-led environmental degradation has been documented as early as the 1950s by scholars such as Smil (1984) and Shapiro (2001). Later works by Day (2005), Han and Zhang (2006) and Hayes (2007) also discuss in detail the alarming scale and rate of environmental destruction, intensified by the open door reforms and industrialization process of the 1970s and 1980s. Institutional constraints such as the lack of coordination between central and provincial government and the gap between policy formulation and implementation have often been given as the main reasons for the failure in environmental protection (Jahiel 1997; Sinkule and Ortolano 1995; Tilt 2007; Carter and Mol 2007; Van Rooij 2006). Other scholars have attributed this to the inherent nature of market liberalization and the dilemmas of perceived trade-offs between economic growth and environmental protection (Sanders 1999) combined with a lack of public participation (Brettell 2003; Buesgen 2008; Sun and Zhao 2008). This section will assess Chinese international environmental diplomacy, especially in Africa, by looking internally at the domestic reforms in China's environmental governance and how perceptions of the environment have evolved through various periods of political and economic change. In particular, the state's capacity to govern environmentally and its interactions with international agencies will be explored here.

Natural resource management in post-independent China was a laissez faire matter with numerous agencies managing various components of the environment, such as forestry and fisheries. There simply was no holistic environmental protection agency. It was not until 1972, after the United Nations Conference on Human Environment in Stockholm, that a formal institution for environmental protection was suggested by Premier Zhou Enlai. Named as the State Environmental Protection Agency (SEPA), it only became a full Ministry in 1988. It was again reorganized as the Ministry of Environmental Protection (MEP) in 2007, during the period of 'Super Ministry Reform' (大部制改革). This Ministry now provides the central leadership for China's environmental protection mechanisms, while on the local level it is the Environmental Protection Bureaus (EPB) that are affiliated to their respective municipal governments (Tilt 2007: 925). It is inevitable with reforms that new spaces of power have emerged with this reconfiguration of administrative authority. Entrenched in the 'guanxi' cultural and social milieu, these new spaces are often occupied by people in friendship networks or familial links. As Fu (2008: 611) puts it, the biggest challenge facing the reforms concerned with enhancing environmental protection in China is to 'regulate the behaviours and relationship of various stakeholders – different levels of government, the industrial sectors, and the public'. Compounded by the absence of an independent judiciary sector and the ambiguity of some environmental laws, enforcement capacity and performance is often poor due to the conflicts of interest between environmental protection and the economic benefits from environmentally irresponsible development projects (Seymour 2005).

However, in the past few years, there have been conscious administrative and legislative efforts to strengthen environmental protection domestically during the process of development. Issues of climate change, environmental conservation and energy featured particularly prominently in the PRC twelfth five-year plan (2011–15). This plan is progressive compared to previous five-year plans as it has binding targets of a 16 per cent cut in energy consumption per unit of GDP, a 17 per cent cut in carbon intensity and an 8 per cent reduction in sulphur dioxide and COD. There were also aims to increase forest cover and reduce water usage and pollutants, which were absent in previous plans (MOFCOM 2011b). By incorporating monitoring and assessment components into the current plan, the Chinese government is beginning to develop and enhance its environmental management and governance capacities and to improve the enforcement and implementation of its legislation. This is reflected in the recent first national census of pollution sources published in February 2010, which took 570,000 staff, US$100 million and over two years to complete (*Xinhua* 2010). The report revealed that water pollution in 2007 was twice as much as shown in the official figures, with discharges totalling 30.3 million tons. This was partly attributed by the poor statistical calculation which excludes agricultural effluence such as fertilizers and pesticides (*New York Times* 9 February 2010).

As such, environmental initiatives such as the project-based Environmental Impact Assessment (EIA) mechanism and the national Environment Monitoring Network have been established along with more than 200 environmental policies, laws and regulations (Fu et al. 2007: 7600). An emerging theme in these initiatives is Corporate Social Responsibility (CSR) and the integration of social and environmental concerns into business operations. CSR is a contested concept with no clear definitions, making theoretical development and measurement difficult (Jansson et al. 2009: 3). The most commonly quoted definition of CSR is from the Commission of European Communities (2001), whereby companies integrate social and environmental concerns into their business operations and in their interaction with the stakeholders on a voluntary basis (Dahlsrud 2006). This highlights the main problem with CSR, as it is a voluntary initiative there has been a lack of compliance from many companies, made worse by the absence of a global regime which encourages national regulations promoting the balance of property rights with obligations linked with labour and environmental issues.

Since the mid-2000s there has been a noticeable increase in China in terms of adoption and compliance with CSR principles, at times through the awards of ISO14001. The ISO14001 is a series of international standards for environmental management which aims to help organizations to minimize the negative environmental impacts from its business operations (ISO 2011). This 'uptake' was further consolidated when CSR guidelines for state-owned enterprises (SOEs) were issued in January 2008 by the State Assets Supervision and Administration Commission (SASAC). These guidelines define CSR as 'based on actions to implement the philosophy of scientific development' and require SOEs to not only develop in a people-centred, 'scientific' way and make profits, but also to 'take responsibility for all stakeholders and the environment, and ultimately to harmonize the enterprise with social and environmental development'. As such, the number of Chinese firms certified with ISO14001 standards increased from 222 in 1999 to 5064 in 2003 (OECD 2003: 8). Similar principles were adopted by the State Council (2007) and a related agency, the China-Africa Business Council (CABC). The latter, an NGO set up in 2005 in conjunction with the UNDP to provide practical business tools to facilitate the strengthening of business ties between China and Africa, has also published CSR guidelines for Chinese enterprises working in Africa. Chinese enterprises with overseas operations are also responding to the increasing call to adopt CSR principles. For example, Sino Steel Group published their *Sustainable Development Report-Africa* in 2008 which states that the company 'puts a high emphasis on resource conservation, recycling, environmental protection, and the safety and health management of its African operations' (Sino steel 2008).

In 2007, China, for its part, developed an environmental database of Chinese companies, requiring commercial banks to review and weigh up each applicant's environmental history before approving credit applications. Along with the Ministry of Environmental Protection (MEP), the China Banking Regulatory Commission (CRBC) established a 'green credit system' which aims to restrict the availability of credit to companies in violation of environmental laws (Bu et al. 2009). For example, the Industrial and Commercial Bank of China has adjusted the structure of its credit policies so that responsibilities and requirements for environmental protection are defined and explicit in investment decision-making (Bu et al. 2009:15). It was only after the implementation of these initiatives that CSR emerged on the agenda of many SOEs partly as a public relations tool and a strategy for the 'greening' of corporate images.

Major Chinese investors, financiers and equipment suppliers have however so far not adopted such standards, or have developed policies that are not necessarily in line with international standards (Bosshard 2008). A July 2007 review of China's environmental performance carried out by the Organisation for Economic Cooperation and Development (OECD) recommended that China 'improve governmental oversight and environmental performance in the overseas operations of Chinese corporations' and 'integrate environmental considerations systematically into China's growing development cooperation programme' (OECD 2007b: 12). Typically China has rebuffed such suggestions by reiterating its commitment to the principle of non-interference in the domestic affairs of partner states. The China ExIm bank adopted an environmental policy in 2004 dealing with issues before, after and during project implementation and more specific guidelines on social and environmental impact assessment were added in 2007. The guidelines require projects to comply with host country policies – but not international standards – regarding environmental assessment, resettlement and consultation (Bosshard 2008). This was partly as a consequence of a campaign led by the International River Networks (IRN) to get ExIm to adopt international best practice on the environment. Indeed, there are examples of how CSR initiatives are adopted either because companies were pressurized by NGOs about environment, community development or global warming (Frynas 2005), or because of the potential of improving public relations by projecting a 'green image'. As a result, CSR activities have generally remained subservient to corporate profit-making objectives (Frynas 2005).

China has also signed over 50 international environmental treaties. Since 2007, China has been the world's largest emitter of greenhouse gases, having released an estimated 6.2 million tonnes of $CO_2$ into the atmosphere (Dwinger 2010). However, China signed the Kyoto Protocol in 1998 and ratified it in 2002 and has assumed a leading role in the Copenhagen Summit on carbon reduction issues. China has also overtaken the United States in its investments in low-carbon energy, investing twice as much and totalling US$44.9 billion in 2009 (UNEP 2011) and is beginning to play an increasingly important role in facilitating the transition to low-carbon energy systems in Africa. China has also moved to 'accelerate industrial restructuring, to upgrade traditional industries using low-carbon technology and to curb the development of high energy-consuming and carbon-emitting industries' (Xie 2010: 25). The Chinese Government also recently embarked on a 10-year plan under the auspices of the newly created National Energy Commission, which aims at having 15 per cent of national energy generated from low-carbon sources by 2020 (Dwinger 2010). This ambitious plan focuses on energy efficiency as well as renewable energy, with the Government planning to set aside billions of dollars for new investments in wind and solar power projects (wind and solar power generation having already doubled year on year over the past 5 years). In addition, legislators intend to introduce a carbon tax in 2012, the revenues of which will go into financing renewable energy R&D and low-carbon energy sources (Dwinger 2010).

In the late 1990s and early 2000s, there were also a series of popular discussions on China's degrading environment and its impacts on the Chinese people. Issues such as poisoned rivers, threats to biodiversity and human health and mega projects which are environmentally destructive such as the Three Gorges Dam, further entrenched the image of China forsaking its environment for economic growth (CNN 1999; WWF 2008). Furthermore, with the accession of China into the World Trade Organization in December 2001, the pursuit of export markets has also led to the vast exploitation of the country's natural resources (Jahiel 2006: 313). It is thus not surprising that foreign commentators and civil society representatives, when confronted with the immense environmental destruction accompanying China's chosen pathways to development, questioned the sustainability of such development trajectories and their feasibility in other parts of the developing world. According to Bosshard (2008: 3), 'China's domestic environmental policies may even encourage China's worst polluters to relocate their production to regions such as Africa' and the 'voracious appetite of the Chinese manufacturing economy serves to exacerbate environmental problems elsewhere' (Jahiel 2006: 323). Indeed, As Mol (2011: 791) highlights, weak environmental regulation and poor implementation in Africa is thought to reflect the nature of business operations within China itself, where industrial and infrastructural operations have been experiencing poor environmental regulation and enforcement.

## Chinese involvement in Africa's resource sectors

In terms of cooperation with Africa, the FOCAC III has so far neglected to deal with the environmental challenges which the intensified trade and investment flows between China and Africa have brought about (Corkin 2009: 5). However, FOCAC IV in 2009 began to show a clear emphasis on the environmental components of Chinese investment in Africa. For example, Wen Jiabao (2009) proposed in Egypt to establish a China–Africa partnership in addressing climate change, enhancing cooperation on satellite weather monitoring, and in developing and using new energy sources. This is vital for Africa as the UN Intergovernmental Panel on Climate Change estimated that between 75 and 250 million people in Africa will be affected by water stress brought on by climate change (IPCC 2007). Deforestation in Africa, where forests are cleared for additional living space or agricultural usage, or where the wood is needed for housing materials, heating and cooking, or to sell and export in order to earn additional income, has also further exacerbated the problem as it contributes to 20–25 per cent of global carbon emissions globally (Dwinger 2010). China's investment in cleaner energy systems in Africa has often been somewhat obscured by popular images of resource- and land-grabs in sub-Saharan Africa and yet renewable energy has become an increasingly prominent feature of China–Africa development cooperation. At the 2009 FOCAC meeting Wen Jiabao also announced that China would construct 100 clean energy projects across the continent focusing on solar power, biogas and small hydropower. China has also held training courses on clean energy sources and climate change for other developing countries (*Xinhua* 2011b). This commitment to small-scale energy projects in Africa's fledgling renewable sector is a break from the previous pattern of China's engagement in Africa's renewable power sector which featured a clear focus on the construction of large hydropower plants (Conrad et al. 2011). Building on its domestic experience and expertise in constructing large hydropower plants, China has either already provided or planned to provide finance and construction capacity to more than 70 projects in 29 African countries (Conrad et al. 2011). According to Foster et al. (2008), by the end of 2007 China was providing US$ 3.3 billion towards the construction of ten major hydropower projects in Africa amounting to some 6000 megawatts (MW) of installed capacity. Once completed, these schemes will increase the total available hydropower generation capacity in sub-Saharan Africa by around 30 per cent.

The depth, drivers and outcomes of China's engagement with renewable energy in Africa are complex and contested in terms of development and its implications for international climate governance and it is important to note that the nature of environmental diplomacy between China and Africa is complex and dynamic. In the context of China–Africa relations, a key issue to explore is the extent to which this 'success' in domestic environmental governance and this commitment to clean energy and low-carbon transition are translating into the African context and how they are impacting on China's relations with African states and their citizens. We will now explore these issues by first looking at Chinese involvement in various resource sectors of Africa, and later by discussing three themes focusing on Chinese enterprises, illegal activities and global environmental governance.

The increasing presence of Chinese investment in various African resource sectors is related to wider issues of land use and the interface between conservation and development. For example, the Chinese obsession with elephant ivory as a status symbol and sign of wealth has had a particular impact on the elephant population of the continent. This huge demand for ivory ornaments, together with buyers from Japan, decimated the population of African and Asian elephants for the last two decades until a 1989 ban on ivory trade. China was a signatory of the Convention on International Trade in Endangered Species (CITES) which saw supplies of ivory in China decrease tremendously. In 2002 the United Nations partially lifted the ban on ivory trade, allowing a few countries to export certain amounts of ivory. In May 2004, the State Forestry Administration enacted a new national ivory registration system requiring ivory dealers and carvers to be registered, which complies with CITES domestic control. In October 2008, CITES granted China and Japan permission to import a total of 108 tons of elephant ivory from African government stockpiles in a one-time auction (*The Telegraph* 05 November 2008). As a result, there were great concerns over the role of Chinese's increasing global power in pressuring international organizations, such as the CITES, to loosen its ivory ban.

In terms of fisheries, due to the declining domestic catch and intensive domestic fishing efforts, the Ministry of Agriculture in China introduced a new regulation on fishing licences which prompted fishers to move away from coastal marine fishing into other production activities in 2002, such as aquaculture and distant fishing. In 2004, China had 88 distant-water fishing enterprises, with 1996 vessels producing 2.42 million tonnes per year for a total value of near US$ 1.2 billion (FAO 2006). The fishing grounds include the high seas of the Pacific Ocean, Atlantic Ocean and Indian Ocean, and the jurisdiction zones of 35 countries (FAO 2006). Although China's distant water fishing (DWF) fleet was only created in the mid-1980s, fishery firms, such as the China National Fishery Corporation (CNFC), have also embarked on the 'going out' strategy recommended by the Chinese government. As such, two-thirds of its catch is from the African seas and it has opened eight representative offices and processing facilities in the continent (FOCAC 2011). There are also smaller firms such as the China Fishery Group, which have done more than just 'plunder' the African seas. They have invested in African countries (e.g. Mauritania) by opening fish-processing factories and by building links with local companies such as the Pacific Andes Group (FIS 26 November 2010).

According to an authoritative source, the number of Chinese fishing vessels in West African waters at any one time could be close to 300 vessels (Wang 2002). Moreover, these Chinese fishing vessels were criticized as worsening food insecurity among the African population, as they targeted small species such as Mackerel, which are the main source of food and income for the small-scale African fishermen (Illegal-fishing info 2009b). For example, the head of the Artisanal Fisheries Council of Senegal noted in 2006 that 'here and there we see infrastructures being built with the support of China, and we say these may be part of the access agreements, but we know nothing about the contents of these agreements' (Bartels et al. 2007: 81). Chinese development assistance in the fishery sectors of various African states, such as Ghana and Angola, has thus been explained by its desire to gain control over primary resources, including oil, timber and fish (Standing 2008: 13). Increasing Chinese aid hence has raised the question of whether this is a diplomatic manoeuvre to gain access to the local fishery industries.

China is the largest importer of forest products in the world, and its imports of forest products have tripled in less than a decade. In 1998, China placed stringent restrictions on domestic logging, forcing the country to import a high percentage of its total wood consumption. Although imports from Africa make up a small proportion of China's total timber imports, China is the main destination of up to 90 per cent of timber for some producer countries on the continent (IUCN, 28 February 2008) (see Figure 7.1 for more details). Regionally, China imports most of its forest products from Central Africa, possibly due to a preference for endemic tree species such as *okoumé* (Canby et al. 2008: 19). Mozambique is one of the biggest exporters with more than 90 per cent of its timber product destined for China. Approximately 70 per cent of Equatorial Guinea's, 50 per cent of the Republic of the Congo's and more than 40 per cent of Gabon's timber were exported to China in 2005. In terms of contributions by export volume to China, Gabon is the top African exporter, delivering 1.1 million m3 logs which accounted for 3.9 per cent share of total Chinese imports in 2009 (Sun and Canby 2011: 12). However, it is important to note that European markets are the biggest importers of African forestry product, with 4.4 million m3 of natural (non-plantation) timber products exported to the EU, compared to 2.1 million m3 sent to China in 2006 (Canby et al. 2008).

China has also been increasing its engagement in the mining sectors of Africa principally in countries such as Botswana, Zambia, Ethiopia,

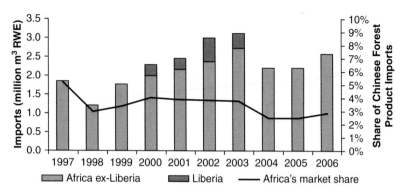

*Figure 7.1*    Share of Chinese forest products import
*Source*: from Forest Trends, Canby et al. 2008: 6.

Ivory Coast, Uganda, Liberia, Zimbabwe and South Africa. Recent developments include the US$7 billion mining agreement with the military government of Guinea in October 2009. In the Democratic Republic of the Congo (DRC), deals were struck between the Congolese government and several Chinese companies for minerals concessions in exchange for infrastructure investments in the Katanga province (Jansson et al. 2009: 33). Joint ventures were also established in Gabon where three agreements were signed on 24 May 2008 between members of the Comibel consortium (comprising the Gabonese state, China National Machinery & Equipment Import & Export Corporation (CMEC) and Panzhihua Iron & Steel Group) to explore iron ore. One of the main criticisms of Chinese engagement in the mining industries is that concessions to these areas are usually negotiated and awarded without competitive bidding and in the absence of environmental concerns.

The hydropower industry has huge potential for the Chinese as African countries are currently only tapping 7 per cent of their technical hydropower potential (Hensengerth 2011) and where the challenge of affordable access to modern energy services is particularly acute. The International Energy Agency (IEA) estimates that access to electricity is at 31 per cent and some 80 per cent of the population are still reliant on the traditional use of biomass (IEA 2011) which has severe health and environmental implications. Some 9.8 per cent of Chinese contractors currently working in African countries are involved in power supply (Chen et al. 2007: 456) and some 33.4 per cent of confirmed Chinese infrastructure commitments in sub-Saharan Africa are in electricity (Foster et al. 2008: 22). According to Hackley and Westhuizen (2011),

Chinese investments in the hydropower industry are worth more than US$9.3 billion. Some of the large-scale hydropower projects currently under construction include the Imboulou dam in the Republic of Congo, the Gibe III dam in Ethiopia, the Kajbar dam in Sudan, the Pubara Hydropower Station in Gabon and Bui Dam in Ghana (CAITEC 2010: 7; Hackley and Westhuizen 2011).

From the point of view of African governments, such investments are greatly welcomed due to the need to boost supply and increase the availability of energy sources. According to Ethiopia's Prime Minister Meles Zenawi, 'hydropower will have to be at the centre of Africa's energy future, as the Gibe III will be instrumental in fighting poverty. It will help to electrify villages, increase irrigation and earn money from electricity exports' (Hackley and Westhuizen 2011). A more interesting but parallel development is happening in the solar energy industry in Africa. Chinese enterprises are now top investors in African solar power and Chinese companies such as Yingli Solar and Suntech Power Holdings Co are establishing joint ventures in South Africa, Benin, Sierra Leone and Mozambique (Hackley and Westhuizen 2011). China's wind power sector has also been expanding into Africa and Chinese wind turbine manufacturers such as the China Longyuan Corporation have been expanding into African markets as the domestic market in China has become increasingly saturated (Conrad et al. 2011).

Through its high-profile oil diplomacy, China has also been very successful in developing its access to African oil and gas reserves. Although Chinese investments in oil fields in African countries have helped to pump more oil out of the fields (Zhang 2007) critics have accused China of fuelling conflicts and human-rights violations in Africa by selling arms to repressive regimes in exchange for oil and minerals (Masaki 2006). In sum, China is accused of mixing business with politics in pursuit of its economic gains in Africa (Zhang 2007: 90). Moreover, cases of infringement or neglect of Environmental Impact Assessments have been common, such as Sinopec's experience in Loango, Gabon, in which drilling operations started before it had been approved by the Ministry of Environment (Jansson et al. 2009: 16).

## The differential impacts of Chinese enterprises on the environment

When we assess Chinese involvement and its impacts in the African resource sectors, a good entry point is to examine and deconstruct the term 'Chinese investment'. The size and capacity of Chinese companies is a key factor in understanding their differential impacts to change the physical environment, which vary considerably between small and medium enterprises (SMEs) and big companies (e.g. CITIC, Sinopec) and depending on whether they are state-owned (e.g. Sinohydro) or private listed enterprises (e.g. China International Fund).

A major growth sector for Chinese SOEs and private firms in recent years has been in engineering and construction. The Chinese now have major infrastructure projects in 35 African countries, most funded by the ExIm bank at 'marginally concessional' rates, and in many cases through natural resource deals. At the same time, SMEs are increasingly common in Africa. For example, in Tanzania, Baregu (2008) notes that out of 147 Chinese companies in the country only 22 had portfolios of more than US$1 million, marking the majority as private SMEs. In addition to these, migrants who are petty entrepreneurs, largely operating in trade, services and in light manufacturing, are establishing themselves in places such as Morocco and Ghana (Colombant 2006), Angola (Corkin 2008b), Cameroon, Namibia and Cape Verde (Haugen and Carling 2005; Mung 2008). These enterprises, regardless of size, also come from different provinces in China and specialize in particular sectors, with differential impacts on the environment. Broadly speaking smaller enterprises, due to the lower investment and project size, tend to be less environmentally impactful compared to larger enterprises such as SOEs.

One example is Sinohydro, with a registered capital of US$122 million with approximately 500–1500 employees on each project, which is becoming a major player in Africa's hydroelectric power (HEP) sector. A key part of the Chinese government's 'going-out' strategy, Sinohydro has been able to bid for overseas engineering projects and receive financial subsidies from the government (Bosshard 2008). Most of these dam projects are funded by the ExIm Bank, such as the new 1500 MW Mphanda Nkuwa dam on the Zambezi River in Mozambique (Biello 2009) and the US$2 billion Merowe Dam along the Nile Valley in Sudan. The Gezhouba group, one of Sinohydro's partners and one of the largest Chinese construction contractors (based in Wuhan) also began work on a 200 MW HEP plant in Nigeria in 2007 and has bidded for projects in Ethiopia, Equatorial Guinea and Algeria (Godrey 2009).

Such large-scale dam projects usually come with huge environmental impacts. They are often located in world heritage sites, protected areas or national parks and have a range of extensive impacts on rivers, watersheds and aquatic ecosystems. These impacts often have led to irreversible loss of species and ecosystems (World Commission on Dams, 2000: xxxi). Moreover, local populations have often been forcibly removed and their livelihoods negatively affected. A case in point is the Chinese constructed Merowe Dam in Sudan, with 50,000 people displaced (Bosshard 2010a). Similarly, in the mining industries, due to the large initial investments in technology and equipment, large SOEs are usually the main operators of these projects, which irrevocably translate to large environmental impacts, especially if the mines are located at inaccessible and ecologically fragile areas. Furthermore, the very nature of the mining operation is environmentally degrading, and any activities in this sector usually generate solid and liquid waste including hazardous products like cyanide and mercury, along with greenhouse gases. While the land degradation caused by the mining is significant, what is more controversial are the harmful health outcomes for mining communities and persons residing in close proximity to such activities (Yelpaala and Ali 2005: 145). Generally, these negative impacts are being mitigated by post mining rehabilitation, involving various processes to remove these chemical discharges in the surrounding areas. However, they have often been flouted due to the lack of compliance or political will to enforce them, and these Chinese projects have tended to commence without EIAs being undertaken and in the absence of sufficient relocation/compensation for the surrounding households. This will be discussed in more depth with reference to the example of the Bui Dam in Ghana in the later section on environmental governance.

## Illegal activities

More threatening to the sustainable extraction of natural resources of African countries are the illegal activities prevalent in certain parts of the continent. For example, the main threat to the elephant population is the existence of a huge illegal black market for ivory, fuelled by the demand from Chinese and Japanese markets. China is the largest importer by weight of illegal ivory in the world (Milliken et al. 2009). According to Esmond Martin, a conservationist who has closely tracked Chinese involvement in the black market ivory trade, 'the elephant poaching has increased in parts of northern Kenya and this is due to various reasons, but most people think it's due to the Chinese demand that's increased the price because most illegal ivory is going to China' (Joselow 2011). Chinese nationals have been arrested and convicted for ivory smuggling in Africa and organized crime gangs are involved in bringing large quantities of illicit ivory into China, according to the London-based Environmental Investigation Agency (Pomfret and Kirkwood 2009).

Although a 2007 field investigation by TRAFFIC, a wildlife trade monitoring network, speaks of an 'unprecedented effort to interdict illicit trade in ivory' and 'confirm China's law enforcement effort scores have improved remarkably' (Holslag 2007: 11), there have been renewed concerns regarding China's outreach and awareness initiatives directed at Chinese communities living abroad. These Chinese nationals are in positions to acquire ivory from illicit sources and transport it back home. Chinese nationals have been arrested within or coming from Africa in at least 134 ivory seizure cases, totalling over 16 tonnes of ivory and another 487 cases representing almost 25 tonnes of ivory originating from Africa was seized en route to China (BBC, 11 November 2009). Indeed some have argued that China continues to hold the key for reversing the upward trend in illicit trade in ivory (CITES 2009: 26). It is difficult however for the Chinese government to manage these individual migrants returning from Africa, despite tightened customs controls both in Africa and China, due to the illicit nature of the trade.

Illegal Chinese fishing is also increasingly being witnessed in African waters. Chinese fishers and fishing boats have been apprehended or monitored while engaged in fishing in Sierra Leone, Guinea and South Africa (Illegal-fishing info, 2009b). Greenpeace and the Environmental Justice Foundation (EJF) have also tracked illegally operating Chinese flagged trawlers from the waters around Guinea (Illegal-fishing info, 2009b). Instead of catching high-end fish like blue fin tuna, they catch smaller species such as mackerel, the main source of income for small-scale African fishermen. This has led to criticism of Chinese fishing vessels for worsening Africa's food crisis and threatening the livelihoods of poor African fishermen (*Donga news*, 17 August 2009). One theory informally circulating in maritime circles posits that piracy in the Gulf of Aden is actually a by-product of overfishing by external powers, who have forced local Somali fishermen into other 'careers' (Goldstein 2009). According to Agnew et al. (2009), many coastal states in Africa license vessels from distant water fishing nations such as China, Taiwan, Korea and Russia to fish in their waters, and there is a significant illegal fishing problem from many of these vessels. They also note that illegal fishing is an important driver of overfishing, which depletes the marine resource base and has ecological impacts. Chinese companies are equally accused of not respecting the fishing quotas assigned to them and of infringing the regulations on fishing zones (Lafargue 2008: 67).

African countries with weak systems of forest governance and law enforcement are seeing similar increases in unsustainable or illegal harvesting, biodiversity loss and the abuse of forest communities' rights, possibly promoted by increased Chinese demand. Exports of timber and other forest-based resources from Africa to China (as well as to developed countries) result in a decline in the capacity of African forests to absorb carbon dioxide and thereby mitigate the effects of fossil fuel emissions (Jansson et al. 2009: 4). One example of this can be seen in the Congo. The Hong Kong-owned Vicwood Pacific is a big player in the global logging industry and acquired the Cameroon subsidiaries of the Thanry Group in 1997. Thanry has been one of the principle loggers and international timber traders in the Congo River Basin. Between 2000 and 2002, Thanry was fined over US$1.3 million for violating forestry laws, including cutting undersized trees, logging outside legal boundaries, and logging in unallocated concessions (Chan-Fishel 2007: 147).

What is more crucial is the presence of illegal logging in Africa and the involvement of mainland Chinese companies in this trade. According to Watts (2005), much of Chinese wood imports comes from countries with poor forest stewardship (many of which are in Africa) and is often illegally purchased. The Royal Institute of International Affairs in London estimates that 70 per cent of China's timber import from sub-Saharan Africa is illegal (Illegal-logging info 2007). For example, in Equatorial Guinea, annual timber extraction exceeds the maximum legally allowed limit by 40–60 per cent. It is also estimated that up to 90 per cent of the total harvest going to China is illegal (Hewitt 2002). Moreover, according to some analysts, China's influence in the sector encourages 'flagrant disregard for the law', and taxes are not paid on 60 per cent of the area allocated as forest concessions (Chan-Fishel 2006). According to one merchant based in China the source of the wood involved is not a major concern: 'we know it's not always legal, where it comes from but it's no problem for us on the Chinese side' (quoted in Watts 2005).

As such, the National Guidelines on Sustainable Overseas Silviculture and on Sustainable Overseas Forestry Development and Utilisation for Chinese Enterprises were introduced by the Chinese government in 2007 and 2009 (WWF 2011) although they are non-mandatory. The non-mandatory nature, similar to the voluntary nature of CSR, places the responsibilities for sustainable timber extraction on the shoulders of the private companies.

### Roles of multi-stakeholders in global environmental governance

Other than the local capacity of the African states to enforce legislation and the Chinese companies' willingness to comply with international environmental standards, what is also vital in successful environmental governance is the presence of local and global civil society. As indicated in the discussion of the political ecology framework, the state still plays an important role in environmental governance, amidst a changing governance structure which is more inclusive and that is beginning to incorporate non-state actors in monitoring actions. The Chinese and African states hence could utilize non-state stakeholders as an extension for environmental management, governance and monitoring.

One of the major debates about increasing Chinese engagement in the African resources sector is that Chinese companies promote the lack of good governance and transparency through their engagement with weak states, and a willingness to engage in commercial activities without considerations of international environmental norms, resulting in further deterioration of the African environment. However, some scholars have argued that China has little to do with these impacts, as the major authority lies with the African governments to implement and enforce their own legislation. For example, Jansson et al. (2009) argue that China has little to do with the deterioration of the Congo environment, as the 'Congolese pattern of political authority and networks are notoriously resilient, and there are no signs that Chinese involvement is going to have a transformative impact on the nature of the Congolese state'.

Dams are once again under the spotlight due to the impending need to reduce carbon emissions to curb climate change and the essential nature of affordable access to electricity for development. As an alternative source of energy to fossil fuel with lower carbon emissions, there has been a growing focus on dam construction for HEP generation. In particular, Chinese investment in hydropower in Africa has received considerable attention due to the sheer scale and pace of Chinese dam construction in the continent. Although these dams are providing cleaner energy and more affordable access to energy for African people, they often come with huge environmental, social, economic and cultural costs. As a result, many non-state actors such as NGOs and civil society representatives have questioned the long-term benefits and the real benefactors of these dams, highlighting issues of social justice, equity, governance and power relations.

There have been many documented examples of the negative environmental and ecosystem implications created by large dams as documented by Chatterjee (1997), McCartney (2007, 2009) and Seddon (2000). Various NGOs in Mozambique, for example, have begun to express concern over the environmental impacts of the Mpanda Nkuwa mega dam on the ecosystem of the Zambezi valley. Daniel Ribeiro, a biologist and the head of Justiça Ambiental (Environmental Justice), a local NGO, argued that 'No serious environmental impact study was conducted, the people whose land will be flooded were not consulted or properly compensated. No doubts that we need electricity and to modernize our agriculture [*sic*]. But at what cost?' (Horta 2009: 12).

Another issue with large dam building is the resettlement process. The Merowe Dam in Sudan displaced approximately 50,000 people and they were resettled on inferior agricultural land (Bosshard 2010b). Their demands to be relocated to viable plots of farmland have been met with violence and several villagers protesting against forced resettlement were killed by local police. According to Ali Askouri, 'Chinese engineers on the dam site are fully aware of the repression going on around them but they never interact with local people. It is hard to speak of any sense of development when those who are supposed to promote it are hiding in camps guarded 24-hours by professional security companies' (Bezlova 2007). The United Nations has also complained about other human-rights abuses and the suppression of anti-dam activism in Sudan.

These issues surrounding dam building are also evident in Ghana. Infrastructure is arguably the area of greatest cooperation between China and Ghana and several agreements have been drawn up over the years for Chinese firms to undertake construction projects including most recently, a hydroelectric dam (Tsikata et al. 2008: 5). Demand for electricity in Ghana has increased tremendously over the years, at an average of 10–15 per cent per annum for the last two decades (ISSER 2005) while The Energy Commission (EC) of Ghana estimates that residential demand may reach anywhere between 7000 and 13,000 Gigawatt hour (GWh) and commercial and industrial consumption between 3000 to 10,000 GWh by 2020 (ISSER 2005). It has been estimated that a year-long power crisis in the industrial sector caused growth to decline from 9.5 per cent in 2006 to 7.4 per cent in 2007 (Idun-Arkhurst 2008). It is hence imperative for the Ghanaian government to ensure a consistent and reliable supply of electricity for its economic growth with hydro-power dams considered a good alternative to non-renewable energy sources, such as coal and diesel.

The Bui Dam built by Sinohydro is an 'EPC' project, meaning 'engineering, procurement, construction' which has been the preferred route for many African governments since the price is agreed up front and fixed. Like many Chinese-funded infrastructure projects the majority of the money comes from ExIm Bank. The Chinese favoured the dam project as opposed to the Ghanaian Government's preferred option of a railway from the coast to Burkina Faso, because the sale of electricity to Mali, Cote d'Ivoire and Burkina Faso would guarantee repayment in a way that a railway could not. This revenue will be paid into an escrow account and these escrow funds used to service the debt. In addition there is a special arrangement with the Ghana Cocoa Board to supply cocoa at current market prices as part payment of the debt.

As mentioned before, hydropower projects usually come with huge environmental impacts which have often led to the irreversible loss of species and ecosystems and also considerable damage and disruption to human livelihoods. In Ghana, one of the most contentious issues with the Bui Dam has been the gap between the recommendations of the EIA and its actual implementation. Sutcliffe (2009), in her field research at the Bui Dam in 2007 assessing the developmental outcomes of the EIA recommendations, saw many of the recommendations, such as participation and consultation with the local people, health and livelihood security, adequate compensation, free access to information and equity in justice, blatantly flouted. There are also no Environmental Resource Management (ERM) or procedural documents pertaining to Sinohydro, a major stakeholder in this project (Sutcliffe 2009: 7). A non-state actor, the 'Ghana Dams Dialogue' has argued that the mitigation measures that were put in place at Bui Dam to deal with the social, environmental, health and livelihood impacts of the existing dams have been inadequate (International Water Power and Dam Construction 2009). The Ghana Dams Dialogue started in 2006 with its mission to lobby for greater transparency and dialogue in dam planning and construction and has to date organized a series of high profile forums. As such, they were involved in the Bui resettlement issue through fact finding visits and brokering between local communities and the Bui Power Authority. Indeed ongoing research and debate suggests that the hydro-ecological impacts have not been thought through with climate change lowering water levels and increasing dam siltation, and selective downstream irrigation likely to affect the local rainfall patterns and decrease the dam's generating capacity (Ghana Dams Dialogue 2009: 4).

Indeed, not all Ghanaian stakeholders, particularly the non-state actors, are enthusiastic about the Bui Hydropower project (BHP) because of the social and environmental problems. Among the social concerns raised regarding the BHP are the socio-cultural and economic impacts of resettling about 2500 people; the biophysical, socio-economic and cultural implications associated with the likely influx of guest workers during construction; and public health issues (BKS Acres 2001; ERM 2007) which might not be easy to mitigate.

The environmental concerns are the wildlife and habitat losses within the Bui National Park (BNP) due to flooding of approximately 21 per cent of the Park. In particular, the rare black Hippopotamus is of major concern as it is highly threatened and the flooded area constitutes part of its habitat (Conservation news, 4 December 2008). Increases in rainfall due to deforestation and climate change will also increase erosion and sedimentation of the river and its banks which will ultimately decrease the life span and productivity of the dam (Ghana Dams Dialogue 2009: 4). This will then also affect river flows around fisheries and the potential proliferation of water and vector-borne diseases and aquatic weeds (Alhassan 2009).

There has also been tension around the dam over resettlement. Studies show that although new accommodation seems appropriate, the local people affected were hardly consulted. Further, some people have yet to be rehoused or compensated at all with local grass-roots leaders getting involved. The new government have sent high-level representatives to the area to calm matters which is part of an electoral payback since there was a rerun of the presidential vote in the Tain constituency where Bui is located which went the National Democratic Congress (NDC)'s way.

Other than environmental and resettlement issues, another contentious issue is the working conditions of the labourers on the BHP project. Working conditions are harsh and the Ghana Trade Union Congress (Ghana TUC) has found that all Ghanaian workers are on temporary contracts and have often been dismissed for fairly minor issues. Chinese corporations in general do not encourage trade unions, and originally did not allow for it at Bui. But a deputation from the Ghana TUC argued that it was enshrined both in Ghanaian law and the contract and hence foreign companies must oblige by the local laws. The Ghana TUC has pushed for less crowded accommodation and for better protection from the debilitating black fly (*Simuliidae*).

It is indeed a difficult task for all dam builders to balance the demand for the construction of alternative hydropower with the need to ensure environmental sustainability, social justice and equity for the affected population. Although China has considerable domestic experience in dam construction, it is perhaps still learning about how to cope with these wider implications on foreign soil, where civil society organizations are more actively engaged with these debates. Although the state is trying to mitigate the environmental and socio-political impacts arising from the construction of the dams, it was demonstrated that the non-state actors, such as the Ghana Dams Dialogue and Ghana TUC have more success in negotiating with the Chinese companies in terms of compliance. Indeed, the state's hands are tied in some ways, as lax investment and environmental laws are attractive to foreign investors as it reduces the cost and time in terms of carrying out these projects.

The Bui Dam example illustrated how state and non-state actors could collaborate in terms of environmental governance and mitigating the impacts from a large-scale development project. This success is however not replicated in the oil sector of Angola, due to the domestic political situation and the lack of non-state actors. In Angola, oil provides some 80 per cent of state revenue, accounting for 61 per cent of GDP and 90 per cent of export earnings in 2005 (Sogge 2006). Employing fewer than eleven thousand people and with almost no forward or backward linkages with the onshore economy, the oil industry is an enclave.

In Angola, within months of the end of the war some of the major Chinese policy banks (such as the China Construction Bank and ExIm bank) had begun to open credit lines to Angola. The environmental implications of China-Angola cooperation in the natural resource sector may have been further exacerbated by the preference in Chinese lending for using natural resources as repayment for concessional loans, as it arguably encourages profligate exploitation of resources. The most exemplary case to date is the '"Angola mode"... where repayment of loans for infrastructure development is made in natural resources (oil in the case of Angola)' (Vines et al. 2009: 32; see also McDonald et al. 2009). The extraction of oil and gas has also had many negative impacts on Angola's marine ecosystems and biological resources. Hazardous wastes and its impacts on water and air quality (both in the immediate vicinity of the oil project and in relation to global concerns such as ozone depleting substances and greenhouse gases) have endangered the health of local populations near oil installations and pipelines and destroyed local livelihoods such as farming and fishing (Karl 2007: 26). While in the last decade Angola has developed wide-ranging environmental legislation and produced several expensively assembled volumes claiming to outline its vision of development in the medium term (2009–13) and long term (up to 2025) (Ministério do Planeamento 2007a, 2007b) in reality Angola has no clear and coherent strategy for development (Shaxson et al. 2008). Furthermore, although there has been increased engagement with regional and international bodies and partners, there needs to be more coordination of environmental issues across state agencies.

For example, the Environment Framework Law (1998) encourages community participation on environmental issues but there is no evidence that this participation has been a feature of the dialogue between China and Angola which has largely been conducted at a narrow, elite business level. There is also no evidence from our field-work to indicate that the original ExIm or China International Fund (CIF) loans were assessed in terms of the environmental impacts they might have prior to approval. Further, because many of the loans from China have been managed by the Gabinete de Reconstrução Nacional (GRN; Office for National Reconstruction) projects, they have often been implemented without consultation with other Angolan state agencies and without wider public participation in decision-making.

However some Chinese oil companies such as the China National Petroleum Corporation (CNPC) have made concerted efforts to support CSR initiatives, such as donating US$50 million to Sudan for construction of hospitals and schools and building the world's largest biodegradable waste water treatment facility in Sudan's Block 1/2/4 oil fields to eliminate the discharge of effluents (CAITEC 2010: 5). But Sinopec, unlike other oil companies such as British Petroleum (BP 2008) and Chevron (Chevron 2011), has not conducted a single EIA or published a CSR report, identifying the environmental implications arising from the exploratory/extractive platforms in Angola to date. In terms of CSR the Angolan government has insisted that transnational corporations operating in Angola devote 15 per cent of their annual budget to development-related activities (Alexander and Gilbert 2008) but this process is managed by Sonangol and it is not at all clear that the same rules apply to Chinese oil companies like Sinopec or to the new quasinational companies being set up like the CSIH or SSI.

More generally, the progress in Angola of other international initiatives such as the Extractive Industries Transparency Initiative (EITI) has also been limited by the proliferation of credit from China (although the loans are only a small fraction of the value of Angolan oil production in recent years). EITI is necessary for better governance of Africa's oil sector, but not sufficient. Transparency, autonomous and transparent management of revenues (involving separation of the government from private sector), the creation of autonomous funds to manage revenue and the careful management of government resources and their fair distribution are also important (Yates 2009). In particular by focusing on the nature of governance and on the exact revenues generated by natural resources EITI underlines what funds *should* be available for promoting national development, making it clear when these funds have been misappropriated. Despite growing pressure from domestic and international NGOs and intergovernmental organizations on the issue of transparency within Angola's oil (and diamond) industry, the credit available from China has arguably allowed the Angolan state to ignore these pressures and concerns about the use to which the profits from extractive resources are put, with potentially far-reaching implications for the future of Angola and its citizens.

However, issues with environmental governance in the oil industry are not only exclusive to Chinese enterprises. For example, multinational oil companies such as Shell, Chevron, Texaco, Exxon and Elf commonly use gas flaring in the Niger Delta as the preferred means to dispose of waste gas associated with oil exploration (Dung et al. 2008: 297). Despite flaring in the Niger Delta being environmentally damaging and contributing to a measurable percentage of the world's total emissions of green house gases, these multinational oil companies state that 'nothing is unethical and immoral in flaring gas, as there is no alternative at present' (Eweje 2006: 39–40). Moreover, major investors in the largest oil producing countries such as Angola and Nigeria are western companies Chevron Texaco and Exxon Mobil (United States).

What makes China's increasing involvement in African oil sector so controversial is probably China's willingness to engage states such as Sudan and Guinea, countries in which atrocities (which United States and other nations have branded genocide) are common. Numerous human rights groups have accused Sudan of systematically massacring civilians and chasing them from ancestral lands to clear oil-producing areas (Rone 2003). Beijing's aggressive pursuit of this type of oil diplomacy without consideration of the international community's concerns may benefit China in the short term, but may have much more damaging long-term implications.

## Conclusion: globalizing China's environmental responsibilities

Chinese strategies in both domestic and overseas environmental management has evolved quite considerably in the last two decades. Domestically, calls from non-state actors such as the public and media have prompted the Chinese government to revamp Chinese environmental legislation and enforcement while interactions with international environmental agencies through multilateral platforms such as the CITES and United Nations Framework Convention on Climate Change have also introduced global environmental norms to the Chinese state which are beginning to be adopted domestically. Chinese national environmental responsibility now extends well beyond Chinese boundaries due to considerable increases in outward investments into resource extraction activities in Africa (as well as into other regions), attracting significant attention from western observers and international civil society organizations who have highlighted the significant environmental degradation accompanying China's chosen domestic development path and questioned the sustainability of such trajectories and their feasibility in other parts of the world. Hence non-state actors, such as environmental NGOs like the World Wildlife Fund, International River Networks and Ghana Dams Dialogue are increasing their efforts to pressure China into mitigating its environmental impacts overseas. As such, in 2006, China vowed to help African countries to turn 'their advantages in energy and resources into development strengths, protecting the local environment and promoting sustainable social and economic development in the local areas' (FOCAC 2006a). One specific measure was the dispatching of environmental protection administrators to Africa and the funding of a China–Africa Environment Centre that works under the banner of the United Nations Environment Programme. In the Declaration of Sharm el-Sheikh of the 2009 FOCAC and the accompanying Action Plan, there was significant emphasis on the environmental aspects of the engagement between China and Africa.

In Africa, in terms of localized environmental impacts from Chinese FDI, the Chinese SOEs are of particular importance given the scale of their projects and investments in Africa and their differential capacities to impact on the environment. As there is a direct relation between these SOEs and the Chinese government, it is generally expected that the Chinese government could do something to ensure its overseas investments are properly governed. However, this is not the case due to the variety and sheer numbers of actors involved, as discussed in Chapter 4. Similarly, although the smaller SMEs tend to be less environmentally impactful due to their smaller investment and project sizes, the Chinese government has little control over these actors. It is among these actors in particular that we see a more worrying trend of illegal activities, such as ivory smuggling and illegal fishing. These activities are threatening to the sustainable extraction of natural resources and jeopardize the food and environmental security of the African communities concerned. In the timber industry, the environmental implications of illegal or unsustainable extraction will extend beyond China and Africa given that the decrease in forest cover to absorb carbon dioxide will inevitably contribute to climate change and further rises in global temperature. Furthermore, African and international civil society organizations are also concerned with the violation of EIAs on social and environmental issues and the infringement of human rights and labour laws, as demonstrated in the case study of the Bui Dam in Ghana.

These illegal activities and violations of EIAs are often more prevalent in states with weak governance structures, such as Somalia, the DRC and Equatorial Guinea. At the same time, the importance of the local government's will to implement, govern and mitigate environmental impacts needs to be re-emphasized as it is ultimately these projects and investments that fall within the jurisdiction and sovereignty of African states. As such there is a need to promote and enhance the local capacity of these states to implement and enforce laws and regulations for overseas investors as well as a strong need for collective dialogue and action from African states concerning possible strategies for managing the environmental implications of these foreign investments (e.g. through the African Union). The examples of Ghana and Angola discussed above illustrate how state and non-state actors may or may not come together to play pivotal roles in ensuring compliance from international companies.

The changes in China's domestic and overseas environmental management strategies can partly be attributed to the global efforts of 'socializing' China into global norms, which are spearheaded by various multilateral organizations, such as the International Monetary Fund, the World Bank Group and civil society actors such as the WWF, Amnesty International, the International Rivers Network and Trade Union alliances. There is also a growing realization and acceptance in China of the important role that China has to play in global environmental governance and of the importance of engaging with a variety of non-state actors in Africa. This was exemplified by the first ever non-governmental exchange between NGOs from China and Africa held in Nairobi, Kenya on 20 August 2011. The China-Africa People's Forum was organized by the China NGO Network for International Exchanges and the Kenyan Non-Governmental Organisations Coordination Board with more than 200 Chinese and African representatives engaging in a dialogue and exchange on issues such as climate change and energy insecurity (*China Daily* 31 August 2011; UN 2011).

Questions of responsibility beyond borders, between places, and between place and space, have always been central for geographers and are also key questions for postcolonial theory (Raghuram et al. 2009). In recent years, following the intervention of Massey (2004) there has been a growing disciplinary interest in geographies of responsibility which raise important questions of considerable relevance to the emerging debates around China–Africa relations. Alongside this there has been a growing pressure on China to assume more 'responsibility' as a world power, much of which has focused on China's role in Sudan's oil industry and its complicity in the perpetuation of conflict in Darfur. It is thus necessary to critically explore the emerging notions of responsibility *to*, responsibility *for* and responsibility *over* African spaces of development as they are articulated through contemporary China–Africa encounters.

As mentioned earlier, there is also perhaps a risk of overstating China's role here – African states also have questions to answer about their own senses of responsibility *for* 'development', *to* their own citizens and *over* their own domestic resource endowments. This means asking questions about the nature of the states with which China cooperates and the wider extent of their extraversion. Furthermore, as Downs (2007) has argued, one of the greatest 'fictions' about China's overseas strategy is that Beijing has complete control over what its companies do and an exaggerated assumption that what Chinese firms do is substantially different from the activities of many western enterprises. While conventional wisdom posits that Chinese multinationals are less concerned with environmental issues than their Western counterparts, not enough research has been done to actually prove this hypothesis. What is clear, however, is that Chinese companies are quickly generating the same kinds of environmental damage and community opposition that Western companies have spawned around the world.

Despite the inherent problems of the concept of CSR and other global mechanisms as non-binding agreements, it is highly dependent on the political will of governments and companies and on an increasing role for environmentally focused civil society movements to ensure there is compliance. Although major international NGOs, such as the International Rivers Network, have assumed responsibility for 'socializing' Sinohydro into global norms of livelihood and environmental protection, it is ultimately the company's will to implement CSR. On the other hand, African civil society also plays an increasingly imperative role. The issue is that if African countries are to avoid another (or deeper) resource curse, the benefits must be distributed by a democratic developmental state. So, Tjønneland et al. (2006) see support for African civil society organizations (CSOs) as a key priority for donors. But civil society is not a homogenous realm unilaterally acting in the good of poor Africans nor is it easy for CSOs to effect changes within Chinese policy. Therefore there is an urgent need to create legislative and institutional frameworks to address Chinese investment in Africa especially in the area of natural resource extraction (Rupp in Rotberg 2008: 84). The overarching aim is to ensure Africa's resources are managed and distributed in a more sustainable and equitable manner.

# 8
# The Geopolitics of China–Africa Engagement

## Introduction: China's oil diplomacy and 'soft power'

Few aspects of China's recent (re)engagement with Africa have attracted as much attention in recent years as what some observers refer to as China's 'oil diplomacy'. Many commentators have highlighted how China has used notionally unconditional aid, low-interest loans and technical cooperation agreements to cement bilateral deals over oil supply, engineering contracts and trade agreements. Beijing is then said to be using the central pillars of its foreign policy, notably unconditional respect for state sovereignty and its corollary, non-interference, in the pursuit of its interests, be they energy security, multipolarity or the 'One China' principle (Tull 2006). Some have even gone further in suggesting that to achieve these goals, Beijing 'is prepared to defend autocratic regimes that commit human rights abuses and forestall democratic reforms for narrow ends of regime survival' (Tull 2006: 476). Others have suggested that to quench its oil thirst, China will resort to any means to extract all available oil and gas resources, thereby destabilizing the regional and even global order. This assertion has been a regular feature of some of the popular geopolitical discourses mentioned in the introduction to this book. It is also quite closely related to the 'rogue aid' discourses and the notion that China is underwriting a world that is 'more corrupt, chaotic and authoritarian' (Naím 2007: 95). It can also be linked to the wider idea of the BRICS as a new version of domination for Africa, accused of neocolonialism, which has emerged in the context of China's growing involvement in the continent (Alden 2007; Alden et al. 2008). International commentators highlight how the operations of China's national oil companies in Africa – China National Offshore Oil Corporation (CNOOC), China National Petroleum Corporation

221

(CNPC), China Petrochemical Corporation (Sinopec) – are closely tied if not driven by Chinese strategic interests (Shaw et al. 2009).

Current interpretations of the 'China Inc.' euphemism emphasize the degree of coherence between Chinese state companies and Beijing's strategic agenda but often this is considerably overplayed. One of the most sweeping arguments following from such discourses is that in future China may enter wars over access to strategic resources, including oil, gas and water, around the world. Here the spectre of a 'global resource war' (Kornegay and Landsberg 2009: 173) looms large. Bajpaee (2005) for example, writing in the *Asian Times* declares that China's quest for oil may 'endanger international security' (Bajpaee 2005). A report by the International Crisis Group in 2008 entitled 'China's thirst for Oil' also notes that China's energy needs have generated concerns about global and regional security but recognizes that 'these are largely overstated' (ICG 2008: i). Klare (2001) boldly predicts that overlapping claims over oil and gas resources in the South China Sea could trigger armed conflict between China and other claimant states and that conflicting claims in the East China Sea by China and Japan may erupt into naval clashes. Moreover, several analysts argue that China's efforts to gain overseas oil supplies could undermine US national security,[1] undercut US efforts to stabilize the Middle East (and reform regimes there) and could even reduce US oil imports (Lai 2007). There is thus the implication that China's foreign policy is being focused solely on the pursuit of energy security, that this has potentially very destablizing consequences for the international political system and that China is prepared to go to war to defend these interests.

China's recent growth has clearly required a concerted economic internationalization and with it changing foreign policy discourses, that bring China closer binationally and multilaterally to other countries. As a result China's foreign policy is understood by some to be shifting from a concern with 'ideology' to a preoccupation with 'business', using what Joseph Nye (2004) terms 'soft power' (recently reformulated as 'smart power') to cajole client states into accepting Chinese contracts (Nye himself has served as an advisor to the Chinese on how best to utilize this form of power). As Nye conceived of it soft power involves three resources – culture, political values and foreign policies – representing 'the ability to get what you want through attraction rather than coercion' exercised through a combination of tangible offers of aid and economic assistance along with intangible efforts to elevate the nature of a country's cultural and political engagement with the forums of world governance.

Yet as Cammack (2008) has shown there are many weaknesses to Nye's conception as he is unable to imagine any situation other than one in which the United States unequivocally takes the lead and there is perhaps too much emphasis on America's national interest. Further, Nye regularly conflates the need to cooperate with the need to lead and for all the talk of soft power in the end the United States clearly does rely on 'hard' power. Further, as Bilgin and Eliş (2008) have argued, Nye's analysis does not offer a theory of power that reflects upon its own moment(s) and site(s) of production and expression nor does it reflect on how US culture, political ideas and policies came to be considered 'attractive' by the rest of the world. Nonetheless there is still value in Nye's (soft) power analysis and his conception has been widely discussed and drawn upon in China itself.[2] The Central Committee of the Chinese Communist Party recently named the promotion of cultural development and the raising of China's 'cultural soft power' as one of the priorities in the twelfth five-year plan for 2011–15 (Kallio 2011). Thus China has recently sought to woo the world with a 'charm offensive' involving diplomacy, trade incentives, cultural and educational exchange opportunities and other techniques, to project a benign national image, to pose as a model of social and economic success and to develop stronger international alliances. Kurlantzick (2007) argues that Beijing's new soft power diplomacy has altered the political landscape in Southeast Asia and far beyond, changing the dynamics of China's relationships with other countries and actively working to take advantage of American policy mistakes in the process.

It is however very important to situate China's contemporary use of 'soft power' in a historical context. As we saw in Chapter 2, the current terms of China–Africa engagement build on longer term geopolitical traditions and histories of cooperation and interaction. We have argued elsewhere that this history of Chinese foreign policy discourses (and the wider geopolitical traditions upon which they rest) today functions as a discursive field through which current foreign policy is legitimized (Power and Mohan 2010). While this history of China–Africa linkages is important for shaping contemporary development it is also used ideologically by China to legitimize its recent commercially centred activities despite the fact that Chinese diplomats have long insisted that commercial enterprise is considered quite separate from political affairs (Srinavasan 2008). Senior Chinese officials have regularly spoken of a sense of historical mutuality with African countries around shared experiences of colonialism and this is used to defend China's current interventions in Africa against accusations of imperialism and to situate

China discursively as part of both the 'developing' and 'developed' world. As if to undeline this, the official policy paper on *China's Foreign Aid* (Government of China 2011) even starts with the sentence 'China is a developing country'.

The two most important pillars of China's foreign policy[3] are that of the 'One China' principle and an uncompromising stance on non-interference in the domestic matters of other states (Zheng 2005). Only a handful of states globally continue to recognize Taiwan instead of Mainland China (Figure 8.1). Indeed, in Africa alone, recent years have seen the reversal of Senegal, Chad and Malawi's diplomatic relations, all of whom have switched to recognition of the People's Republic of China (PRC) government. Thus there are a range of important geopolitical traditions that are said to form the foundations of China's current engagement with Africa, which are usually traced back to the revolutionary period of Chinese foreign policy from 1950 to the early 1970s when China's foreign policy was fiercely critical of the bipolar Cold War world and sought to wrest the leadership of the non-aligned nations away from Moscow (Snow 1988; Jung and Halliday 2006). For Taylor (2006a, 2006b) the link connecting all Chinese foreign policy over the

*Figure 8.1* 'We will definitely free Taiwan!'. 1971. Stefan R. Landsberger collection, International Institute of Social History (Amsterdam)

past 50 years is a desire to diminish and contain the influence of hege-monic powers and also to carve out a rightful place for China in the world, born from a sense that China has been 'muscled out' of inter-national relations. China's confrontation with the United States in the 1950s and 1960s and with the Soviet Union in the 1960s and 1970s were particularly important here. The early days of PRC diplomacy therefore primarily involved attempts to counter the international recognition of Taiwan and to compete with Western and Russian influence in the continent (Lyman 2005). The concept of Afro-Asian solidarity, forged in the crucible of independence struggles, would also go on to provide an important political foundation for the evolving China–Africa relation-ship (Figure 8.2). According to the post-conference analysis produced by the US administration's Office of Intelligence Research (OIR) in 1955,[4] Bandung had been a psychological milestone, advancing the prospect of both ad hoc and formal Afro-Asian partnership and signalling the end of a 'lingering sense of inferiority' that might combine to create a stronger and friendlier region even one 'more ready to cooperate with the West'.

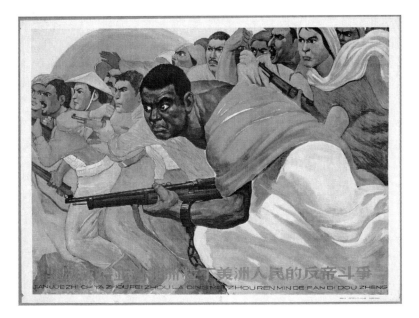

*Figure 8.2* 'Vigorously support the anti-imperialist struggle of the peoples of Asia, Africa and Latin America'. 1964. Stefan R. Landsberger collection, International Institute of Social History (Amsterdam)

The events and aftermath surrounding Tiananmen Square also provided a crucial geopolitical moment in the expansion of China's relations with Africa. As one commentator noted, 'the events of June 1989 ... did not affect the PRC's relations with the Third World as it did with the Western world...What changed [was] the PRC's attitude towards the Third World countries, which...turned from one of benign neglect to one of renewed emphasis' (Gu 1995: 125). The fragile relations with the West undoubtedly compelled Beijing to reconsider its relations with the 'developing world'. In certain quarters it was felt that western critiques of the Chinese government's actions in response to the student democracy movement at Tiananmen Square had less to do with human rights issues and were more oriented towards undermining China's rapid modernization – a sentiment shared by many African leaders and which became a powerful tool in rallying them to support China's cause (Taylor 2004). With the demise of the Cold War altering the balance of power in the global system towards unilateralism, China took advantage of the situation to push for a multipolar world order that resisted Western and, in particular, US hegemony.

In this chapter we want to move beyond the notion of China as a 'monolithic strategic actor' (Wissenbach 2009: 6) and to disaggregate China and the increasingly diverse range of foreign policy actors involved in this 'soft power' charm offensive, debunking the myth that China has only recently engaged the African continent as part of its oil diplomacy and seeking to situate the rise of China as part of a wider contemporary 'scramble for Africa'. The chapter begins by considering the geoeconomic and geopolitical rivalry emerging around Africa and highlights the growing importance of Africa and the competition for strategic influence there among the BRICs in particular but also the competition among other emerging and established players. How do China's emerging economic and political agendas relate to those of other 'rising powers' in Africa (particularly Brazil, India and Russia)? The chapter then considers the range of foreign policy actors that can be considered part of this charm offensive, looking at the role of China's provinces and foreign policy think tanks, the Chinese military, Chinese state-owned enterprises (SOEs) and the 'quiet diplomacy' (Shambaugh 2007a) practised by the International Department of the Chinese Communist Party. The discussion here also explores the news and communications aspects of China's global 'soft power' push as an important strategic attempt to grapple with the domestic and international challenges emerging in the age of globalized information (Bandurski 2009). The chapter then moves on to focus on China's recent shifts in foreign policy discourses and its vision of the evolving international political system following controversy about China's role in Sudan and Zimbabwe and reflecting upon the long-term tenability of China's established principles for foreign cooperation (e.g. non-interference, respect for state sovereignty). The focus is not just on how China seeks to engage the world but also on how the world has come to view China. Recent debates about multilateralism and multipolarity in China (given China's accession to the World Trade Organization (WTO) and its contemporary role within the United Nations (UN)) are particularly revealing in this regard and these are considered alongside recent attempts to encourage China to consider questions of international 'responsibility'. The chapter then goes on to explore the growing importance of peacekeeping, security and military cooperation between China and Africa. The chapter concludes by setting out a framework for a critical geopolitics of China–Africa relations.

## The new 'scramble for Africa'

When examining the range of countries currently seeking economic and political 'partnerships' in Africa, China is clearly not the only show in town and Chinese engagement with Africa therefore needs to be understood in the context of the wider contemporary 'scramble for Africa' of which it is a part. This includes the efforts of the European Union (EU), of the US Africa Command (AFRICOM), the India–Africa Forum, the Turkey–Africa Summit and the Tokyo International Conference on African Development (TICAD). Africa is also becoming amenable to the persuasions of India, Brazil, Russia, the Gulf States and rising Southeast Asian giants like Malaysia, Singapore and South Korea. Russia has intensified its efforts to engage with Africa in recent years but as with Chinese engagement with the continent, this has an important historical context.[5] The role of the Soviet Union in shaping the coordinates of 'third world' geopolitics is a neglected theme in the literature and little is known about the instrumentalization of the Soviet model in development practice (Laïdi 1988, 1990). During the Cold War the USSR played on its ambiguous position as both 'inside' the international system and 'outside' it, presenting itself as the natural 'midwife' for completing the independence of 'new-born' states (Laïdi 1988).

The importance of Russia as a trading partner to African countries is still relatively minimal when compared with the EU, China, India Brazil or the United States but between 1994 and 2008 it has increased almost tenfold from US$740 million to US$7.3 billion (AfDB 2011). During this time the Russian government embraced a new foreign policy towards Africa, undertook high-level official visits to some African countries, and advocated for conflict resolution, humanitarian assistance and debt relief. One of the main attractions for Russia's energy and other natural resource industries are the vast reserves of natural resources in Africa and as a result Russian companies led by Gazprom, Rusal, Nornikel, Alrosa and Renova have invested billions in sub-Saharan Africa (Matthews 2007). Others, like metal group Evraz and oil giant Lukoil are also active, as are a number of banks, including Vneshtorgbank, which has opened the first Angolan bank to have predominantly foreign ownership (Matthews 2007). Rosatom, the Russian state nuclear energy group, has been expanding its worldwide uranium reserves including the US$1.15bn acquisition of a project in Tanzania and a ten-year agreement on the delivery of enriched uranium with South Africa, having already invested in Namibia. Russia has strongly encouraged its companies to buy assets around the world because it suited former President Vladimir Putin's philosophy of restoring Russia's international position. In September 2006 Putin made a whistle-stop tour of Africa with several top Russian oligarchs in tow – including Russian oligarch and President of the Renova group Viktor Vekselberg, who pledged to invest US$2 billion in metal and mining projects in Africa. The importance Russia places on expanding its engagement with Africa was also illustrated by Russian President Dmitry Medvedev's visit to Egypt, Nigeria, Namibia and Angola in June 2009 (the second visit to Africa in three years by a Russian President) to sign natural gas deals involving Russian state-owned gas giant Gazprom and to discuss commercial opportunities for Russia (UPI 2009). Russian official sources presented the visit as purely economic, stressing that its goals were to assist Russian businesses and to develop mutually beneficial relations with African countries. Accompanied by a 400-strong business delegation President Medvedev signed a number of important economic agreements in the sphere of energy resources and nuclear power (Filatova 2009).

Russia's outward investment is thus dominated by large resource-based corporations that seek to gain greater access to the African markets of fuel, energy and metallurgy, and expand Russian investment flows to African countries, including Algeria, Angola, Botswana, Côte d'Ivoire, the Democratic Republic of Congo (DRC), Egypt, Gabon, Guinea, Namibia, Nigeria and South Africa. The Russian private sector however – unlike the Chinese, Brazilian, Indian and US private sector – has so far failed to build the requisite networks in Africa. The necessary interests have thus not emerged to push for closer trade between

Africa and Russia. Further, Russia's own enormous energy resources are located in areas that are not easily accessible, sparsely populated and have extremely unfriendly climatic conditions – so developing them would be a much costlier business than developing the same resources in Africa (Filatova 2009). Unlike China, Russia currently has little need of African resources but is keen to sell Russian nuclear technology and possibly armaments to African countries. Russia may even be seeking to control the access that other countries have to Africa's resources by forming cartels with African oil and gas producers.[6] In effect, Medvedev's visit to Africa should be seen as a move to create a bloc of countries rich in energy resources (Kornegay and Landsberg 2009). The existence of such a bloc, in Russia's thinking, would increase the political weight of its participants and thus change the balance of power and influence in the world (Filatova 2009).

As with China and Russia, India's alliances with Africa were forged during the 1950s and 1960s in the context of debates about non-alignment and decolonization (Dubey 1990; Beri 2003). There is considerable anxiety in India about China's growing influence on the continent and a growing desire to mimic the close economic and commercial ties forged by Beijing in recent years. India's trade with Africa has soared from just under US$1 billion in 1991, the year the Indian economy began to open up to the outside world, to around US$50 billion in 2010. Some 250 Indian companies have invested, mainly in telecommunications, chemical and mining companies (*The Guardian*, 23 May 2011). The value of China's trade with Africa, worth less than India's in 1999, had leapt to more than US$100bn by 2010. African exports to China surged 48 per cent between 1999 and 2004, compared with 14 per cent growth in exports to India (*Financial Times* 2008). India woke up to Chinese influence in Africa when Beijing hosted the third FOCAC meeting in 2006 and following similar conferences to promote cooperation organized by Japan, Turkey and the EU, the first India–Africa Forum, a two-day summit in New Delhi attended by eight heads of African states and delegations from 14 African countries, was held in 2008. At the conference Manmohan Singh, India's prime minister, said India would more than double the size of credit lines to projects in Africa, from US$2.15bn to US$5.4bn between 2003–04 and 2008–09. He also promised to boost India's aid budget to Africa, pledging grants of US$500m (€318m, £252m) for projects over the next five to six years and announced duty-free access to Indian markets for the world's 50 least developed countries (LDCs), 34 of which are in Africa, as part of a package of measures designed to highlight New Delhi's commitment to deepening relations with the continent. The scheme would provide preferential market access on tariff lines that comprise 92.5 per cent of all LDC exports, including diamonds, cotton, cocoa, aluminium ore and copper ore. Declaring India's intent to become 'a close partner in Africa's resurgence', Mr Singh called for a 'new architecture' in relations, launching an 'Africa-India Framework for Co-operation' and a 'Delhi Declaration'. At the second India–Africa Forum summit in Addis Ababa in May 2011 India announced a US$5.7 billion loan package (including US$5 billion in lines of credit and US$700 million for new institutions and training programmes), US$300 million for a railway line between Ethiopia and Djibouti and even US$2 million for the African Union mission in Somalia.

Energy, particularly oil, coal and uranium, have been at the forefront of India's strategy in Africa. India imported 12 per cent of its crude oil from Nigeria alone in 2010 and has increasingly looked to Africa to diversify its energy sources, and to reduce its dependency on the Middle East, which accounts for two-thirds of its imports (Vines 2010b). India is dependent on oil for roughly 33 per cent of its energy needs, 65 per cent of which it imports and currently India is the fifth largest consumer of energy in the world, accounting for about 3.75 per cent of global consumption. With rapid economic growth and industrialization, India is expected to double its energy consumption by 2030, overtaking Japan and Russia to become the world's third largest consumer, after the United States and China (Shrivastava 2009). The significance of the Indian Ocean to India's economic development and security is thus particularly immense (Vines and Oruitemeka 2008; Vines 2009b; Vines and Campos 2010). Most of India's trade is by sea and nearly 89 per cent of India's oil arrives by sea. Maintaining energy security is one of the major policy challenges facing India. Not unlike China, India also views Africa as a possible source of raw materials and energy for its industrial growth. Africa currently accounts for about 20 per cent of India's oil imports, a figure that is likely to rise in the future.

India is now scaling up its diplomatic initiatives within Africa and there are plans to add to the 25 existing Indian embassies and high commissions on the continent. Keen to protect its military and security presence in the Western Indian Ocean region the Indian government has been alarmed by recent Chinese efforts in the Seychelles and Mauritius (Vines 2009b). New Delhi was particularly alarmed that Chinese President Hu Jintao ended his tour of eight African states in early 2007 by visiting the Seychelles (Aiyar 2007) while Mauritius is the location for a US$730 million Chinese special economic zone (SEZ). As

India seeks to deepen its defence and commercial engagement with the Seychelles, Madagascar, Mauritius and Mozambique, Sino-Indian rivalries are likely to increase further. That said there are perceptible differences in India's foreign policy in the East African, West African and the Indian Ocean regions (Shrivastava 2009).

The Indian economy has grown steadily over the last two decades. The largest democracy in the world has also become one of the fastest growing, with an average annual GDP growth rate of 5.7 per cent in the 1980s and the 1990s, and 9 per cent and above from 2001 to 2007 (Shrivastava 2009: 126). Since 2000, the overall thrust of Indian foreign policy has been to seek geopolitical partnerships in multiple directions to serve its national interests and India has started to play a more involved role in a wide spectrum of multilateral and regional institutions. India is however not necessarily perceived as a 'champion' of the global South. In spite of taking a leading role in South–South initiatives such as the G20 in the WTO and the India–Brazil–South Africa (IBSA) Dialogue Forum (see below), the Indian approach has not been radical enough concerning the transformation of the existing international economic or political structures, nor does it articulate a concrete agenda to promote Southern interests, or the interests of non-members (see Alden and Vieira 2005). Further, the Nehruvian notion of non-interference, which retains a considerable influence on India's policy-making, has much in common with the Chinese foreign cooperation principle of non-interference in the affairs of foreign states. Unlike China however, Indian investment is notably more diverse in terms of its regional as well as sectoral spreads (Naidu 2008a). India also has a significant diaspora in Africa which is an important conduit and increasingly plays a significant role in furthering the relationship. Indian multinationals such as the Tata group and Mahindra and Mahindra have been present in Africa for several decades (Pal, 2008) while Indian NGOs and civil society are becoming increasingly active at an international level (Price 2011). However, the outward investments of Indian companies are set to rise sharply, partly in response to the government's 'Focus Africa Programme' and the 'Go Global' policy. Unlike China however few of the companies involved are state-owned.

Brazil has also been attempting to engage with Africa in a big way in recent years. The current pro-Africa stance in Brazil can be traced back to Brazilian diplomatic attempts in the 1960s and 1970s to establish economic, political and cultural relations with the continent (Freitas Barbosa et al. 2009). In the 1970s Brazil sought to diversify the country's economic partners, seeking to relativize the prominence given to the United States by increasing the role of European countries and Japan, but also by fostering technical cooperation and establishing new ties with countries perceived to be at the same level of development. Following the progress of decolonization in Africa Brazil's cooperation with the continent increased considerably (Vizentini 2005). Common action in UN fora, two-way diplomatic missions, technical cooperation and increasing trade primarily with Portuguese ex-colonies, Nigeria, and southern African countries, were the constitutive features of Brazilian relations with Africa in this period. Stimulated by this new political climate, in 1979, Petrobras made its first investment in Angola, followed by the construction company Norberto Odebrecht in 1982. Following this, other firms from this sector came in, not restricting themselves to Portuguese-speaking countries (Ribeiro 2007). During the 1980s and the 1990s, as the Brazilian economy successively faced internal crises and a new pattern of integration into the world economy was put in place – leading to a foreign policy rearrangement – the country's relationship with Africa suffered an intense decline (Ribeiro 2007).

Brazil's recent escalation of its cooperation with Africa can be traced in particular to the emergence of President Lula's administration in 2003. Brazil's exports increased rising by a factor of 2.8 from 1999 to 2007, reaching a trade surplus of US$46 billion in 2006, the fifth largest in the world (WTO 2008). Booming commodity prices and a reasonably competitive industrial sector were key factors determining this outcome (Freitas Barbosa et al. 2009). From 1999 to 2007, the bilateral current of trade (exports and imports) increased by 459 per cent, almost reaching US$20 billion in the last year of the period. By 2010 bilateral trade stood at about US$25 billion (BBC 2011b). Much of this activity is geographically concentrated however. Some 66.8 per cent of the country's exports to Africa go to South Africa, Nigeria, Angola and Egypt (Freitas Barbosa et al. 2009). Brazilian transnational companies, some of which are in direct competition with firms from India, China and Russia 'either come from sectors in which the country combines resource advantages with technological capacities, such as mining, oil and steel; or from somewhat isolated industrial sectors – aircraft, bus manufacture, auto parts – that have developed new products and processes, or from the heavy construction sector' (Freitas Barbosa et al. 2009: 70).

Brazilian attempts to establish greater cooperation with Africa are marked by a clear effort to depict relations as being 'special'.[7] This rhetoric is heavily based on the African heritage within Brazilian culture, on Brazil's historical debt to Africa for perpetuating slavery for centuries as well as on the fact that African countries are also developing ex-colonies that have much to gain from cooperation with Brazil in multilateral fora. Lula has made eight trips to 19 countries in Africa since coming to power while Brazil opened 12 new embassies in Africa between 2003 and 2007 alone (Freitas-Barbosa et al. 2009). Another important step in developing Brazilian engagement with Africa was the creation in 2003 of the IBSA Dialogue Forum. IBSA is a state-led trilateral development initiative between India, Brazil and South Africa to promote South–South cooperation and exchange (Taylor 2009). As regional leaders, with similar positions in multilateral organizations and a common wish to integrate a reformed UN Security Council, India, Brazil and South Africa established a strategic partnership. However, the economic ties between these partners are not as strong as they could be and the forum seems not to go much beyond informal consultations and small-scale technical partnership agreements.

In a 2008 speech given by President Lula at GE Transportation South America, in the state of Minas Gerais, he criticized Brazilian firms' 'timid' participation in Africa vis-á-vis that of Chinese firms, arguing that 'Brazil cannot afford to sit and wait while things are happening in the African continent without our participation' (*Valor Econômico* 28 May 2008). Brazilian companies are by no means on a level playing field with their Chinese competitors however as the latter's expansion in Africa relies heavily on a multiplicity of governmental mechanisms that Brazil is simply not in a position to offer. Brazil does not have enough foreign policy instruments to sustain the observance of economic interests in Africa and as a result the presence of Brazilian companies in Africa cannot be credited to an efficient and pragmatic foreign policy (Freitas-Barbosa et al. 2009). We might therefore categorize the Lula government's renewed interest in Africa in terms of three main objectives: South–South diplomacy as a means of strengthening global leadership; Brazil's bid for a UN Security Council seat; and the biofuels agenda (Freitas-Barbosa et al. 2009). Nevertheless, while these geopolitical motivations are largely reflected in the rhetoric informing Brazilian policy towards Africa – as well as in the various diplomatic trips made by President Lula to the continent in an effort to open new embassies in the region – the extent to which the agreements are being implemented is unclear.

## Disaggregating Chinese foreign policy: the diversity of 'actors'

One important point of distinction between China and the other 'rising powers' is the diversity of actors involved in its foreign policy. China's major foreign policy decisions are often seen as being made exclusively by leaders at the apex of China's political hierarchy, while their idiosyncrasies and personal policy preferences were frequently understood to determine the course of Chinese foreign policy. While this may have been true in Mao Zedong's era individual supremacy in foreign policy decision-making has been significantly reduced since the 1990s as a wider range of actors come into play (Martin 2010). Similarly Lieberthal (1992) has argued that the post-reform Chinese state is characterized by 'fragmented authoritarianism', suggesting that while the state has retained its dominant role in economic and social spheres, authority below the very peak of the system has become more fragmented and disjointed as a result of economic reform and administrative decentralization. Although Foreign policy-making remains quite centralized there has thus been a considerable diversification of the range of actors involved.

The Chinese Foreign Ministry is viewed (appropriately) as the primary institutional locus of foreign policy-making and implementation in China and thus receives the lion's share of attention in Chinese diplomacy. There are a range of other important actors involved however. Over the past two decades China's international relations (IR) think tanks have come to play increasingly important roles in China's foreign policy-making and intelligence analysis, as well as serving as an increasingly important liaison to officials and specialists in foreign countries (Shambaugh 2002). Many of China's IR institutes are the 'stepchild' of the imported Soviet system, although their development since the 1980s has been spurred by an increased appreciation of the role played by think tanks in the United States and other nations (Shambaugh 2002). Some of the most prominent include the Chinese Academy of Social Sciences (CASS), the Shanghai Institute of International Studies (SIIS) and the China Institute of Contemporary International Relations (CICIR). Almost all of these operate within administrative hierarchies under a State Council ministry, a Central Committee department or one of the general departments of the People's Liberation Army (PLA). Think tank influence has certainly grown commensurate with China's involvement in global affairs as 'ministries, localities, and even private companies and educational institutions have needed information on foreign countries and international affairs, and this demand has created important new revenue streams for think tanks, as their government "customers" have had fewer financial resources to provide' (Shambaugh 2002: 581). Cumulatively, they have gained in importance (although there are exceptions to this generalization) and today they must be considered important actors in the foreign policy-making process in the PRC. The think tanks should thus 'not be dismissed as purveyors of propaganda or disseminators of disinformation. They are serious professional research institutions, both for current intelligence and for scholarly purposes' (Shambaugh 2002: 581).

While the Foreign Ministry is involved in *making* foreign policy in China, it is also well understood that many foreign policy issues are debated and decisions made among Chinese leaders through the Foreign Affairs Leading Group (FALG), which exercises supervision on foreign affairs. It is currently chaired by Hu Jintao and contains several senior members of the PRC leadership leaving the Foreign Ministry (and other organs) to implement them (Shambaugh 2007b). The FALG became increasingly influential in the 1990s becoming simultaneously a policy-deliberative body, a policy-making organ and a policy co-ordination institution. Beyond the FALG one of the most important, but least well understood, organs of China's foreign affairs system (*waishi xitong*) is the International Department of the Chinese Communist Party (CCP-ID) which deals with party-to-party relations. Over the past eight decades of the Department's existence, it has performed a mixture of positive and negative roles:

> On the negative side, it has sought to subvert foreign governments and has smuggled weapons to insurgent groups. It has been a missionary of revolution, a propaganda agent, an intelligence collector, and supporter of brutal regimes such as the Khmer Rouge. More positively and more recently, however, the ID has served as an alternative diplomatic channel and secret envoy in sensitive negotiations with North Korea (and possibly Iran), a vehicle to learn from abroad to aid China's modernisation, a conduit to introduce foreign officials and experts to China and as a means to build ties with foreign societies and political parties. (Shambaugh 2007a: 28)

Before and after the 1955 meeting of the Afro-Asian People's Solidarity Organisation conference in Bandung, Indonesia, the International Liaison Department (ILD; the predecessor of ID) expanded its links with socialist parties and movements in Africa and the Middle East (Figure 8.3). This included inviting numbers of youth, women's and worker's delegations from these countries to China. The ILD was also given responsibility for establishing party relations with African liberation movements in 1977 (to compete with the Soviet Union) (Shambaugh 2007a). Today, the Chinese Communist Party (through the ID) maintains ties

觉醒了的人民,必将得到最后的胜利!

*Figure 8.3* 'Awakened peoples, you will certainly attain the ultimate victory!' September, 1963. Stefan R. Landsberger collection, International Institute of Social History (Amsterdam)

with around 400 political parties and organizations in over 140 countries (Shambaugh 2007a). Bureau IV of the CCP/ID deals with Africa and Bureau III with West Asian and North African affairs and these bureaus rotate their personnel through appropriate embassies abroad. In 2004 the ID exchanged 2–3 delegations with almost every African country except for Angola (which had six) and South Africa (which had four). Travel abroad for all Politburo and Central Committee members who do not hold a government position is arranged through ID channels (Shambaugh 2007a). The ID also sends abroad provincial and municipal Party secretaries. The ILD played a key role in getting heads of state from five of these countries to attend the October 2006 China–Africa Summit in Beijing (despite the absence of diplomatic relations).

For some commentators, the SOEs should also be regarded as important agents of Chinese foreign policy. They argue that since senior managers of SOEs are appointed by the Party, they have important incentives to adhere to central policies. SOEs clearly remain a key component of the state apparatus as can be seen in the ownership structures and administrative arrangements they are subject to (Chan 2009) and the central position they occupy in the 'go out' strategy. Schuller and Turner (2005), for example, argue that Chinese companies are seen by the State as part of its 'geopolitical positioning' in Africa since SOEs contribute to an overall programme of foreign economic policy. Similarly Gonzalez-Vicente (2011: 3) argues that 'Chinese SOEs operate as the spearheads of a developmental and geopolitical vision that emanates primarily from the central state'. Focusing on the 'go out' process, Gonzalez-Vicente (2011: 3) examines the expansion of agents and entities of the state to external contexts 'through which the Chinese state directly alters geopolitical and developmental spaces outside its borders'. Yet there are significant tensions between different actors within the Chinese state (Liou 2009) and many of the companies concerned do not see their role in Africa as part of some wider geopolitical practice while there are multiple points of disjuncture between the activities of some SOEs and this wider foreign policy. As Liou (2009: 673) argues '[w]hen an overseas project involves multiple Chinese SOEs, economic considerations and bureaucratic fragmentation often make them compete in ways that harm overriding state interests'. Although senior SOE managers are appointed by the central state, several state agencies are often involved in evaluating their performance so an increasingly fragmented bureaucratic structure potentially weakens central state control over the investment decisions made by SOEs. Neither does SASAC have the strength of authority to retain complete oversight of state assets abroad as is often assumed by many commentators. McGregor (2008) notes how SOEs have often 'hijacked' China's diplomatic initiatives in Africa (especially in Sudan), pursuing profit at the expense of broader national interests while Liou (2009) also uses the example of Sudan to illustrate how Chinese oil firms like Sinopec have their own commercial interests and (as a result of their enhanced coroporate autonomy following restructuring) are able to pursue them despite opposition from the central state.

In seeking to move beyond the heavy focus on centrally owned Chinese firms or on centrally administered Chinese state agencies like the Ministry of Foreign Affairs (MFA) we might also however attend to the important role of China's provinces as foreign policy actors (Zhimin and Junbo 2009). China contains 33 province-level divisions, including 22 provinces, 5 autonomous regions (Guangxi Zhuang, Inner Mongolia, Ningxia Hui, Xinjiang Uyghur and Tibet Autonomous Regions); 4 municipalities (Beijing, Tianjin, Shanghai and Chongqing), and 2 special administrative regions (Hong Kong and Macau). In 1978, under the leadership of Deng Xiaoping, the new economic reform and opening-up policies launched a process of transformation in China, changing it from a highly centralized state that was economically inward looking to one that is much more decentralized and internationalized. This gave much more power to provinces as well as responsibility for managing the province's economy and as a result China's decentralization and internationalization has produced unprecedented economic success in the country. For Gerald Segal (1994) these twin processes call for a need to 'deconstruct' China's foreign relations and to see the coastal provinces as somewhat independent actors separate from the central government. Segal (1994: 352) argued that 'the only way to ensure China does not become more dangerous as it grows richer and stronger is to ensure that in practice, if not in law, there is more than one China to deal with'. After three decades of rapid economic development, a number of provinces have become middle-income economies in their own right.

Since 1994 through the process of recentralization, the central government–provincial relationship has been reshaped into a model of 'strong localities and strong center' (Zhimin and Junbo 2009). Chinese provinces have since developed a sophisticated local foreign affairs management system. This is usually led by a small leading group dealing with foreign affairs headed by either the provincial governor or party secretary. The system also includes a variety of less prominent government organs dealing with foreign relations, such as the Overseas Chinese Affairs Office, and quasi-governmental bodies, such as People's Friendship Associations (Zhimin and Junbo 2009). The provincial foreign affairs offices have the responsibilities of implementing the national foreign policy locally; arranging for the reception of foreign VIPs and for overseas visits of local leaders; administering passport and visa matters for local official business trips abroad; organizing and promoting activities with sister cities and provinces of other countries; administering consular and foreign media affairs and guiding the foreign affairs related work of other local government departments (Zhimin and Junbo 2009). While retaining control over policy direction, in the areas of local foreign consular affairs, foreign media affairs, overseas Chinese affairs, and receiving foreign state or government leaders, the central government relies on provincial governments to perform the actual administrative and operational work. Provinces – as non-sovereign actors in interstate relations – can also act as an agent of the central government charged with conducting 'informal diplomacy' through direct contacts with countries that have no diplomatic relations with China or in those cases when state–state relationships are suspended (Zhimin and Junbo 2009). Furthermore, the coastal provinces have developed their own extensive global networks.

Through their sister city networks and the networks of multinational companies investing in their jurisdictions, these provinces are able to command a variety of channels to gain access to foreign countries' foreign policy-making processes. Through these channels, the central government may ask provincial leaders to assist its efforts to influence foreign countries. Provincial leaders have begun to lead local trade delegations to Africa, which is a fairly new phenomenon compared to a few years ago, when trade delegations mostly went to Europe, North America, Japan and other developed countries (Zhimin and Junbo 2009). While national firms have been dominant in the Chinese construction industry, provincial companies, even as latecomers in this market, have been expanding very rapidly in recent years. Provinces have also started to provide aid to their African counterparts in their own capacity and there have been many twinning relationships established by Chinese provinces and cities with provinces and cities in Africa. What is new in the contemporary period is the fact that, unlike previously, the Chinese provinces are 'not just agents of the central government in Africa, but also its partners' (Zhimin and Junbo 2009: 15).

It is also important to acknowledge the significant role of the Chinese military in foreign policy decision-making (Lanteigne 2009). The PLA has always had a key role in shaping and implementing PRC foreign policy and there has been massive investment in recent years in its modernization. There is evidence that the opinions of PLA officers are becoming increasingly influential as it has dramatically expanded its foreign military relations programme to foster good relations with other countries. In this sense it is important to understand the significant role the PLA plays in Chinese foreign policy through military cooperation and exchanges, through arms transfers, through its significant global network of defence attaché offices and through its growing involvement in peacekeeping (see below). The Central Military Affairs Commission (CMAC), which constitutes the civilian oversight body for the PLA, is also a significant actor in the making of Chinese foreign policy, institutionalizing the party's control over the armed forces and their nuclear arsenal. CMAC has the final say on all decisions relating to the PLA, including senior appointments, troop deployments and arms spending. Almost all the members are senior generals, but the most important posts have always been held by the party's most senior leaders. The chairmanship was held by Mao Zedong and then Deng Xiaoping, who stayed in the job after he had resigned from all other positions, suggesting to some analysts that this is the real source of power in China.

Other, less obvious, foreign policy 'actors' might also be included here such as the growing number of Chinese NGOs, lobby groups and international NGOs (INGOs) that are now active in China (Lanteigne 2009). Before 1978, there were only about 6000 so-called social organizations in China. By the end of 2007, the number of registered NGOs had reached 387,000 (Lu 2009) although precise numbers are hard to come by as many Chinese NGOs are not actually registered. The social organizations that existed before the reforms were fully controlled by the state and served the state's objectives but the fragmentation of state power in the reform era has created much manoeuvring space for Chinese NGOs. While some of the registered NGOs today are best described as government-organized NGOs (GONGOs), many were born of private initiatives and are organized in a bottom-up fashion while many unregistered grass-roots organizations have also been very active (Lu 2009). Both GONGOs and popular NGOs, both the most and the least autonomous NGOs, both self-funded and state-subsidized NGOs, need to draw one form of support or another from the state in order to operate (Lu 2009). Current Chinese government regulations require every NGO to place itself under the 'professional management' of a state organ with responsibilities in its area of work, in addition to being registered and vetted annually by Civil Affairs departments. Chinese NGOs have however expanded their connections with Transnational Civil Society and with INGOs in particular which has further enhanced the growth of Chinese NGOs domestically. Chinese NGOs have benefited from transnational cooperation in capacity building, programme planning, management and accountability (Jie 2009) with important implications for Chinese politics and foreign policy. Estimates suggest that more than 490 INGOs and major international foundations have set up projects and opened offices in China (Jie 2009). There are between 3000 and 6000 foreign NGOs based in China, including about 2000 foundations, 1000 implementing groups, 2500 chambers of commerce, and 1000 religion-based organizations (Wang Ming 2005). China's membership in INGOs has increased steadily in the reform era, from 71 INGOs in 1977 to 484 in 1986 and 2297 in 2002 (YIO 2002–03: 1611).

A growing number of observers are also beginning to point to the wider 'cultural diplomacy' of Confucius Institutes and the future role they might play in rolling out Chinese foreign policy overseas although so far very little in the way of a coherent strategy has emerged as to how they can be integrated into the mainstream of Chinese foreign policy (Simons 2009). The Hanban – the Chinese National Office for teaching Chinese as a Foreign Language – began spreading them from 2004 when it set up the first Confucius Institute in the South Korean capital of Seoul. The use of the 'Confucius' tag is however somewhat confusing here since the rise of the CCP was a negative reaction to the entrenchment of Confucian thought in Chinese society.

During the Cultural Revolution of 1966–76, Confucius was reviled, seen as an obstacle to social change and a throwback to the past, yet Confucius is 'back in fashion' (Paradise 2009: 648) lending a basis for ideas such as the 'harmonious society', which is essentially a Confucian concept. Furthermore, the hierarchical layering of power and rigidity of moral precepts that are fundamental to Confucius' system are thoroughly out of place in China's present vision of its role in a fast-globalizing modern world. The Confucius Institutes headquarters' website counts 23 Confucius Institutes from 18 countries in Africa, with some of these classified as 'classrooms' in existing African universities, along with others in the offing. At the end of 2010 there were 322 Confucius Institutes and 369 Confucius classrooms in 96 countries (Hanban 2011). A set of draft guidelines for the Institutes notes that: 'Overseas Confucius Institutes must abide by the One-China Policy, preserve the independence and unity of the People's Republic of China, and ... refrain from participating in any political, religious or ethnic activities in the country where they are located'. These Institutes are thus a growing part of China's 'charm offensive', and an instrument of China's 'soft power'. Beyond the Confucius Institutes Gillespie (2009) argues that academic and student exchange schemes, which see African students coming to China, also have a bearing on China's changing foreign policy and on China's vision of South–South cooperation more generally.

China's media are also increasingly playing a role in disseminating Chinese foreign policy overseas and are becoming a key part of its 'soft power' diplomacy as a result of a centralized strategy underpinned by hard media controls at home and by the monopolization and manipulation of information (Bandurski 2009: 2). The Chinese government invested a reported US$8.7 billion in 2009–10 in its 'external publicity work' – primarily on the 'Big Four': China Central Television (CCTV), China Radio International (CRI), Xinhua News Agency and the *China Daily* newspaper (Shambaugh 2010). Some specific efforts include Xinhua TV now operating a 24-hour news channel that is trying to imitate Al Jazeera; CCTV News trying to compete with CNN and BBC and CRI buying more air time in a number of AM and FM radio markets in the United States and Europe, while broadcasting directly into Africa, the Middle East and Latin America (Shambaugh 2010). Xinhua News Agency in particular is penetrating deeply into the developing world, becoming one of the principal sources of news for people in Africa (Shambaugh 2010). Thus it is important to recognize the increasingly global footprint of China's audio-visual and print media and the variety of languages now being used in Chinese broadcasting: CCTV now broadcasts six international channels in five languages and claims a total global audience of about 125 million (Shambaugh 2010). Furthermore, some of China's provincial television stations (in Chongqing, Shanghai and Hunan) are also now seeking a niche in the foreign broadcast market (Shambaugh 2010).

## Recent shifts in Chinese foreign policy

Foreign policy is often described as the interplay between various political *agents* (including individuals with specific needs and wants) and *structures* formed by social relationships (such as the state as well as organizations and rules which are commonly constructed) (Lanteigne 2009: 1). As was illustrated in the previous section, with respect to China one of the most significant changes in the country's foreign policy development has been 'the expansion of the number of "agents" involved, directly or indirectly, in foreign policymaking processes, and in the number of China's international interests as well as global level structures with which it [China] can interact' (Lanteigne 2009: 1). As a result, over the past decade China's stance on foreign relations has clearly shifted. China's transformation from a revolutionary power to a post-revolutionary state is reflected in the apparent shift in national priorities since the birth of the PRC in 1949 between the two major periods of PRC history: the era of 'revolution' under Mao Zedong (1949–76) and the era of 'modernization' under Deng Xiaoping (since 1978) (Zhao 2007). As Easley (2008) notes, Chinese foreign policy discourses are shifting as multilateralism is prioritized over concerns with multipolarity, anti-hegemonism and non-interference (which underpinned much of the Mao era) and as a new vision of a strong and globally engaged China ('peaceful rise', 'win-win' diplomacy and 'harmonious world') starts to emerge.

Beijing's advancement of the concept of multipolarity, defined as the construction of more or less flexible alliances to contain every form of hegemony and to build a new and just international order, has often motivated China's increasing engagement in Africa (Tull

2006: 476). In the second phase Leonard (2008) sees a broad left-right schism within the PRC, with old guard communists being much more belligerent towards other international powers and seeing the need to enhance domestic military capability. The 'new right' are a small but influential group (although their influence has waned since the mid-1990s) who want complete liberalization and a market-oriented foreign policy. The current leaderships are variously described as 'populist' (Zhengxu and Tin Seng 2007) and 'new left' (Leonard 2008), because they espouse a belief in markets but tempered by the need to reduce inequality. Within them is a liberal internationalist group that wants engagement with the norms of the international community based on the idea of 'peaceful ascendance'. Since late 2003, top-level Chinese officials have used the notion of a 'peaceful ascendance' to describe an ideal growth plan for Chinese economic, political and military expansion but the implications of this policy remain ambiguous.

Chinese discourses of partnership also relate to its role in multilateral organizations, to its contestation of hegemony and to its desire to become a major centre of influence in a multipolar world (Gu et al. 2008). Along with an additional tool of Chinese foreign policy, the provision of preferential trade access to African 'partners', these discourses and initiatives construct China as a viable alternative to the West while simultaneously signalling China's role as a generous global power (Alves 2008). As China engages with a wider set of global multilateral fora it has adopted a cautious, reactive and pragmatic diplomatic approach (Gu et al. 2008). As a result China has become a major driver of global change and *de facto* a significant global governance actor. Different global governance arenas, characterized by different interest structures and institutional settings, are following different political logics yet China does not yet have an irrevocably defined and comprehensive global governance strategy:

> Chinese actors are still learning (rapidly) how to build up global governance capabilities in many global governance arenas, and how to balance national interests with regional and global challenges and responsibilities. Furthermore, the Chinese government seems to be very aware of the fact that international stability and a positive international perception of its global rise are important preconditions for a smooth domestic transformation process. This makes China sensitive for external criticism and amenable for a constructive engagement with Western countries. (Gu et al. 2008: 289)

On 11 December 2001, China formally entered the WTO, a move that promised among other things to further liberalize the Chinese economy, accelerate economic growth, increase the country's international prestige and enhance the flagging legitimacy of the CCP (Jahiel 2006). The implications of WTO membership for the economy, society and politics have been heatedly debated in the period surrounding China's accession (see Wang 2000; Fewsmith 2001; Lee 2001; Hsiung 2003) but it is clear that the WTO's prioritization of economic growth has reinforced the ideological foundation of China's reform era. It has also arguably intensified socio-economic disparities, heightened self-serving actions by local political leaders and increased environmental degradation in the countryside, leading to a surge of social discontent (Jahiel 2006). As part of its liberal internationalism and its ascension to the WTO, China thus increasingly recognizes that it needs to court votes to protect and promote its interests. African votes were crucial, for example, in blocking resolutions at the UN Commission on Human Rights condemning alleged human rights abuses in China or in garnering sufficient support to win a second bid to host the Olympics in 2008.

Despite Jeffrey Sachs's romanticized assertion that Beijing's reluctance to 'interfere' in politics was 'an asset, not a liability' (Sachs quoted in Reuters 2006) there is clear evidence that China's policy of non-interference is softening. Respect for sovereignty and non-interference represent two key phrases that have been repeated in China's rhetoric surrounding the engagement with Africa (Power and Mohan 2010). This rhetoric encourages the impression that China is not imposing its political views, ideals or principles onto recipient countries (Davies et al. 2008: 57) and reinforces the perception that China is now 'non-ideological' and pragmatic, since its concerns are for securing resources rather than transforming hearts and minds. At the same time there is a discourse of mutual interdependence, which fits with China's foreign policy doctrine of peaceful ascendance. At the core is an acknowledgement that '[a]lthough Africa might need China, China definitely needs Africa more for her development process' (Li Anshan 2006: 10). We would argue however that non-interference has always been a flexible practice, depending on the circumstances, and also that such a principle necessarily cannot be permanent. Where deals are signed with unpopular dictatorial regimes that could later be revised by a new government, it becomes necessary for the Chinese to protect such regimes. Carmody and Taylor (2010) characterize China's resource or geo-economic strategy in Africa as being 'embodied by different strands of engagement and modes of governance: clientelism, proxy force and hegemony'. Together these constitute an incipient new form of what they term 'flexigemony', whereby Chinese actors 'adapt their strategies geographically to suit the particular histories and geographies of the African states with which they engage'. Karumbidza (2007) is probably correct then when he says that 'the Chinese are themselves well aware' that their non-interference stance is untenable in Africa. Given that the economic relationship matters to China, its government has a vested interest in long-term stability, and its current rhetoric suggests an understanding that this is best procured by 'harmony' and the careful balancing of interests, not by force. Non-interference is a principle that is certainly breaking down as shown by China's recent involvement in Sudan and the DRC and by the use of other terms in China such as 'proactive non-interference' and 'constructive mediation' (Raine 2009: 155). Nonetheless, expectations of changes in Chinese policy, especially surrounding issues such as non-interference, should not be overestimated: any changes are likely to remain 'piecemeal, limited, and tactical, rather than broad-ranging and strategic' (Raine 2009: 162).

The Sudan case is pivotal for illustrating how the Chinese principle of non-interference is beginning to change. Over the past 10 years China's support for various Khartoum governments in return for uninterrupted running of the oil industry by the Chinese National Petroleum Corporation (CNPC) has had massive political impacts. China's commercial role in Sudan's oil industry was exposed to international scrutiny and criticism after lobby groups based in the United States began, in 2006, associating Darfur with China's hosting of the Summer Olympics in August 2008, in what became known as the 'Genocide Olympics'. Beijing concurrently doubled its diplomatic efforts in Khartoum, appointing a Special Envoy to Africa, Lu Guozong, to act as a mediator. Shortly after this, Ambassador Liu Guijin was appointed the first Special Representative of China to Africa and assigned the Darfur crisis as his priority area of focus. Chinese pressure greatly contributed to the Khartoum regime's eventual agreement to UN Secretary-General Kofi Annan's three-phase plan for the resolution of the conflict, including the deployment of a joint AU-UN peacekeeping force in Darfur. It is telling however, that Ambassador Liu modified Beijing's position from non-interference to the ambiguous-sounding 'using influence without interference' (*Mail & Guardian*, 27 July 2007). China has supplied arms to Sudan and helped develop northern Sudan's arms manufacturing industry and such practices demonstrate its willingness to look the other way when sovereign states commit genocide and persecution of its citizenry, if it serves China's national interests – in this case, access to oil. China's diplomacy on Darfur became more public from 2006 to the point where it cannot be said to be not 'interfering'. Beijing exerted pressure on Sudan to curb its militias and took the lead in winning Khartoum's acceptance of a hybrid African Union–UN peacekeeping force (Figure 8.4) in 2006 (Large 2008b). Chinese commentators defend the actions of their firms by claiming that they have changed Sudan from an oil-importing to an oil-exporting economy, providing the wealth needed for a move towards political stability. In addition they point out that their government has provided substantial amounts of 'humanitarian' aid. Yet they are also painfully aware of the damage that their presence in Sudan is doing to China's 'soft power' (Alden and Hughes 2009). Beijing has however underestimated the political risk posed by Darfur to its interests in Sudan, as well as its standing in Africa and on the international stage. The appointment of a new special Ambassador in May 2007 was part of China's efforts to bolster its image and contribute to solutions (such as increasing aid provision to Darfur). Such moves also enabled China to promote its own interests through more vocal diplomacy and participation in multilateral forums

*Figure 8.4*   Chinese peacekeepers that are part of the African Union/United Nations Hybrid Operation in Darfur (UNAMID) form a guard of honour and protect a borehole operated by a Chinese engineering company in Nyala (South Darfur) for UNAMID contingents. Photograph by Albert Gonzalez Farran/UNAMID

and initiatives on Darfur. Yet China's more proactive diplomacy was accompanied by continuity in defending the sovereignty of Sudan and arguing against further sanctions, as well as deepening economic links. Beijing has also continued to adopt a state-centric approach, failing to consider other non-state actors in Darfur such as private militias and rebel movements.

Even as China responded to international pressure to nudge the Sudanese regime towards the settlement of the Darfur crisis, it was woefully late. There is also certainly no indication China will fundamentally reassess its indiscriminate arms sale practices in Sudan or in other parts of the continent like Zimbabwe. Further, as Large (2009) points out, China's response to the specific context of Sudan should not be too strongly interpreted as a deepening of China's bilateral engagement on African conflicts. According to the US Congressional Research Service (CRS) China's US$600 million worth of arms trade agreements made it the largest single supplier to sub-Saharan Africa from 2006 to 2009 (Grimmett 2010). The growing influence of African engagement on China's foreign policy is also evident in China's modifying stance on UN and AU intervention in the civil conflict in Darfur. Despite a previously strong stance on non-interference and support of Khartoum's rejection of UN intervention, the Chinese leadership was eventually instrumental in persuading Khartoum to accept a joint UN–AU taskforce. Despite supporting various liberation parties in Africa throughout the Cold War, China refused to participate in peacekeeping missions at that time, claiming this was in conflict with its non-interference policy. China is now a substantial contributor to UN peacekeeping missions, particularly in Africa (see below). This is largely to counterbalance the perception that China is only interested in Africa for commodities extraction. Furthermore, reluctantly it seems, Beijing has accepted that to be taken seriously as a responsible global power intent on a 'peaceful rise', participation in such institutions is required (He, Y. 2007: 11).

China's relationship with Zimbabwe has also attracted increasing attention in recent years (Sachikonye 2008) and further illustrates the way in which this 'influence without interference' has provided a lifeline for some of Africa's most problematic political regimes. In April 2008 a Chinese shipment of arms[8] destined for Zimbabwe had to be recalled after southern African countries refused to allow the weapons to be unloaded. The Chinese ship,[9] *An Yue Jiang*, first ran into trouble in South Africa where dock workers refused to unload it as a gesture of solidarity with their fellow workers in Zimbabwe. Other countries followed the example set by South African trade unionists (though notably not by President Thabo Mbeki) and refused to let the Chinese ship dock. Zambia, then chair of the Southern African Development Community, said the weapons could deepen Zimbabwe's election crisis. China recalled the ship after its fruitless mission and defended the shipment on the grounds that the contract for the weapons had been signed in 2007 and was unconnected to the current crisis in Zimbabwe noting that China had been very 'responsible and cautious' with regards to weapons exports (*The Guardian*, 24 April 2008). China's relationship with Zimbabwe dates back to the liberation struggle of the 1970s, when troops were trained by Chinese advisers – as well as those from North Korea and elsewhere. Military relations between the two countries date back even further to 1963, when Zimbabwe African National Union (ZANU) cadres began to train at Nanjing military academy for the Rhodesian bush war (Spiegel and Le Billon 2009). China's support for Mugabe waned in the early 1980s as China sought strong economic partners in Africa. Mugabe showed little interest in this policy and began to turn to the West for support. The situation changed however after Tiananmen Square in 1989 when China actively sought African support for its position on human rights issues in international fora. Mugabe obliged China by defending its actions in Tiananmen Square. Zimbabwe subsequently developed a 'Look East' policy, which included closer ties with Indonesia, India, Iran, Malaysia, North Korea, and especially China. China–Zimbabwe relations then expanded politically, economically and militarily at a fast pace. With Zimbabwe's economic isolation in recent years – and its spiralling troubles, including 700 per cent inflation and 70 per cent unemployment – the relationship has strengthened even further (BBC 2004; Sachikonye 2008).

In 2005 Zimbabwe engaged in a controversial policy of slum demolition around Harare and Bulawayo that eventually left some 700,000 persons homeless in a scheme called *Operation Murambatsvina* ('Drive Out Rubbish') – intended to crack down on black-market trading and other criminal activity in slum areas. China publicly endorsed the action and, along with Russia, opposed any discussion of the subject in the UN Security Council on the grounds it would amount to meddling in Zimbabwe's internal affairs. Prominent scholars such as Lloyd Sachikonye, John Makumbe and Eldred Masunungure agreed on the view that the clean-up campaign was motivated by the government's quest to create space for Chinese businesses in Zimbabwe's urban centres (Norwegian Refugee Council Report 2005). Mugabe was actually in China for a week-long visit at the height of international outrage about this operation. Although mutual support on human rights issues where China and Zimbabwe are under fire is not the principal reason for close ties, it is arguably a significant factor. Lloyd Sachikonye (2008) has argued that it is China's appetite for natural resources that largely explains its increased engagement in Zimbabwe. China's non-interference policy also clearly dovetails with Mugabe's concept of a desirable foreign partner. After the West ended military sales to Zimbabwe, Mugabe turned increasingly to China as a source of equipment. Since 2005, for example, Zimbabwe has ordered twelve K-8 advanced jet trainers from China valued at US$240 million. Human rights activists say China has also sold riot control equipment, small arms and air force trainer jets worth US$200 million to Mr. Mugabe's government (Spiegel and Le Billon 2009).

China is now Zimbabwe's largest export market for tobacco and is becoming more active in mining ventures in Zimbabwe. Bilateral trade in 2010 between China and Zimbabwe was only about US$400 million (Business Diary 2011), which is actually much smaller than China's trade with Africa's major oil and mineral exporting countries. In return for bailing out Robert Mugabe's regime with injections of cash, machinery, equipment and military supplies, Chinese SOEs have assembled a portfolio of shares in some of Zimbabwe's prize assets including a 70 per cent stake in Zimbabwe's only electricity generation facilities at Hwange and Kariba and stakes in the national railway. In 2009 Zimbabwe secured lines of credit worth US$950 million from China (China Forum, 2009) and a further US$10 billion of lending from the China Development Bank was agreed in early 2011 to support the mining and agriculture sectors, just as the country had seen a reduction in international funding due to the non-implementation of issues in the Global Political Agreement. In addition to the weaponry, Beijing has also given several gifts to President Mugabe and his allies. The tiles that decorate the president's palatial Harare home were a 'goodwill donation' from China, for example. There are limits, however, to what both countries get out of this relationship. Since 1991 the Chinese foreign minister has made his overseas visit to Africa each year, visiting a wide range of countries (some on multiple occasions) yet only one of these visits took the foreign minister to Zimbabwe. Harare has also defaulted on some Chinese loans in recent years. Further, Beijing did not publicly support a government crackdown on the Zimbabwean political opposition in 2007 (Shinn 2008a). Over the longer term, China has profound doubts about the stability and viability of the Zimbabwean government. As it looks to portray itself as a neutral force rather than an unequivocal backer of government repression, it has made efforts to develop ties with other groupings, reaching out to a number of different factions in ZANU-PF and possible successors to Mugabe (Small 2008: 5).

## China as a 'responsible' great power: peacekeeping and security cooperation

China's evolving foreign policy also shows a new commitment to advancing global security cooperation in a number of areas. In particular China has been keen to portray an image of itself as a responsible great power (*fuzeren de daguo*) an impulse which arguably stems from China's fears about a hostile response to its growth as a major power and the possible harm this may do to its relationships with the United States and the European Union. Goldstein (2005: 175) argues that China has what amounts to a 'grand strategy' that is manifest through its 'increased participation in multilateral forums, restrained currency policy, and active cultivation of major power partnerships [which] are designed to mute perceptions of a "China threat", to build China's reputation as a responsible actor, and to convince others of the benefits of engagement with China as well as the counterproductive consequences of attempting to threaten, isolate or contain it'. In this regard China 'has quickly realized that Africa will become an important stage where its image as a responsible global actor is forged' (Huang 2010: 8). In late 2008, for example, China actively pushed the governments of the DRC and Rwanda to resolve the conflict in eastern DRC, where Rwanda was supporting rebel groups. China has also played an active and constructive role in promoting nuclear non-proliferation on the Korean peninsula while Beijing has also worked through the Shanghai Co-operation Organisation (SCO) and the ASEAN Regional Security Policy Conference to advance stability in the Asian region.

One particularly significant way in which China is projecting itself as a responsible great power is with regard to Beijing's increasing involvement and contribution to United Nations peacekeeping[10] operations (UNPKOs) in Africa (Shelton 2008; Taylor 2008). Taking a more hands-on approach to conflict resolution and peace operations in Africa arguably also helps China reverse some of the negativity it has encountered about its expanding role and allows China to cast itself as a nation that is intimately concerned about peace and the welfare of Africans and is – unlike the United States, for example – willing to put its troops on the frontline in furtherance of this stance (Taylor 2008). Formerly, Beijing was highly sceptical of the UN's peace efforts, primarily because of the way the Chinese leadership perceived how the UN was utilized at the time of the Korean War, to legitimize and sanction what was seen as an aggressive military intervention (Taylor 2008). In addition, outside of the UN for many years and thus incapable of having any influence, China's position on peace operations was understandably suspicious. Consequently, even after Beijing took up its UN seat the position on peace operations remained guarded and China refused to contribute to peace budgets for many years (even though as a member of the Security Council it had a responsibility to do so) (Chen 2009). Yet in recent years there has been a sea change in China's attitude to peace operations and Beijing has emerged as a significant contributor. China has increased its troop contributions to UN peacekeeping missions 20-fold since 2000, with the majority based in Africa (Saferworld 2011) and has also taken part in multilateral anti-piracy efforts in the Gulf of Aden. Since 1989, China has contributed over 10,000 peacekeepers to 22 UN peacekeeping missions (International Crisis Group 2009). As of July 2010, 2013 Chinese peacekeepers were serving on 9 of the 15 UN peacekeeping operations around the world with the great majority (1622) deployed in Africa. As of October 2011, China was the seventh top provider of financial contributions to UN peacekeeping operations, after the United States, Japan, the United Kingdom, Germany, France and Italy. While the number of Chinese peacekeepers worldwide is much smaller than that of Bangladesh (10,654), India (8,423) and Pakistan (10,626) (Saferworld 2011), China currently ranks as the largest contributor to UN peacekeeping operations among the five permanent members of the Security Council which 'somewhat puts to shame the reluctance of other great powers to get involved' (Taylor 2008: 6).

Through peacekeeping, China is thus able to build its image as a responsible great power and play an expanding role in advancing global peace and stability. This is seen to complement China's 'peaceful rise' and efforts to promote a 'harmonious world' (*hexie shijie*). The need for stable markets in Africa and a positive trade environment also underpins Beijing's increasing commitment to UNPKOs. Given China's significant military capacity, in terms of personnel numbers and the urgent need to build peace in Africa 'a positive synergy is increasingly evident' (Shelton 2008: 4). China has sent personnel to peacekeeping operations in Mozambique, Sierra Leone, Liberia, the DRC, Côte d'Ivoire, Burundi, Sudan, Western Sahara, Ethiopia and Eritrea and China is currently involved in the African Union–United Nations Hybrid Operation in Darfur (UNAMID), the UN Mission for the Referendum in Western Sahara (MINURSO), the UN Stabilisation Mission in the Democratic

Republic of Congo (MONUSCO), the UN Mission in Liberia (UNMIL) the UN Mission in Sudan (UNMIS) and the UN Mission in Cote d'Ivoire (UNOCI) (Saferworld 2011). On 27 August 2007, a Chinese general was appointed to lead a UN peacekeeping mission for the first time. General Zhao Jingmin took control of the UN mission in Western Sahara, confirming China's status as an important participant in UN peace-keeping operations (Shelton 2008). China has not however – as of yet – contributed any combat troops to UN missions. Its peacekeepers instead hold positions as military observers, civilian police, with the majority acting as 'force enablers', that is, those units that provide infrastructure, medical, logistical and transport support (Saferworld 2011).

Thus China is increasingly viewed as a constructive partner, which can use its influence for positive outcomes in conflict situations. According to an International Crisis Group (ICG) report in 2009 the end result has been 'a public relations success' in terms of how the PLA is viewed over-seas and how China's foreign policy is received more broadly (ICG 2009: 9). During a visit to Africa in 2006, Foreign Minister Li Zhaoxing specif-ically pledged Beijing's support for an expanded UN role in addressing African conflicts, while he promised increased Chinese involvement in UNPKOs. China is also seeking to strengthen the role of the UN Security Council in authorizing, managing and terminating peacekeeping oper-ations. China opposes premature deployment, which could result in high casualties and has encouraged the UN to focus on the eradica-tion of the causes of conflict, rather than conflict containment (Shelton 2008). In the future China may seek to further strengthen this process through the training of African peacekeepers in China, the greater use of Chinese military equipment in PKOs, through expanded links with Chinese military communications systems, through increased joint Africa–Chinese peacekeeping deployments[11] and through an enhanced role for the African Union (AU) in cooperating with Chinese peace-keeping efforts (Shelton 2008). One area of peace operations where China has yet to play a significant role howsever is in peace*building*, that is, the use of a wider spectrum of security, civilian, administrative, political, humanitarian, human rights and economic tools and inter-ventions to build the foundations for longer term peace in post-conflict countries (Saferworld 2011).

Beijing's Africa strategy to promote China's economic (resource access and trade) and political (one-China recognition) interests explicitly tie in the PLA to support overall peace and security for its interests in Africa (Puska 2007). This commitment (outlined in the 2006 Africa Strategy and also in FOCAC action plans) tasks the PLA with conducting high-level and technological military cooperation and exchanges, training African military personnel and 'support[ing] defence and army building' in African countries. By taking part in such operations, Chinese troops and the PLA in general stand to benefit in terms of training and experience, while not having to expend significant resources from the annual budget. This helps facilitate – albeit in a small way –the modernization of the PLA while enabling military cadres to test equipment and techniques in the field (Taylor 2008). The PLA now has two dedicated peacekeeping training facilities at Nanjing (Jiangsu province) and Langfang (Hebei) intended to train and prepare troops for a range of overseas peacekeeping tasks and missions (Shelton 2008). In addition to its involvement in UNPKOs the PLA and police also support China's Africa strategy through participation in non-traditional missions, such as combating terrorism and piracy, small-arms smuggling, drug trafficking and transnational economic crimes. Consequently, the PLA now maintains a growing military presence on the African continent. Estimates range from approximately 1200 soldiers, including PKO forces, to more than 5000. China's bilateral military cooperation (although extremely opaque) extends throughout the continent, reaching at least 43 countries to provide a network of military relations from which to shape its future role in Africa. According to Shinn (2008b) ten countries have more established military ties with China than others: Algeria, Angola, Egypt, Ghana, Nigeria, South Africa, Sudan, Uganda, Zambia and Zimbabwe. Chinese Embassy defence attaché offices throughout Africa provide the diplomatic foundation for China's military contacts. Accredited defence attachés link the PLA to host country militaries. Since 1985 China itself has nearly doubled its number of defence attachés worldwide from 59 to 109. However in Africa the increase has been far more modest, from nine to fifteen (Saferworld 2011). Defence attaché duties vary, but as a minimum, they report on local matters from a military and/or security perspective and facilitate contacts with local armed forces. China currently maintains bilateral diplomatic military relations with at least 25 African countries, spread across the main regions of the continent. At least 14 of the 107 Chinese military attaché offices worldwide are in African countries (Algeria, DRC, Egypt, Ethiopia, Liberia, Libya, Morocco, Mozambique, Namibia, Nigeria, Sudan, Tunisia, Zambia and Zimbabwe). In Beijing, 18 African countries maintain permanent defence attaché offices, 7 of which are directly reciprocal: Algeria (which has continuously maintained a defence attaché in Beijing since January 1971), Egypt, Namibia, Nigeria, Sudan, Zambia and Zimbabwe).

Between 2001 and 2006, Chinese military leaders visited Africa over 30 times, touring virtually every country that recognizes China. These visits often included more than one country, but several of the countries received multiple stopovers by Chinese military leaders (15 visits to Egypt, for example, during the course of these six years). Additionally, China's still rare naval ship visits have included stops in Africa. Rear Admiral Huang Jiang led the first PLA Navy (PLAN) ship visit, consisting of the *Shenzhen*, China's newest Luhai-class guided missile destroyer at the time, and the Nancang supply ship, to Africa in July 2000. There have also been suggestions from some Chinese military officials that China should establish a permanent military base in Africa to support its operations in the Gulf of Aden. China also engages in bilateral security consultations although to date these have been largely centred on South Africa (through the Sino South African Defence Committee set up in April 2003 in Pretoria). China's military-military activities in Africa also include working-level professional contacts, such as military aid and assistance to local militaries in the form of 'donations' and technical support, training and exchanges, arms-sales related support and professional education. Further, much of the assistance which China provides to African governments to finance military infrastructure development is in turn spent on Chinese companies who carry out the implementation of the projects.

China's military-to-military activities in Africa, including defence attaché presence, naval ship visits, arms sales and other missions to support military cooperation can be expected to expand to keep pace with China's growing national interests throughout the region. Resource access and associated security needs would likely influence any expansion of China's defence attaché offices in Africa – four of the six countries (Algeria, Egypt, Nigeria and Sudan) that China currently maintains reciprocal, resident defence attaché offices with, are among those countries where China has interests in petroleum and other resources. Gabon and Equatorial Guinea, which are among the main producers of petroleum in Africa and already have established defence attaché offices in Beijing, would be logical additions. China may also increasingly be challenged to respond to security threats to Chinese property and personnel in the region that may necessitate a re-evaluation of the role of China's military. Certain questions about these developments remain however:

> Interestingly, Beijing will increasingly have to contend with the impulses generated by a rising China and expectations of it to play

a greater and greater role in international affairs and the goal of seeking to control any evolution in the definition of sovereignty, which threatens to be outside of China's control. Managing the debate and delimiting discussions of what sovereignty is and when it might be transgressed is therefore central to Beijing's position on intervention and peacekeeping. (Taylor 2008: 7)

China still 'resolutely opposes actions perceived as interfering in the domestic affairs and sovereignty of other states and will only agree to a peace operation if the host government concurs' (Taylor 2008: 6). Further, Beijing remains suspicious that interventions carried out in the name of humanitarianism 'have been motivated by interests other than charity or international solidarity' and that the United States in particular attempts to utilize the UN as a means to project its own interests and policies (Taylor 2008: 6). Thus China remains sceptical about certain calls for action and closely interrogates the claims made when advancing demands for intervention (Taylor 2008). Consequently, Beijing's involvement in peace operations in Africa in the future 'is likely to develop as and when Beijing is comfortable with such missions' (Taylor 2008: 7). This will in turn be connected to China's changing position on state sovereignty.

## Conclusion: a 'critical geopolitics' of China–Africa relations

The rapid economic growth registered by 'rising powers' like China, Brazil and India in recent years and the growing evidence of cooperation around a broad spectrum of issues among states of the global South have revived the hope (or spectre) of a new 'Bandung'– just over a half-century after leaders of 29 African and Asian states met in that Indonesian hill resort town to 'inject the voice of reason in world affairs', as President Sukarno put it. Indeed the so-called New Asia Africa Strategic Partnership (NAASP) launched at the Bandung revival and the fiftieth anniversary commemoration in April 2005 co-hosted by South Africa and Indonesia (DFA 2006: 70–71) is one such attempt to resurrect the Bandung spirit in the contemporary era. What is becoming clear is that the rapid and steady intrusion and recognition of a set of major emerging economies is challenging the established global order, 'wrenching global relations into flux' (Shaw et al. 2009: 27). Africa is thus moving from being 'quite a central *object* in the evolving international relations of the twentieth century' to a position where 'the continent has more fully acquired *subject* status in the international system' (Cornelissen

2009: 24, emphasis in original). That said it remains a concern that the AU, as the key body of the inter-African regime 'lacks a coherent strategy for managing the proliferation of multi-bilateral relationships with the continent' (Kornegay and Landsberg 2009: 189) and that limited progress has been made in developing a common African position on managing relationships with the emerging (as well as established) powers.

China is not the only 'rising power' seeking to secure strategic influence in Africa and despite their different intentions these (re)emerging powers share commonalities in terms of the means that they use to reach their goals as all of them use soft power as a means of promoting their national interests. While none of them are African, they affect the continent's present and future in the world economy and by asserting their newfound influence, these countries seek a reorientation of power towards multipolarity with important implications for the way we conceptualize international relations. Articulated through an economics-led diplomacy, they have demanded a new set of international norms, a new trade agenda and equitable representation in the multilateral arena. It is also possible that the deepening contact between the BRICs and Africa is giving rise to a new 'top-down' multilateralism in the twenty-first century, a new multilateralism that is superseding the 'bottom-up' multilateralism of the late 1990s (Shaw et al. 2009). IBSA – and similar groupings – will provide the platform for emerging countries to work around the familiar institutions of international relations in the years ahead and the creation of such dialogue forums demonstrates a frustration with institutions such as the WTO, from which countries of the South feel neglected and thus seek to address the imbalance.

The rapid resurgence of China in recent years is beginning to radically alter the global geopolitical ecology of investment, production and trade (Power and Mohan 2010). For commentators like Giovanni Arrighi, China holds up the possibility of a 'new Bandung' and a 'commonwealth of civilisations on an economic basis'. Similarly Snow (2008: xvi) goes as far as to say that China's resurgence represents a constellation of engagements that resembles 'the emergence of a Chinese Commonwealth' (2008: xvi). China's involvement in Africa does permit the 'revival of triangulation' (Large 2008c) which means African states can pursue relations with more than one external state but the debate is perhaps really about whether Africa's leverage from its Chinese engagement vis-á-vis its Northern development partners is viable (Naidu et al. 2009). Palat (2009) argues to the contrary, that 'neither the Chinese corporations nor the Chinese government has done anything to benefit trade unions or social justice movements in Africa'. This, indeed, demonstrates that the 'leverage' argument must distinguish between the actors we are discussing: African leaders, women, soldiers, businessmen, children, workers, the poor? (Naidu et al. 2009). As multiple actors arrive in increasing numbers in Africa, it is becoming increasingly evident that the notion of a coherent, mono- lithic 'China Inc' is a myth and that the argument that this is centrally regulated and managed coherently by a central Chinese government is fallacious. There are a wide range of foreign policy actors involved (many of whom are in competition with each other) while it is also necessary to go beyond the state-to-state level of analysis and see 'the complexity of the problems in China–Africa relations as arising from the much larger historical process of the erosion of the barrier between China's domestic politics and its foreign relations' (Alden and Hughes 2009: 584).

From the case of China in Africa we have elsewhere called for an intensification of the dialogue between critical geopolitics and crit- ical development theory (Power and Mohan 2010; Power 2010). Geopolitics and development theory are conventionally kept apart by a well- established social scientific division of labour which assumes that the domain of the (geo)political is discrete and separable from the supposedly economic and technical domain of development (Ó Tuathail 1994). Indeed it is impossible to understand the contemporary making of development theory and practice *without* reference to geopolitics and the geopolitical imagination of non-western societies (Power 2010). As Slater argues: 'power and knowledge ... cannot be adequately grasped if abstracted from the gravity of imperial encounters and the geopol- itical history of West/non-West relations' (Slater 2004). All concep- tualizations of development thus contain and express a geopolitical imagination which condition and enframe its meanings and relations (Slater 1993). China's contemporary vision of development does not envisage a domain completely separate from foreign policy concerns and actively mobilizes historical discourses of geopolitics (respect for sovereignty, non-interference in political affairs, anti-hegemonism) and the language of commonality and mutuality (solidarity, friendship, anti-imperialism) in order to justify and legitimate its contemporary Africa policy (Figure 8.5). Cowen and Smith (2009) have argued that there has been a recent recasting of traditional geopolitical logics and practices in the context of (among other things) globalization and that these may better be captured today by a 'geoeconomic' conception of

*Figure 8.5*   A large sign, extolling the benefits of China–Africa dealings, outside the Xiamen Trade Fair Exhibition Hall in China. Source: Speak-it Productions Ltd

space, power and security, which sees geopolitical forms 'recalibrated by market logics'. Thus it could be argued that geoeconomics is crucial to any interpretation of contemporary China–Africa engagement and to our understanding of the spatial reconfiguration of contemporary political geographies that results from this engagement.

A critical geopolitics must examine how China's historical imagination of geopolitics has enframed the meanings attached to 'aid' and 'development' and the relations forged with African 'partners' as a result. This historical imagination of geopolitics remains crucial since it forms a discursive field through which current foreign policy is legitimized. Further engagement with Chinese (and African) approaches to IR is an important first step in this regard. We would also argue that a critical geopolitics also needs to focus more directly on the range of impacts China is having on forms of African governance (especially in 'pariah states' like Sudan and Zimbabwe), on the role China takes in situations of conflict, in peacekeeping and military cooperation programmes and on the relations China has with local, regional and global institutions. We would also echo Gonzalez-Vicente's (2011) contention that it is increasingly important to problematize the Chinese state as it becomes re-territorialized outside China's borders and to interrogate more fully the ways in which deals and collaborations with foreign states are reshaping the structural environment in which Chinese firms operate overseas. In some important ways therefore entities of the Chinese state are becoming actors in political processes directed by governmental actors within African states.

China would appear to be increasingly faced with a dilemma. It is outwardly supportive of international norms and institutions, as the current global order has been very conducive to its growth thus far. China actively supports institutions that foster the international environment conducive to its continual growth (He, Y. 2007: 10). However, these international norms and institutions are increasingly propounded to be at odds with some of China's activities in Africa. Over recent years there has been a considerable growth in China's diplomatic self-confidence in shaping diplomatic processes, and determining clear Chinese policy objectives when dealing with diplomatic crises. Beijing has also come to see the value of ensuring that there is a political process in place to deal with these crises that it can point to in order to hold back consideration of coercive resolutions at the UN Security Council (Small 2008). As a result it is becoming clear that some of the long-standing principles (e.g. non-interference) that have shaped China's engagement with Africa over many decades are becoming untenable and that as its presence in Africa develops and intensifies, managing the debate and delimiting discussions of what sovereignty is and when it might be transgressed is likely to become more complex, albeit central to Beijing's future position on intervention in Africa.

# 9
# Changing Contexts and the Future of China–Africa Relations

## Introduction

> We are however concerned that China's foreign assistance and investment practices in Africa have not always been consistent with generally accepted international norms of transparency and good governance, and that it has not always utilized the talents of the African people in pursuing its business interests
>
> Hillary Clinton, 11 June 2011, Dar es Salaam, Tanzania

> I believe the model of authoritarian capitalism [in China] we are seeing will fall short in the long term ... When people get economically richer they make legitimate demands for political freedoms to match their economic freedoms. This model is unable to respond.
>
> David Cameron, 20 July 2011, Lagos, Nigeria

These two extracts from speeches delivered on the African continent by US Secretary of State Hillary Clinton and the UK Prime Minister David Cameron thrust the nature of China's involvement in Africa into the global media spotlight again. Criticizing both China's domestic and overseas capitalist practices, these western politicians reiterated the inability of the Chinese political and economic model to meet the global norms around good governance and the demands of its citizens. The comments also reconfirm our introductory statements that popular perceptions of China–Africa relations are still very much presented from the perspective of western powers and interests. Despite this apparent continuity in discourses around China things have changed, particularly our understanding of how China's domestic agendas shape its interventions in Africa and how the mediation of such interventions by African actors conditions the impacts on the ground.

Conscious of this need to understand the Chinese 'way of doing things' in order to explain its overseas practices in African and global contexts, this book was oriented around four arguments. First, we investigated the 'Chinese model' by looking at the various domestic agents of economic transformation, environmental governance, overseas aid activities and international engagement. This was historicized to argue that while China has clearly stepped up its engagements with Africa they are part of a much longer and dynamic set of relationships between the two. Second, we explored the political interface between Chinese and African actors focusing on both the state and civil society, as well as multilateral actors that shape this political sphere, largely – though not exclusively – through aid. Third, to understand this mediation and its effects we took a case study approach of Chinese investments, development aid activities and environmental governance. Throughout the book we strived to 'ground' these debates by focusing not just on the role of states and transnational institutions but also on the specific impacts of China in Africa as experienced by ordinary people and local communities. Finally, we scrutinized the wider geopolitical shifts and geoeconomic rivalries between China and the rest of world, which are concretized in 'China–Africa' relations but have broader political implications around shifting hegemony. In this final chapter we summarize the key findings, revisit some of the theoretical debates with which we started, and look to the future in terms of emerging trends.

## Current and emerging patterns of engagement

Perhaps the first key point to note is that in terms of Africa, the Chinese are neither new to the continent in terms of trade nor in developmental aid. While clearly a monumental break with the past, the earliest recorded encounters showed that China–Africa engagement did not begin with the birth of the People's Republic of China (PRC) in 1949. Migrant flows have fluctuated across different historical periods reflecting different economic and political conditions in China and the changing scope of China's international engagements.

Later relations forged during the anti-colonial struggles in Africa and the revolutionary period of Chinese foreign policy in the 1950s strived to wrest the leadership of the international communist movement from the Soviet Union (Snow 1988). Afro-Asian solidarity in particular and the Asian–African conference held in Bandung, Indonesia in 1955 went on to provide an important political foundation for the evolving China–Africa relationship. These were built on the five principles of 'respect for territorial integrity; non-aggression; non-interference in each others' affairs, equality and mutual benefits in relations and peaceful coexistence' (Jones 2005: 851), which still guide much development cooperation (Xinhua 2011b). The Tazara railway is an illustrative example of a successful aid project which still serves its public today and is held up as a symbol of this earlier peaceful solidarity. Today, Chinese officials regularly engage these historical narratives to demonstrate that China has been an 'all-weather' friend and therefore, by implication, that its relations with Africa are also legitimate and built sensitively but directly on historical precedents.

Despite the evocation of past connections, contemporary Chinese involvement with Africa has evolved from ideologically driven interaction during the Cold War to a combination of pragmatic economic and political means. However, the Ministry of Foreign Affairs still stresses that the China–Africa partnership is conducted on the basis of the five principles of peaceful coexistence (Ministry of Foreign Affairs PRC 2006). That these principles have become 'set in aspic' (Strauss and Saavedra 2009: 558) leaves very little rhetorical room for the Chinese government to encompass other discursive rhetorics to legitimate and explain its actions domestically and abroad. The geopolitical world has moved on since these principles were first enunciated, particularly the waning of US hegemony in the pre- and post-2008 financial crisis and the tapering off of traditional western sources of political influence. One upshot of this is that African countries have been turning towards the Chinese and other emerging economies such as India, Brazil and South Africa, which may be resulting in a new set of international norms and coalitions that pose a challenge to the established global order. Besides these major players we are also seeing Southeast Asian countries such as Malaysia, Singapore and South Korea taking major stakes in Africa's natural resources sector, notably the timber and mining industries. Through various mechanisms, like multilateral forums such as the Forum on China–Africa Cooperation (FOCAC), the Tokyo International Conference on African Development (TICAD), India–Africa Forum and various bilateral trade and aid agreements, the emerging global competitors are jostling for Africa's attention. With this new found confidence, both the 'rising powers' and the African states have demanded a new set of international norms, a new trade agenda and equitable representation in the multilateral arena. Reciprocally traditional geopolitical players in Africa, such as the European Union (EU) and the United States, are also intensifying their engagement in the continent to counteract the growing influence of new rising powers.

The shifting geopolitics is underpinned by China's unique approach to the economy and development more generally. We discussed this in terms of the combination of Chinese Socialism with 'neoliberal' approaches to the economy, which in turn creates a potentially new trajectory of development for Africa. This new landscape is reflected in the economic mechanisms of the FOCAC, such as the focus on SEZs, which were in part affirmations of the successful experiences that China had with these enclavic economic spaces. Utilizing the China–Africa Development Fund (CADFund), Chinese companies have been taking responsibility for designing, building and managing the SEZs. Although the CADFund was set up to promote economic cooperation between China and Africa, its aim is to ultimately support the Chinese 'going out' strategy and finance the market entry of Chinese firms into African economies. Access for African enterprises to this fund can only be achieved through joint ventures with their Chinese counterparts (CADF 2010), which reflects the point made by Murray Li that the 'Chinese government's biopolitical priority is the provisioning of its own population' (2010: 76). While 'win-win' benefits may accrue we have to be clear that despite the rhetoric of partnership the Chinese are, like other powers before them, primarily driven by self-interest. But, as we discuss later, this is not to say that Africans are powerless in this relationship.

A further feature of Chinese 'capitalism' in Africa, which goes against those homogenizing discourses which treat China's agenda as a statist and singular one, are the multitude of actors we see there. Most notable and visible are the Chinese SOEs that tend to be in oil and gas, mining, hydropower and other resource-based industries which require huge initial investments that act as barriers to entry for the small and medium enterprises (SMEs). Moreover, numerous successful Macao firms were found operating in Angola due to colonial and linguistic connections and in general these colonial treaty ports still act as important conduits in and out of Africa, as the 88 Queensway Group in Hong Kong attests. Other than economic actors such as SOEs and SMEs, political actors such as provincial governments and leaders also entered the economic sphere and are significant players in Africa. Through sister city and corporate networks, provinces have been able to command a variety of channels with which to gain access to African states (Gill and Reilly 2007).

The outcome of political and economic ties are the burgeoning volumes of Chinese aid, trade and investment. In terms of concrete data, bilateral trade rose from US$10.6 billion to US$91.07 billion from 2000 to 2009 (CAITEC 2010) and in the first half of 2011 China–Africa imports and exports totalled US$79.01 billion, an increase of 29.1 per cent year-on-year (Chinese Customs 2011). Using empirical data from Angola and Ghana, which represent different examples of China's development 'partnerships' in Africa, we inspected the varied gains and losses between China and different African countries. For resource-rich countries like Angola, China's presence could create a two-sided 'resource curse' insofar as it may raise oil rents which go to elites whereas trade competition reduces the diversity of the economy and cuts both employment and export revenue. For countries like Ghana, the impacts were varied in different sectors as Chinese goods displaced locally produced ones without countervailing gains from mineral exports. However, infrastructural gains on the Ghanaian state, such as hydro-power dams and roads built by Chinese assistance brought benefits to the general population and development of the country.

In terms of the impacts of China's policy directives on individual African states, we argued that political systems vary widely across the African continent, which in turn created a diverse investment environment. Furthermore, when formal state support is unviable due to weak institutions, cooperation is organized through informal private entities, which created differential outcomes and impacts in the various countries. Here the Gabinete de Reconstrução Nacional (Office for National Reconstruction; GRN) in Angola (and its successor 'Sonangol Imobiliária'/Sonangol Real Estate) is one such example of a semi-official arrangement and within the Chinese SME sector we see various local patrons providing the political entry and protection required for these 'middlemen minorities' to operate at the frontiers of market opportunities.

Along with its economic presence and political implications, China has also rapidly expanded its environmental footprint and impacts in Africa. An important objective of China's Africa strategy has been to extract natural resources which have so far not been accessible to China or are in increasingly greater demand within the Chinese mainland. Such resources are often located in fragile ecosystems and countries plagued by corruption and conflict. Further, China has become involved in some very large mining projects in Africa and its construction companies are increasingly seeking to source building materials locally. As a long-term partner in Africa's development and in response to global pressure, China needs to demonstrate an interest in addressing the environmental impacts of its projects. The Chinese government's concern to issue guidelines to Chinese companies on the impacts of their overseas investments has been one important step in this regard. Contrary to popular images of Chinese-led resource- and land-grabs in sub-Saharan Africa, China's investment in renewable energy and cleaner energy systems in Africa (which are becoming an important feature of China–Africa development cooperation) suggests that China is becoming increasingly conscious of its environmental responsibilities in its engagements with Africa.

In addition to exploring macro inter-state connections, we also looked at the less visible exchanges such as commodity flows, the movement of people and the emergence of diasporic spaces. The micro-politics embedded in these everyday interactions are vital for understanding the impacts of economic practices. During our field research in Angola and Ghana we found that many African people were positive about the role that Chinese business plays or about the role that China can play more generally in African development. However, we have the politicization of the migrant/host relationship for domestic political advantage (as exemplified by Sata of Zambia). So, while in most states the Chinese are welcomed, in some localities and at certain times they are treated with resentment and occasionally subjected to violence. For example, in Dar es Salaam, Chinese traders are now banned from selling in markets, as the Tanzanian Government proclaimed that the Chinese were welcome as investors but not as 'vendors or shoe-shiners' (*Economist* 20 April 2011).

## China, Africa and theories of development

In the opening chapter we discussed a number of concepts which we used to set up a series of questions. The queries related to how we understand development, the role of states and regimes in brokering a relational view of development, and how this played out socially and geographically in terms of new transnational configurations such as enclaves. Here we revisit these questions in light of the analysis presented in the preceding chapters. We noted in the opening chapter that the China in Africa discourse tends to treat Africa as passive and the relationship as only benefitting China. While we must be wary of reversing the analytical lens too far we can think in more relational terms about the interconnectedness of China with Africa, which points to a more mixed and complex picture. A key finding is that we need to move beyond economism and ethnocentrism in discussing China and Africa. The dominant 'China Inc.' assumptions tend to reduce Chinese motivations to singular, rational economic ones, but our data – while not disputing this general picture of self-interest – reveals much more complex motives.

This required a disaggregation of firm types but also a focus on individuals within these organizations. Here we saw major differences between the agendas of Chinese SOEs, which had the backing of the Chinese state, and independent Chinese business people. In the former we did see highly enclaved investments with concessional lending essentially tied to the use of Chinese SOEs. The developmental impact in Africa, then, was more limited to some degree. Local employment of Africans varied but was significantly lower in Angola than Ghana. In the Egypt Suez SEZ, there were job opportunities for over 1800 locals and only 80 Chinese staff were imported (Brautigam and Tang 2011). These turnkey projects also brought in a great deal of their own equipment and inputs so that local suppliers hardly benefitted with the Chinese workers being paid directly into their Chinese bank accounts and residing in labour camps so that local multipliers were further reduced. That said, these projects were delivering infrastructure that was urgently needed and so the net developmental impacts are mixed and only time will tell how far these investments in things like roads, ports, electricity and ICT infrastructures will yield economic and social benefits, but one can only imagine that the effects will be positive. When we looked at Chinese independent SMEs we saw that the motivations for betterment were strong. But many did not just regard Africa as a site of short-term economic opportunity but were interested in longer-term strategies for investment. This refutes the short-termist and exploitative assumptions we often hear about.

The second major aspect of our analysis which we rooted in postcolonial and neo-Marxist theory was around development as hybrid and relational and in this, African agency is vitally important. In discussing China in Africa, Africa is spoken of or spoken for in all these representations. At best elite Africans appear in diplomatic set pieces or western journalists – like Hitchens with whom we started this book – select some horror show regarding 'poor' Africans and extrapolate to the whole continent. Even the 'Asian Drivers' agenda (Kaplinsky 2008), which we discussed in Chapter 6, is premised on a conflation of all Asian countries as sharing some essential characteristics and is based on the assumption that they do the 'driving', which denies African agency in this relationship. In turn this leads to (or arguably stems from) 'Africa' and 'China' being treated as singular and homogenous.

Our data showed Africans negotiating their relationships with the Chinese and in some cases contesting their presence. This agency is found at the individual level, but also within more organized civil society activity and within parts of the African state at both a central and 'street' level. However, what has hitherto been overlooked in these relationships and struggles is a strong class and interest-based dimension (Mohan and Power 2008). For example, cross-cultural friendships – especially business partnerships – tend to be elite-based with well-educated Africans working with Chinese peers. In terms of protest, civil society action is often – but not exclusively – about protecting the class privileges of the African petit-bourgeoisie and the labour aristocracy. The preponderance of activism from trade unions and business associations suggests that it is those that stand to lose most from cheap imports and labour importation that have become the most organized elements in Africa. Finally this class-based agency is located within the African state. We noted in the opening chapter, and in more detail in Chapter 6, that the idea of 'failed states' is unhelpful and that we have to examine actually existing state–capital dynamics and the repertoire of political strategies used by Africans. The case of the Queensway-CIF-GRN in Angola showed that agency was at work especially for those sections of the state that benefit from (and so fight for) Chinese investment. But, this is a selected elite so that the 'China–Africa' relationship is organized through hybrid and enclaved, yet spatially diffuse 'state' institutions which are detached from national democratic processes.

Moreover the extension of the 'China Inc.' assumptions into Africa tends to suggest that ethnic economies are internally coherent and enclavic. But this is clearly misplaced as our evidence showed hard capitalist logic determining business behaviour as opposed to favouring of co-ethnic and complex migrant trajectories were such that there was no inherent trust within a 'Chinese' community, and extensive relationships with African businesses. That is not to say that these relationships are random, but that ethnicity and nationality are over-determined in the literature on Chinese migrant businesses, which in turn diverts attention from the potential benefit to African economies. For example, recent research in Zambia (Fessehaie and Morris 2011) suggests that the Chinese are not as enclaved as earlier reports suggested and Zambian firms have secured a growing number of contracts.

At a more everyday level the interactions between Chinese migrants and local populations are often welcomed for the transparency of the relationship which is founded on a clear business footing. The Chinese are often either employers or suppliers, and the transactions are devoid of the racial connotations attached to European colonization. However, there is evidence that the Chinese exhibit racism and bewilderment at the structures in which African societies are organized. The 'bewilderment' suggests that ideas of parity and 'South–South' exchange are still in the embryonic stage. Additionally some Africans exhibit attitudes towards the Chinese that are steeped in negative stereotypes, even though African traders in China have noted a better reception than, say, in Europe.

## Future engagements: globalizing Africa–China relations

This discussion of African agency is based on a potential space opening up for new directions in African development. The rising powers undoubtedly provide new sources of finance for Africa as well as some ideological models with which to contest the dominant approaches to development. What these new sources of finance provide for recipient countries, technical debates aside, is some leverage; what has been termed the 'revival of triangulation' (Large 2008c). Yet on the face of it China's interests do not radically alter the role Africa plays in the global division of labour (Tull 2006), but what is interesting to analyse is whether individual African states are able to harness this hegemonic rivalry for their own ends. It is also important to distinguish between the actors we are discussing when highlighting this enhanced 'leverage' when the main beneficiaries would appear to be state and business elites rather than (for example) trade unions, social justice movements or the poor (Palat 2009).

Certainly in the recent Democratic Republic of the Congo (DRC) deal with the Chinese (Vandaele 2008), which was a classic 'resource-for-equity' swap on a massive scale, the DRC negotiators were novel for seeking to secure local deals for Congolese sub-contractors and workers. As yet, we do not know how far it was feasible to use local firms or whether these clauses in the loan agreements are being honoured, but it does suggest that African states can harness the rivalry between donors and investors to drive forward their own development agendas. The donor harmonization process provides another example of how shrewd and domestically focused 'triangulation' can deliver benefits. However, while an elite commitment to development that the Chinese help realize may be beneficial and allow a policy space to open up things are dynamic. The result is that the policy space and state autonomy may be closed down. The first factor which might reduce the ability of African states to manoeuvre is the growing role of China in African politics.

The second concerns the convergence of donors around certain norms which will mean that apparent policy alternatives are not so different and hence the space to manoeuvre is reduced.

In terms of China's growing role in African politics Sudan has been a real test case. Here we saw that the Chinese were initially 'blindly' supportive of Bashir, but were roundly condemned by the international community for their complicity in the atrocities in Darfur. Although the Chinese began high profile diplomacy and aid missions around the Southern Sudan and Darfur issues, they were all the time manoeuvring smartly to ensure access to oil and markets following the Comprehensive Peace Agreement and ultimate secession of Southern Sudan. So, the linkages between development cooperation and regime legitimacy are fluid and poorly understood. What it does show is that 'non-interference' is breaking down as the Chinese government increasingly refers instead to 'proactive non-interference' and 'constructive mediation' (Raine 2009: 155).

Moreover despite the tangible evidence of modernization that Chinese projects bring there are growing signs of disaffection with the Chinese among Africans and a possible counter-attack by the Chinese that will take them deeper into African politics. The Sata case in Zambia has taken a new (possible) twist. In the 2011 elections that Sata eventually won the incumbent Movement for Multiparty Democracy's campaign was allegedly bankrolled by the Chinese in an attempt to stifle Sata's chances (Redvers 2011). Clearly, if this proves to have even a grain of truth, it counters any claims by the Chinese towards 'non-interference' in local politics and may presage a phase of deepening direct engagement in domestic politics. As we saw, at the 2009 meeting of the Forum on China–African Cooperation (FOCAC) the Chinese stressed building African capacity as a priority and the question was raised: capacity for what?

The onset of FOCAC as a multilateral platform has also thrust the role of African regional institutions (such as New Partnership for African Development [NEPAD], the African Union [AU] and Southern African Development Community [SADC]) into the limelight. For example, an organization such as the NEPAD Business Foundation (NBF), a private sector body spun out from the NEPAD Secretariat, is working to prioritize and coordinate infrastructure development around key development corridors, but its efforts are largely applicable to the southern African region only. The NEPAD Secretariat and NBF engaged with the Chinese Government around the FOCAC Forum in November 2006, but neither has the mandate to negotiate project investment on behalf of African governments or other private sector stakeholders. Rather its role appears to be the marketing and coordination of prioritized corridors or so-called spatial development initiatives (Davies 2010: 22). As corporate relations with the Chinese mature, African governments are becoming more proactive in managing their relations with the Chinese. Ultimately, to increase the benefits of Chinese engagement in Africa, it is highly reliant on the willingness of the Chinese to further integrate economically and socially into African countries, and improve its global standings on various issues of governance and responsibility.

In terms of regimes gaining legitimacy from new sources of finance and tangible development outputs, the recent Zambian election suggests the relationship between inward investment and legitimacy are not clear-cut. Thus we may see a backlash against foreigners in a similar vein to Uganda in the 1970s. Further, bound up in these moves is a manipulation of racist sentiment on both sides of the 'Africa' and 'Asia' divide (Nyiri 2006). Again, this is an unfolding issue which needs monitoring across different countries. Likewise the level of contestation from civil society in many countries has been mute, and even the most powerful civil society organizations (CSOs), such as trade unions, lack the power after 25 years of neo-liberal rollback to make much difference. Given the wider geopolitical concerns about the rise of Asian powers, in particular among international policymakers and civil society, we are likely to see more 'domestic' campaigns being orchestrated by international actors.

The second factor that might close down the policy space opened by the 'rising powers' is a gradual convergence around the ideology of development. We noted that some responses to the new donors have been realist and 'hawkish', reflecting deeper concerns about global hegemony and the (possible) waning of US supremacy. More sanguine responses see the rising powers doing some things differently and in this difference there is opportunity for learning and collaboration based on the 'comparative advantage' of each donor (GRIPS 2008). The start of this is 'dialogue' with the Chinese which has over the past five years become the mainstay of the European donors. We also discussed at some length the idea that China shares many neo-liberal approaches with western economic actors. What this might mean is that rather than being an alternative for African states, which enables some form of triangulation, we gradually see a new liberal order emerging (Ikenberry 2008) that is not the same as the US-led one of the past 60 years but is also not that different.

China, aware of its growing global responsibilities as a rising power, has managed to deflect criticism of its action by evoking its 'non-interference' stance and more recently towards promoting a 'harmonious' world order. China's evolving foreign policy has demonstrated a new commitment to advancing global security cooperation in a number of areas such as peacekeeping. China has begun to play an active and constructive role, using it to influence and promote positive outcomes in conflict situations, such as promoting nuclear non-proliferation on the Korean Peninsula or by increasing its troop contributions to UN peacekeeping missions 20-fold since 2000, with the majority based in Africa. There has thus been a growing recognition in China that Africa will become an important stage where its image as a responsible global actor is forged (Huang 2010).

But as we noted there is an increasingly wide array of Chinese actors, combined with the lack of an effective mechanism bridging the gap between China's Africa policy and its implementation, as incidents of exploitation and mismanagement sprung up throughout the continent. The combination of multiple oversight bureaucracies (which do not always enjoy direct lines of authority over Chinese corporations overseas), competing companies and their conflicting interests means that it is becoming increasingly more difficult and challenging for the Chinese government to manage and coordinate the activities of Chinese actors on the continent. Indeed, in the past few years, there have been conscious administrative and legislative efforts to strengthen, for example, the environmental protection measures in play both domestically and in the governance of Chinese corporations operating overseas. There is also a growing recognition in China of the importance of Corporate Social Responsibility (CSR) along with some significant recent increases in the adoption of CSR standards by major Chinese firms including many SOEs. Further, interactions with international environmental agencies through multilateral platforms (such as the United Nations Framework Convention on Climate Change) and the signing of over 500 international environmental treaties have led to global environmental norms being increasingly embraced by the Chinese state. This illustrates that China's interactions with the international community are enhancing China's capacity to consider and respond to environmental impacts.

However, while the Chinese echo some of the concepts and make some concessions to international norms, it is unlikely that they will wholeheartedly throw themselves into these institutional processes. Their own development models are too powerful and different for them to, for example, suddenly start championing civil society and governance reform, but as we noted there is space for consensus around business-led growth. So, we are likely to see interesting discursive and ideological battles in the coming few years as both sides seek to influence the other, and if the 'China model' is used ideologically by recipient states in Africa to oppose reform then the discursive field of development will become even muddier.

# Notes

## 2 Contextualizing China–Africa Relations

1. According to the Chinese historical records ('Shi Ji') written by the famous historian Si Machien over one hundred years BC, the Emperor Wuti of the Han Dynasty sent envoys to the far west to make alliance with friendly 'tribes' against the powerful Huns in the north. These envoys reached many distant countries originally unknown to China, including Pathia, Babylonia, Seleuid Media, and lastly a place named Likan. They also brought back a Likan magician presented as a gift by the King of Pathia. Likan was identified as Alexandria in Egypt (Jinyuan 1984).
2. As is officially recorded in China, the state of Mogadishu had sent its ambassadors to China three times between 1416 and 1423 (Jinyuan 1984).
3. Taiwan is important for the Africa migration story for three reasons (Mohan and Tan-Mullins 2009). First, it is one of the most significant parts of the Chinese diaspora, around 22 million, and many Taiwanese firms operate in Africa (Pickles and Woods 1989). Second, political tensions between supporters of the PRC and ROC still exist among diaspora communities. Third, the PRC has pursued its 'One China' Policy since the formation of Taiwan and has given favourable aid terms to African countries which support its claims to Taiwan.
4. In 1966 Mao launched the so-called Great Proletarian Cultural Revolution, a post-revolutionary struggle for the purification of the Party against alleged 'bourgeois' and 'intellectual' tendencies. Teachers, professors and judges became the target of vicious attacks by young Red Guards. Millions were forced into manual labour and tens of thousands were executed, resulting in massive civil unrest and economic disorder.
5. Egypt became the first African country to establish diplomatic relations with China in 1956.
6. Sudan was the fourth African state to recognize the PRC, and the Chinese have never forgotten this diplomatic debt 'from their own days of isolation and pariah-statehood' (Chan 2008: 4).
7. The Sino-Indian crisis of the 1960s not only intensified the already deteriorating Sino-Soviet relations by making Moscow openly pro-India, but also ended the myth of 'Afro-Asian Solidarity' by creating new cleavages within the 'Third World' (Wei 1982).
8. For an interesting discussion of Nkrumah's attempt to settle the conflict which had brought China and the United States to the brink of hostilities (the Vietnam war) see Snow (1988: 109).
9. Sino-Egyptian diplomatic relations, established in 1956, soured in 1959, and relations with Ghana were suspended in 1966, following a coup which deposed Nkrumah. It was also deeply involved in rebellions in the Democratic Republic of the Congo led by Gaston Soumialot and Pierre Mulele in 1964 (Davidson 1981: 102–9).

10. Based in Beijing, the IPRCC was jointly initiated and established by the Chinese government, the United Nations Development Programme (UNDP) and other international organizations in December 2004. Specifically, the Centre aims to optimize poverty reduction policies and strategies through an intensive research programme, facilitating and strengthening international exchange and collaboration by organizing a wide range of activities, and promoting knowledge sharing and South-South learning through training courses. The Africa–China Forum on Poverty Reduction and Development is co-organized by the IPRCC and the UNDP and is designed to promote exchanges and cooperation between African countries and China in the area of poverty reduction and social development.

11. See Snow's chapter 'The poor help the poor' (1988: 144–85) for fascinating detail on China's early aid architecture. A more lurid account of Mao's motives for overseas aid is contained in Jung and Halliday (2006: 465–8, 561–3).

12. The Great Leap forward was indeed a (man-made) disaster causing between 16 and 40 million deaths in rural China.

13. Snow's account of the Zhou Enlai tour can be found in *Beijing Review*, 3 January 3 1964, page 94.

14. Peking also suffered other diplomatic setbacks in the Congo, Burundi, Angola and Mozambique and following the military coup in Indonesia.

15. Zhao, who during the so-called Cultural Revolution was paraded through Canton (Guangzhou) in a dunce's cap, was 'rehabilitated' by Zhou Enlai in 1973 and sent to China's largest province, Sichuan, as first party secretary. There he instituted rural land 'reforms', the abolition of the commune system and a raft of other pro-market measures. This gained the attention of Deng Xiaoping who drafted him into the Politburo in the late 1970s. Zhao became prime minister in 1980 and assumed, in addition, the post of CCP General Secretary in January 1987. For a detailed account of Zhao's tour see Beri (1983).

16. The strictness of the (non)use of 'aid' as a term has always differed among actors; originally, the key term was 'external' or 'foreign' assistance instead of 'aid', thereby explicitly distancing China from Western definitions and practice (cf. Grimm et al. 2011). The semantic debate seems to have relaxed considerably – and most visibly so with the publication of an official policy paper on *China's Foreign Aid* in 2011 (GoC 2011). According to the figures published in this document, the (relative) majority of aid in 2009 went to Africa (45.7%, attributed to 51 countries), with Asia following (32.8% to 30 countries overall) and Latin America and the Caribbean being the third most important region (12.7% to 18 countries). It is important to highlight that China usually does not differentiate between sub-Saharan Africa and Northern Africa. The document also notes that 'by the end of 2009, China had provided a total of 256.29 billion Yuan [US$ 39.59 billion] in aid to foreign countries, including 106.2 billion Yuan in grants [US$ 16.4 billion], 76.54 billion Yuan in interest-free loans [US$ 11.82billion] and 73.55 billion Yuan in concessional loans [US$ 11.35 billion]' (GoC 2011). China seems to be overcoming its initial reluctance to using the term 'aid' as such.

17. There have been suggestions however that China has used aid to discourage African governments from supporting Japan's case for a seat on the UN security council (Lancaster 2007).

18. This was as a consequence of China joining the World Bank in 1980 and the African Development Bank in 1985 (Brautigam 1985).
19. Marcum (1981: 230, 419 n30). Savimbi himself later claimed in 1975 that the Chinese did not support him (Jackson 1995).
20. Although no longer publicly supplying arms to any group in Angola, Beijing authorized the release of Chinese arms from Zairean army arsenals for use by the FNLA in July 1975. In addition, the Chinese also apparently lent support to Daniel Chipenda's former Eastern Revolt faction of the MPLA which had split from its parent body and joined the FNLA in February 1975. The Chinese also revived the dormant relationship with UNITA (Jackson 1995).
21. An anonymous Chinese official quoted in Arthur Gavshon, *Crisis in Africa: Battleground of East and West* (Harmondsworth: Penguin Books, 1981: 139).
22. In addition to the state-backed migrants there are petty entrepreneurs who largely operate in trade, services and in light manufacturing (Mohan and Tan-Mullins 2009).
23. 'Premier Wen's Several Talks During Europe Visit', Xinhua (2004). Wen sounded similar themes during a spring 2005 trip to South Asia. See Xiao Qiang, 'Premier Wen's South Asian Tour Produces Abundant Results', *Renmin Ribao*, 13 April 2005.

# 3  Chinese Policies and Their Implications for Africa

1. For more on this see Brautigam and Tang (2009).

# 4  Towards a Chinese 'Socialist Market Economy'

1. It is difficult, however, to make a precise evaluation of China's outflowing FDI because of discrepancies in statistics.
2. These cities were: Dalian, Qinhuangdao, Tianjin, Yantai, Qingdao, Lianyungang, Nantong, Shanghai, Ningbo, Wenzhou, Fuzhou, Guangzhou, Zhanjiang and Beihai. Since 1992, the State Council has opened a number of border cities, and in addition, opened all the capital cities of inland provinces and autonomous regions. In addition, free trade zones, state-level economic and technological development zones and high-tech industrial development zones have been established in large and medium-sized cities.
3. This was focused on the Yangtze River Delta, Pearl River Delta, Xiamen-Zhangzhou-Quanzhou Triangle in south Fujian, Shandong Peninsula, Liaodong Peninsula, Hebei and Guangxi. In 1990, the Chinese government decided to open the Pudong New Zone in Shanghai to overseas investment, and opened more cities in the Yangtze River valley. Deng Xiaoping was instrumental in the opening of the Pudong New Area, revitalizing the city as China's economic hub.
4. More importantly, it reflected the changing conceptions of some leaders of the long-term benefits of restricting domestic sectors from competition, and their concerns over the type of capitalism that was emerging in China (Breslin 2004).

5. The Chinese do not use the term 'privatization' relying instead on several other terms such as 'transformation of ownership' (*zhuanzhi*) or 'readjustment of ownership structure' (*suoyouzhi jiegou tiaozheng*). Similarly, the Chinese often use 'non-public ownership' as a substitute for 'private ownership'.

6. For the full text of the Decision see *Beijing Review* 36, No. 47, 22–28 November 1993, pp. 12–31.

7. The government has also embarked on a project to provide 40% of China's exporters with their own reputable *brand* by 2010 (*Peoples Daily*, 9 June 2005; *Peoples Daily*, 11 December 2005).

8. 125 'central SOEs' are currently listed on the SASAC website: http://www.sasac.gov.cn/n2963340/n2971121/n4956567/4956583.html

9. In 2005 the Administration for Foreign Exchange (SAFE) made it easier for financial institutions to invest abroad.

10. The CIC website can be found at: http://www.china-inv.cn/

11. Many Chinese enterprises conduct investment 'round-tripping', i.e. relocating funds into an offshore incorporated entity, then directing the funds back as a 'foreign' investor (see UNCTAD Investment Brief, 2007). Some of these enterprises also list on the Hong Kong stock exchange to raise more capital, before re-investing in China.

12. The Chairperson of the CIF, Ms Lo Fung Hung, is also the Vice-Chairperson of the CSIH.

13. It is worth noting however that Hong Kong was placed at the top of this list in first place. The Index measures the economic freedom of countries based on trade freedom, business freedom, investment freedom and property rights.

14. While party members were exhorted to study the theory of the three represents, the concept of a xiaokang 小康 society was promoted for the wider population. The concept of xiaokang is sometimes associated with a 'middle class' society and is better understood as referring to the creation of a moderately well off society – 'less affluent than "well-off" but better off than freedom from want' (Xinhua 2002).

# 8    The Geopolitics of China–Africa Engagement

1. Maganheim (2007) argues that that the rise of China and its moves to secure sea-lanes has implications for US operational access to African seaports and that American military planners must confront the reality that access for the largest class of vessels capable of delivering sizeable amounts of equipment and material into available African seaports may be denied due to conflict with China's commercial interests in African ports.

2. The first use of 'soft power' in China's official party media came on 15 November 2001, in *Guangming Daily*, a newspaper published by the Central Propaganda Department (Bandurski 2009). In 2007 President Hu Jintao told the 17th Communist Party Congress that China needed to increase its soft power. A useful discussion on the use of the term in China can be found in Paradise (2009).

3. For more on China's foreign policy see also A. Doak Barnett, *The Making of Foreign Policy in China: Structure and Process* (Boulder: Westview Press, 1985); Lu Ning, *The Dynamics of Foreign Policy Decision Making in China* (Boulder: Westview Press, 2000); David M. Lampton (ed.), *The Making of Chinese Foreign and Security Policy in the Era of Reform* (Stanford: Stanford University Press, 2001); Yufan Hao and Lin Su (eds.), *China's Foreign Policy Making* (Burlington, VT: Ashgate, 2005).

4. Report, Office of Intelligence Research (OIR) no. 6903, 'Results of the Bandung Conference: A Preliminary Analysis', 27 April 1955, attached to Memorandum, Staats to OCB, 12 May 1955, OCB Central File Series, WHO-NSC, Box 86, f: 'OCB 092.3 [file #2] (2) April–November 1955,' DDEL.

5. For more on the history of Russian relations with Africa see Matusevich (2006) and Shubin (2008).

6. According to Kornegay and Landsberg (2009: 180) 'The Russian goal, well advanced, is to knit together an East–West energy grid of Moscow-dominated pipeline routes in a cooperative network of strategic nodal points involving other producers, such as Iran in Central Eurasia and Algeria and Libya along the southern Mediterranean, in order to consolidate an encircling dependency of the European market on the one hand and the emerging Asian markets on the other'.

7. Angola with its strong lingusitic, historical and cultural connections to Brazil is a case in point and has been one of the biggest receipients of Brazilian investment. The Angola Credit line from Brazil started out in 2006 as a means of financing the purchase of equipment to be used in infrastructure projects in Angola conducted by Brazilian firms with a budget of US$750 million. During the seventh presidential trip to Africa, in October 2007, President Lula officially granted another US$1 billion to the credit line when visiting Angola. These resources are used in projects that are priorities for the Angolan government and are mostly infrastructure-related.

8. The European Union has an arms embargo against Zimbabwe, part of sanctions in place since 2002 which bars the 27 EU states from supplying arms or equipment intended for military operations. The United States has also imposed sanctions on Mugabe's government (*The Guardian* 24 April 2008).

9. The ship was said to have carried 3 million 7.62 rounds, 3224 mortar shells and 31 tubes and 1500 rocketpropelled grenades. The shipment weighed 90.5 tonnes and was billed at $1,245,000. See copies of invoices from www.noseweek.co.za and Jessica Lasky-Fink and Jeff Abramson, 'Chinese arms shipment sparks outrage', *Arms Control Today*, 1 June 2008. The ship's owner was the parastatal Chinese Ocean Shipping Company and it was carrying cases of weaponry and ammunition in six containers. The shipper of the arms was Poly Technologies Inc. of Beijing, a subsidiary of China Poly Group Corporation, the delivery address on the shipping documents was the Zimbabwe Defence Force, Harare, and the point of origin on the cargo manifest was Beijing. The invoice was dated 21 January 2008 and the shipment left Tianjin on 15 March (Spiegel and LeBillon 2009).

10. 'Peacekeepers' includes personnel performing a variety of functions within a peacekeeping mission, including combat troops (which China has yet to

contribute), police, medical specialists, engineers, military observers and other supporting personnel.

11. This is distinct from the joint military exercises China has been involved with. Between August 2005 and December 2006, China conducted joint military exercises (including maritime search and rescue and counter-terrorism scenarios) with India, Pakistan, Russia, Tajikistan, Thailand, the Shanghai Cooperation Organization (SCO), and the United States but no African states have yet been included in the joint exercises with China, either bilaterally or multilaterally.

# Bibliography

Accenture Consulting Group (2005) 'China spreads its wings: Chinese companies go global,' http://www.accenture.com/us-en/Pages/insight-china-spreads-wings-chinese-companies-go-global-summary.aspx (accessed 29 September 2011).

ACET (African Center for Economic Transformation) (2009) 'Looking East, a guide for Africa's policy-makers, Volume 2: Key dimensions of Chinese engagements in African countries', http://acetforafrica.org/site/wp-content/uploads/2009/05/lookingeastv2.pdf (accessed 29 September 2011).

ADB (Asian Development Bank) (2003) The Development of Private Enterprise in the People's Republic of China (Manila: ADB).

Adie, W. A. C. (1964) 'Chou En-Lai on Safari', The China Quarterly 18 (Apr–Jun): 174–94.

AfDB (African Development Bank) (2011) 'Russia's economic engagement with Africa', Africa Economic Brief, Volume 2, Issue 7, May 11, http://www.afdb.org/fileadmin/uploads/afdb/Documents/Publications/Russia's_Economic_Engagement_with_Africa.pdf

AFRODAD (2008) 'Mapping Chinese development assistance in Africa: A synthesis of Angola, Mozambique, Zambia and Zimbabwe', AFRODAD, Harare. http://www.afrodad.org/downloads/publications/China%20in%20Africa%20Draft.pdf/ (accessed 12 September 2009).

Agência Angola Press (2009) 'Premier wants food production research', 29 April, http://www.portalangop.co.ao/motix/en_us/noticias/economia/Premier-wants-food-production-research,2f1bec58-fc80–475c-b187-f9990198d44f.html (accessed 17 August 2010).

Agnew, D., Pearce, J., Pramod, G., Peatman, T., Watson, R., Beddington, J. and Pitcher, T. (2009) Estimating the worldwide extent of illegal fishing. PLoS one 4 (20). http://www.ncbi.nlm.nih.gov/pmc/articles/PMC2646833/

Aiyar, P. (2007) 'China continues to court Africa', The Hindu, 1 February.

Alavi, H. (1972) 'The state in post-colonial societies: Pakistan and Bangladesh', New left Review 74 (July–August): 145–73.

Alden, C. (2005) 'China in Africa', Survival 47(3): 147–64.

Alden, C. (2007) China in Africa (London: Zed).

Alden, C. (2008) 'Africa without Europeans'. In C. Alden, D. Large and R. Soares de Oliveira (eds), China Returns to Africa: A Rising Power and a Continent Embrace (London: Hurst), 349–59.

Alden, C. and Davies, M. (2006) 'Chinese multinational corporations in Africa', http://www.cctr.ust.hk/materials/conference/china-africa/papers/Chris_Alden_Chinese_Multinational_Corporations.pdf (accessed 27 September 2011).

Alden, C. and Hughes, C. R. (2009) 'Harmony and discord in China's Africa strategy: Some implications for foreign policy', The China Quarterly 199: 563–84.

Alden, C. and Vieira, M. A. (2005) 'The new diplomacy of the South: South Africa, Brazil, India and Trilateralism', Third World Quarterly 26(7): 1077–95.

Alden, C., Large, D. and Soares de Oliveira, R. (eds) (2008) *China Returns to Africa: A Rising Power and a Continent Embrace* (London: Hurst).

Alexander, K. and Gilbert, S. (2008) 'Oil and governance report: A case study of Chad, Angola, Gabon, and Sao Tome é Principe', Pretoria: IDASA, http://www.idasa.org/our_products/resources/output/oil_and_governance_report/?pid=political_governance_programme (accessed 27 September 2011).

Alhassan, H. S. (2009) 'Viewpoint – Butterflies vs. hydropower: Reflections on large dams in contemporary Africa', *Water Alternatives* 2(1): 148–60

Ali, A. A. (2007) 'The political economy of relations between Sudan and China'. In G. Le Pere (ed.), *China in Africa: Mercantilist Predator or Partner in Development?* (Braamfontein: Institute for Global Dialogue and South African Institute for International Affairs).

AllAfrica (2011) 'Ghana: Ecobank, Bank of China to boost trade', http://allafrica.com/stories/201104190701.html (accessed 27 September 2011).

Allbusiness (23 September 2010) 'Ghana loan furthers China's Africa strategy'.

Allen, F., Qian, J. and Qian, M. (2005) 'Law, finance, and economic growth in China', *Journal of Financial Economics* 77: 57–116.

Alphaliner (2010) 'Top 100 operated fleets as per 16 January 2010', http://coordination-maree-noire.eu/IMG/pdf_fleet2010.pdf (accessed 27 September 2011).

Alves, P. (2008) 'China's Preferential Trade Policy as a Foreign Policy Tool'. In H. Edinger, H. Herman and J. Jansson (eds), *New Impulses from the South: China's Engagement of Africa* (Stellenbosch: CCCS).

Amankwah, A. (2005) '23,000 jobs gone to the wind, AllAfrica.com, http://www.modernghana.com/news/88758/1/23000-jobs-gone-with-the-wind.html (accessed 20 October 2011).

Amin, S., Bond, P., Dembele, D. M. and Sharife, K. (2009) *Aid to Africa: Redeemer or Coloniser?* (Oxford: Pambazuka Press).

Amit, V. (2002) 'The Trouble with Community'. In V. Amit and N. Rapport (eds) *The Trouble with Community* (London: Pluto Press).

Ampiah, K. and Naidu, S. (eds) (2008) *Crouching Tiger, Hidden Dragon? Africa and China* (Scottsville, SA: University of KwaZulu-Natal Press).

Anagnost, A. (2004) 'The corporeal politics of quality (Suzhi)', *Public Culture* 16: 189–208.

Andrae, G. and Beckman, B. (1999) *Union Power in the Nigerian Textile Industry: Labour Regime and Adjustment* (New Jersey, Transaction Publishers).

ANGOP (Angola Press Agency) (2006) 'Kwanza Sul: China funds USD40 Million cotton project', http://www.portalangop.co.ao/motix/en_us/noticias/economia/2006/10/45/Kwanza-Sul-China-Funds-USD-Million-Cotton-Project,fbe5bac2-fee3–4b0e-b7ae-04e48d54002c.html (accessed 20 October 2011).

ANGOP (2009a) 'Public Work Minister proceeds work in Uige province', http://www.portalangop.co.ao/motix/en_us/noticias/sociedade/Public-Work-minister-proceeds-work-Uige-Province,7af84c7e-983c-4831–8f80–23718870f0f6.html (accessed 11 October 2011).

ANGOP (2009b) 'CAN 2010 stadiums to cost USd 600 million', 31 January, http://www.portalangop.co.ao/motix/en_us/noticias/desporto/2009/0/5/CAN2010-stadiums-cost-Usd-600-million,e0d813e6–38da-47a8–8d4b-ddb87be4c600.html, (accessed 16 March 2010).

Arrighi, G. (2007) *Adam Smith in Beijing* (London: Verso).

Askouri, A. (2007) 'China's Investment in Sudan: Displacing Villages and Destroying Communities'. In F. Manji and S. Marks (eds), *African Perspectives on China in Africa* (London: Pambazuka books), 71–86.

Baah, A. Y. and Jauch, H. (2009) *Chinese Investments in Africa: A Labour Perspective* (Sutcliffe: African Labour Research Network).

Bajpaee, C. (2005) 'China fuels energy Cold War', *Asian Times*, 2 March.

Bandurski, D. (2009) 'Is China's new communications worldview coming of age?', China Media Project, http://cmp.hku.hk/2009/11/12/2926/comment-page-1/#comment-1092 (accessed 20 October 2011).

Baregu, M. (2008) 'The Three Faces of the Dragon: Tanzania-China Relations in Historical Perspective'. In K. Ampiah and S. Naidu (eds) *Crouching Tiger, Hidden Dragon? Africa and China* (Scottsville, SA: University of KwaZulu-Natal Press), 152–66.

Bartels, L., De la Fayette, L., Davies, I. and Campling, L. (2007) Policy Coherence for Development and the Effects of EU Fisheries Policies on Development in West Africa (Brussels: European Parliament).

Bayart, J. (1993) The State in Africa: The Politics of the Belly (Harlow: Longman).

BBC (British Broadcasting Corporation) (2004) 'China raises stakes in Zimbabwe', http://news.bbc.co.uk/1/hi/business/4031969.stm (accessed 05 October 2011).

BBC (2011a) 'Crime rings boost ivory smuggling', 11 November, Http://news.bbc.co.uk/2/hi/8355527.stm (accessed 04 October 2011).

BBC (2011b) 'World Cup handover puts spotlight on Africa-Brazil ties', http://www.bbc.co.uk/news/10541108 (accessed 20 October 2011).

Begum, H. (2010) 'China: From Recipient to Donor? What Have We Learned?'. In K. King (ed.), *A Brave New World of 'Emerging', 'Non-DAC' Donors and their Differences from Traditional Donors*, NORRAG News No 44, September 2010, http://www.norrag.org/issues/latest.

Benn, H. (2004) *China and the UK: Partners in International Development*, Hilary Benn, Secretary of State for International Development, United Kingdom, Fudan University, Shanghai, 25 May 2004, http://www.dfid.gov.uk/countries/asia/China/benn-speech-english.pdf.

Bennett, T. (2007) 'Is China annexing Africa?', *Moneyweek*, http://www.money-week.com/news-and-charts/economics/is-china-annexing-africa/ (accessed 26 September 2011).

Berger, S. (2008) 'Anti-China candidate Michael Sata hopes to become Zambia president', *The Telegraph*, 30 October, http://www.telegraph.co.uk/news/worldnews/africaandindianocean/zambia/3287332/Anti-China-candidate-Michael-Sata-hopes-to-become-Zambia-president.html

Bergesen, A. (2008) 'The new surgical colonialism: China, Africa, and oil' Paper presented at the American Sociological Association Annual Meeting, Sheraton Boston and the Boston Marriott Copley Place, Boston, MA, 31 July 2008.

Beri, H. M. L. (1983) 'Zhao in Africa', *Strategic Analysis* 6(10): 637–43.

Beri, R. (2003) 'India's Africa policy in the post-Cold War era: An assessment', http://www.idsa.in/publications/strategic-analysis/2003/april/Ruchita%20Beri.pdf/ (accessed 17 April 2010).

Berkes, F. (2009) 'Evolution of co-management: Role of knowledge generation, bridging organizations and social learning', *Journal of Environmental Management* 90: 1692–702.

Bernstein, T. P. and Xiaobo Lu (2003) *Taxation without Representation in Contemporary Rural China* (New York, NY: Cambridge University Press).

Bezlova, A. (2007) 'China– new promoter of mega dams', 23 May 2007. http://ipsnews.net/news.asp?idnews=37844 (accessed 07 October 2011).

Bhabha, H. (1994) *The Location of Culture* (London: Routledge).

Biao, X. (2003) 'Emigration from China: A sending country perspective', *International Migration* 41(3): 21–48.

Biello, D. (2009) 'The dam building boom: Right path to clean energy', 23 February, http://e360.yale.edu/content/feature.msp?id=2119 (accessed 07 October 2011).

Bilgin, P. (2008) 'Thinking past 'Western' IR', *Third World Quarterly*, 29(1): 5–23.

Bilgin, P. and Eliş, B. (2008) 'Hard power, Soft power: Toward a more realistic power analysis', *Insight Turkey*, http://www.bilkent.edu.tr/~pbilgin/Bilgin-Elis-IT-2008.pdf (accessed 07 October 2011).

Birdsall, N. (2008) 'Seven deadly sins: Reflection on donor failings'. In W. Easterly (ed.), *Reinventing Foreign Aid* (US: MIT Press), 515–51.

BKS Acres (2001) *Bui Hydropower Project. Environmental Impact Assessment: Scoping Report* (Accra, Ghana).

Bolton, G. (2008) Aid and Other Dirty Business: How Good Intentions Have Failed the World's Poor (London: Ebury Press).

Bosshard, P. (2007) China's role in financing African infrastructure, international rivers network, http://www.irn.org/pdf/china/ChinaEximBankAfrica.pdf (accessed 20 October 2011).

Bosshard, P. (2008) 'China's Environmental Footprint in Africa', China in Africa Policy Briefing (SAIIA), 3: 1–12.

Bosshard, P. (2009) 'China dams the world', *Wold Policy Journal* 26(4): 43–5.

Bosshard, P. (2010a) 'Sudan's Merowe dam: German company brought to justice?', *Pambazuka News*, 13 May, http://pambazuka.org/en/category/comment/64399 (accessed 20 October 2011).

Bosshard, P. (2010b) 'China not a rogue dam builder we feared it would be', http://www.internationalrivers.org/en/blog/peter-bosshard/china-not-rogue-dam-builder-we-feared-it-would-be/ (accessed 05 October 2011).

Bottelier, P. (2007) 'China and the World Bank: How a partnership was built', *Journal of Contemporary China*, 16(51): 239–58.

BP (British Petroleum) (2011) *BP Statistical Review of World Energy 2011* (London: BP).

BP (2008) 'BP in Angola sustainability report 2008', http://www.bp.com/liveassets/bp_internet/globalbp/STAGING/global_assets/e_s_assets/e_s_assets_2008/downloads/Angola_sustainability_review_2009_English.pdf (accessed 07 October 2011).

Brautigam, D. (1998) *Chinese Aid and African Development: Exporting Green Revolution* (Basingstoke: Macmillan and New York: St Martin's).

Brautigam, D. (2003) 'Close encounters: Chinese business networks as Industrial catalysts in Sub-Saharan Africa', *African Affairs* 102: 447–67.

Brautigam, D. (2007) 'China's Foreign Aid in Africa: What do we know?' Paper presented at the Conference on 'China in Africa: Geopolitical and Geoeconomic considerations', 31 May–2 June 2007, J. F. Kennedy School of Government, Harvard University.

Brautigam, D. (2008) 'China Foreign Aid in Africa: What Do We Know?', in R. Rotberg (ed.) *China into Africa: Trade, Aid and Influence* (Washington DC: Brookings Institution Press).

Brautigam, D. (2009) The Dragon's Gift: The Real Story of China in Africa (Oxford: OUP).

Brautigam, D. and Tang, X. (2009) 'China's engagement in African agriculture: "down to the countryside"', *The China Quarterly* 199: 686–706.

Brautigam, D. and Tang, X. (2011) 'African Shenzhen: China's special economic zones in Africa', *Journal of Modern African Studies* 49(1): 27–54.

Brenner, N. (1999) 'Beyond state centrism? Space, territoriality, and geographical scale in globalization studies', *Theory and Society* 28: 39–78.

Breslin, S. (2004) 'Capitalism with Chinese characteristics: The public, the private and the International', Murdoch University, Asia Research Centre, Working Paper No. 104.

Breslin, S. (2006) 'Serving the Market or Serving the Party: Neo-liberalism in China'. In R. Robison (ed.), *The Neo-liberal Revolution: Forging the Market State* (New York: Palgrave Macmillan), 14–34.

Brettel, A. (2003) 'The Politics of Public Participation and the Emergence of Environmental Proto-Movements in China'. PhD dissertation from University of Maryland.

Bridgland, F. (1986) *Jonas Savimbi: A Key to Africa* (Edinburgh: Mainstream).

Broadman, H. (2007) Africa's Silk Road: China and India's New Economics Frontier (Washington DC: World Bank).

Brooks, S. (02 February 2011) 'A new 'southern tour': Chinese investment enters a new decade', Consultancy Africa Intelligence, http://www.consultancyafrica.com/index.php?option=com_content&view=article&id=659:a-new-southern-tour-chinese-investment-enters-a-new-decade&catid=58:asia-dimension-discussion-papers&Itemid=264 (accessed 01 September 2011).

Brown, K. and Chun, Z. (2009) 'China in Africa –– Preparing for the next forum for China Africa cooperation', Asia Programme Briefing Note: ASP 2009/02, http://www.chathamhouse.org/sites/default/files/public/Research/Asia/0609ch_af.pdf (accessed 29 September 2011).

Brown, W. (2006) 'Africa and International Relations: a comment on IR Theory, anarchy and Statehood', *Review of International Studies* 32(1): 119–43.

Brunson, J. E. (1985) Black Jade: The African Presence in the Ancient East and Other Essays (DeKalb: Kara).

Brunson, J. E. (1995) 'The African Presence in Early China', in R. Rashidi and I. Van Sertima (eds), *African Presence in Early Asia* (New Brunswick: Transaction Press), 120–37.

Bryant, R. (1996) 'The Politics of Forestry in Burma'. In P. Hirsch and C. Warren (eds), *Politics and Environment in Southeast Asia: Resources and Resistance* (Routledge: London), 107–21.

Bryant R. (1997) 'Beyond the impasse: The power of political ecology in Third World environment research', *Area* 29(1): 5–19.

Bryant, R. and Bailey, S. (1997) *Third World Political Ecology* (London: Routledge).

Bu, Y. X., Zhu, H. M., Chen, Y. M. and Wu, Z. (2009) *Towards Sustainable Development: The Role of China's Financial Sector* (China: WWF and People's Bank of China).

Buesgen, M. (2008) 'Environmental NGOs' role in expanding social spaces – diversification with Chinese characteristics: A case study of ENGOs opposition to the Nujiang dam in China's Yunnan Province', *China Journal of Social Work* 1(2): 160–71.

*Business Daily Update* (2006) 'Policy Banks Should Play Key Role In International Trade', 29 April.

Business Diary (2011) 'China to strengthen bilateral ties with Zimbabwe', 28 February, http://www.thebusinessdiary.co.bw/?p=1479 (accessed 29 September 2011).

CADF (China Africa Development Fund) (2010) 'About CADF', http://www.cadfund.com/NewsInfo.aspx?NId=393 (accessed 10 October 2011).

CAITEC (Chinese Academy of International Trade and Economic Cooperation) (2010) 'China-Africa trade and economic relationship annual report 2010', http://www.focac.org/eng/zxxx/t832788.htm (accessed 28 September 2011).

Calderisi, R. (2007) *The Trouble with Africa* (New Haven: Yale University Press).

Callahan, W. (2008) 'Chinese visions of world order: Post-hegemonic or a new hegemony?' *International Studies Review* 10: 749–61.

Cammack, P. (2008) 'Smart power and US leadership: A critique of Joseph Nye', *49th Parallel* 22 (Autumn) 4–20.

Campos, I. and Vines, A. (2008) Angola and China: A pragmatic partnership?, http://www.csis.org/media/csis/pubs/080306_angolachina.pdf (accessed 11 March 2009).

Canby, K., Hewitt, J., Bailey, L., Katsigris, E. and Sun, H. (2008) 'China and the global market for forest products; Implications for forests and livelihoods', http://www.forest-trends.org/documents/files/doc_515.pdf (accessed 27 September 2011).

Cao, Y., Qian, Y. and Weingast, B. (1999) 'From federalism, Chinese style, to privatization, Chinese style', *Economics of Transition* March, 7(1): 103–31.

Carmody, P. (2011) *The New Scramble for Africa* (London: Polity Press).

Carmody, P. and Taylor, I. (2010) 'Flexigemony and force in China's geoeconomic strategy in Africa: Sudan and Zambia compared', *Geopolitics* 15(3): 495–515.

Carroll, R. (2006) 'China's Goldmine', *The Guardian*, http://www.guardian.co.uk/business/2006/mar/28/china.g2, 28 March, (accessed 09 October 2011).

Carter, N. T. and Mol, A. P. J. (2007) (eds) *Environmental Governance in China* (New York: Routledge).

CASS (2008) Interview with Dr. Liu Haifang, CASS, 04 September 2008, in CASS Beijing.

CCCS (Centre for Contemporary Chinese Studies) (2011) 'The management of Chinese Foreign Direct Investment', Policy Briefing, March, http://www.ccs.org.za/wp-content/uploads/2011/04/Policy-Briefing-final_180411.pdf (accessed 09 October 2011).

CCPIT (China Council for the Promotion of International Trade) (2010) 'Zhong Guo Zou Chu Qu Zhan Lu:e De Xing Cheng. The making of our country's 'Go Out' strategy', http://www.ccpit.org/Contents/Channel_1276/2007/0327/30814/content_30814.htm (accessed 09 October 2011).

CCS (Centre for Chinese Studies) (2007) *China's Interest and Activity in Africa's Construction and Infrastructure Sectors* (Stellenbosch: CCS, Stellenbosch University).

CCS (2011), China's special economic zone: A bright future for Africa? http://www.ccs.org.za/wp-content/uploads/2011/09/China_Monitor_SEP_2011.pdf (accessed 15 March 2012).

Centre for conflict resolution (2009) 'Taming the dragon? Defining Africa's interest at the Forum on China-Africa Cooperation' (FOCAC) Seminar Report Number 32, http://www.ccr.org.za/images/stories/Vol_32_taming_the_dragon.pdf (accessed 11 October 2011).

Chabal, P. and Daloz, J. P. (1999) *Africa Works: Disorder as Political Instrument* (Oxford: James Currey).

Chakrabarty, D. (1992) 'Provincializing Europe: Postcoloniality and the critique of history', *Cultural Studies* 6(3): 337–57.

Chan, H. S. (2009) 'Politics over markets: Integrating state-owned enterprises into Chinese socialist market', *Public Administration and Development* 29(1): 43–54.

Chan, S. (2008) 'Ten Caveats and One Sunrise in Our Contemplation of China and Africa'. In C. Alden, D. Large and R. Soares de Oliveira (eds), *China Returns to Africa: A Rising Power and a Continent Embrace* (London: Hurst), 339–47.

Chan, T., Tracy, N. and Wenhui, Z. (1999) *China's Export Miracle* (London and New York: MacMillan).

Chan-Fishel, M. (2006) 'Environmental impact: More of the same?' Pambazuka News Issue 282. http://www.pambazuka.org/en/category/comment/38851

Chan-Fishel, M. (2007) 'Environmental Impact: More of the Same?'. In F. Manji and S. Marks (eds), *African Perspectives of China in Africa* (Kenya: Fahamu), 139–52.

Chan-Fishel, M. and Lawson, R. (2007) 'Quid pro quo? China's investment for resource swaps in Africa', *Development* 50(3): 63–8.

Chang, S. (1968) 'The distribution and occupations of overseas Chinese', *Geographical Review* 58(1): 89–107.

Chatterjee, P. (1997) 'Dam busting', *New Scientist* 34–7.

Chavan, R. S. (1979) *Chinese Foreign Policy: The Chou En-lai Era* (New Delhi: Sterling Publishers).

Chen, C., Chiu, P., Orr, R. and Goldstein, A. (2007) 'An Empirical Analysis of Chinese Construction Firms into Africa'. Paper presented at the CRIOCM2007 International Symposium on Advancement of Construction Management and Real Estate, 8–13 August 2007, Sydney, Australia, http://crgp.stanford.edu/publications/conference_papers/Chen_Chiu_Orr_Goldstein_Emp_analysis_Chinese_Africa.pdf (accessed 12 September 2011).

Chen, C. and Orr, R. (2009) 'Chinese contractors in Africa: Home government support, coordination mechanisms, and market entry strategies', *Journal of Construction Engineering and Management* 135(11): 1201–10.

Chen, G., Firth, M. and Xu, L. (2009) 'Does the type of ownership control matter? Evidence from China's listed companies', *Journal of Banking and Finance* 33(1): 171–81.

Chen, J. J. (2005) 'Corporatisation of China's State-Owned Enterprises and Corporate Governance'. In D. Brown and A. Macbean (eds), *Challenges for China's Development: An Enterprise Perspective* (London & NY: Routledge), 58–71.

Chen, J. (2009) 'Explaining the change in China's attitude toward UN peace-keeping: A norm change perspective', *Journal of Contemporary China* 18(58): 157–73.

Chen, S. and Ravallion, M. (2008) 'The Developing World is Poorer than We Thought, but no Less Successful in the Fight against Poverty', World Bank, Washington.

Chen, Z. (2009) 'International Responsibility and China's Foreign Policy'. In M. Lida (ed.) *China's Shift: Global Strategy of the Rising Power* (Japan: The National Institute of Defense Studies), 7–28.

Chen, Z. and Jian, J. (2009) 'Chinese Provinces as Foreign Policy Actors in Africa', South African Institute of International Affairs, SAIIA Occasional paper number 22, China in Africa programme.

Cheng, J. Y. S. and Shi, H. (2009) 'China's Africa policy in the post-Cold War era', *Journal of Contemporary Asia* 39(1).

Chevron, (2011) 'Angola Fact Sheet', March 2011, http://www.chevron.com/documents/pdf/angolafactsheet.pdf (accessed 07 October 2011).

Chidaushe, M. (2007) 'China's grand re-entrance into Africa – mirage or oasis?'. In M. Manji and S. Marks (eds), *African Perspectives on China and Africa* (Cape Town, Nairobi and Oxford: Fahamu), 107–18.

*China Daily* (19 April 2009) http://www.chinadaily.com.cn/m/tianjin/e/2009–04/19/content_7962798.htm (accessed 14 March 2012).

*China Daily* (9 November 2009a) 'Wen's speech at 4th Ministerial Conference of Forum on China-Africa Co-operation' (full text), http://www.chinadaily.com.cn/china/2009–11/09/content_8929621_2.htm. (accessed 09 December 2009).

*China Daily* (9 November 2009b) 'China fulfills promised aid and loans to Africa', http://www.chinadaily.com.cn/china/200911/09/content_8933696.htm (accessed 28 September 2011).

*China Daily* (25 December 2009) 'China revises 2008 GDP growth up to 9.6%'.

*China Daily* (21 January 2010) 'China's GDP grows 8.7% in 2009'.

*China Daily* (20 July 2010) 'Overseas projects fuel big dreams for workers'.

*China Daily* (28 August 2010) 'China's crackdown on illegal labour export heats up'.

*China Daily* (7 September 2010) 'China's first special economic zone marks 30th anniversary'.

*China Daily* (21 September 2010) 'Chinese SMEs prefer to trade in Asia-Pacific'.

*China Daily* (14 October 2010) 'China-Africa trade volume set to hit new record high', http://www.chinadaily.com.cn/china/2010–10/14/content_11412120.htm (accessed 09 October 2011).

*China Daily* (31 August 2011) Li Jinjun: NGOs do what governments don't. http://www.chinadaily.com.cn/china/chinaafricaforum/2011–08/31/content_13227364.htm (accessed 09 October 2011).

*China Economic Review* (2011) 'Into Africa', http://www.chinaeconomicreview.com/en/node/25346 (accessed 01 September 2011).

China Forum (2009) 'Why does China give Mugabe $1 billion?', http://bbs.chinadaily.com.cn/thread-640330-1-1.html, (accessed 28 March 2012).

Chinese Customs (2011) 'China-Africa trade statistics', http://www.e-to-china.com/2011/0823/96699.html (accessed 01 September 2011).

CIC (China Investment Corporation) (2011) Annual Report, http://www.china-inv.cn/cicen/annals/annals.html (accessed 24 September 2011).

CITES (2009) 'CITES ivory sale will increase poaching and illegal trade'. http://www.telegraph.co.uk/earth/earthcomment/3394968/CITES-ivory-sale-will-increase-poaching-and-illegal-trade.html (accessed 28 September 2011).

Clapham, C. (2006) 'Fitting China In', Brenthurst Foundation, Paper 8/2006 (Johannesburg: Brenthurst Discussion).

CNN (1999) 'China's Three Gorges Dam. CNN Indepth Specials – Visions of China', http://edition.cnn.com/SPECIALS/1999/china.50/asian.superpower/three.gorges/

Coker, C. (1985) *NATO, The Warsaw Pact and Africa* (New York: St Martin's).

Collier, P. (2006) 'Is aid oil? An analysis of whether Africa can absorb more aid', *World Development* 34(9): 1482–97.

Collier, P. (2008) The Bottom Billion, Why are the Poorest Countries Failing and What can be Done about it? (United Kingdom: Oxford University Press).

Colombant, N. (2006) 'West Africa attracts influx of Chinese entrepreneurs', Voice of America News, 19 May 2006, http://www.voanews.com/english/news/a-13-2006-05-19-voa52.html (accessed 28 September 2011).

Commission of European Communities (2001) 'Sustainable and responsible business, Corporate Social Responsibility (CSR)', http://ec.europa.eu/enterprise/policies/sustainable-business/corporate-social-responsibility/index_en.htm (accessed 27 September 2011).

Conrad, B., Fernandez, M. and Houshyani, B. (2011) 'Towards an energizing partnership? Exploring China's role as catalyst of renewable energy development in Africa', World Wildlife Fund, http://www.gppi.net/fileadmin/media/pub/2011/conrad-et-al_2011_sino-african-energy-relations.pdf (accessed 27 September 2011).

Conservation News (2008) 'Environmental concerns as Ghana Bui Dam starts construction', http://www.africanconservation.org/200812041259/conservation-news-section/environmental-concerns-as-ghanas-bui-dam-starts-construction.html (accessed 27 September 2011).

Conservative Party (2010) 'One World Conservatism: A Conservative Agenda for International Development', Policy Green Paper No. 11. Conservative Party, London.

Copson, R. (2007) 'US Response to China's Rise in Africa: Policy and Policy Options'. In M. Kittisou (ed.) *Africa in China's Global Strategy* (London: Adonis and Abbey).

Corkin, L. (2008a) 'All's Fair in Loans and War: The Development of China-Angola Relations'. In: K. Ampiah and S. Naidu (eds), *Crouching Tiger, Hidden Dragon? Africa and China* (Scottsville, SA: University of KwaZulu-Natal Press), 108–23.

Corkin, L. (2008b) 'Chinese migrants to Africa: A historical overview', *The China Monitor* 26: 4–5.

Corkin, L. (2009) 'China, Africa and the environment: A briefing paper on the forum on China-Africa co-operation for international rivers', http://www.internationalrivers.org/africa/chinese-dams-africa/china-africa-and-environment (accessed 27 September 2011).

Corkin, L. (2010) 'The State of Play: China Exim Bank's Evolving Relations with Angola', unpublished paper.

Cornelissen, S. (2009) 'Awkward embraces: Emerging and established powers and the shifting fortunes of Africa's IR in the twenty-first century', *Politikon* 36(1): 5–26.

Cowen, D. and Smith, N. (2009) 'After geopolitics? From the geopolitical social to geoeconomics', *Antipode* 41: 22–48.

Crawford, D. (2000) 'Chinese capitalism: Cultures, the Southeast Asian region and economic globalization', *Third World Quarterly* 21(1): 69–86.

Curtis, D. (2008) 'Partner or Predator in the Heart of Africa? Chinese Engagement with the DRC'. In K. Ampiah and S. Naidu (eds) *Crouching Tiger, Hidden Dragon? Africa and China* (Scottsville, SA: University of KwaZulu-Natal Press), 86–107.

Dahlsrud, A. (2006) 'How Corporate Social Responsibility is defined: An analysis of 37 definitions', *Corporate Social Responsibility Environmental Management* 15: 1–13.

Dalby, S. (2007) 'Anthropocene geopolitics: Globalisation, empire, environment and critique', *Geography Compass* 1(1): 103–18.

Dauvergne, P. (1994) 'The politics of deforestation in Indonesia', *Pacific Affairs* 66(4): 497–518.

Davidson, B. (1959) *Old Africa Rediscovered* (London: Gollancz).

Davidson, B. (1981) The People's Cause. A History of Guerrillas in Africa (Harlow: Longman).

Davidson, B. (1992) The Black Man's Burden: Africa and the Curse of the Nation-State (Oxford: James Currey).

Davies, M. (2008) 'How Chinese delivers development assistance to Africa', (Stellenbosch; Centre of Chinese Studies) http://collection.europarchive.org/tna/20080305120132/http://dfid.gov.uk/pubs/files/china-dev-africa.pdf (accessed 11 October 2011).

Davies, M. (2010) 'How China is Influencing Africa's Development', Background Paper for the *Perspectives on Global Development 2010 Shifting Wealth*, http://www.oecd.org/dataoecd/34/39/45068325.pdf (accessed 11 October 2011).

Davies, M., Edinger, H., Tay, N. and Naidu, S. (2008) *How China Delivers Development Assistance to Africa* (South Africa: Centre for Chinese Studies, University of Stellenbosch).

Davies, P. (2009) Think piece on aid and development cooperation post Accra and beyond – steps towards a development dialogue for the 21st century. http://www.eurodad.org/uploadedfiles/whats_new/news/post%20accra%20china-africa%20think%20piece%20january%202009.pdf

Davies, P. (2010) 'Roles and activities of the "new development partners"'. In K. King (ed.) *A Brave New World of 'Emerging', 'Non-DAC' Donors and their Differences from Traditional Donors,* NORRAG News No 44, http://www.norrag.org/issues/article/1318/en/roles-and-activities-of-the-_new-development-partners.html?PHPSESSID=34227322ff4f8994954c5e1376e9018c (accessed 11 October 2011).

Day, K. (2005) *China's Environment and the Challenge of Sustainable Development* (Armonk, NY: M.E. Sharpe).

De Beule, F. and Van den Bulcke, D. (2010) 'The global crisis, Foreign Direct Investment and China', *BICCS Asia Paper* 5(6): 1–31.

De Haan, A. (2009) *How the Aid Industry Works: An Introduction to International Development* (Sterling, VA: Kumarian Press).

De Haan, A. (2010) 'Facts and fiction about development aid & what it means for China', unpublished paper given at the ESRC Rising Powers Workshop 1: The understanding and practice of development in China and the European Union, School of Public Policy and Management, Tsinghua University, 15–16 July 2010.

De Renzio, P. (2006) 'Aid, budgets and accountability: A survey article', *Development Policy Review* 24(6): 627–45.

Deutscher, E. (2010) 'DAC Approach to new Donors'. In K. King, K (ed.), *A Brave New World of 'Emerging', 'Non-DAC' Donors and their Differences from Traditional Donors*, NORRAG News No 44, September 2010, http://www.norrag.org/issues/article/1323/en/dac-approach-to-the-new-donors.html?PHPSESSID=34227322ff4f8994954c5e1376e9018c (accessed 11 October 2011).

DFA (Department of Foreign Affairs) (2006) *Annual Report 2005–06* (South Africa: Tshwane-Pretoria).

Dicken, P. (2003) Global Shift: Reshaping the Global Economic Map in the 21st Century, 4th edn. (New York: Guilford Press).

Dickinson, S. (2010) 'China energy shortages and their impact on your business', http://www.chinalawblog.com/2010/12/china_energy_shortages_and_their_impact_on_your_business.html (accessed 11 October 2011).

Dickson, B. (2002) 'Cooptation and corporatism in China: The logic of party adaptation', *Political Science Quarterly* 115(4): 517–40.

Dickson, B. (2003) Red Capitalists in China: The Party, Private Entrepreneurs, and Prospects for Political Change (Cambridge: Cambridge University Press).

Dickson, B. (2007) 'Integrating wealth and power in China: The Communist Party's embrace of the private sector', *The China Quarterly* 192: 827–54.

Ding, X. (2000a) 'Informal privatization through internationalization: The rise of nomenklatura capitalism in China's offshore business', *British Journal of Political Science* 30(1): 121–46.

Ding, X. (2000b) 'The illicit asset stripping of China's state firms', *China Journal* (43) January: 1–28.

Dirlik, A. (1997) 'Critical reflections on "Chinese capitalism" as paradigm', *Identities*, 3(3): 303–30.

Dobler, G. (2008) 'Solidarity, Xenophobia and the Regulation of Chinese Businesses in Namibia'. In C. Alden, D. Large and R. Soares de Oliveira (eds), *China Returns to Africa: A Rising Power and a Continent Embrace* (London: Hurst), 237–55.

Dollar, D. (2008) 'Lessons from China for Africa', Research Working Paper No. 4531, World Bank East Asia and Pacific Region.

Doornbos, M. (2010) 'Researching African statehood dynamics: Negotiability and its limits', *Development and Change* 41(4): 747–69.

Downs, E. (2007) 'The fact and fiction of Sino-African energy relations', *China Security* 3(3): 42–68.

Dreher, A., Nunnenkamp, P. and Thiele, R. (2010) 'Are New Donors Different?' In K. King (ed.), *A Brave New World of 'Emerging', 'Non-DAC' Donors and their Differences from Traditional Donors*, NORRAG News No 44, http://www.norrag.org/issues/article/1320/en/are-_new-donors-different.html (accessed 11 October 2011).

Dubey, A. K. (1990) Indo-African Relations in the Post-Nehru Era (1965–1985) (Delhi: Kalinga Publications).

Dung, E. J., Bombom, L. S. and Agusomu, T. D. (2008) 'The effects of gas flaring on crops in the Niger Delta, Nigeria', *GeoJournal* 73: 297–305.

Dunn, K. (2001) 'Introduction: Africa and International Relations Theory'. In K. C. Dunn and T. M. Shaw (eds) *Africa's Challenge to International Relations Theory* (Basingstoke: Palgrave), 1–8.

Dwinger, F. (2010) 'Combating Climate Change: China's Contribution to the Expansion of Africa' Renewable energy sector. http://www.consultancyafrica.

com/index.php?option=com_content&view=article&id=479:combating-climate-change-chinas-contribution-to-the-expansion-of-africas-renewable-energy-sector&catid=58:asia-dimension-discussion-papers&Itemid=264

Eadie, G. A. and Grizzell, D. M. (1979) 'China's Foreign Aid, 1975–78', *The China's Quarterly* 77: 217–34.

Easley, Leif-Eric (2008) 'Multilateralism, not multipolarity should be goal', *The China Post*, 29 March http://www.chinapost.com.tw/commentary/the-china-post/leif-eric-easley/2008/03/29/149402/p3/Multilateralism-not.htm. (accessed 11 October 2011).

Easterly, W. (2007) The White Man's Burden: Why the West's Efforts to Aid the Rest Have Done So Much Ill and So Little Good (Oxford: Oxford University Press).

Easterly, W. (ed.) (2008) *Reinventing Foreign Aid* (Harvard: MIT Press).

Economy, E. (2004) The River Runs Black: The Environmental Challenge to China's Future (Ithaca: Cornell University Press).

Economy, E. (2005) 'Environmental Enforcement in China'. In K. Day (ed.), *China's Environment and the Challenge of Sustainable Development* (Armonk and London: ME Sharpe), 102–20.

ECOWAS-SWAC/OECD (2006) 'Atlas on regional integration in West Africa', www.atlas-westafrica.org (accessed 11 October 2011).

Edmonds, R. L. (1994) Patterns of China's Lost Harmony: A Survey of the Country's Environmental Degradation and Protection (London & New York: Routledge).

EIA (Energy Information Administration) (2010) 'Angolan oil: Overview' http://www.eia.gov/countries/country-data.cfm?fips=AO (accessed 22 February 2010).

EIA (2011) International Energy Outlook 2011. http://www.eia.gov/forecasts/ieo/pdf/0484(2011).pdf

Ellis, L. J. (2007) 'China Exim Bank in Africa', http://legacy.wilsoncenter.org/ondemand/index.cfm?fuseaction=media.play&mediaid=FA160714-CB89-C09C-EB8D7DEDF2015CD9 (accessed 29 September 2011).

Elvin, M. (2004) The Retreat of Elephants: An Environmental History of China (New Haven: Yale University Press).

Elvin, M. and Ts'ui-jung, Liu (1998) *Sediments of Time: Environment and Society in Chinese History* (Cambridge: Cambridge University Press).

Epstein, G. and Braunstein, E. (2002) 'Bargaining power and foreign direct investment in China: Can 1.3 billion consumers tame the multinationals?', Working Papers, wp45, Political Economy Research Institute, University of Massachusetts at Amherst.

ERM (Environmental Resources Management) (2007) 'Environmental and Social Impact Assessment of the Bui Hydropower Project: Final Report', annex volume, Accra.

Escobar, A. (1995) *Encountering Development: The Making and Unmaking of the Third World* (Princeton: Princeton University Press).

Esteves, D. (2008) Relações de Cooperação China-África: O Caso de Angola (Coimbra: Almedina).

Esty, D. C. and Ivanova, M. H. (2004) 'Globalization and environmental protection: A global governance perspective', Yale Center for Environmental law & Policy Working Paper Series No. 0402. http://envirocenter.yale.edu/uploads/workingpapers/0402%20esty-ivanova.pdf (accessed 27 September 2011).

Eweje, G. (2006) 'Environmental costs and responsibilities resulting from oil exploitation in developing countries: The case of the Niger Delta of Nigeria', *Journal of Business Ethnics* 69: 27–56.

Eyben, R (2006) 'The road not taken: International aid's choice of Copenhagen over Beijing', *Third World Quarterly* 27(6).

FAO (Food and Agricultural Organisation) (2004) 'Fishery and aquaculture country profiles', China, http://www.fao.org/fishery/countrysector/FI-CP_CN/en (accessed 27 September 2011).

FAO (2006) 'Fishery and aquaculture country profiles: China' http://www.fao.org/fishery/countrysector/FI-CP_CN/en (accessed 01 October 2011).

Fei, Z. (1995) 'Deep friendship between China and Africa', *Chinafrica* 51: 23–32.

Ferguson, J. (2005) 'Seeing like an oil company: Space, security, and global capital in neoliberal Africa', *American Anthropologist* 107(3): 377–82.

Ferguson, J. (2006) *Global Shadows: Africa in the Neoliberal World Order* (Durham NC and London: Duke University Press).

Ferguson, J. and Gupta, A. (2002) 'Spatializing states: towards an ethnography of neoliberal governmentality', *American Ethnologist* 29(4): 981–1002.

Fernández-Gilberto, A. E. and Hogenboom, B. (2007) 'Developing regions facing China in a Neoliberalized world', *Journal of Developing Areas* 23: 305–39.

Fessehaie, J. and Morris, M. (2011) Value Chain Dynamics of Chinese Copper Mining in Zambia: Enclave or Linkage Development? Paper submitted to the special issue of Development and Change on China as a development actor.

Fewsmith, J. (2001) 'The political and social implications of China's accession to the WTO', *China Quarterly* 167(1): 573–91.

Filatova, I. (2009) 'Russia's plans for Africa', *The Guardian*, Friday 26 June, http://www.guardian.co.uk/commentisfree/2009/jun/26/russia-africa-dmitry-medvedev (accessed 01 October 2011).

*Financial Times* (2008) 'India follows China's path with Africa overture', http://www.ft.com/cms/s/0/1c23aec2-05cf-11dd-a9e0-0000779fd2ac.html#axzz1bJs5HkZI (accessed 01 October 2011).

FIS World News (2010) 'China Fishery embraces African seafood and market', 26 November 2010 http://fis.com/fis/worldnews/worldnews.asp?monthyear=&day=26&id=39425&l=e&special=0&ndb=0 (accessed 01 October 2011).

Fishman, T. C. (2005) China, Inc.: How the Rise of the Next Superpower Challenges America and the World (London: Simon and Schuster).

FOCAC (Forum for China-Africa Co-operation) (2006a) 'Beijing Summit and Third Ministerial Conference on China-Africa Co-operation', http://english.mofcom.gov.cn/subject/focac/index.shtml (accessed 20 September 2011).

FOCAC (2006b) 'Chinese, African entrepreneurs sign billion dollar worth agreements', http://www.fmprc.gov.cn/zflt/eng/zxxx/t279809.htm (accessed 29 September 2011).

FOCAC (20 March 2009), 'Secretariat of Chinese Follow-up Committee of FOCAC Formally Launches Preparation for 4th Ministerial Conference', http://big5.fmprc.gov.cn/gate/big5/www.fmprc.gov.cn/zflt/eng/dsjbzjhy/hycb/t619614.htm

FOCAC (2011) 'CNFC: 25 years of fishing and shrimping in Africa', http://www.focac.org/eng/zfgx/t829517.htm (accessed 01 October 2011).

Foreign and Commonwealth Office (2009) 'Lord Malloch-Brown visit to Africa' http://www.fco.gov.uk/malloch-brown-africa-150609 (accessed 06 August 2011).

Foster, V., Butterfield, W., Chuan, C. and Pushak, N. (2008) *Building Bridges: China's Growing Role as Infrastructure Financier for sub-Saharan Africa* (Washington DC: World Bank).

France Diplomatie (2008) 'Mineral resources and development in Africa', http://www.diplomatie.gouv.fr/fr/IMG/pdf/mineral_resources_DOS_2010.pdf (accessed 29 September 2011).

Fraser, A. and Lungu, J. (2007) 'For whom the windfalls? Winners and losers in the privatization of Zambia's copper mines', Civil Society Trade Network of Zambia, Lusaka, http://www.sarpn.org/documents/d0002403/1-Zambia_copper-mines_Lungu_Fraser.pdf (accessed 29 September 2011).

Frederick, J. (2004) 'Time to cool down', *Time*, 24 May 2004, 163(20): 42–4.

Freitas Barbosa, A., Narciso, F. and Biancalana, M. (2009) 'Brazil in Africa: Another emerging power in the continent?', *Politikon* 36(1): 59–86.

French, H. 2004. *China in Africa: All Trade, With No Political Baggage* (New York Times, 8 August 2004).

French, H. and Polgreen, L. (2007) 'Chinese flocking in numbers to a new frontier: Africa', *International Herald Tribune*, 17 August, http://www.iht.com/articles/2007/08/17/news/malawi.php (accessed 29 September 2011).

Friedman, E. (2009) 'How economic superpower China could transform Africa', *Journal of Chinese Political Science* 14: 1–20.

Fritz, B. and Horn, J. (2011) 'Reel China: Hollywood tries to stay on China's good side', *Los Angeles Times*, 16 March *http://articles.latimes.com/2011/mar/16/entertainment/la-et-china-red-dawn-20110316* (accessed 21 October 2011).

Frontier Advisory (2009) 'Angola: Africa's foremost emerging market. Seminar held at Johannesburg Stock Exchange, South Africa, 21 July 2009, http://www.frontieradvisory.com/events (accessed 03 November 2009).

Frynas, J. G. (2005) 'Oil in Nigeria: conflict and litigation between oil companies and village communities', *International Affairs* 81(3): 581–98.

Fu, B. (2008) 'Blue skies for China', *Science*, 321: 611.

Fu, B. J., Zhuang, X. ., Jiang, G. B., Shi, J. B. and Lu, Y. H. (2007) 'Environmental problems and challenges in China', *Chinese Academy of Sciences*, http://www.aseanenvironment.info/Abstract/41016309.pdf (accessed 28 September 2011).

Gao, S. (1996) *China's Economic Reforms* (London/New York: MacMillan).

Gavshon, A. (1981) *Crisis in Africa: Battleground of East and West* (Harmondsworth: Penguin Books).

Ghana Business News Website (2010) 'Will Ghana choose China over ExxonMobil for Kosmos' Jubilee stake?' at Ghana business news website, http://www.ghana-businessnews.com/2010/08/16/will-ghana-choose-china-over-exxonmobil-for-kosmos%E2%80%99-jubilee-stake/ (accessed 29 September 2011).

Ghana Dams Dialogue (2009) 'Ghana Dams Dialogue Newsletter', Issue 4, December 2009, http://ghanadamsdialogue.iwmi.org/Data/Sites/2/Documents/gdd_newsletter-issue4(latest).pdf (accessed 07 October 2011).

Gibson-Graham, J. . (1996) The End of Capitalism (As We Knew It): A Feminist Critique of Political Economy (Oxford: Blackwell).

Gill, B. and Huang, Y. (2006) Sources and limits of Chinese 'Soft Power', *Survival* 48(2): 17–36.

Gill, B. and Reilly, J. (2007) The tenuous hold of China Inc in Africa, *The Washington Quarterly* (Summer): 37–52.

Gillespie, S. (2009) 'African Students in China: Past and Present'. In: L. Chisholm and G. Steiner-Khamsi (eds), *South-South Cooperation in Education and Development* (New York: Teachers College Press), 210–25.

Gilroy, P. (1987) *There Ain't No Black in the Union Jack: The Cultural Politics of Race and Nation* (London: Unwin Hyman).

Gilroy, P. (2004) *After Empire* (London: Routledge).

GIPC (2008) 'Second Quarter 2008 Investment Report', *The GIPC Quarterly Update*, Volume 4, Issue 2, http://www.gipc.org.gh/UploadFiles/Publications/2nd%20Quarterly%20Update%20July%202080917124854.pdf (accessed 11 October 2011).

Glassman, J. (1999) 'State power beyond the 'Territorial Trap': The internationalization of the state', *Political Geography* 18(6): 669–96.

Glassman, J. (2006) 'Primitive accumulation, accumulations by dispossession, accumulations by 'extra-economic' means', *Progress in Human Geography* 30(5): 608–25.

Global Witness (2009) 'IMF risks condoning corruption with new loan to Angola', press release 05/10/2009. http://www.globalwitness.org/ru/node/3855 (accessed 05 October 2011).

Glosny, M. (2006) 'Meeting the development challenge in the 21st century: American and Chinese perspectives on Foreign Aid National Committee on US-China relations', http://www.ncuscr.org/files/6.%20Foreign%20Aid%20(21).pdf (accessed 18 November 2009).

GOC (Government of China) (2011) *China's Foreign Aid*. Information Office of the State Council, People's Republic of China, Beijing, 21 April 2011.

Godrey, M. (2009) 'A global hydropower', 6 March 2009. http://www.cibmagazine.com.cn/html/Print/Show.asp?id=854&a_global_hydro_power.html (accessed 05 October 2011).

Goldbourne, H. (ed.) (1979) *Politics and the State in the Third World* (London: Macmillan).

Goldstein, A. (2005) Rising to the Challenge: China's Grand Strategy and International Security (Stanford: Stanford University Press).

Goldstein, L. J. (2009) 'Strategic implications of Chinese fisheries development', *China Brief* 9(16).

Gong, S. (2007) 'Chinese workers in Africa: Working conditions and potential conflict', unpublished paper presented at the conference 'Rethinking Africa's 'China Factor': Identifying Players, Strategies, and Practices', 27 April 2007, http://www.international.ucla.edu/africa/grca/publications/article.asp?parentid=107298 (accessed 20 October 2011).

Gonzalez-Vicente, R. (2011) 'The internationalization of the Chinese state', *Political Geography* 30(7): 402–11.

Goodman, D. and Segal, G. (eds) (1994) *China Deconstructs: Politics, Trade and Regionalism* (New York/ London: Routledge).

Goodman, D. S. G. (2009) 'Sixty years of the People's Republic: Local perspectives on the evolution of the state in China', *The Pacific Review* 22(4): 429–50.

Gould, W. (1995) 'Ideology and data analysis in African population policies in the case of Kenya', *Applied Geography* 15(3): 203–18.

Grant, A. (2009) Digging deep for profits and development? Reflections on enhancing the governance of Africa's mining sector. SAIIA Occasional Paper No 49. October 2009. South Africa: South Africa Institute of International Affairs.

Greenhalgh, S. and Winckler, E. A. (2005) *Governing China's Population: From Leninist to Neoliberal Biopolitics* (Stanford, CA: Stanford University Press).

Griffin, L. (2008) 'The North Sea fisheries crisis and good governance', *Geography Compass* 22: 452–75.

Grimm, S., Rank, R., McDonald, M. and Schickerling, E. (2011) *Transparency of Chinese Aid: An Analysis of the Published Information on Chinese External Financial Flows* (Stellenbosch, South Africa: Centre for Contemporary Chinese Studies).

Grimmett, R. (2010) *Conventional Arms Transfers to Developing Nations, 2002– 2009*, United States Congressional Research Service.

GRIPS (2008) Diversity and Complementarity in Development Aid: East Asian Lessons for African Growth (Tokyo: GRIPS Development Forum).

Groves, J. (2011) 'Cameron warns Africans over the 'Chinese invasion' as they pour billions into the continent', *Daily Mail*, 20 July, http://www.dailymail. co.uk/news/article-2016677/Cameron-warns-Africans-Chinese-invasion-pour-billions-continent.html?ITO=1490 (accessed 20 October 2011).

Gu, J. (2009) 'China's private enterprises in Africa and the implications for African development', *European Journal of Development Research* 21(4): 570–87.

Gu, J. and Schiere, R. (2010) 'Post crisis prospect for China-Africa relations', Africa Development Bank Group Working Paper Series No. 124, May 2010.

Gu, J., Humphrey, J. and Messner, D. (2008) 'Global governance and developing countries: The implications of the rise of China', *World Development* 36(2): 274–92.

Gu, W. (1995) Politics of Divided Nations: The Case of China and Korea (Westport: Praeger).

Guan, X. P. (2001) 'Globalization, inequality and social policy: China on the threshold of entry into the World Trade Organization', *Social Policy and Administration* 35(3): 242–57.

Guerin, E. (2008) 'Chinese assistance to Africa: Characterization and position regarding the global governance of developmental aid', Institut du développement durable et des relations internationales, *Global Governance* 3: 1–10.

Guijin, L. (2008) 'China in Africa: A sincere, co-operative and equal partner', http://www.chinese-embassy.org.za/eng/zfgx/zfhzlt/t277443.htm (accessed 29 February 2008).

Guimarães, A. (1998) *The Origins of the Angolan Civil War: Foreign Intervention and Domestic Political Conflict* (London: Macmillan Press Ltd).

Hackley, R. and Westhuizen, L. (2011) 'Africa's friend China finances $9.3 billion of hydropower', 10 September, http://www.bloomberg.com/news/2011-09-09/ africa-s-new-friend-china-finances-9-3-billion-of-hydropower.html (accessed 05 October 2011).

Hagmann, T. and Peclard, D. (2010) 'Negotiating statehood: Dynamics of power and domination in Africa', *Development and Change* 41(4): 539–62.

Hairong, Y. (2003) 'Neoliberal governmentality and neohumanism: Organizing suzhi/value flow through labor recruitment networks', *Cultural Anthropology* 18(4), 493–523.

Han Shi and Zhang Lei (2006) 'China's environmental governance of rapid industrialisation', *Environmental Politics* 15(2): 271–92.

Han, Y.. (2011) 'Chinese investment boosts African economic development', 09 May 2011, China and Africa Journal, http://www.focac.org/eng/zfgx/t821032. htm (accessed 01 September 2011).

Hanban (2011) 'About Confucius Institute/Classroom', http://www.chinese.cn/ hanban_en/node_10971.htm (accessed 01 September 2011).

Harding, H. (1987) *China's Second revolution, Reform after Mao* (Washington DC: Brookings Institution).

Harding, H. (1995) 'China's Co-operative Behaviour'. In T. W. Robinson and D. Shambaugh (eds), *Chinese Foreign Policy: Theory and Practice* (London: Clarendon), 375–400.

Harrison, G. (2004) The World Bank and Africa: The Construction of Governance States (London: Routledge).

Hart, G. (1996) 'Global connections: The rise and fall of a Taiwanese production network on the South African Periphery', Working Paper No. 6, University of California (Berkeley, California: Institute of International Studies).

Hart, G. (2001) 'Development critiques in the 1990s: cul de sac and promising paths', *Progress in Human Geography* 25(4): 649–58.

Hart, G. (2004) 'Geography and development: critical ethnographies', *Progress in Human Geography* 28(1): 91–100.

Harvey, D. (2003) *The New Imperialism* (Oxford: Oxford University Press).

Harvey, D. (2005) *A Brief History of Neoliberalism* (Oxford: Oxford University Press).

Haugen, H. and Carling, J. (2005) 'On the edge of the Chinese diaspora: The surge of baihuo business in an African city', *Ethnic and Racial Studies* 28(4): 639–62.

Hawksley, H. (2010) UK seeks China aid partnership in Africa. http://www.bbc. co.uk/news/world-africa-11444441

Hayes, J. (2007) 'The recent environmental history of tiger leaping gorge: Environmental degradation and local land development in northern Yunnan', *Journal of Contemporary China* 16(52): 499–516.

Hayter, T. (1971) *Aid as Imperialism* (London: Penguin).

He, S. and Wu, F. (2009) 'China's emerging neoliberal urbanism: Perspectives from urban redevelopment', *Antipode* 41(2): 282–304.

He, W. P. (2007) 'The balancing act of China's Africa policy', *China Security* 3(3): 23–40.

He, Y. (2007) 'China's changing policy on peace keeping operations, Institute for Security and Development Policy, Occasional Paper, July, 1–71.

Hecht, D. and Simone, A. M. (1994) *Invisible Governance: The Art of African Micro-Politics* (New York: Autonomedia).

Heggelund, G., Abdresen, S. and Sun, Y. (2005) 'Performance of the Global Environmental Facility (GEF) in China: Achievements and challenges as seen by the Chinese', *International Environmental Agreements* 5: 323–48.

Heimer, M. and Thogersen, S. (2006) *Doing Fieldwork in China* (Denmark: NIAS Press).

Heller P. (2001) 'Moving the State: The politics of democratic decentralization in Kerala, South Africa, and Porto Alegre', *Politics & Society* 29(1): 1–28.

Henderson, J. (2008) 'China and global development: Towards a global Asian era?' *Contemporary Politics* 14(4): 375–92.

Hensengerth, O. (2011) Interaction of Chinese Institutions with Host Governments in Dam Construction: The Bui Dam in Ghana (Bonn, DE, German Development Institute).

Heritage Foundation (2011) *2010 Index of Economic Freedom* (Washington DC: Heritage Foundation).

Hewitt, J. (2002) 'China: Illegal imports and exports', *Global Timber*, July.

Hilsum, L. 2006. 'We Love China', in The View from Africa, *Granta* No. 92, January 15th 2006, http://www.granta.com/extracts/2616.

Himley, M. (2008) 'Geographies of environmental governance: The nexus of nature and neoliberalism', *Geography Compass* 2(2): 433–51.

Hitchens, P. (2008) 'How China has created a new slave empire in Africa', *The Mail Online*, 28 September, http://www.dailymail.co.uk/news/article-1063198/PETER-HITCHENS-How-China-created-new-slave-empire-Africa.html (accessed 20 September 2011).

Ho, C. (2008) 'The "Doing" and "Undoing" of community: Chinese networks in Ghana', *China Aktuell* 3: 45–76.

Ho, P. and Edmonds, R. L. (2008) China's Embedded Activism: Opportunities and Constraints of a Social Movement (London & New York: Routledge).

Hodges, D. (2001) Angola from Afro-Stalinism to Petro-Diamond Capitalism (Oxford: James Currey).

Hoffmann, S. (1977) 'An American social science: International relations', *Daedalus* 3: 41–60.

Holmes, J. R. (2007) 'Soft Power' at sea: Zheng He and China's maritime diplomacy, *Virgina Review of Asian Studies*, http://vcas.wlu.edu/VRAS/2007/Holmes.pdf (accessed 20 September 2011).

Holslag, J. (2006) 'A new phase in China's economic development', *BICCS Asia paper*, 1(1): 1–13.

Holslag, J. (2007) 'Friendly giant? China's evolving Africa policy', *Asia Paper* 2(5).

Hon, T., Jansson, J., Shelton, G., Liu, H., Burke, C. and Kiala, C. (2010) 'Examining China's FOCAC commitments to Africa and mapping the way ahead', Centre for Chinese Studies, University of Stellenbosch, prepared for Rockefeller Foundation, January 2010, http://www.ccs.org.za/wp-content/uploads/2010/03/ENGLISH-Evaluating-Chinas-FOCAC-commitments-to-Africa-2010.pdf (accessed 29 September 2011).

Hoogvelt, A. (1997) Globalisation and the Postcolonial World: The New Political Economy of Development (London: Macmillan).

Hope, N. C., Yang, D. T. and Li, M. Y. (2003) *How Far Across the River? Chinese Policy Reform at the Millennium* (Stanford, California: Stanford University Press).

Horta, L. (2009) 'Food security in Africa. China's new rice bowl', China Brief (Jamestown Foundation), Issue 11, 27 May 2009.

Hsiung, J. (2003) 'The aftermath of China's accession to the World Trade Organisation', *Independent Review* 8(1): 87–112.

Hsu, E. (2007) 'Zanzibar and its Chinese communities', *Populations, Space and Place* 13(2): 113–24.

Huang, C. H. (2010) 'China, the UN and African security: The way forward', paper presented at the China-Africa Civil Society Forum on Peace and Development, Beijing, 2–4 June 2010.

Huang, X. (2011) 'Corporate governance and Chinese FDI in Australia', East Asia Forum, 5 June 2011, http://www.eastasiaforum.org/2011/06/05/corporate-governance-and-chinese-fdi-in-australia/#more-19336 (accessed 01 September 2011).

Huang, Y. (2007) 'A comparative study of China's foreign aid', *Contemporary International Relations*, 17(3): 81–93.

Hubbard, P. (2008) 'Chinese Concessional Loans'. In R. Rotberg (ed.), *China Into Africa, Trade, Aid and Influence* (Washington DC; Brooking Institution Press), 217–30.

IDE-JETRO (2010) 'China in Africa', http://www.ide.go.jp/English/Data/Africa_file/Manualreport/cia_11.html (accessed 01 September 2011).

Idun-Arkhurst, I. (2008) 'China and Ghana: A case study of engagement', Paper presented at the African Union Conference, South African Institute of International Affairs, Johannesburg, South Africa http://www.africa-union.org/root/ua/Conferences/2008/sept/EA/08sept/2008%20I%20Arkhurst.pdf (accessed 28 December 2009).

IEA (International Energy Agency) (2011) 'Energy for all: Financing access for the poor. Special early excerpt of the World Energy Outlook 2011', http://www.iea.org/papers/2011/weo2011_Energy_for_all.pdf

Ikenberry, J. (2008) 'The rise of China and the future of the West', *Foreign Affairs* 87(1): 23–37.

Illegal-fishing info (2009a) 'China', http://www.illegal-fishing.info/sub_approach.php?subApproach_id=116 (accessed 01 October 2011).

Illegal-fishing info (2009b) 'Illegal Chinese fishing fuel global conflicts', 14 August, http://illegal-fishing.info/item_single.php?item=news&item_id=4002&approach_id=12 (accessed 01 October 2011).

Illegal-logging info (2007) 'China's rise:: Hope or doom for Africa?', 16 June, http://www.illegal-logging.info/item_single.php?it_id=2168&it=news (accessed 05 October 2011).

Imai, K. (2009) 'Exploring the Persistence of State Corporate Ownership in China'. In N. Islam (ed.), *Resurgent China: Issues for the Future* (London: Palgrave Macmillan), 237–57.

International Crisis Group (2008) 'China's thirst for oil', Asia Report, 153, 9 June.

International Crisis Group (2009) 'China's growing role in UN peacekeeping', Asia Report No.166, http://www.voltairenet.org/IMG/pdf/China_and_UN_Peacekeeping.pdf (accessed 05 October 2011).

International Rivers Network (2009) 'China's leading hydropower dam company', http://www.internationalrivers.org/en/node/3600 (accessed 22 February 2010).

International Water Power and Dam Construction (2009) 'The Ghana dams dialogue', http://www.waterpowermagazine.com/storyprint.asp?sc=2054100 (accessed 27 September 2011).

IPCC (Intergovernmental Panel on Climate Change) (2007) 'Summary for policymakers: An assessment of the intergovernmental panel on climate change', http://www.ipcc.ch/pdf/assessment-report/ar4/syr/ar4_syr_spm.pdf (accessed 01 October 2011).

IPR (2005) "Go Out' covers 200 countries and regions', 26 October.

Ismael, T. (1971) The People's Republic of China and Africa, *The Journal of Modern African Studies* 9(4): 507–29.

ISO (International Organization for Standardization) (2011) 'ISO14001 essentials' http://www.iso.org/iso/iso_14000_essentials (accessed 09 October 2011).

ISSER (Institute of Statisical, Social and Economic Research) (2005) Guide to electric power in Ghana. Ghana: University of Ghana http://www.beg.utexas.edu/energyecon/IDA/USAID/RC/Guide_to_Electric%20Power_in_Ghana.pdf

IT News Africa (2007) 'Egypt welcomes Chinese investment in various sectors', 30 March 2007 http://www.itnewsafrica.com/2007/05/egypt-welcomes-chinese-investment-in-various-sectors/ (accessed 11 October 2011).

IUCN (International Union for Conservation of Nature) (2011) 'China important to African timber producers', 28 February 2008, http://www.iucn.org/about/work/programmes/forest/fp_our_work/fp_our_work_thematic/fp_our_work_flg/?731 (accessed 07 October 2011).

Jackson, S. F. (1995) 'China's Third World foreign policy: The case of Angola and Mozambique', 1961–93, *China Quarterly* 142: 388–422.

Jacoby, U. (2007) 'Getting together', *Finance and Development Quarterly Magazine of IMF*, 44(2), http://www.imf.org/external/pubs/ft/fandd/2007/06/jacoby.htm (accessed 30 December 2007).

Jacques, M. (2009) When China Rules the World: The Rise of the Middle Kingdom and the End of the Western World (London: Allen Lane).

Jahiel, A. R. (1997) 'Research note: The contradictory impact of reform on environmental protection in China', *The China Quarterly* 149: 81–103.

Jahiel, A. R. (2006) 'China, the WTO and implications for the environment', *Environmental Politics* 15(2): 310–29.

Jansson, J., Burke, C. and Jiang, W. R. (2009) Chinese Companies in the Extractive Industries of Gabon and DRC: Perceptions of Transparency ( Stellenbosch: CCS).

Jessop, B. (1990) State Theory: Putting Capitalist States in their Place (Cambridge: Polity Press).

Jessop, B. (2002) *The Future of Capitalist State* (Cambridge: Polity Press).

Jiang, W. and Jing, J. (2010) 'Deepening Chinese stakes in West Africa: The case of Ghana', China Brief, Volume 10(4), 18 February, http://www.jamestown.org/uploads/media/cb_010_18.pdf (accessed 12 September 2011).

Jie, C. (2009) 'The NGO community in China: Expanding linkages with transnational civil society and their democratic implications', *China Perspectives*, http://chinaperspectives.revues.org/3083#quotation (accessed 12 September 2011).

Jintao, H. (2007) Speech by Chinese President Hu Jintao at the University of Pretoria on China-Africa Cooperation, 'Enhance China-Africa Unity and Cooperation To Build a Harmonious World,' delivered on 7 February 2007, http://www.internationalepolitik.de/ (accessed 05 October 2008).

Jinyuan, G. (1984) 'China and Africa: The development of relations over many centuries, *African Affairs* 83(331): 241–50.

Jones, M. (2005) 'A 'Segregated' Asia? Race, the Bandung Conference, and Pan-Asianist fears in American thought and policy, 1954–1955', *Diplomatic History* 29(5).

Joselow, B. (2011) 'China's demand for ivory threatens Kenya's elephants', 12 October, http://www.voanews.com/english/news/africa/Chinese-Demand-for-Ivory-Threatens-Kenyas-Elephants-131600618 (accessed 05 October 2011).

Juma, C. (2007) 'Lessons Africans must learn from Chinese expansion', *Business Daily*, 13 July, http://belfercenter.ksg.harvard.edu/publication/1722/lessons_africa_must_learn_from_chinese_expansion.html (accessed 22 September 2011).

Jung, C. and Halliday, J. (2006) *Mao: The Unknown Story* (London: Vintage Books).

Junger, S. (2007) 'Enter China, the giant', *Vanity Fair*, July 2007, http://www.vanityfair.com/ontheweb/features/2007/07/africalinks200707#junger (accessed 22 September 2011).

Kallio, J. (2011) Tradition in Chinese Politics: The Party-State's Reinvention of the Past and the Critical Response from Public Intellectuals (Helsinki: Finnish Institute of International Affairs).

Kaplinsky, R. (2008) 'What does the rise of China do for industrialisation in Sub-Saharan Africa?', *Review of African Political Economy* 115: 7–22.

Kaplinsky, R. and Messner, D. (2008) 'Introduction: The impact of Asian drivers on the developing world', *World Development* 36(2): 197–209.

Kaplinsky, R. and Morris, M. (2006) 'The Asian Drivers and SSA: MFA quota removal and the portents for African industrialisation', http://asiandrivers.open.ac.uk/documents/Kaplinsky_Morris_ADs_and_SSA_OECD_Final_May_06.pdf (accessed 07 October 2011).

Kapoor, I. (2008) *The Postcolonial Politics of Development* (London: Routledge).

Karl, T. (2007) 'Oil led development: Social, political and environmental consequences', CDDRL Working Paper, Number 80, January 2007. http://iis-db.stanford.edu/pubs/21537/No_80_Terry_Karl_-_Effects_of_Oil_Development.pdf (accessed 07 October 2011).

Karumbidza, J. (2007) 'Win-win Economic Co-operation: Can China Save Zimbabwe's Economy?'. In F. Manji and S. Marks (eds), *African Perspectives on China in Africa* (Nairobi and Oxford, Fahamu), 87–106.

Keck, M. and Sikkink, K. (1998) Activists Beyond Borders: Advocacy Networks in International Politics (London: Cornell University Press).

Kerr, D. (2007) 'Has China abandoned self-reliance?' *Review of International Political Economy* 14(1).

Kiala, C. (2010) 'The impact of China-Africa aid relations: The case of Angola', *Policy Brief*, Issue 1.

King, K. (2006) 'Aid within the wider China-Africa partnership: A view from the Beijing Summit', http://www.cctr.ust.hk/materials/conference/china-africa/papers/King,Kenneth.pdf (accessed 01 January 2008).

King, K. (2007) 'The Beijing China-Africa summit of 2006', *China Report* 43(3), 337–47.

King, K. (2010) 'New Actors: Old Paradigms?'. In K. King (ed.) *A Brave New World of 'Emerging', 'Non-DAC' Donors and their Differences from Traditional Donors*, NORRAG News No 44, September 2010, http://www.norrag.org/issues/article/1317/en/editorial-new-actors – old-paradigms-%5B1%5D.html?PHPSESSID=34227322ff4f8994954c5e1376e9018c (accessed 01 October 2011).

Kirby, W. (2006) 'China's internationalization in the early People's Republic: Dreams of a socialist world economy', *China Quarterly* 188: 870–90.

Klare, M. (2001) Resource Wars: The New Landscape of Global Conflict (New York: Henry Holt).

Kohli, J. (2009) 'The dragon on safari: China's Africa policy', Institute of Peace and Conflict Studies, New Delhi, http://www.ipcs.org/pdf_file/issue/SR86-China-Kohli-Final.pdf (accessed 01 October 2011).

Kornegay, F. A. and Landsberg, C. (2009) 'Engaging emerging powers: Africa's search for a common position', *Politikon* 36(1): 171–91.

Kragelund, P. (2008) 'The return of non-DAC donors to Africa: New prospects for African development?', *Development Policy Review* 26(5): 555–84.

Kurlantzick, J. (2007) *Charm Offensive: How China's Soft Power Is Transforming the World* (New Haven, CT: Yale University Press).

Lafargue, F. (2008) 'New economic actors in the Mediterranean, China in North Africa', MEDS: 64–68, http://www.iemed.org/anuari/2008/aarticles/EN64.pdf (accessed 01 October 2011).

Lai, H. H. (2007) 'China's oil diplomacy: Is it a global security threat?', *Third World Quarterly* 28(3): 519–37.

Laïdi, Z. (ed.) (1988) 'Introduction: What use is the Soviet Union?' In *The Third World and the Soviet Union* (London: Zed Books), 1–23.

Laidi, Z. (1990) The Superpowers and Africa: The Constraints of a Rivalry 1960–1990 (London:, Chicago Press).

Lampton, D. M. (2008) *The Three Faces of Chinese Power: Might, Money and Minds* (Berkeley: University of California Press).

Lancaster, C. (2007) 'The Chinese aid system', Centre for Global Development, http://www.cgdev.org/content/publications/detail/13953/ (accessed 26 December 2007) (accessed 01 October 2011).

Lanteigne, M. (2009) *Chinese Foreign Policy: An Introduction* (London, Routledge).

Lardy, N. R. (2005) 'China: The Great New Economic Challenge?'. In C. F. Bergsten (ed.), *The United States and the World Economy: Foreign Economic Policy for the Next Decade* (Washington, DC: Institute for International Economics), 121–41.

Large, D. (2008a) 'Beyond 'Dragon in the Bush': The study of China-Africa relations', *African Affairs* 107(426): 45–61.

Large, D. (2008b) 'From Non-Interference to Constructive Engagement? China's Evolving Relations with Sudan'. In C. Alden, D. Large and R. Soares de Oliveira (eds), *China Returns to Africa: A Rising Power and a Continent Embrace* (London: C.R. Hurst), 275–94.

Large, D. (2008c) 'China & the contradictions of 'Non-interference' in Sudan', *Review of African Political Economy* 115: 93–106.

Large, D. (2009) 'China's Sudan engagement: Changing northern and southern political trajectories in peace and war', *The China Quarterly* 199: 610–26.

Larkin, B. (1971) China and Africa, 1949–70: The Foreign Policy of the People's Republic of China (Berkeley and Los Angeles: University of California Press).

Le Billon, P. (2001) 'The political ecology of war: Natural resources and armed conflict', *Political Geography*, 20, 561–584.

Lee, C. (2009) 'Raw encounters: Chinese managers, African workers and the politics of casualization in Africa's Chinese enclaves', *The China Quarterly* 199: 647–66.

Lee, F. (2005) 'Public Environmental Consciousness in China: Early Empirical Evidence'. In K. Day (ed.), *China's Environment and the Challenge of Sustainable Development* (Armonk and London: ME Sharpe), 35–65.

Lee, K. W. (2001) 'China's accession to the WTO: Effects and social challenges', *China Perspectives* 33: 13.

Lee, M. (2007) 'Uganda and China: Unleashing the power of the dragon'. In M. C. Lee, H. Melber, S. Naidu and I. Taylor (eds) *China in Africa* (Uppsala: Nordiska Afrikainstitutet). 26–40

Lee, M. (2011) 'Hilary Clinton warns Africa of 'New Colonialism', *Huff Post*, 11 June 2011, http://www.huffingtonpost.com/2011/06/11/hillary-clinton-africa-new-colonialism_n_875318.html, (accessed 01 October 2011).

Lee, M. C., Melber, H., Naidu, S. and Taylor, I. (2007) *China in Africa*, Current African Issues No. 33 (Uppsala: Nordiska Afrikaininstitutet).

Leonard, M. (2008) *What Does China Think?* (London: Fourth Estate).

Levitt, P. and de la Dehesa, R. (2003) 'Transnational migration and the redefinition of the state: Variations and explanations', *Ethnic and Racial Studies* 26(4): 587–611.

Levkowitz, L., Ross, M. M. and Warner, J. R. (2009) 'The 88 Queensway group: A case study in Chinese investors operations in Angola and Beyond', US-China Economic and Security Review Commission, http://www.uscc.gov/The_88_Queensway_Group.pdf (accessed 19 December 2009).

Leys, C. (1996) *The Rise and Fall of Development Theory, EAEP* (London: Indiana University Press and James Currey).

Li, A. (2005) *Chinese Diaspora in Africa* (Beijing: Peking University Centre on Overseas Chinese).

Li Anshan (2006) 'Transformation of China's policy towards Africa', Center on China's Transnational Relations, Working Paper No. 20, The Hong Kong University of Science and Technology.

Li, Xiaoyun (2009) 'China's foreign aid and aid to Africa: Overview'. Unpublished paper.

Li, Z., Xue, D., Lyons, M. and Brown, A. (2007) 'Ethnic enclave of transnational migrants in Guangzhou: A case study of Xiaobei', http://www.hkbu.edu.hk/~curs/Abstracts%20and%20Fullpapers/05/07.doc, (accessed 01 October 2011).

Lieberthal, K. G. (1992) 'Introduction: The "Fragmented Authoritarianism" Model and Its Limitations'. In K. G. Lieberthal and D. M. Lampton (eds), *Bureaucracy, Politics, and Decision Making in Post-Mao China* (Berkeley, CA: University of California Press).

Liew, L. H. (2005) 'China's engagement with neo-liberalism: Path dependency, geography and party self-reinvention', *Journal of Development Studies* 41(2): 331–52.

Lim, K. F. (2010) 'On China's growing geo-economic influence and the evolution of variegated capitalism', *Geoforum* 41: 677–88.

Lin, C. (2006) *The Transformation of Chinese Socialism* (Durham, NC: Duke University Press).

Lin, G. C. S. (1999) 'State policy and spatial restructuring in post-reform China, 1978– 1995', *International Journal of Urban and Regional Research* 23(4): 670–96.

Liou, C. S. (2009) 'Bureaucratic politics and overseas investment by Chinese State-owned oil companies', *Asian Survey* 49(4): 670–90.

Liu, J. and Diamond, J. (2005) 'China's environment in a globalizing world. How China and the rest of the world affect each other', *Nature* 435: 1179–86.

Liu, Y., Pan, W., Shen, M., Song, G., Bertrand, V., Child, M. and Shapiro, J. (2006) 'The Politics and Ethics of Going Green in China: Air Pollution Control in Benxi City and Wetland Preservation in the Sanjiang Plain'. In J. Bauer (ed.), *Forging Environmentalism: Justice, Livelihood, and Contested Environments* (Armonk and London: ME Sharpe): 31–102.

Live, Y. (2005) 'Reunion Island'. In L. Pan (ed.) *The Encyclopedia of the Chinese Overseas* (Singapore: Nanyang Technological University).

Lo, C. W-H and Tang, S. Y. (2007) 'Institutional Reform, Economic Changes, and Local Environmental Management in China: The Case of Guangdong Province'. In N. T. Carter and A. P. J. Mol (eds), *Environmental Governance in China* (London & New York: Routledge), 42–62.

Loong Yu, A. (2009) 'China: End of a Model ... or Birth of a new one?', *New Politics*, XII-3, http://newpolitics.mayfirst.org/print/node/88?nid=88 (accessed 25 September 2011).

Lu, M. and Feng, M. (2008) 'Reforming the welfare system in the People's Republic of China', *Asian Development Review* 25 (1&2): 58–80.

Lu, Y. (2009) Non-Governmental Organisations in China: The Rise of Dependent Autonomy (London and New York: Routledge).

Lunding, A. (2006) 'Global champions in waiting: Perspectives on China's overseas direct investment', *Current Issues* (China Special), (4 August), http://www.dbresearch.com/PROD/DBR_INTERNET_EN-PROD/PROD0000000000201318.PDF (accessed 25 September 2011).

Lyman, P. (2005) 'China's rising role in Africa', Council on Foreign relations, http://www.cfr.org/publication/8436/chinas_rising_role_in_africa.html?breadcrumb=default (accessed 25 September 2007).

Ma, L. (2002) 'Space, Place and Transnationalism in the Chinese Diaspora'. In L. Ma and C. Cartier (eds), *The Chinese Diaspora: Space, Place, Mobility and Identity* (Lanham, MD: Roman & Littlefield), 1–50.

Ma, S. Y. (1998) 'Third World studies, development studies and post-communist studies: Definitions, distance and dynamism', *Third World Quarterly* 19(3): 339–56.

Ma, X. and Ortolano, L. (2000) *Environmental Regulation in China: Institutions, Enforcement and Compliance* (Lanham: Rowman and Littlefield Publishers).

MacAndrews, C. (1994) 'Politics of the environment in Indonesia', *Asian Survey* XXXIV (4), 376–7.

MacLeod, G. and Goodwin, M. (1999) 'Space, scale and state strategy: Rethinking urban and regional governance', *Progress in Human Geography* 23(4): 503–27.

Maganheim, G. S. (2007) 'Chinese influence on US operational access to African seaports', *JFQ Forum* 45: 22–7.

Magee, D. (2006) 'New Energy Geographics: Powershed Polities and Hydropower Decision Making in Yunnan, China', PhD dissertation for University of Washington.

*Mail & Guardian* (27 July 2007) 'China defends Darfur stance as pressure grows', http://mg.co.za/article/2007–07–27-china-defends-darfur-stance-as-pressure-grows (accessed 10 October 2011).

Mamdani, M. (1996) *Citizen and Subject: Contemporary Africa and the Legacy of Later Colonialism* (Princeton: Princeton University Press).

Manji, F. (2007) 'Preface'. In: F. Manji and S. Marks (eds), *African Perspectives on China in Africa* (Cape Town, Nairobi and Oxford: Fahamu/Pambazuka), vii-viii.

Manji, M. and Marks, S. (eds) (2007) *African Perspectives on China in Africa*, (Cape Town, Nairobi and Oxford: Fahamu).

Manning, R. (2006) 'Will 'emerging donors' change the face of international cooperation', *Development Policy Review* 24(4): 371–85.

Marcum, J. A. (1981) The Angolan Revolution, Volume II: Exile Politics and Guerrilla Warfare (1962–1976), (Cambridge, MA: MIT Press).

Marks, R. (1998) Tiger, Rice, Silk and Silt: Environment and Economy in Late Imperial South China (Cambridge: Cambridge University Press).

Marks, S (2006) 'China in Africa – the new imperialism?', Pambazuka news. http://www.pambazuka.org/en/category/features/32432 (accessed 10 October 2011).

Marks, S. (2009) 'Africa's freedom railway', Pambazuka News, 3 September, http://www.pambazuka.org/en/category/africa_china/58442 (accessed 10 October 2011).

Martin, M. (2010) 'Understanding China's political system', Fderation of American Scientists, Congressional Research Service, R41007, http://www.fas.org/sgp/crs/row/R41007.pdf, (accessed 26 March 2012).

Masaki, H. (2006) 'Japan takes on China in Africa', *Asia Times,* 15 August, http://www.atimes.com/atimes/Japan/HH15Dh01.html (accessed 17 September 2011).

Massey, D. (2004) 'Geographies of responsibility', *Geografiska Annaler* B, 86: 5–18.

Matthews, O. (2007) 'Racing for new riches: Russian and Chinese investors are battling for African resources to fuel their growing empires', *Newsweek*, 19 November, http://www.newsweek.com/id/68910 (accessed 17 September 2011).

Mattlin, M. (2009) 'Chinese strategic state-owned enterprises and ownership control', BICCS Asia paper, vol. 4(6): 1–28.

Matusevich, M. (ed.) (2006) *Africa in Russia, Russia in Africa: Three Centuries of Encounters* (Trenton, NJ and Asmara: Africa World Press).

Mawdsley, E. (2008) 'Fu Manchu versus Dr Livingstone in the Dark Continent? Representing China, Africa and the West in British Broadsheet Newspapers', *Political Geography* 27(5): 509–29.

Mbembe, A. (2001) *On the Postcolony* (London: University of California Press).

McCartney, M. P. (2007) 'Decision support systems for large dam planning and operation in Africa', Colombo, Sri Lanka: International Water Management Institute. 47 p. (IWMI Working Paper No. 119).

McCartney, M. P. (2009) 'Living with dams: Managing the environmental impacts', *Water Policy* 11(1) 121–39.

McCaskie, T. (2008) 'The United States, Ghana and oil: Global and local perspectives', *African Affairs* 107/428: 313–32.

McCormick, D., Kaplinsky, R. and Morris, M. (2006) *The Impact of China on Sub-Saharan Africa* UK: DFID.

McDonald, K., Bosshard, P. and Brewer, N. (2009) 'Exporting dams: China's hydropower industry goes global', *Journal of Environmental Management* 90: S294–S302.

McGreal, C. (2007) 'Thanks China, now go home: Buy-up of Zambia revives old colonial fears', *The Guardian online*, 5 February, http://www.guardian.co.uk/world/2007/feb/05/china.chrismcgreal (accessed 17 September 2011).

McGregor, R. (2008) 'Chinese diplomacy 'hijacked' by companies in Beijing', *Financial Times*, 17 March 2008.

McIlwaine, C. (1998) 'Civil society and development geography', *Progress in Human Geography* 22(3): 415–24.

McKeown, A. (1999) 'Conceptualizing Chinese diasporas, 1842 to 1949', *Journal of Asian Studies* 58(2): 327–30.

McMichael, P. (2000) Development and Social Change: A Global Perspective. California: Pine Forge Press.

McWilliams, A., Siegel, D. and Wright, P. (2006) 'Corporate social responsibility: Strategic implications', *Journal of Management Studies* 43(1): 1–18.

Meisner, M. (1999) *Mao's China and After: A History of the People's Republic*, 3rd edn. (New York: The Free Press).

Mercer, C. Mohan, G. and Power, M. (2003) 'Towards a critical political geography of African development', *Geoforum* 34(4): 419–36.

Meyer, M. (2008) *Last Days of Old Beijing: Life on the Vanished Backstreets of a City Transformed* (New York: Walker and Company).

MFA (Ministry of Foreign Affairs) China (2000) 'Premier Zhou Enlai's tour of three Asian and African countries', http://www.fmprc.gov.cn/eng/ziliao/3602/3604/t18001.htm, (accessed 22 September 2009).

MFA (2006) 'China's African Policy', http://www.fmprc.gov.cn/eng/zxxx/t230615.htm (accessed 09 December 2009).

Michel, S., Beuret, M. and Woods, P. (2009) *China Safari: On the Trail of Beijing's Expansion in Africa* (New York: Nation Books).

Migdal, J. (1994) 'The State in Society: An Approach to Struggles for Domination'. In J. S. Migdal, A. Kohli and V. Shue (eds), *State Power and Social Forces. Domination and Transformation in the Third World* (Cambridge: Cambridge University Press).

Milliken, T. Burn, R. and Sangalakula, L. (2009) The Elephant Trade Information System (ETIS) and the Illicit Trade in Ivory: A report to the 15th meeting of the Conference of the Parties to CITES. Report for CITES CoP15 Annex 1.

Ministério do Planeamento (2007a) *Plano de Desenvolvimento de Médio Prazo 2009–13*. [Medium-term development plan 2009–13]. República de Angola.

Ministério do Planeamento (2007b) Angola 2025: Angola um país com futuro – *sustentabilidade, equidade, modernidade: Estratégia de Desenvolvimento a longo prazo para Angola (2025), Volumes I–II*. [Angola 2025: Angola a country with a future – sustainability, equity, modernity: long-term development strategy for Angola (2025)]. República de Angola.

Minqi Li (2005) 'The rise of China and the demise of the capitalist world-economy: exploring historical possibilities in the 21st century', *Science & Society* 69(3): 442–8.

Mittelman, J. H. (2006) 'Globalization and development: Learning from debates in China', *Globalizations* 3(3): 277–91.

MOFCOM (Ministry of Commerce) (2007) Small-Medium Enterprises International Market Development Fund', Press Office Release, 17 January.

MOFCOM, PRC (2008) Trade statistics. http://english.mofcom.gov.cn/statistic/statistic.html (accessed 17 July 2009).

MOFCOM (2009) '2008 Statistical bulletin of China's outward foreign direct investment', Beijing: Ministry of Commerce (MOFCOM), Department of Outward Investment and Economic Cooperation, http://hzs2.mofcom.gov.cn/aarticle/statistic/200909/20090906535723.html (accessed 12 October 2009).

MOFCOM (2010) 'Full text of China-Africa Economic and Trade Cooperation White Paper', http://www.gov.cn/english/official/2010–12/23/content_1771603.htm (accessed 01 September 2011).

MOFCOM (2011a) 'China's Foreign Aid', http://news.xinhuanet.com/english2010/china/2011–04/21/c_13839683_14.htm (accessed 01 September 2011).

MOFCOM (2011b) '12th five year plan: China's scientific and peaceful development', http://www.fmprc.gov.cn/eng/wjb/zwjg/zwbd/t807552.htm (accessed 09 October 2011).

Mohan, G. (2002) 'The disappointments of civil society: NGOs, citizenship and institution building in Northern Ghana', *Political Geography* 21(1): 125–54.

Mohan, G. (2008) 'China in Africa: A review essay', *Review of African Political Economy* 35(1): 155–73.

Mohan, G. and Mohan, J. (2002) 'Placing social capital', *Progress in Human Geography* 26(2): 191–210.

Mohan, G. and Power, M. (2008) 'New African choices? The politics of Chinese engagement', *Review of African Political Economy* 35(115): 23–42.

Mohan, G. and Power, M. (2009) 'Africa, China and the "new" economic geography of development', *Singapore Journal of Tropical Geography* 30: 24–8

Mohan, G. and Stokke, K. (2000) 'Participatory development and empowerment', *Third World Quarterly* 21(2): 266–80.

Mohan, G. and Tan-Mullins, M. (2009) 'Chinese migrants in Africa as new agents of development? An analytical framework', *European Journal of Development Research* 21: 588–605.

Mohan, G., Brown, E. and Milward, B. (2000) *Structural Adjustment, Practices, Theory and Impacts* (UK: Routledge).

Mol, A. (2011) 'China's ascent and Africa's environment', *Global Environmental Change* 21: 785–94.

Monson, J. (2009) Africa's Freedom Railway: How a Chinese Development Project Changed Lives and Livelihoods in Tanzania (Bloomington: Indiana University Press).

Morton, K. (2005) International Aid and China's Environment: Taming the Yellow Dragon (London & New York: Routledge).

Moss, N. with Nicolas van de Walle and Gunilla Pettersson (2008) 'An Aid-Institutions Paradox? Aid dependency and state building in sub-Saharan Africa'. In William Easterly (ed.), *Reinventing Aid* (Cambridge: MIT Press).

Moyo, D. (2009) *Dead Aid: Why Aid is not Working and how there is a Better Way for Africa* (London: Allen Lane).

Muekalia, D. (2004) 'Africa and China's strategic partnership', *African Security Review* 13(1): 5–11, http://www.iss.co.za/pubs/ASR/13No1/F1.pdf (accessed 01 November 2007).

Mung, M. E. (2000) *La diaspora chinoise: géographie d'une migration* (Paris: Ophrys).

Mung, M. E. (2008) 'Chinese migration and China's foreign policy in Africa', *Journal of Overseas Chinese* 4: 91–109.

Murray Li, T. (2007) *The Will to Improve: Governmentality, Development, and the Practice of Politics* (Durham, NC: Duke University Press).

Murray Li, T. (2010) 'To Make Live or Let Die? Rural Dispossession and the Protection of Surplus Populations'. In: N. Castree *et al* (eds) *The Point is to Change It: Geographies of Hope and Survival in an Age of Crisis* (Antipode Supplement, Chichester: Wiley-Blackwell), 66–93.

Murray, G. and Cook, I. G. (2002) *Green China: Seeking Ecological Alternatives* (London & New York: Routledge).

Mutume, G. (2007) 'Organised crime targets weak African states', 21(2) *African Renewal*, 21: 23.

Naidu, S. (2008a) 'India's growing African strategy', *Review of African Political Economy* 35(1): 116–28.

Naidu, S. (2008b) 'Balancing a Strategic Partnership? South Africa-China Relations'. In: K. Ampiah and S. Naidu (eds) *Crouching Tiger, Hidden Dragon? Africa and China* (Scottsville, SA: University of KwaZulu-Natal Press), 167–91.

Naidu, S., Corkin, L. and Herman, H. (2009) 'China's (re) emerging relations with Africa: Forging a new consensus?' *Politikon* 36(1): 87–115.

Naim, M. (2007), 'Rogue aid', *Foreign Policy*, March/April 2007, 159: 95–6.

Natsios, A. S. (2006) 'Five debates on international development: The US perspective', *Development Policy Review* 24(2): 131–9.

Ndulo, M. (2008) 'Chinese Investments in Africa: A Case Study of Zambia'. In: K. Ampiah and S. Naidu (eds), *Crouching Tiger, Hidden Dragon? Africa and China* (Scottsville, SA: University of KwaZulu-Natal Press), 138–51.

Neuhauser, C. (1968) Third World Politics: China and the Afro-Asian People's Solidarity Organisation (Cambridge: Harvard University Press).

*New York Times* (2010) 'China report shows more pollution in waterways', 9 February, http://www.nytimes.com/2010/02/10/world/asia/10pollute.html (accessed 18 September 2011).

Ngome, I. (2009) 'Cameroonian perceptions of the Chinese invasion', AfricaFiles, http://www.africafiles.org/article.asp?ID=15986 (accessed 18 September 2011).

Nolan, P. (2002) 'China and the global business revolution', *Cambridge Journal of Economics* 26: 119–37.

Nolan, P. (2004) *China at the Crossroads* (London: Polity).

Nonini, D. M. (2008) 'Is China becoming neoliberal?', *Critique of Anthropology* 28(2): 145–76.

Nordtveit, B. (2010) 'Development as a complex process of change: Conception and analysis of projects, programs and policies', *International Journal of Education and Development* 30: 110–17.

Norwegian Refugee Council Report (2005) 'Zimbabwe's Operation Murambatsvina: The Tipping Point?', Africa Report, No. 97, August, http://www.nrc.ch/8025708F004CE90B/(httpDocuments)/FBFD607BE0680EF480 2570B7005A5854/$file/097_zimbabwe_s_operation_murambatsvina_the_ tipping_point.pdf (accessed 29 September 2011).

Nugent, P. (2010) 'States and social contracts in Africa', *New Left Review* 63, May-June 2010, 35–68.

Nye, J. (2004) Soft Power: The Means to Success in World Politics (New York, Public Affairs).

Nye, J. (2006) 'Assessing China's Power', Op-Ed, *The Boston Globe* (April 19).

Nyiri, P. (2006) 'The yellow man's burden: Chinese migrants on a civilizing mission', *The China Journal* 56: 83–106.

Nyiri, P. (2009) 'Chinese entrepreneurs in poor countries: A transnational 'middlemen minority' and its futures', unpublished paper.

Ó Tuathail, G. (1994) 'Critical geopolitics and development theory: Intensifying the dialogue', *Transactions of the Institute of British Geographers* 19(2): 228–33.

Ó Tuathail, G. (1996) *Critical Geopolitics: The Politics of Writing Global Space.* (Minneapolis: University of Minnesota Press, Volume 6, in the Borderlines series and London: Routledge).

Obi, C. I. (2005) 'Environmental movements in sub-Saharan Africa, a political ecology of power and conflict', Civil Society and Social Movements Programme paper number 15.

Obiorah, N. (2007) 'Who's afraid of China in Africa? Towards an African civil society perspective on China-Africa relations'. In: F. Manji and S. Marks (eds), *African Perspectives on China in Africa* (Cape Town, Nairobi and Oxford: Fahamu/Pambazuka), 35–56.

OECD (2003) 'Corporate responsibility practices of emerging market companies – a fact finding study', Working Paper on international investment. http://www.oecd.org/dataoecd/29/38/35666512.pdf (accessed 09 October 2011) OECD (2007a) 'Aid Statistics', http://stats.oecd.org/Index.aspx?DatasetCode=ODA_RECIPIENT (accessed 29 September 2011).

OECD (2007b) Working party on environmental performance, environmental performance review of China (Final). Paris: OECD.

Ogunsanwo, A. (2008) 'A tale of two giants: Nigeria and China'. In: K. Ampiah and S. Naidu (eds), *Crouching Tiger, Hidden Dragon? Africa and China* (Scottsville, SA: University of KwaZulu-Natal Press), 192–207.

Oi, J. (1995) 'The role of the local state in China's transitional economy', *China Quarterly* (December), 144: 1132–50.

Oliveria, R. (2007) 'Business success, Angola-style: Postcolonial politics and the rise of Sonangol', *The Journal of Modern African Studies* 45: 595–619.

Ong, A. (1999) Flexible citizenship: The cultural logics of transnationality. (Durham NC: Duke University Press).

Ong, A. (2007) 'Neoliberalism as a mobile technology', *Transactions of the Institute of British Geographers* 32(1): 3–8.

Oster, S. (2007) 'China: New dam builder for the world', *The Wall Street Journal*, 28 December 2007, http://online.wsj.com/article/SB119880902773554655.html (accessed 22 February 2010).

Owen, O. and Melville, C. (2005) 'China and Africa: A new era of 'south-south cooperation', http://www.opendemocracy.net/globalization-G8/south_2658.jsp (accessed 25 February 2008).

Oxfam America (2009) 'Ghana's big test: Oil's challenge to democratic development', http://www.oxfamamerica.org/files/ghanas-big-test.pdf (accessed 20 October 2011).

Pal, P. (2008) 'Surge in Indian Outbound FDI to Africa: An Emerging Pattern in Globalization?', Paper presented to the Global Studies conference, 16–18 May 2008, University of Illinois, Chicago, http://203.197.126.76/research/download/OFDI_Partha-pal.pdf, (accessed 28 March 2012).

Palat, R. A. (2008) 'A New Bandung? Economic growth vs. distributive justice among emerging powers', *Futures* 40: 721–34.

Palat, R. A. (2009) 'Rise of the Global South and the Emerging Contours of a New World Order'. In P. J. Nederveen and B. Rehbein (eds), *Globalization and Emerging Societies: Development and Inequality* (Basingstoke: Palgrave).

Pan, C. (2009) 'What is Chinese about Chinese businesses? Locating the 'rise of China' in global production networks', *Journal of Contemporary China* 18(58): 7–25

Pan, L. (ed.) (2005) *The Encyclopedia of the Chinese Overseas* (Singapore: Nanyang Technological University).

Pan, Y. and Zhou, J. (2006) 'The rich consume and the poor suffer the pollution', 27 October, http://www.chinadialogue.net/article/show/single/en/493 – The-rich-consume-and-the-poor-suffer-the-pollution- (accessed 22 October 2011).

Paradise, J. F. (2009) 'China and international harmony: The role of Confucius Institutes in bolstering Beijing's Soft Power', *Asian Survey* 49(4): 647–69.

Park, Y. (2006) 'Sojourners to settlers: Early constructions of Chinese identity in South Africa, 1879–1949', *African Studies* 65(2): 201–31.

Park, Y. (2008) 'State, myth, and agency in the construction of Chinese South African identities 1948–1994', *Journal of Overseas Chinese* 4(1): 69–90.

Park, Y. (2009) *Chinese Migration in Africa*, SAIIA Occasional Paper No 24, January 2009, SAIIA.

Peck, J. and Theodore, N. (2007) 'Variegated capitalism', *Progress in Human Geography* 31(6): 731–72.

Peet, R. and Watts, M. (2004) 'Liberating political ecology'. In R. Peet and M. Watts (eds) *Liberation Ecologies: Environment, Development and Social, Movements* 2nd edn (London: Routledge), 3–47.

Pei, M. (2006) 'The dark side of China's rise', *Foreign Policy*, March/April.

Peluso, N. (1992) *Rich Forest, Poor People: Resources Control and Resistance in Java* (Berkeley: University of California Press).

Peluso, N. and Watts, M. (eds) (2001) *Violent Environment* (Ithaca: Cornell University Press).

*People's Daily* (9 June 2005) 'Ministries' guidebook propping up export brands'.

*People's Daily* (11 December 2005) 'China to earmark 700 mln yuan for brand building in 2006', http://english.peopledaily.com.cn/200512/11/eng20051211_227183.html (accessed 22 October 2011).

Perkins, D. (1994) 'Completing China's move to the market', *Journal of Economic Perspectives* 8(2): 23–46.

PEW Charitable Trusts (2010) *Who's Winning the Clean Energy Race?* (Washington DC: Pew Charitable Trusts).

Phillips, M. (2006) 'G-7 to warn China over costly loans to poor countries', *The Wall Street Journal* (15 September 2006, p. A2).

Pickles, J. and Woods, J. (1989) 'Taiwanese investment in South Africa', *African Affairs* 88: 507–28.

Pomfret, J. and Kirkwood, T. (2009) 'Demand for illegal ivory soars in booming China', *The Independent*, Sunday, 9 November, http://www.independent.co.uk/news/world/africa/demand-for-illegal-ivory-soars-in-booming-china-1820976.html (accessed 22 October 2011).

Porter, M. E. (1998) Clusters and competition: new agendas for companies, governments, and institutions. In M. E. Porter (ed.), *On Competitiveness* (Cambridge, MA: Harvard Business School Press), 197–288.

Portes, A. and Jensen, L. (1987) 'What's an ethnic enclave? The case for conceptual clarity', *American Sociological Review* 52: 768–71.

Portes, A. and Sensenbrenner, J. (1993) 'Embeddedness and immigration: Notes on the social determinants of economic action', *American Journal of Sociology* 98(6): 1320–50.

Poston Jr., D. L., Mao, M. X. and Yu, M.Y. (1994) 'The global distribution of the overseas Chinese around 1990', *Population and Development Review* 20(3): 631–45.

Powell, A. (2007) 'Officials: 74 dead in attack on Chinese oil field in Ethiopia', *The Independent*, 25 April 2007, http://www.independent.co.uk/news/world/africa/officials-74-dead-in-attack-on-chinese-oil-field-in-ethiopia-446063.html (accessed 22 October 2011).

Power, M. (2003) *Rethinking Development Geographies* (London: Routledge).

Power, M. (2010) 'Geopolitics and development: An introduction', *Geopolitics* 15(3): 433–40.

Power, M. (2011) 'Angola 2025: The future of the "world's richest poor country" as seen through a Chinese rear-view mirror', *Antipode*, doi: 10.1111/j.1467–8330.2011.00896.x

Power, M. and Mohan, G. (2010) 'Towards a critical geo-politics of China's engagement with African development', *Geopolitics* 15(3): 462–95.

Price, G. (2011) For the Global Good: India's Developing International Role (London: Chatham House).

Puska, S. (2007) 'Military backs China's Africa adventure', http://www.atimes.com/atimes/China/IF08Ad02.html (accessed 13 October 2011).

Qian, J. and Wu, A. (2007) 'Playing the blame game in Africa', *International Herald Tribune*, 23 July 2007, http://www.nytimes.com/2007/07/23/opinion/23iht-edqian.1.6784986.html?pagewanted=all, (accessed 13 October 2011).

Qian, Y. and Wu, J. (2000) 'China's transition to a market economy: How far across the river?', Paper prepared for the Conference on Policy Reform in China at the Center for Research on Economic Development and Policy Reform (CEDPR), Stanford University, 18–20 November 1999.

QiaoQing (2005) '2002–2004 year book on overseas statistics by the Overseas Chinese Affairs Office of the State Council, CCP, PRC'. Adapted and translated from Zhang WanXin, 2005, HuaJiaoHuaRenGaiShu (Overseas Chinese Brief), Overseas Chinese in Africa, 215–35.

Qinmei, W. (1998) 'Sino-African friendship in the past twenty years', *Chinafrica* 10, 20 October, 16–22.

Raghuram P., Madge, C. and Noxolo, P. (2009) 'Rethinking responsibility and care for a postcolonial world', *Geoforum* 40: 5–13.

Raine, S. (2009) *China's African Challenges* (London: Routledge).

Ramamurti, R. (2009) *Impact of the Crisis on New FDI Players*, Paper, Fourth Columbia International Investment Conference, FDI, the Global Crisis and Sustainable Recovery, Columbia University, New York, November.

Ramo, J. (2004) *The Beijing Consensus* (London: The Foreign Policy Centre).

Ravenhill, J. (2006) 'Is China an economic threat to Southeast Asia?', *Asian Survey* 46(5) 653–74.

Redvers, L. (2011) China's Stake in Zambia's election. http://www.bbc.co.uk/news/world-africa-14952240

Reed, M. G. and Bruyneel, S. (2010) 'Rescaling environmental governance, rethinking the state: A three-dimensional review', *Progress in Human Geography* 34(5): 646–53.

Reilly, J. and Na, W. (2007) 'China's Corporate Engagement in Africa'. In M. Kitissou (ed.), *Africa in China's Global Strategy* (London: Adonis & Abbey Publishers Ltd).

Reisen, H. and Ndoye, S. (2008) 'Prudent versus imprudent lending in Africa: From debt relief to emerging lenders', OECD Development Centre Working Paper no 268, OECD Paris. http://www.oecd.org/dataoecd/62/12/40152567.pdf (accessed 28 September 2011).

Reno, W. (1995) *Corruption and State Politics in Sierra Leone* (Cambridge: Cambridge University Press).

Reuters (2006) 'China's presence a boon to Africa – UN advisor', Reuters (Beijing), 15 August.

Rhodes, R. A. W. (1996) 'The new governance: Governing without government', *Political Studies* 44: 652–67.

Ribeiro, C. O. (2007) 'Relações Político-Comerciais Brasil-África (1985–2006)', PhD thesis, PUC-SP University, São Paulo.

Richardson, P. (1977) 'The recruiting of Chinese indentured labour for the South African goldmines, 1903–1907', *Journal of African History* 18.

Riddell, R. (2007) *'Does Foreign Aid Really Work?'* (Oxford: Oxford University Press).

Robinson, P. (1977) 'The recruiting of Chinese indentured labour for the South African gold-mines, 1903–1908', *The Journal of African History* 18: 85–108.

Rocha, J. (2007) 'A New Frontier in the Exploitation of Africa's Natural Resources: The Emergence of China'. In F. Manji and S. Marks (eds), *African Perspectives on China in Africa* (Nairobi: Fahamu Books), 15–34.

Rofel, L. (2007) Desiring China: Experiments in Neoliberalism, Sexuality, and Public Culture (Durham, NC: Duke University Press).

Rone, J. (2003) *Sudan, Oil and Human Rights* (New York: Human Rights Watch).

Rose, N. (1999) *Powers of Freedom: Reframing Political Thought* (Cambridge: Cambridge University Press).

Rotberg, R. (2008) *China into Africa: Trade, Aid and Influence* (Cambridge: World Peace Foundation).

Ru, J. and Ortolano, L. (2009) 'Development of citizen-organised environmental NGOs in China', *Voluntas* 20: 141–68.

Sachikonye, L. (2008) 'Crouching Tiger, Hidden Agenda? Zimbabwe-China Relations' in K. Ampiah, K and S. Naidu (eds), *Crouching Tiger, Hidden Dragon? Africa and China* (Scottsville SA: University of KwaZulu-Natal Press).

Sachs, J (2007) 'China's lessons for the World Bank', *The Economists View*, http://economistsview.typepad.com/economistsview/2007/05/jeffrey_sachs_c.html/

Saferworld (2011) 'China's growing role in African peace and security', Saferworld, London. http://www.saferworld.org.uk/smartweb/resources/view-resource/500/ (accessed 28 September 2011).

SAIIA (South African Institute for International Affairs) (2009) *Report for China and Africa: Assessing the Relationship on the Eve of FOCAC IV*, Joint AU-SIIA workshop in Addis Ababa, Ethiopia, 25 September 2009 (accessed 28 September 2011).

Sanders, R. (1999) 'The political economy of Chinese environmental protection: Lessons of the Mao and Deng years', *Third World Quarterly* 20(6): 1201–14.

SASAC (State-owned Assets Supervision and Administration Commission of the State Council) (2011) 'Main functions and responsibilities of SASAC', http://www.sasac.gov.cn/n2963340/n2963393/2965120.html (accessed 29 September 2011).

Sautman, B. and Hairong, Y. (2006) 'Honour and Shame? China's Africa Ties in Comparative Perspective'. In L. Wild and D. Mepham (eds), *The New Sinosphere: China in Africa* (London: Institute for Public Policy Research), 54–61.

Sautman, B. and Hairong, Y. (2007) 'Friends and interests: China's distinctive links with Africa', *African Studies Review* 50(3): 75–114.

Sautman, B. and Hairong, Y. (2009) 'African perspectives on China-Africa links', *The China Quarterly* 199: 728–59.

Schmitz, H. (2007) 'The rise of the East: What does it mean for development studies?', *IDS Bulletin* 38(2): 51–8.

Schoeman, M. (2007) China in Africa: The Rise of a Hegemony'. In *China and Africa: Partners in Development and Security?* (Copenhagen: Danish Institute of International Affairs, 23 August).

Schuller, M. and Turner, A. (2005) 'Global companies: Chinese companies spread their wings', *China Aktuell* 4: 3–12.

Schwartz, J. (2003) 'The impact of state capacity on enforcement of environmental policies: The case of China', *The Journal of Environment Development.* 12(50): 50–81.

Seagrave, S. (1996) Lords of the Rim: The Invisible Empire of the Overseas Chinese (London: Corgi Books).

Seddon, M. (2000) 'Molluscan biodiversity and the impact of large dams', Contributing Paper Prepared for Thematic Review II. 1: Dams, ecosystem functions and environmental restoration.

Segal, G. (1994) 'Deconstructing Foreign Relations'. In D. S. G. Goodman and G. Segal (eds), *China Deconstructs: Politics, Trade and Regionalism* (London: Routledge), 322–55.

Selby, J. (2003). 'Introduction'. In: F. Cochrane, S. Duffy and J. Selby (eds), *Global Governance, Conflict and Resistance* (Basingstoke: Palgrave Macmillan), 1–18.

Servant, J. (2005) 'Moscow and Beijing, Asia's roaring economies, China's trade safari in Africa', http://mondediplo.com/2005/05/11chinafrica (accessed 28 September 2011).

Seungho Lee (2006) Water and Development in China: The Political Economy of Shanghai Water Policy (Singapore: World Scientific Publishing).

Seymour, J. D. (2005) 'China's Environment: A Bibliographic Essay'. In K. Day (ed.), *China's Environment and the Challenge of Sustainable Development* (Armonk and London: ME Sharpe), 248–74.

Shambaugh, D. (1994) 'Introduction'. In T. Robinson and D. Shambaugh (eds), *Chinese Foreign Policy: Theory and Practice* (Oxford: Oxford University Press), 1–10.

Shambaugh D. (2002) 'China's international relations think tanks: Evolving structure and process', *The China Quarterly* 171: 575–96.

Shambaugh, D. (2007a) 'China's quiet diplomacy', *China: An International Journal* 5(1): 26–54.

Shambaugh, D. (2007b) 'China's propaganda system: Institutions, processes and efficacy', *The China Journal* 57: 25–58.

Shambaugh, D. (2010) 'China flexes its soft power', *New York Times*, 7 June, http://www.nytimes.com/2010/06/08/opinion/08iht-edshambaugh.html (accessed 28 September 2011).

Shapiro, J. (2001) Mao's War against Nature: Politics and the Environment in Revolutionary China (Cambridge: Cambridge University Press).

Shaw, T. M., Cooper, A. F. and Chin, G. T. (2009) 'Emerging powers and Africa: Implications for/from global governance', *Politikon* 36(1): 27–44.

Shaxson, N., Neves, J. and Pacheco, F. (2008) *Drivers of Change: Angola* (London: Department for International Development).

Shelton, G. (2005) 'China, Africa and South Africa advancing south-south cooperation'. In A. Boron and G. Lechini (eds), *Politics and Social Movements in an Hegemonic World: Lessons from Africa, Asia and Latin America* (Argentina: CLACSO, Consejo Latinoamericano de Ciencias Sociales, Ciudad Autónoma de Buenos Aires), 347–83.

Shelton, G. (2008) 'China: Africa's new peacekeeper', *The China Monitor* 33, Sptember, http://www.ccs.org.za/downloads/monitors/September%20 China%20Monitor.pdf (accessed 28 September 2011).

Shen, I-Yao (2006) *A Century of Chinese Exclusion Abroad* (Beijing: Foreign Languages Press).

Shen, S. (2009) 'A constructed (un)reality on China's re-entry into Africa: The Chinese online community perception of Africa (2006–2008)', *Journal of Modern African Studies* 47(3): 425–48.

*Shenzhen Daily* (5 January 2005) 'Huawei funded for overseas expansion'.

Shinn, D. (2008a) 'China's relations with Zimbabwe, Sudan and the Democratic Republic of the Congo', http://www.gwu.edu/~elliott/news/speeches/ shinn031508.cfm/ (accessed 28 September 2011).

Shinn, D. (2008b) 'Military and Security Relations: China, Africa and the Rest of the World'. In R. Rotberg (ed.), *China into Africa: Trade, Aid, and Influence* (Cambridge: Brookings).

Shrivastava, M. (2009) 'India and Africa: From political alliance to economic partnership', *Politikon* 36(1): 117–43.

Shubin, V. (2008) The Hot 'Cold War': The USSR in Southern Africa (London: Pluto Press).

Sidaway, J. (2007) 'The Geography of Political Geography'. In K. Cox, M. Low and J. Robinson (eds), *The Handbook of Political Geography* (London: Sage).

Si Zoubir, L. (2004) 'Mutations incertaines de la l'économie', *Le Monde Diplomatique*, 27–28 October.

Simons, B. (2009) 'Confucianism' at large in Africa', *Asia Times Online*, 7 August, http://www.atimes.com/atimes/China/KH07Ad03.html (accessed 28 September 2011).

Sinkule, B. J. and Ortolano, L. (1995) *Implementing Environmental Policy in China* (Westport: Greenwood Publishing Group).

Sino Steel (2008) 'Sino Steel Corporation Sustainability Africa Report',. http:// www.sinosteel.com/templates/images/index_8.16/%E9%9D%9E%E6%B4% B2%E6%8A%A5%E5%91%8A_%E8%8B%B1%E6%96%87%E7%89%88.pdf (accessed 09 October 2011).

Six, C. (2009) 'The rise of postcolonial states as donors: A challenge to the development paradigm?', *Third World Quarterly*, 30(6): 1103–21.

Skocpol, T. (1985) 'Bringing the State Back in: Strategies for Analysis in Current Research'. In P. Evans, D. Rueschemeyer and T. Skocpol (eds), *Bringing the State Back in* (New York: Cambridge University Press), 3–43.

Slater, D. (1993) 'The geopolitical imagination and enframing of development theory', *Transactions of the Institute of British Geographers* 18(4): 419–37.

Slater, D. (2004) Geopolitics and the Post-colonial: Rethinking North-South Relations (Oxford: Blackwell).

Slater, D. and Bell, M. (2002) 'Aid and the geopolitics of the post-colonial: Critical reflections on new labour's overseas development strategy', *Development and Change* 33(2): 335–60.

Small, A. (2008) 'China's changing policies towards rogue states', German Marshall Fund of the United States Testimony before the U.S.-China Economic and Security Review Commission China's expanding Global Influence: Foreign Policy Goals, Practices and Tools, 18 March 2008.

Smart, A. (1997) 'Oriental Despotism and Sugar-coated Bullets: Representations of the Market in China'. In J. G. Carrier (ed.), *Meanings of the Market* (New York: Berg), 159–94.

Smil, V. (1980) 'Environmental degradation in China', *Asian Survey* 20(8): 777–88.

Smil, V. (1984) The Bad Earth: Environmental Degradation In China (US, London: Zed).

Smil, V. (1993) China's Environmental Crisis: An Inquiry into the Limits of National Development (Armonk and London: ME Sharpe).

Smil, V. (1998) 'China energy and resources uses: Continuity and change', *China Quarterly* 156: 935–51.

Smil, V. (2004) China's Past, China's Future: Energy, Food, Environment (London and New York).

Smith, N. (2008) *Uneven Development: Nature, Capital and the Production of Space* (Athens, Ga: The University of Georgia Press).

Snow, P. (1988) *The Star Raft: China's Encounter with Africa* (Ithaca, New York: Cornell University Press).

Snow, P. (1995) 'China and Africa: consensus and camouflage'. In T. Robinson and D. Shambaugh (eds), *Chinese Foreign Policy: Theory and Practice* (UK: Oxford Press).

Snow, P. (2008) 'Foreword'. In C. Alden, D. Large and R. Soares de Oliveira(eds), *China Returns to Africa: A Rising Power and a Continent Embrace* (London: Hurst Publishers), xiv–xx.

So, A. (2005) 'Beyond the logic of capital and the polarization model: The state, market reforms, and the plurality of class conflict in China', *Critical Asian Studies* 37(3): 481–94.

Sogge, D. (2002) Give and Take: What's the Matter with Foreign Aid? (London: Zed).

Sogge, D. (2006) 'Angola: Global 'good governance' also needed'. *FRIDE*, Working Paper 23, http://www.fride.org/publication/69/angola-global-good-governance-also-needed (accessed 02 March 2010).

Sörensen, J. (2010) Challenging the Aid Paradigm: Western Currents and Asian Alternatives (London: Palgrave MacMillan).

Spiegel, S. J. and Le Billon, P. (2009) 'China's weapons trade: From ships of shame to the ethics of global resistance', *International Affairs* 85(2): 323–46.

Spivak, G. (1988) 'Can the subaltern speak?'. In C. Nelson and L. Grossberg (eds), *Marxism and the Interpretation of Culture* (Urbana: University of Illinois Press), 271–313.

Srinavasan, S. (2008), 'A Marriage less Convenient'. In K. Ampiah and S. Naidu (eds), *Crouching Tiger, Hidden Dragon? Africa and China* (Scottsville, SA: South Africa: University of Kwazulu Natal Press), 55–87.

Staeheli, L. and Mitchell, D. (2004) 'Spaces of Public and Private: Locating Politics'. In C. Barnett and M. Low (eds), *Spaces of Democracy: Geographical Perspectives on Citizenship, Participation and Representation* (London: Sage), 147–60.

Staehle, S. (2007) 'How to integrate China into the Global Aid Regime. Presentation at China and Africa, who benefits?' Frankfurt Conference, 14–15 Dec 2007, http://www.izo.uni-frankfurt.de/Conf_China_in_Africa_Presentation_Staehle_Final_20071213.pdf (accessed 02 October 2011).

Standing, A. (2008) 'Corruption and industrial fishing in Africa', Chr. Michelsen Institute, Anti Corruption Resource Centre, http://www.cmi.no/publications/file/3188-corruption-and-industrial-fishing-in-africa.pdf (accessed 02 October 2011).

Steiner-Khamsi, G. (2010) '(North-) South-South cooperation in the context of standardized aid', in K. King (ed.) *A Brave New World of 'Emerging', 'Non-DAC' Donors and their Differences from Traditional Donors*, NORRAG News No 44, September 2010, http://www.norrag.org/issues/article/1324/en/(north-)-south-south-cooperation-in-the-context-of-standardized-aid.html?PHPSESSID=ea018508137f54ef257a1f17bbe581fe (accessed 20 October 2011).

Stiglitz, J. (2002) *Globalization and its Discontents* (New York: Norton).

Story, J. (2010) 'China and the global business system: Wrecker or stakeholder?', BICCS Asia paper, 5(1): 1–40.

Stratsis Incite (2010) 'China and Ghana sign Trade deals-Loans worth up to $15 Billion', September 27, http://stratsisincite.wordpress.com/2010/09/27/china-and-ghana-sign-trade-deals-loans-worth-up-to-15-billion/ (accessed 20 October 2011).

Strauss, J. (2006) 'Introduction: In search of PRC history', *The China Quarterly* 188: 855–69.

Strauss, J. (2009) 'The past in the present: Historical and rhetorical lineages in China's relations with Africa', *The China Quarterly* 199: 777–95.

Strauss, J. and Saavedra, M. (2009) 'China, Africa and internationalization', *The China Quarterly* 199: 551–62.

Strauss-Kahn, D. (2010) 'Transcript of a press briefing on IMF reforms by Dominique Strauss-Kahn, Managing Director of the IMF, With Caroline Atkinson, Director of External Relations Department', Friday, 5 November, Washington, D.C, http://www.imf.org/external/np/tr/2010/tr110510.htm (accessed 20 October 2011).

Sun, S. X. and Zhao, J. L. (2008) 'Developing a Workflow Design Framework Based on Dataflow Analysis', Proceedings of the 41st Hawaii International Conference on System Sciences, Big Island, Hawaii, USA, 19–28. .

Sun, X. and Canby, K. (2011) 'China, overview of forest governance, market and trade', Forest Trends for FLEGT Asia Regional Programme, http://www.forest-trends.org/documents/files/doc_2878.pdf (accessed 05 October 2011).

Sutcliffe, C. (2009) 'Interviews with people to be affected by Bui dam: A field report', http://internationalrivers.org/files/Bui%20Field%20Report.pdf (accessed 05 October 2011).

Sylvanus, N. (2007) '"Chinese Devils"? Perceptions of the Chinese in Lomé's Central Market', unpublished paper presented at the conference Rethinking Africa's 'China Factor': Identifying Players, Strategies, and Practices, April 2007, http://www.international.ucla.edu/media/files/82.pdf (accessed 05 October 2011).

Symes, D. (2006) 'Fisheries management and institutional reform: A European perspective', *ICES Journal of Marine Science* 64: 779–85.

Tan-Mullins, May, Mohan, G. and Power, M. (2010) 'Redefining 'Aid' in the China-Africa Context', *Development and Change* 41(5): 857–81.

Tang, J. and Zhang, C. (2011) 'SMEs play 'big role' in Africa', 29 August, *International Business Journal*, http://www.focac.org/eng/zfgx/jmhz/t859358.htm (accessed 01 September 2011).

Taylor, I. (1998) 'China's foreign policy towards Africa in the 1990s', *The Journal of Modern African Studies* 36(3): 443–60.

Taylor, I. (2004) 'The "All-Weather Friend"? Sino-African Interaction in the Twenty-First Century'. In I. Taylor and P. Williams (eds), *Africa in International Politics: External Involvement in Africa* (London: Routledge).

Taylor, I. (2006a) China and Africa: Engagement and Compromise (London: Routledge).

Taylor, I. (2006b) 'China's oil diplomacy in Africa', *International Affairs* 82(5): 937–59.

Taylor, I. (2007a) 'Governance in Africa and Sino-African relations: Contradictions or confluence?', *Politics* 27(3): 139–46.

Taylor, I. (2007b) 'Unpacking China's Resource Diplomacy in Africa'. In H. Melber (ed.), *China in Africa* (Uppsala: Nordiska Afrikainstitutet). 10–25.

Taylor, I. (2008) 'China's role in peacekeeping in Africa', *The China Monitor* 33, 6–9 September.

Taylor, I. (2009) 'The South will rise again? New alliances and global govern-ance: The India-Brazil-South Africa dialogue forum', *Politikon* 36(1): 45–58.

Taylor, I. (2011) *The Forum on China-Africa Cooperation* (FOCAC) (London: Routledge).

Taylor, I. and Xiao, Y. (2009) 'A case of mistaken identity: China Inc. and its imperialism in sub-Saharan Africa', *Asian Politics and Society* 1(4):709–25.

Teng, L. (2009) 'China's First Equity Investment to facilitate the African Continent', Presentation by the Southern African Representative of the China-Africa Development Fund (CADFund) at the opening of the Asian Business Centre at the Gordon Institute of Business Science (GIBS), Johannesburg, South Africa, 26 March.

Terra Daily (6 July 2010), 'Chinese built hospital risks collapse in Angola: State Radio', http://www.terradaily.com/reports/Chinese-built_hospital_risks_collapse_in_Angola_state_radio_999.html

*The Economist* (2008) 'The new colonialists: China's thirst for resources' (13 March).

*The Guardian* (24 April 2008) 'Zimbabwe arms shipment returns to China', http://www.guardian.co.uk/world/2008/apr/24/zimbabwe.china (accessed 09 October 2011).

*The Telegraph* (05 November 2008) 'CITES ivory sales will increase poaching and illegal trade', http://www.telegraph.co.uk/earth/earthcomment/3394968/CITES-ivory-sale-will-increase-poaching-and-illegal-trade.html (accessed 09 October 2011).

Thomas, G. (2005) *The UK and China: Taking forward a partnership on development*, speech by Gareth Thomas, given at the Chinese Academy of Social Sciences, 1st December 2005, http://www.dfid.gov.uk/news/files/Speeches/gareth-china-speech.pdf.

Thornton, P. M. (2010) 'From liberating production to unleashing consumption: Mapping landscapes of power in Beijing', *Political Geography* 29(6): 302–10.

Thuno, M. (2001) 'Reaching out and incorporating Chinese overseas: The trans-territorial scope of the PRC by the end of the 20th century', *The China Quarterly* 168: 910–29.

Tickell, A. and Peck, J. (2003) 'Making global rules: Globalization or neoliberalization'. In J. Peck and H. Yeung (eds), *Remaking the Global Economy: Economic-Geographical Perspectives* (London: Sage), 163–81.

Tilt, B. (2007) 'The political ecology of pollution enforcement in China: A cCase from Sichuan's rural industrial sector', *The China Quarterly* 192: 915–32.

Tjonneland, E., Brandtzaeg, B., Kolas, A. and Le Pere, G. (2006) 'China in Africa: Implications for Norwegian foreign and development policies', CHR Michelsen Institute, CMI, Norway, http://www.cmi.no/publications/publication/?2438=china-in-africa-implications-for-norwegian (accessed 23 August 2011).

Tong, Y. (2007) 'Bureaucracy meets the environment: Elite perceptions in six Chinese cities', *The China Quarterly* 189: 100–21.

Tradeinvest Africa (2009), 'Development fund strengthens Sino-African partnership',http://www.tradeinvestafrica.com/feature_articles/224685.htm, (accessed 28 September 2011).

Trofimov, Y. (2007) 'New management: In Africa China's expansion begins to stir resentment: Investment boom fuels colonialism charges; a tragedy in Zambia', *The Wall Street Journal*, 2 February 2007, p. A1.

Tsai, K. S. (2007) Capitalism Without Democracy: The Private Sector in Contemporary China (Ithaca and London: Cornell University Press).

Tsai, L. (2007) Accountability without Democracy: Solidary Groups and Public Goods Provision in Rural China (Cambridge: Cambridge University Press).

Tsikata, D., Fenny, A. P. and Aryeetey, E. (2008) *China Africa Relations; A Case Study of Ghana* (South Africa: African Economic Research Consortium).

Tull, D. (2006) 'China's engagement in Africa: Scope, significance and consequences', *Journal of Modern African Studies* 44(3): 459–79.

UNDP (United Nations Development Programme) China (2008) *Human Development Report China 2007/08* (Beijing: China Translation and Publishing Corporation).

UNEP (United Nations Environment Programme) (2009) *Global Trends in Sustainable Energy Investment* (Geneva: UNEP).

UNEP (2011) *Global Trends in Renewable Energy Investment* (Geneva: UNEP).

United Nations (2007) Asian Foreign Direct Investment in Africa: Towards a new era of cooperation among developing countries (New York: United Nations).

United Nations (2011) 'Secretary General's Message to China-Africa People's Forum', presentation in Nairobi, Kenya on 29 August 2011 http://www.un.org/apps/sg/sgstats.asp?nid=5480 (accessed 04 October 2011).

UPI (United Press International) (2009) 'Russia horns in on China in Africa', 25 June, Http://www.upi.com/Science_News/Resource-Wars/2009/06/25/Russia-horns-in-on-China-in-Africa/UPI-85411245943929/ (accessed 04 October 2011).

U.S. Congress (1973) Congressional Record – House, Washington: U.S. Government Printing Office, 18 January 1973.

Vandaele, J. (2008) 'China Outdoes Europeans in Congo', 8 February, http://ipsnews.net/news.asp?idnews=41125 (accessed 14 October 2010).

Van Rooij, B. (2006) 'Implementation of Chinese environmental law: Regular enforcement and political campaigns', *Development and Change* 37(1): 57–74.

Van Sertima, I. (1976) They Came Before Columbus: The African Presence in Ancient America (New York: Random House).

Vines, A. (2009a) 'Angola as a global player: Closing remarks', Chatham House Africa Programme Conference to mark the 10th anniversary of the Chatham House Angola Forum, 24 July 2009, http://www.chathamhouse.org.uk/files/14445_240709vines.pdf/ (accessed 01 August 2009).

Vines, A. (2009b) 'India's Strategy in Africa: Looking Beyond the India-Africa Forum', *South African Yearbook of International Affairs 2008/9*, SAIIA.

Vines, A. (2010a) 'India in Africa: Expert comment', http://www.chathamhouse.org/media/comment/view/162831 (accessed 01 August 2009).

Vines, A (2010b) 'India's Africa engagement: Prospects for the 2011 India-Africa Forum', Chatham House programme paper AFP 2010/01, http://www.chathamhouse.org/sites/default/files/public/Research/Africa/1210vines.pdf, (accessed 26 March 2012).

Vines, A. and Oruitemeka, B. (2008) 'India's engagement with the African Indian Ocean rim states', *South African Journal of International Affairs* 14(2): 111–25.

Vines, A. and Campos, I. (2010) 'China and India in Angola'. In F. Cheru and C. Obi (eds), *The Rise of China and India in Africa: Challenges, Opportunities and Critical Interventions* (Zed Press).

Vines, A. Wong, L., Weimer, M. and Campos, I. (2009) *Thirst for African Oil: Asian National Oil Companies in Nigeria and Angola* (London: Chatham House).

Viviano, F. (2005) 'China's Great Armada', *National Geographic*, July, 34–53.

Vizentini, P. (2005) *Relações Internacionais do Brasil: de Vargas a Lula*, 2nd edn (São Paulo: Editora Perseu Abamo).

Walder, A. (2002) 'Privatization and elite mobility: Rural China, 1979–1996', Stanford Institute for International Studies, A/PARC Working Paper.

Wang, J. (1994) 'International Relations Theory and the Study of Chinese Foreign Policy: A Chinsese Perspective'. In T. Robinson and D. Shambaugh (eds) *Chinese Foreign Policy: Theory and Practice* (Oxford: OUP), 482.

Wang, H. (2003) *China's New Order: Society, Politics and Economy in Transition* (Cambridge, MA: Harvard University Press,).

Wang Ming (2005) *Southern Weekend ( Nanfang Zhoumo)* (internet edition), 19 May.

Wang, N. (ed.) (2002) Handbook on Long-Distance Fishing Technology and Economy (Beijing: Ocean Press).

Wang, S. (2000) 'The social and political implications of China's WTO membership', *Journal of Contemporary China* 25: 373–405.

Wang, Y., Yao, Y. and Ju, M. (2008) 'Wise use of wetlands: Current state of protection and utilisation of Chinese wetlands and recommendations for improvement', *Environmental Management* 41: 793–808.

Wang, Z. (2007) Zouxiang Shijie de Zhongguo Kuaguo Gongsi, China Commerce Press.

Wang, Z. and Lim, T. S. (2007) 'China's growing interest in Africa'. In G. Wang and J. Wong (eds), *Interpreting China's Development* (Singapore: World Scientific Publishing), 256–60.

Warah, R. (2008) *Missionaries, Mercenaries and Misfits* (London: AuthorHouse).

Waterpower (2009) 'Chinese investment in African hydro' (06 Nov 2009), http://www.waterpowermagazine.com/story.asp?storyCode=2054628 (accessed 27 September 2011).

Watson, J., Byrne, R., Stua, M., Ockwell, D., Xiliang, Z., Da, Z., Tianhou, Z., Xiaofeng, Z. and Xunmin, O. (2011) *UK-China Collaborative Study on Low Carbon Technology Transfer: Final Report*. Report to the Department of Energy and Climate Change (Brighton: University of Sussex).

Watson, S. (2004) 'Cultures of Democracy: Spaces of Democratic Possibility'. In C. Barnett and M. Low (eds) *Spaces of Democracy: Geographical Perspectives on Citizenship, Participation and Representation* (London: Sage), 207–22.

Watts, J. (2005) 'China consumes forests of smuggled timber', *The Guardian*, 22 April, http://www.guardian.co.uk/world/2005/apr/22/china.jonathanwatts (accessed 07 October 2011).

Watts, J. (2010) When a Billion Chinese Jump: How China Will Save Mankind – Or Destroy It (London: Faber and Faber).

Watts, M. (2003) 'Development and governmentality', *Singapore Journal of Tropical Geography* 24(1): 6–34.

Wei, L. T. (1982) *Peking Versus Taipei in Africa 1960–1978* (Taiwan: The Asia and World Institute).

Weidenbaum, M. and Hughes, S. (1996) The Bamboo Network: How Expatriate Chinese Entrepreneurs Are Creating a New Economic Superpower in Asia (New York: Martin Kessler Books).

Weigelin-Schwiedrzik, S. (2006) 'In search of a master narrative for 20th-century Chinese history', *China Quarterly* 188: 1070–91.

Weil, R. (1996) Red Cat, White Cat: China and the Contradictions of Market Socialism (New York: Review Press).

Wen, J. B. (2009) 'Full text of Wen Jiabao Speech at FOCAC IV', http://www.chinadaily.com.cn/china/2009–11/09/content_8929621_2.htm (accessed 01 March 2010).

Weng Ming (1995) 'Person Selected Right Before the Journey: Lord Qiao's first visit to the UN'. In Fu Hao and Li Tongcheng (eds), *World Affairs: Diplomats in the UN* (Beijing: Chinese Overseas Publishing House).

Wheeler, N, (2004) 'A civic trend within ethnic transnationalism? Some insights from classical social theory and the Chinese American experience', *Global Networks* 4 (4): 391–408.

Whitfield, L. and Jones, E. (2007) 'Ghana: The political dimensions of aid dependence', Global Economic Governance Programme, WP 2007/32 Oxford University, http://www.globaleconomicgovernance.org/wp-content/uploads/Whitfield%20Jones%20Final.pdf (accessed 01 March 2010).

Wild, L. and Mepham, D. (eds) (2006)*The New Sinosphere: China in Africa* (London: IPPR).

Wilhelm, J. (2006) 'The Chinese communities in South Africa'. In S. Buhlungu, J. Daniel, R. Southall and J. Lutchman (eds) *State of the Nation: South Africa 2005–2006* (Cape Town, Nairobi and Oxford: HSRC Press), 350–68.

Wilson, E. (2005) 'China's Influence in Africa: Implication for US policies', Centre for International Development and conflict management, US: University of Maryland.

Winrow, G. M. (1990) *The Foreign Policy of the GDR in Africa* (Cambridge: Cambridge University Press).

Winters, C. A. (1984) 'Blacks in ancient China, Pt. 1: The founders of Xia and Shang', *Journal of Black Studies* (1984): 8–13.

Wissenbach, U. (2009) 'The EU's response to China's Africa safari: Can triangulation match needs?, *European Journal of Development Research Special Issue* 21: 662–74.

Wissenbach, U. (2010) 'Understanding Europe's Development Policy', unpublished paper given at the ESRC Rising Powers Workshop 1: The understanding and practice of development in China and the European Union, School of Public Policy and Management, Tsinghua University, 15–16 July 2010.

Woetzel, J. R. (2008) 'Reassessing China's state-owned enterprises', *The McKinsey Quarterly*3: 59–65.

Wong, M. (2006) 'Chinese workers in the garment industry in Africa: Implications of the contract labour dispatch system on the international labour movement', *Labour, Capital and Society* 39(1): 69–111.

Woods, N. (2008) 'Whose aid? Whose influence? China, emerging donors and the silent revolution in development assistance', *International Affairs* 84(6): 1205–21.

Workman, D. (2009) 'China trade statistics 2009', International Trade @ suite 101, http://daniel-workman.suite101.com/china-trade-statistics-2009-a205058 (accessed 26 March 2012).

World Bank (1992) China: Strategies for Reducing Poverty in the 1990s, A World Bank country Study (Washington: World Bank).

World Bank (2005) *China: An Evaluation of World Bank Assistance* (Washington: World Bank).

World Bank (2006) Country Partnership Strategy for the People's Republic of China for the Period of 2006–2010 (Washington: World Bank).

World Bank (2007a) *Africa Development Indicators 2007–8* (Washington: World Bank).

World Bank (2007b) China and the World Bank: A Partnership for Innovation (Washington: World Bank).

World Bank (2008) *Africa Development Indicators 2008–9* (Washington: World Bank).

World Bank (2009a) *Macro-brief: Angola* (Luanda: World Bank).

World Bank (2009b) 'Economy-Wide Impact of Oil Discovery in Ghana', 30 November,http://siteresources.worldbank.org/INTGHANA/Resources/Economy-Wide_Impact_of_Oil_Discovery_in_Ghana.pdf (accessed 17 March 2010).

World Bank (2010) *The World Bank Operational Manual*, http://go.worldbank.org/DZDZ9038D0 (accessed 17 March 2010).

World Bank policy note (2005) 'SOE dividends: How much to pay and to whom? http://www.worldbank.org/research/2005/10/12769917/soe-dividends-much (accessed 17 March 2010).

World Commissions on Dams (2000) 'Dams and development; A report to the World Commission on Dams', http://www.unep.org/dams/WCD/report/WCD_DAMS%20report.pdf (accessed 27 September 2011).

World Markets Analysis (2006) 'Chinese ODI in Africa: Oil, arms, aid and non-interference', 17 February.

World Rainforest Movement (2005) 'Mozambique: Forestry in Zambezia province, Chinese takeaway!', http://www.wrm.org.uy/bulletin/96/AF.html#Mozambique (accessed 27 September 2011).

WTO (World Trade Organization) (2008) *International Trade Statistics 2008* (Geneva: WTO).WTO (2009) *International Trade Statistics* (Geneva, WTO).

Wu, F. (2002) 'China's changing urban governance in the transition towards a more market-oriented economy', *Urban Studies* 39: 1071–93.

Wu, F. (2004) 'Residential relocation under market-oriented redevelopment: The process and outcomes in urban China', *Geoforum* 35(4): 453–70.

Wu, F. (2008) 'China's great transformation: Neoliberalization as establishing a market society', *Geoforum* 39: 1093–96.

WWF (World Wildlife Fund) (2008) 'Report on ecological footprint in China', http://www.wwfchina.org/english/downloads/China%20Footprint/chna_footprint_report_final.pdf (accessed 28 September 2011).

WWF (2009) 'Data shows illegal ivory trade on the rise', http://wwf.panda.org/?uNewsID=180702 (accessed 28 September 2011).

WWF (2011) 'China and Africa – Poverty and Environment: Facilitating dialogue and engagement for sustainable trade and investment', http://assets.wwf.org.uk/downloads/china_africa_poverty_environment.pdf (accessed 07 October 2011).

Xiang, B. (2005) 'Promoting knowledge exchange through diaspora networks: The case of the PRC', Compas Report, http://www.adb.org/Documents/Reports/GCF/reta6117-prc.pdf (accessed 07 October 2011).

Xie, Z. (2010) 'China's policies and actions to address climate change', *China Today* 59(11): 22–5.

Xing, Y. (2006) 'Why is China so attractive for FDI? The role of exchange rates', *China Economic Review* 17: 198–209.

*Xinhua* (2002) 'All About Xiaokang', *Xinhuanet*, 10 November.

*Xinhua* (2004) 'China celebrates ancient mariner to demonstrate peaceful rise', 7 July, http://english.peopledaily.com.cn/200407/08/eng20040708_148861.html (accessed 01 September 2011).

*Xinhua* (2006) 'Characteristics of FOCAC', http://www.china.org.cn/english/features/focac/183733.htm (accessed 01 September 2011).

*Xinhua* (2008a) 'Chinese envoy: China to provide more humanitarian aid to Darfur', 26 February 2008, http://news.xinhuanet.com/english/2008–02/26/content_7669108.htm (accessed 29 February 2008).

*Xinhua* (2008b) 'Three Chinese workers kidnapped in South Nigeria', 09 May, http://www.china.org.cn/international/news/2008–05/09/content_15129136.htm, (accessed 17 September 2008).

*Xinhua* (2009) 'Made in China' ad campaign wins applause in China', http://news.xinhuanet.com/english/2009–12/05/content_12594805.htm (accessed 26 March 2012).

*Xinhua* (2010) 'China issues national census of pollution sources', http://www. chinadaily.com.cn/china/2010–02/09/content_9451095.htm

*Xinhua* (2011a) 'Full text: China's foreign aid', http://news.xinhuanet.com/ english2010/china/2011–04/21/c_13839683.htm (accessed 07 October 2011).

*Xinhua* (2011b) 'China issues 1st national census of pollution sources', 10 February, http://english.mep.gov.cn/News_service/media_news/201002/ t20100210_185653.htm (accessed 09 October 2011).

Xue, G. (2006) 'China's distant water fisheries and its response to flag state responsibilities', *Marine Policy* 30: 653.

Yates, D. (2009), 'Enhancing the governance of Africa's oil sector', Occasional paper, Number 51, Governance of Africa's resources programme (South Africa: South African Institute of International Affairs).

Yelpaala, K. and Ali, S. H. (2005) 'Multiple scales of diamond mining in Akwatia, Ghana: Addressing environmental and human development impact', *Resources Policy* 30: 145–55.

Yiming, Y., Guo, H., Hongfei, Xu, Weiqi, L., Shanshan, L. and Haiqing, L. (2011) 'The development of the Shenzhen special economic zone in China', *The China Monitor* 65: 4–9.

Yin, D. (2009) 'China's attitude toward foreign NGOs', *Washington University Global Studies Law Review* 8: 521–43.

YIO (Yearbook of International Organisations) (2002–03), Volume 2. *International Organization Participation: Country Directory of Secretariats and Membership* (Belgium: Union of International Associations).

Young, N. and Shih, J. (2003) *The Chinese Diaspora and Philanthropy, Global Equity Initiative* (Harvard: Harvard University Press).

Yu, G. (1966) 'China's Failure in Africa', *Asian Survey* 6(8): 461–8.

Yu, G. (1977) 'China and the Third World', *Asian Survey*, 17(11): 1036–48.

Yu, G. (1980) 'The Tanzania-Zambian Railway: A Case Study in Chinese Economic Aid to Africa'. In W. Weinstein and T. H. Henriksen (eds), *Soviet and Chinese Aid to African Nations* (New York: Praeger Publishers), 117–44.

Yu, G. T. (1965) 'Sino-African relations: A survey', *Asian Survey* 5(7): 321–32.

Yu, G. T. (1988) 'Africa in Chinese Foreign Policy', *Asian Survey* 28(8): 849–62.

Yu, N. (2011) 'Paving the way', *Beijing Review*, http://www.bjreview.com/ special/2011–09/02/content_387691.htm (accessed 02 September 2011).

Zadek, S., Xiaohong, C., Zhaoxi, L., Tao, J., Yan, Z., Yu, K., Forstater, M. and Morgan, G. (2009) 'Responsible business in Africa: Chinese business leaders' perspectives on performance and enhancement opportunities', Corporate Social Responsibility Initiative, Working Paper No. 54, http://www.hks. harvard.edu/m-rcbg/CSRI/publications/workingpaper_54_zadeketal.pdf (accessed 28 September 2011).

Zetter, R., Griffiths, D., Sigona, N., Flynn, D., Pasha, T. and Beynon, R. (2006) 'Immigration, social cohesion and social capital: What are the links?', http:// www.jrf.org.uk/bookshop/eBooks/9781899354440.pdf (accessed 02 September 2011).

Zhang, J. (2004) *Catch-up and Competitiveness in China: The Case of Large Firms in the Oil Industry* (London: Routledge).

Zhang, L. and Ong, A. (2008) *Privatizing China: Socialism from Afar* (New York: Cornell University Press).

Zhang, W. (2006) 'The allure of the Chinese model', *International Herald Tribune*, 2 November.

Zhang, W. *et al* (ed.) (1993) *HuaqiaoHuaRenGaiShu*, Overseas Chinese Affairs Office of the State Council, CCP, PRC.

Zhang, Y. (2002) 'Review: International Relations Theory in China today: The state of the field', *The China Journal* 47: 101–8.

Zhang, Z. X. (2007) 'China's hunt for oil in Africa in perspective', *Energy & Environment* 18(1): 87–92.

Zhao, S. (2007) 'China's geostrategic thrust: Patterns of engagement'. In G. Le Pere (ed.), *China in Africa: Mercantilist Predator or Partner in Development?*, (Braamfontein: Institute for Global Dialogue and South African Institute for International Affairs), 33–53.

Zhao, S. (2011) 'The geopolitics of China-African oil', China Briefing. http://www.china-briefing.com/news/2011/04/13/the-geopolitics-of-china-african-oil.html (accessed 09 October 2011).

Zheng, B. (2005) 'Peacefully rising to great-power status', *Foreign Affairs* 88, September–October, 18–24.

Zhengxu, W. and Tin Seng, L. (2007) 'China's growing interest in Africa'. In Wang Gungwu and John Wong (eds), *Interpreting China's Development* (Singapore: World Scientific Publishing), 256–60.

Zhimin, C. and Junbo, J. (2009) Chinese provinces as foreign policy actors in Africa', SAIIA Occasional paper 22 (Pretoria, SAIIA).

Zusman, E. and Jennifer L. Turner (2005) 'Beyond the Bureaucracy: Changing China's Policymaking Environment'. In K. Day (ed.), *China's Environment and the Challenge of Sustainable Development* (Armonk and London: ME Sharpe): 121–49.

Zweig, D. (2009) 'A new "trading state" meets the developing world', Center on China's Transnational Relations, Working Paper No. 31.

Zweig, D. and Chen, Z. (eds) (2007) *China's Reforms and International Political Economy* (London: Routledge).

# Index

accountability, 24, 159, 160
Accra Agenda for Action, 132, 152
accumulation
  crisis of, 92–100
  by dispossession, 15, 18
Africa
  *see also* China-Africa relations;
    *specific countries*
  aid diplomacy in, 127–59
  Brazil and, 231–3
  China as economic role model for,
    123–6
  Chinese aid projects in, 43–8
  Chinese communities in, 28, 34,
    172–7
  Chinese migration to, 32–6, 58,
    166, 171–7, 267–8
  Chinese policies in, 62–87
  civil society, 178–88, 267, 270
  development in, 49, 63, 127–8
  environmental issues, 191–220
  exploitation of, 15–16
  governance systems, 160–71
  impact of China in, 263–5
  India and, 229–31
  national liberation movements in,
    37–9, 47, 54–7
  natural resources, 192, 200–16
  popular responses to Chinese in,
    178–88
  representations of, 5–7
  resource sectors, 200–16
  Russia and, 227–9
  'scramble' for, 227–33
African agency, 9, 17, 18–21
African state, 14, 19, 161–4
African Union (AU), 62, 269
Africa Strategy, 25, 62–87, 189, 252–3
Afro-Asian People's Solidarity
  Organization (AAPSO), 39, 40
Afro-Asian solidarity, 29, 36–43
agency, African, 9, 17, 18–21

agriculture, 21, 81–2, 157
aid
  to Angola, 141–5, 167–9
  bundling of, 24
  China as recipient of, 136
  China's policy on, 43–8, 51, 128–59
  comparative perspective on, 139–41
  definition of, 134
  development and, 127–8
  donor responses to, 151–8
  emerging donors and, 15, 24, 128–
    32, 139, 151–8
  to Ghana, 145–51
  history of, 29
  investment and, 136–7
  logics, modalities and
    conditionalities, 132–9
  medical, 46–7, 80
  non-interference policy, 138–9, 154
  in practice, 141–51
  rogue, 130–1, 137, 141
  tied, 21, 63–4, 137–8
aid diplomacy, 127–59
aid projects, 43–8, 51
  in Angola, 141–5
  in Ghana, 145–51
  joint ventures, 53
  quality of, 87
  sustainability of, 87
  Tazara Railway, 48–50, 61
  types of, 87
Akosombo Dam, 187
Alavi, Hamza, 162
ancient China, 30–2
Angola, 22, 23, 47
  Chinese in, 11, 29, 54–7, 77–80, 175
  civil war, 54–7
  development relations in, 141–5,
    167–9
  donor harmonization in, 157–8
  loans to, 114
  natural resources, 214, 215–16

Asian-African Conference, 39
Asian Driver phenomena, 19, 165, 266
assemblages, 22, 188
automobile manufacturing, 79

Bandung Conference, 39, 41, 60
banking sector, 107–9
Bank of China, 85
Battuta, Ibn, 31
Beijing Consensus, 7, 129
Beijing Olympics, 188
bilateral trade, 62–3, 264
bourgeoisie, 99, 162
Brazil, 231–3
bribery, 190
Bui Dam, 82, 87, 150–1, 169–71, 187, 211–13, 214
business associations, 184–6, 267
business practices, 86

cadres, 98, 99
Cameron, David, 260
Cameroon, 37, 179
Canga, Pedro, 116
capital
    financial, 125
    state and, 17–18, 161–4
capitalism, 11–12, 15, 19, 95, 96, 98, 110, 119–20, 162–3
capitalist class, 98–9
causality, 22
Central Military Affairs Commission (CMAC), 239–40
Chiang, Kai-shek, 36–7, 39
China
    *see also* China-Africa relations
    African aid projects by, 43–8
    aid diplomacy, 127–59
    in Angola, 11, 29, 54–7, 77–80
    demonization of, 1–5
    development strategy, 90–2
    environmental protections in, 197–200
    in Ghana, 11, 80–2
    as great power, 250–5
    media in, 241–2
    natural resource management in, 196

neoliberalism in, 18–21, 91, 96, 263
oil diplomacy, 221–7
rise of, 1–2, 7, 130, 165, 255–7
China-Africa Business Council (CABC), 85–6
China-Africa Development Fund (CADFund), 62, 68, 263
China-Africa diplomacy, 64–77
China-Africa relations
    contextualization of, 26–61
    critical genealogy of, 26–8
    current patterns of engagement, 261–t5
    direction of, 64–77
    disaggregated analysis of, 7, 9, 24
    dynamics of, 9–10
    future of, 260–72
    geopolitics of, 221–59
    globalization of, 268–72
    history of, 24, 26–43, 58–61
    initial encounters, 28–32
    introduction to, 1–23
    'lost decade' in, 50–4
    popular responses to, 178–88
    representations of, 2–7
China Development Bank (CDB), 107–8
China Inc., 7, 137, 175, 222, 266, 267
China International Fund (CIF), 115–16, 167–8, 169, 215
China International Trust and Investment Corporation (CITIC), 78
China Investment Corporation (CIC), 109
China National Offshore Oil Corporation (CNOOC), 105
China Road and Bridge Corporation (CRBC), 78
Chinese aid
    *see also* aid
    comparative perspective on, 139–41
    donor responses to, 151–8
    in practice, 141–51
Chinese businesses, 17, 110–16, 125, 166–7
Chinese Communist Party (CCP), 6, 17, 27–9, 36–7, 58, 84, 89–91, 97, 98, 133

Chinese communities, in Africa, 28, 34, 172–7
Chinese diaspora, 28, 32–6, 58, 113, 166, 171–7, 265, 267–8
Chinese economy, 88–126
  as African role model, 123–6
  central government control of, 103
  'go out' strategy, 100–10, 125, 206, 237, 263
  growth of, 20, 88–92, 124–6
  modernization of, 51–3, 60
  neoliberalism and, 18–21, 116–23
  state-owned enterprises (SEOs), 100–10
  state socialism, 92–100
  transnational corporations and, 110–16
Chinese Foreign Ministry, 234, 235
Chinese foreign policy, 13, 224–5
  Angola and, 54–7
  diversity of actors in, 233–42
  peacekeeping and security cooperation, 250–5
  postcolonial era, 39
  post-Mao, 50–4
  principles of, 60
  'scramble' for Africa and, 227–33
  shifts in, 60–1, 242–50
  soft power and, 221–7
  Soviet Union and, 40–1, 50–1, 55–6
Chinese military, 239–40
Chinese policies, 18, 24
  *see also* Chinese foreign policy
  in Africa, 62–87
  in Angola, 77–80
  challenges of, 83–7
  differential impacts of, 77–82
  'go out' strategy, 81, 85, 91, 100–10, 113, 125, 206, 237, 263
  impacts of, 77–82
  lack of coordination in, 83–7
  'open door' policies, 91, 93
  opportunities and challenges of, 82–7
Chinese workers, 28, 34–6, 86, 138, 174, 184
civil society, 20, 25, 178–88, 267, 270
climate change, 21, 191–2, 200–1
Clinton, Hillary, 145, 260

coercive social contract, 164
Cold War, 28–9, 133, 135, 262
colonialism, 9, 28, 33, 42, 61, 189
  surgical, 14–16
Confucius Institutes, 240–1
Convention on International Trade in Endangered Species (CITES), 202
convivial culture, 180
coolie labour, 15–16, 33–6
corporate social responsibility (CSR), 85–6, 197–8, 219–20, 271
corruption, 63, 127–8
critical geopolitics, 2, 255–9
cultural diplomacy, 240–1
Cultural Revolution, 37, 47, 50, 52, 60, 92, 99, 241
currency valuation, 93, 95

dam projects, 206–7, 210–14
Darfur, 189, 246, 247, 269
Davidson, Basil, 22
Democratic Republic of Congo (DRC), 79, 153, 268
Deng, Xiaoping, 51, 57, 91, 92, 96, 97, 101, 124
Department of Foreign Economic Cooperation (DFEC), 109–10
Department of International Development (DFID), 152–3, 155
dependency theory, 17
development
  African, 49, 63, 127–8
  aid and, 127–8
  cooperation, 63–4
  ideology, 270–2
  infrastructure, 78–9
  political economy of, 10–14
  theories of, 265–8
Development Assistance Committee (DAC), 15, 127, 129, 130, 131, 134
diplomacy
  China-Africa, 64–77
  cultural, 240–1
  oil, 205, 221–7
diplomatic relations, 46
direct investment, 63
disaggregation, 7, 9, 24, 164–5, 233–42, 266

Dos Santos, Jose Eduardo, 57, 169
double movement, 10–11

East Asia, 100
economic liberalization, 18–21
Egypt, 39, 40, 75–6, 266
elites, 24, 98, 167, 168, 189, 267
emerging donors, 15, 24, 128–32, 139,
    151–8
employment opportunities, 78–9, 266
enclaves, 14–16, 17, 22, 185–6
endangered species, 202, 207–8
energy issues, 165, 204–5
entrepreneurs, 25, 99, 172–6
environmental change, 21
environmental impact assessments
    (EIAs), 169–70, 197, 205, 207,
    218–19
environmental issues, 18–21, 25,
    191–220, 265
  domestic discourses on, 195–200
  globalization of, 216–20
  impact of Chinese enterprises,
    205–7
  internationalization of, 195–200
  power relations and, 194–5
Environment Framework Law, 214–15
Ethiopia, 39, 205
Eurocentrism, 17
European Union (EU), 153–4, 165,
    263
Export-Import Bank (ExIm), 77, 84,
    85, 108–9, 137, 143–4, 149–50,
    156, 166, 206, 215
Export Processing Zones (EPZs), 93
exports, 20, 52, 63, 80–1, 91, 95, 264
Extractive Industries Transparency
    Initiative (EITI), 215–16
extroversion, 167–71

Ferguson, James, 14–15, 17, 18
financial capital, 125
fishing industry, 81–2, 202–3, 208
'five principles', 41
flexigemony, 171, 245
foreign aid, *see* aid
foreign direct investment (FDI),
    89–90, 93, 104, 110, 112, 115,
    123–4, 165

foreign-funded enterprises (FFEs),
    112, 114
foreign invested enterprises (FIEs), 95
foreign policy, *see* Chinese foreign
    policy
forestry, 203, 204, 208–9, 217–18
Forum on China-Africa Cooperation
    (FOCAC), 5, 24, 62, 64–73, 77–8,
    82–5, 87, 161, 200, 262–3, 269–70

Gabon, 204
Gaye, Adama, 3, 5
Genocide Olympics campaign, 188
geopolitics
  of China-Africa engagement,
    221–59
  critical, 2, 255–9
  postcolonial, 10–21
  of representation, 1–10
  shifts in, 7, 260–5
Ghana, 22, 23, 44
  Chinese involvement in, 11, 80–2
  Chinese migrants in, 174–6
  dam building in, 211–12
  development relations in, 145–51
  donor harmonization in, 155–6
  independence for, 39
  migrants to, 36
  oil exploration in, 156–7
global capitalism, 11–12, 110, 119–20
global economy, 12
global environmental governance,
    195–200, 209–16
global governance, 243–4, 246–7
globalization, 10–14
gold, 34
'go out' strategy, 81, 85, 91, 100–10,
    113, 125, 206, 237, 263
governance, 160–1
  African, 160–71
  corruption, 63, 127–8
  global, 243–4, 246–7
  global environmental, 195–200,
    209–16
  municipal, 85, 95–6, 238–9
governmentality, 11, 19
graft, 25
Great Leap Forward, 44, 92
greenhouse gases, 21, 191–2, 201

guerilla warfare, 39
Guinea, 44

Hart, Gillian, 10
Harvey, David, 117
hegemony, 9, 11
Hong Kong, 115–16, 263
Hoogvelt, A., 11–12
human rights, 160, 161, 249
hybridity, 167–71
hydropower plants, 201, 204–7,
    210–14

identity politics, 176
ideology, 29, 270–2
illegal activities, 207–9, 218–19
imperialism, 42, 60
imports, 63
India, 41, 60, 129, 130, 140, 229–31
inequalities, 21, 90–1, 126
infrastructure investment, 21, 45, 63,
    64, 78–9, 82
    *see also* aid projects
integration, 176–7
inter-cultural interpretation, 23
international capital, 17–18
International Monetary Fund (IMF),
    142, 156
International Poverty Reduction
    Centre in China (IPRCC), 43
international relations, 10–14, 234
inward investment, 169
ISO14001, 198
ivory trade, 202, 207–8

Japan, 52, 53
Jessop, B., 162–3
Jiang, Zemin, 102
joint ventures, 93, 112, 204

kidnapping, 179
Kilamba Kiaxi Housing Project, 78
knowledge, power and, 11
Korea, 157
Korean War, 37
Kuomintang (KMT), 36

labour
    African, 174, 266

cheap, 15–16, 33–6
Chinese, 28, 34–6, 86, 138, 174, 184
    unrest, 86
land, 21
Lekki Free Trade Zone, 75, 76
Li, Murray, 11, 19, 97
liberation movements, 37–9, 47, 54–7
Liberia, 39
local governments, 95–6
logging, 209
'lost decade', 50–4

Mali, 44, 76
manufacturing sector, 93, 95, 112
Maoism, 13, 50
Mao Zedong, 36, 37, 42, 45, 46, 50
market economy, transition to
    socialist, 88–126
Marxist theory, 162
Mauritius, 75
media, 241–2
medical aid, 46–7, 80
Merowe Dam, 187–8, 206, 207, 211
micro-politics, 171–7, 265
migration, Chinese, to Africa, 32–6,
    58, 166, 171–7, 267–8
Millennium Development Goals
    (MDGs), 141
mineral reserves, 192
Ming Dynasty, 28, 30, 59
mining sectors, 203–4
Ministry of Commerce (MOFCOM),
    101, 106, 109–10, 137, 166
Ministry of Foreign Affairs (MFA),
    101, 237–8
modernization theory, 17
Moyo, Dambisa, 127
Mozambique, 47, 210–11
MPLA, 41, 54–6
multilateral organizations, 243–4,
    246–7
multipolarity, 242–3
multi-stakeholders, 209–16
municipal government, 85, 95–6,
    238–9

nationalism, 49
national liberation movements, 37–9,
    47, 54–7

natural resources, 21, 24, 171, 192, 200–16
  exploitation of, 161
  illegal extraction of, 207–9
Nehru, Jawaharlal, 41
neocolonialism, 15–16
neo-communists, 13
neoliberalism, 11, 15, 18–21, 91, 96, 116–23, 263
neo-Marxism, 17, 162–3, 266
NEPAD Business Foundation (NBF), 269
Neto, Agostinho, 57
New Left, 122–3, 126
Nigeria, 75, 189
non-aligned movement, 41, 43
non-governmental organizations (NGOs), 11, 123, 163, 240
non-interference policy, 60, 138–9, 154, 244–5, 259, 271
non-Western perspectives, 13–14

Official Development Assistance (ODA), 134
  *see also* aid
Ogun Zone, 75
oil companies, 167–9, 215–16, 221–2
oil diplomacy, 205, 221–7
oil exploration, 156–7
'One China' principle, 224
'open door' policies, 91, 93
Opium Wars, 33
Organizations of African Unity (OAU), 54
outsourcing, 110
Overseas Chinese, 32–6
overseas contracts, 106

Pan-Africanism, 49
Paris Declaration on Aid Effectiveness, 131–2, 152
patronage, 25
peacekeeping, 246–7, 250–5
People's Liberation Army (PLA), 28, 36, 108, 234, 239–40
People's Republic of China (PRC), 27, 28, 35, 37, 39, 58
Pires, Tome, 31–2
planned economy, 103

political ecology, 20–1, 194–5
political economy, 10–14, 20, 161–2, 167
political engagement, 176
political processes, 167–71
politics, 25, 176, 264–5, 268–9
popular culture, 2
postcolonial geopolitical economy, 10–21
postcolonialism, 10, 14
postcolonial theory, 9, 167, 219–20, 266
power, knowledge and, 11
power relations
  in environment sector, 194–5
  shifts in, 1–2, 7, 21
privatization, 98, 104
provincial government, 95–6, 238–9

Qian, Qichen, 53

racism, 178–9
regimes, 164–71, 270
remittances, 174–5
renewable energy, 193, 201–2, 204–5
representation, geopolitics of, 1–10
Republic of China (ROC), 37
resource curse thesis, 161, 264
resource-for-equity swaps, 168–9
resource sectors, 200–16
responsibility, 219–20
rogue aid, 130–1, 137, 141
Russia, 227–9

Sata, Michael, 178, 269
Savimbi, Jonas, 55
scientific development, 133
Sector-Wide Approaches (SWAPs), 132
security cooperation, 250–5
Shang/Yin Dynasty, 31
Shenzhen, 88–9
shock therapy, 18
Sinohydro, 78, 82, 106, 149, 151, 170–1, 186, 187, 206
slavery, 33
small and medium enterprises (SMEs), 76, 86, 91, 206, 218, 263
social capital, 163
socialist market economy, 88–126

social relations, 171–7
social welfare programs, 117
soft power, 24, 27, 131, 221–7, 247
South Africa, 34, 39, 47, 49, 54
South-South cooperation, 29, 36–43,
    140–1, 189
sovereign-backed debt, 79
sovereignty, 18, 60, 259
Soviet Union, 37, 39–42, 47, 50–1,
    55–6, 133, 225
spatial development initiatives, 270
Special Economic Zones (SEZs),
    49–50, 68, 73–7, 86–9, 93, 94,
    113, 124
State Assets Supervision and
    Administration Commission
    (SASAC), 106–7
state-capital dynamics, 17–18,
    161–4
State Grid Corporation of China
    (SGCC), 105
state-owned enterprises (SOEs), 23,
    85, 91, 100–10, 166, 172, 198,
    206, 236–7, 266
states
    African, 14, 19, 161–4
    role of, 17–18
state socialism, 92–100
Sudan, 139, 245–6, 247, 269
Suez Canal, 75, 266
Sung Dynasty, 30
surgical colonialism, 14–16
sustainability, 87
Swahili sailors, 31

Taiwan, 37, 47, 52, 53, 224–5
Tamh Dynasty, 31–2
Tanzania, 183–4
Taylor, Ian, 162
Tazara Railway, 48–50, 61
telecommunications sector, 79, 81
Third World alliance, 42, 133
Tiananmen square, 53, 117, 226
tied aid, 21, 63–4, 137–8
timber industry, 208–9, 217–18
trade
    Africa-Chinese, 62–3, 185–6, 264
    Chinese-Angola, 145
    Chinese-Ghana, 80–1, 145–6

early, between Africa and China,
    29–30
trade unions, 182, 184, 186–7, 189,
    267
traditional donors, 15, 128–9, 151–8
transnational corporations (TNCs),
    17, 89, 110–16, 166
transparency, 22, 86, 134, 159, 189
transportation costs, 79
trilateral cooperation, 154

Uganda, 185, 270
unitary capital, 17
United Nations peacekeeping
    operations (UNPKOs), 250–5
United States, 37, 50, 51, 112, 165,
    166, 263

varieties of capitalism, 19, 119–20

Washington Consensus, 129, 130
Wen, Jiabao, 58, 62
West, 13, 61
Wolfowitz, Paul, 136
World Bank, 156, 157, 168
world-systems theory, 13
World Trade Organization (WTO), 43,
    95, 244

Xia Dynasty, 31

yuan, 93, 95
Yuan Dynasty, 30

Zambia, 73–5, 178, 182–3,
    269, 270
Zanzibar, 35–6
Zhao, Ziyang, 51, 53
Zheng, He, 27–8, 30–2, 42,
    58–9
Zhong Xing Telecommunication
    (ZTE), 79
Zhou, Enlai, 41–2, 44, 45, 50, 51
Zhou Dynasty, 31
Zhu, Rongji, 100–1
Zhu, Siben, 30
Zimbabwe, 49, 247–50
Zimbabwe African National Union
    (ZANU), 2, 4